DAVE HEEREN'S BASKETBALL ABSTRACT
1991–92 Edition

Dave Heeren

PRENTICE HALL
Englewood Cliffs, New Jersey 07632

Prentice-Hall International (UK) Limited, *London*
Prentice-Hall of Australia Pty. Limited, *Sydney*
Prentice-Hall Canada, Inc., *Toronto*
Prentice-Hall Hispanoamericana, S.A., *Mexico*
Prentice-Hall of India Private Limited, *New Delhi*
Prentice-Hall of Japan, Inc., *Tokyo*
Simon & Schuster Asia Pte. Ltd., *Singapore*
Editora Prentice-Hall do Brasil, Ltda., *Rio de Janeiro*

© 1992 *by*
PRENTICE-HALL, Inc.
Englewood Cliffs, NJ

10 9 8 7 6 5 4 3 2 1

ISSN 1051–1849

ISBN 0-13-202995-2

PRENTICE HALL
Business Information & Publishing Division
Englewood Cliffs, NJ 07632
Simon & Schuster, A Paramount Communications Company

To my wife Joan

   for putting up with a basketball fanatic
for 27 years.

Contents

Introduction

Official credit for inventing basketball goes to Dr. James Naismith, who in 1891 asked a custodian to nail two peach baskets to the balcony of a YMCA gymnasium in Springfield, Massachusetts. An old photograph shows Naismith as a mustachioed gentleman, dressed in a three-piece suit, holding a peach basket under his left arm, and a soccer ball in his right hand.

Good promoter, Dr. Naismith.

But was he really the first person to invent a game in which a ball was thrown into a larger receptacle? I doubt it. The instinct to throw small round objects at or into larger objects is probably as old as Eden.

A small boy throws a stone at a tree or into a pond, or a wad of paper into a trash can. I can recall throwing various small items into the inkwell of my first-grade desk and keeping score.

The noise is crucial. Whack of stone against tree. Plop of rock in water. Clunk of trash can. Thud of school desk. Creak of peach basket. These days it is the swish of nets. Show me a hoop without a net hanging from it and I'll show you one that probably isn't put to much use.

Noise or no noise, it was Dr. Naismith who had the vision to develop the game into an organized sport and to let the media in on it. That's the key: The media. Suppose he had not had the presence of mind to call his local newspaper. How then would we know that there ever was a peach basket hanging in the Springfield YMCA?

But he did, and we do, so officially the sport of basketball is 100 years old. What better time to reflect on the greatest players, coaches, and teams in the sport's history than its 100th anniversary? That's what this book is about—the greatest.

- ◇ Greatest players, greatest coaches, greatest teams.
- ◇ Greatest collegians, greatest pros.
- ◇ Greatest old-timers, greatest contemporaries.
- ◇ Greatest scorers, shooters, rebounders.
- ◇ Greatest playmakers, shot-blockers, ball-thieves.
- ◇ Greatest centers.
- ◇ Greatest forwards.
- ◇ Greatest guards.

The greatest players are *not* necessarily the ones who score the most points. This is not a simplistic statement; all-star basketball teams are still being selected at all levels based almost exclusively on scoring averages.

The greatest scorers are not even necessarily the ones who score the most points. There are other factors to be considered about each player—the number of minutes he plays, the number of shots he takes, the number of points scored by his team. A player who averages 25 points for a team that averages 75 is a better scorer than one who averages 30 for a team that scores 120.

Efficiency is the crucial element: How well does a player do based on his number of opportunities? What percentage of his team's points does he score? What percentage of the total rebounds in a game does he collect? What percentage of his teammates' field goals does he assist on? How many points does he average per shot?

Greg Thomas suggested the idea of rebounding efficiency with an "abstraction" he wrote for the 1990 edition of *The Basketball Abstract.* He entitled it "available rebounds." The same principle has been applied in this edition to every statistical category. Only one player in professional basketball history qualifies among the all-time leaders in five statistical categories. Read this book and find out who he is.

Find out, too, who are really the *greatest* players, coaches, and teams of all-time. Not all of the TENDEX honorees are to be found in the Naismith Hall of Fame. And not all Naismith honorees make it with TENDEX. Politics don't count with TENDEX. But they sometimes do with Naismith, and so does television exposure.

A player who spent his entire NBA career in Kansas City has as good a chance to make the TENDEX Hall as a Los Angeles Laker or a Boston Celtic.

The difference between this and other evaluations of basketball's all-time greats is that this one is based on a careful analysis of statistics. You won't find the greatest NBA team of all-time overlooked entirely in this book. Which team was truly the best of all-time? Read this book and find out.

The best method of statistical evaluation for individual players is TENDEX, a formula that places into calculation each player's points, rebounds, assists, steals, blocked shots, turnovers, minutes played, and shooting percentages. Plus a game-pace factor that puts into perspective his number of opportunities for statistical production based on the number of ball possessions of his team.

Each ball-possession that ends with a shot being taken is worth almost exactly one point. So each point counts as one TENDEX point. So does each assist that converts a normal one-point possession into an easy two-point basket. So does a rebound or steal that acquires ball possession. And so does a blocked shot, which has defensive intimidation value that makes up for the fact that not all blocks result in turnovers.

On the minus-one side are turnovers that lose possession and all missed shots (this is where shooting percentages figure into the equation).

The total from all these additions and subtractions is divided by the player's total of minutes played and then a second division is made based on his team's game-pace. For college players only, a third division is made based on the team's strength-of-schedule.

The TENDEX rating of a team is based on the difference between the composite ratings of all its players and the ratings of its composite opponents.

A coach's rating reflects the difference between his team's rating and its winning percentage. Some coaches get more out of their players than they should. Others get less. The best coaches are the ones who get the most out of their players. Who were the greatest coaches of all-time? Read this book and find out.

The highest rated players, teams, and coaches are the ones chosen for the TENDEX Hall of Fame.

Unlike the Baseball Hall of Fame, there is no one in the TENDEX Basketball Hall based on exaggerated credentials. Nobody makes it just because he gave articulate interviews that made him popular with sportswriters. Nobody gets in because he happened to have great teammates who won a few championship rings for him.

Welcome to the TENDEX Hall of Fame: Enter on merit.

—DAVE HEEREN

SECTION I

THE TENDEX
HALL OF FAME

1
The Pointmakers

All are but parts of one stupendous whole—
Alexander Pope

In the three previous editions of *The Basketball Abstract,* the emphasis was on the "stupendous whole," that is, the TENDEX Rating, which gives an overview of a basketball player's ability based on a consolidation of ten statistical categories. In this edition, the emphasis still is on the whole, but not to the exclusion of the parts. The greatest players are to be determined in each category (scoring, rebounding, etc.) and then we shall consider which of these players belong with the all-time greats in the Hall of Fame.

It will be interesting to see how many players are exceptional in one or more categories without being Hall of Famers, and equally interesting to see if anyone qualifies for the Hall of Fame without rating at or near the top in any one aspect of play.

The formula for TENDEX ratings is:

Points + Assists + Rebounds + Steals + Blocked Shots – Turnovers – Missed Field-Goal Attempts – Missed Free-Throw Attempts/ Minutes Played/Game Pace = TENDEX.

With the inclusion in college ratings of strength-of-schedule, the formula probably should be called ELEVENDEX.

In practical language, TENDEX represents the number of points per minute a player is worth to his team. High-scoring players are not necessarily the highest rated unless they are good in other categories of play. The only player ever to achieve a rating of 1.000 (one point per minute) for a full season was Wilt Chamberlain, who did it three times. It was Chamberlain's rebounding as much as his scoring that gave him such high ratings.

SHOOTERS VS. SCORERS

Although TENDEX is able to pinpoint the skill level of most players, there are other significant statistical percentages and ratios. Let's begin with scoring. There are good scorers who don't shoot well, and good shooters who don't score well, so shooters are to be rated in another chapter. This is for players who score a lot of points regardless of how well they shoot.

For the first 23 years of the National Basketball Association's existence, from the 1946–47 season through the 1968–69 season, statistical titles were awarded on the basis of total points, total assists, and total rebounds. It was not until 1969–70 that a change was made to per-game averages for determining these three individual champions. The antiquated bulk-total rating method cost Joe Fulks a scoring title in 1947–48 and cost Oscar Robertson scoring and assists titles in 1967–68.

It was not that Fulks and Robertson played too few games to qualify. Fulks missed only five games in 1947–48 and is listed in official NBA records as the No. 2 scorer that year. He scored 949 points. Official scoring leader Max Zaslofsky scored 1,007. But Fulks' scoring average was 22.1; Zaslofsky's was 21.0. Fulks should have been named the scoring champ and the system should have been permanently changed beginning with that season.

In 1967–68, Oscar Robertson was the dominant player in the NBA. The Boston Celtics, who went on to win the league title that season, had so much trouble with Robertson throughout the regular season that they purposely played reserves in losing the final game of the season to Detroit and then were able to play the Pistons instead of Robertson's Cincinnati team in the first round of the playoffs.

Only five individual statistical categories were tabulated at that time and Robertson should have been honored as the winner in three of them. He won in free-throw percentage, but was listed only No. 3 in assists and No. 6 in scoring, despite having the best per-game averages in both categories. He averaged 29.2 points per game. Official scoring champion Dave Bing averaged 27.1. Robertson averaged 9.7 assists per game. Official assists champion Wilt Chamberlain averaged 8.6. Robertson played in 65 of the 82 games that season.

The NBA was publicly criticized by television commentators for its outmoded statistical system. It was doubly embarrassing for the established league because that season was the first of the American Basketball Association, which began immediately listing its leaders on the basis of per-game averages. If the ABA had adopted the ancient ways of the NBA, the ABA's first scoring champion would have been Doug Moe, who averaged 24.2 points per game while scoring 1,884 points, instead of actual champ Connie Hawkins, who averaged 26.8 while scoring 1,875 points. The abashed NBA changed its system after playing one

more season but to this day hasn't changed its inconsistent record book.

It may be time to change the system again.

During recent years, several statisticians have come up with statistical percentages superior to the official ones used by the NBA, and I don't mean only comprehensive stats such as TENDEX. In each category, there are better methods than per-game percentage to determine the most proficient players.

PER-GAME VS. PER-MINUTE

Much better than per-game is per-minute, which serves as the basis for TENDEX and has been used in all editions of *The Basketball Abstract*. Per-minute works better than per-game for the same reason per-game works better than bulk totals. It is one step more advanced in evaluating the performance of players. With a minimum of 10,000 points scored, here are the all-time top ten NBA-ABA players in total points, points-per-game and points-per-minute:

TOTAL POINTS

Player (Seasons)	Points
1. Kareem Abdul-Jabbar (20)	38,387
2. Wilt Chamberlain (14)	31,419
3. Julius Erving (16)	30,026
4. Moses Malone (17)	27,908
5. Dan Issel (15)	27,482
6. Elvin Hayes (16)	27,313
7. Oscar Robertson (14)	26,710
8. George Gervin (14)	26,595
9. John Havlicek (16)	26,395
10. Alex English (15)	25,613

POINTS PER GAME

1. Michael Jordan (7)	32.6
2. Wilt Chamberlain (14)	30.1
3. Elgin Baylor (14)	27.4
4. Jerry West (14)	27.0
5. Bob Pettit (11)	26.4
6. Dominique Wilkins (9)	26.1
7. Oscar Robertson (14)	25.7
8. Karl Malone (6)	25.6
9. George Gervin (14)	25.1
10. Rick Barry (14)	24.8

POINTS PER MINUTE

1. Michael Jordan (7) .... .8436
2. George Gervin (14) .... .7471
3. Dominique Wilkins (9) .... .7064
4. John Drew (11) .... .7005
5. David Thompson (9) .... .6916
6. Karl Malone (6) .... .6913
7. Jerry West (14) .... .6889
8. Mark Aguirre (10) .... .6888
9. Elgin Baylor (14) .... .6836
10. Bob Pettit (11) .... .6826

The total-points list closely approximates the all-time top ten in minutes played. It reflects the fact that the more time a player spends on the floor, the more points he is likely to score. The only players on this list who did not make the top ten in minutes played are Gervin and English. They replace Artis Gilmore and Bill Russell.

Abdul-Jabbar, the all-time leader in minutes played, is No. 1 on the total-points list but does not make the top ten in points-per-game or points-per-minute. Chamberlain, who ranks No. 1 in minutes per game, is No. 2 on the points-per-game list but does not make the points-per-minute list. Abdul-Jabbar and Chamberlain were excellent scorers, but their standing atop all-time scoring lists is attributable to very high minutes-played totals. In an efficiency statistic such as points-per-minute, neither man makes the top ten. Jordan is actually a much more prolific scorer than either of the two great centers.

But even points-per-minute may not be the best measure of a player's scoring effectiveness. Suppose Player A spends most of his career on a team, such as Denver, which plays at a fast pace year after year, while Player B is on a team, such as Detroit, which plays at a slower pace. The way to equalize the two players is to compare their scoring totals with their teams' scoring totals. This yields two other equations:

$$PTP/TTP = SP$$
$$PPM/TPM = SE$$

The first equation is Player's Total Points divided by Team's Total Points equals Scoring Productivity. The high-scoring players who

play a lot of minutes per season will dominate this statistic. Here are the all-time top ten:

SCORING PRODUCTIVITY

1. Michael Jordan (7) .... .2685
2. George Mikan (7) .... .2475
3. Wilt Chamberlain (14) .... .2382
4. Karl Malone (6) .... .2381
5. Bob Pettit (11) .... .2331
6. Paul Arizin (10) .... .2136
7. Dominique Wilkins (9) .... .2086
8. Kareem Abdul-Jabbar (20) .... .2075
9. Julius Erving (16) .... .2040
10. Oscar Robertson (14) .... .2037

All of these players scored more than 20 percent of their team's total points for their full careers. It is an intriguing statistic because it brings into focus players who played during the earliest era of the NBA when teams were scoring only 70 or 80 points per game. Obviously, if you average 25 points per game for a team averaging 75 points, you are a more productive scorer than somebody who averages 25 for a team that averages 125.

Mikan actually would have led this list if he hadn't played his final season, 1955–56, when he scored only 390 points. For his other six seasons, he scored nearly 29 percent of his team's points, higher than Jordan's percentage.

In Mikan's best season, 1950–51, he scored 34.3 percent of his team's points. He averaged 28.4 points per game. His team, Minneapolis, averaged 82.8 points per game. The runnerup in scoring that season, Alex Groza of Indianapolis, was far behind at 21.7.

The single-season record holder for scoring the highest percentage of his team's points was Wilt Chamberlain with 40.2 percent in 1961–62. Chamberlain averaged 50.4 points per game. His team, Philadelphia, averaged 125.4.

The second equation, PPM/TPM = SE, is Points per Minute divided by Team Points per Minute equals Scoring Efficiency. This is the best statistic for evaluating scorers. Each team has five players on the court at once, so the norm for this statistic is one-fifth or .2000. No player ever has doubled the norm. The best of all-time is Michael Jordan, who scores slightly more than 38 percent of his team's points during his minutes of playing time.

Here is a list of the all-time top fifty players in scoring efficiency, based on the ratio of points they scored to points their teams scored during their minutes on the court (minimum 10,000 points):

SCORING EFFICIENCY

1. Michael Jordan (7) .... .3822
2. John Drew (11) .... .3223
3. George Gervin (14) .... .3204
4. Karl Malone (6) .... .3161
5. Dominique Wilkins (9) .... .3136
6. Bernard King (14) .... .3104
7. Bob Pettit (11) .... .3094
8. Adrian Dantley (14) .... .3071
9. Mark Aguirre (10) .... .3057
10. George Mikan (7) .... .3055
11. Patrick Ewing (6) .... .3028
12. World B Free (13) .... .3009
13. Pete Maravich (10) .... .2968
14. Walter Davis (14) .... .2965
15. David Thompson (9) .... .2943
16. Bob McAdoo (14) .... .2937
17. Jerry West (14) .... .2915
18. Julius Erving (16) .... .2907
19. Elgin Baylor (14) .... .2902
20. Kareem Abdul-Jabbar (20) .... .2890
21. Rick Barry (14) .... .2879
22. Alex English (15) .... .2853
23. Clyde Lovellette (11) .... .2849
24. Neil Johnston (8) .... .2843
25. Hakeem Olajuwon (7) .... .2814
26. Terry Cummings (9) .... .2811
27. Charles Barkley (7) .... .2804
28. Jeff Malone (8) .... .2800
29. Dale Ellis (8) .... .2782
30. Larry Bird (12) .... .2772
31. Paul Arizin (10) .... .2769
32. Kiki Vandeweghe (11) .... .2758
33. Paul Westphal (12) .... .2757
34. Dan Issel (15) .... .2756
35. Wilt Chamberlain (14) .... .2735
36. Moses Malone (17) .... .2727
37. Bob Lanier (14) .... .2713
38. Tom Chambers (10) ..,.,........... .2709
39. Cliff Hagan (13) .... .2704
40. George McGinnis (11) .... .2693
41. Jack Twyman (11) .... .2677
42. Purvis Short (12) .... .2676
43. Mike Mitchell (10) .... .2668
44. Tom Heinsohn (9) .... .2667
45. Lou Hudson (13) .... .2664
46. Sam Jones (12) .... .2659
47. Calvin Murphy (13) .... .2655
48. Spencer Haywood (13) .... .2636
49. Fred Brown (13) .....,............. .2633
50. Earl Monroe (13) .... .2616

ABSTRACTION 1

Extraneous Production

Baseball has an amusing statistic called runs-produced. It's amusing because it's so ridiculous, but the sad thing is there's a basketball statistic just like it that is receiving unwarranted attention.

Runs-produced is the total of a baseball player's runs scored plus his runs-batted-in, minus his home runs (don't ask me why they subtract home runs). So in a game in which a team scores five runs, the team's individual players are likely to be credited with producing ten runs—five runs and five RBIs—unless, heaven forbid, somebody should blow the whole thing by hitting a home run. Then it would be only nine.

During a full season, a team will "produce" nearly twice as many runs as it scores. Now there's one for Ripley's Museum.

Here's a basketball stat that is just as absurd. It's called points-produced or points-accounted-for and it is the total of a player's points plus twice the total of his assists. As the spurious reasoning goes, an assist leads to a basket and is therefore worth two points. So backcourtman Smith who accumulates 20 points and 10 assists in a game is said to have produced or accounted for 40 points.

If a team scores 100 points and has 40 assists for a game, its total point "production" for the game is 180.

The problem with both the baseball runs-produced and basketball points-produced is duplication.

Let's say for example that all 10 of backcourtman Smith's assists go to backcourtman Jones. But Jones is a good playmaker also. He has 10 assists, one on each of Smith's baskets. Like Smith, Jones has "produced" 40 points on 20 points and 10 assists.

Trouble is, on the scoreboard the combination of backcourtmen Smith and Jones does not total 80 points but 40. All 20 of their assists are invested in the 40 total points scored between the two of them. Now it's true this particular scenario is unlikely to happen, but it does illustrate the fallacy of the points-produced statistic.

And it singles out one of the problems of TENDEX: Why give out awards for assists at all? In the TENDEX system, with each assist counted as having a value of one point, an assisted basket is worth three points while an unassisted one is worth only two points even though both count the same on the scoreboard.

It's better than counting four for an assisted basket (as the points-producers do), but still it's not accurate.

The primary reason why I include one point in the TENDEX formula for each assist is that an assist converts a normal one-point ball-possession into a two-point basket.

The value of an assist can be appreciated in contrast to a defensive statistic that causes an opposite effect, a blocked shot.

A blocked shot forces a miss that may or may not result in a team losing possession of the ball without scoring. It makes it much more unlikely that the offensive team will score.

A great pass leads to an easy shot and makes it much more likely that the offensive team will score. If the team does score, of course, the player who made the pass is credited with an assist in addition to the two points credited to the player who makes the shot.

I think it is fair to credit one TENDEX point to a player who makes a pass leading directly to an easy basket.

But two points? No way.

2
Boards & Bounds

Just look at the record book: Wilt Chamberlain and Bill Russell are the greatest rebounders. Despite Kareem Abdul-Jabbar's surplus of minutes played, Chamberlain and Russell are the only players in NBA-ABA history to total 20,000 or more rebounds. They are also the only players to average more than 20 rebounds per game for their full careers. Chamberlain (22.9) and Russell (22.5) averaged six-plus rebounds per game more than No. 3 man Bob Pettit (16.2). This means Chamberlain and Russell were the greatest rebounders of all-time, and all we need to do is figure out which one was better, right?

Maybe not.

The intangible factor is shooting:

◇ During the late 1940s, NBA players averaged about 70 percent on free-throw shooting and less than 30 percent on field-goal shooting.

◇ During the 1950s, the shooting improved slightly. League-wide field-goal percentages climbed above .300 but at no time reached .400. Free-throw percentages rose to about .750.

◇ Free-throw percentages haven't changed much since the 1950s, but field-goal percentages climbed into the low .400's during the 1960s.

◇ Another increase occurred during the 1970s: Field-goal percentages rose steadily. For the decade, the percentage was about .450.

◇ Despite the emergence of the low-percentage three-point shot during the 1980s, the field-goal percentage climbed above .475. By the end of the decade, the league-wide average in two-point field-goal percentage was nearly .500.

So what is the meaning of these shooting statistics when we are talking about rebounding? Just this: The higher the shooting percentages, the fewer missed shots there are to be rebounded. In the 1990 edition of *The Basketball Abstract*, Greg Thomas introduced a statistic he called "available rebounds." This is what we are talking about: There were more rebounds available during the 1950s and 1960s to Chamberlain and Russell and Pettit than to the great rebounders of the 1970s and 1980s.

During the 1959–60 and 1960–61 seasons, peak years for Chamberlain and Russell, the league-wide rebounding average was more than 73 per team per game. During the entire decade of the 1980s, the league-wide rebounding average was less than 44. We are talking about a difference of almost 30 available rebounds per team per game.

As we did with scoring, let's proceed step by step and see who ranks high on the all-time rebounding lists, beginning with the least important rebounding statistics, total rebounds, and ending with the most important, percentage of available rebounds.

The total-rebounds list is easy. It comes right out of the record book. Here is the top ten:

TOTAL REBOUNDS

Player (Seasons)	Rebounds
1. Wilt Chamberlain (14)	23,924
2. Bill Russell (13)	21,721
3. Kareem Abdul-Jabbar (20)	17,106
4. Moses Malone (17)	16,772
5. Artis Gilmore (17)	16,330
6. Elvin Hayes (16)	16,279
7. Nate Thurmond (14)	14,464
8. Walt Bellamy (14)	14,241
9. Wes Unseld (13)	13,679
10. Jerry Lucas (11)	12,942

Notice that there is only one player on this list who played most of his career during the 1980s, Moses Malone. The other players all played the majority of their careers during the 1960s or 1970s. Chamberlain and Russell were the only players on this list who began their careers during the poor-shooting 1950s.

The only thing this list proves is that Chamberlain and Russell snared more rebounds than anybody else. The rebounds-per-game top ten list is only slightly more significant. Again, Chamberlain and Russell are on top:

REBOUNDS PER GAME

1. Wilt Chamberlain (14)	22.89
2. Bill Russell (13)	22.56
3. Bob Pettit (11)	16.23
4. Jerry Lucas (11)	15.61
5. Nate Thurmond (14)	15.00
6. Wes Unseld (13)	13.99
7. Walt Bellamy (14)	13.65
8. Dave Cowens (11)	13.63
9. Elgin Baylor (14)	13.55
10. George Mikan (7)	13.40

Mikan's average is listed for the five seasons he played in which rebounds were counted. It is assumed he averaged the same his first two

seasons, although the likelihood is his average was higher for those two seasons. If all of his statistics were known, he could stand as high as No. 7 on this list.

The most noticeable thing about this list is that there is not an active player on it. Moses Malone, the active player with the highest average, is No. 12, with a rebounding average just under 13 per game. The only other active players who average 10 or more rebounds per game for careers of 10 seasons or longer are Buck Williams, Bill Laimbeer, Robert Parish, and Larry Bird. Jack Sikma's average dropped under 10 last season and Parish and Bird are expected to slip under 10 this season.

Charles Oakley, Dennis Rodman, Hakeem Olajuwon, Charles Barkley, Karl Malone, Patrick Ewing, and David Robinson also have double-figure rebounding averages, but their careers have not entered the declining stages as yet.

Since Chamberlain and Russell more than doubled the per-game rebounding averages of most of the best active players, this reaffirms the fact that it has become difficult to accumulate big rebounding totals in recent years because of increased shooting accuracy.

Another factor is that during the era of Russell and Chamberlain most teams had only one big man. Today, most teams have at least two and sometimes three strong rebounders. A good example is the Boston Celtics. Larry Bird is the same height as Russell (6' 9"), but he has played the small forward position most of his career for the Celtics, with 7-foot Robert Parish and 6' 11" Kevin McHale handling the center and power forward positions.

A third factor is that Chamberlain and Russell had high minutes-per-game averages. This shows up on the rebounds-per-minute list, where they are not quite as dominant as on the previous two lists. There are no active players on this top ten list (minimum 5,000 rebounds):

REBOUNDS PER MINUTE

1. Bill Russell (13)	.533
2. Wilt Chamberlain (14)	.500
3. Walter Dukes (8)	.424
4. Mel Daniels (9)	.424

5. Bob Pettit (11) .... .420
6. Nate Thurmond (14) .... .403
7. Jerry Lucas (11) .... .403
8. Swen Nater (11) .... .402
9. Wes Unseld (13) .... .384
10. George Mikan (7) .... .384

After placing third on the list of most total rebounds, Kareem Abdul-Jabbar did not make either the per-game or per-minute list. He did not come close to making the list with his percentage of .304 rebounds per minute. Making an appearance on this list, ironically, is Swen Nater who, during his college career, was called the world's best second-string center. He was Bill Walton's substitute at UCLA but later became a strong player in both the ABA and NBA. Although not a scorer, passer, or defensive intimidator to rival Walton, Nater was a powerful rebounder.

The final two rebounding lists also are affected by minutes played. The first one, Rebounding Productivity, is dominated by iron-man players because it compares a player's total rebounds to the number of rebounds available in all games his team played. A player who does not play a high percentage of his team's minutes has no chance to make this list (minimum of 5,000 rebounds):

REBOUNDING PRODUCTIVITY

1. Wilt Chamberlain (14) .... .1650
2. Bill Russell (13) .... .1531
3. Moses Malone (17) .... .1350
4. Buck Williams (10) .... .1293
5. Wes Unseld (13) .... .1285
6. Hakeem Olajuwon (7) .... .1282
7. Artis Gilmore (17) .... .1276
8. Charles Barkley (7) .... .1272
9. Charles Oakley (6) .... .1260
10. Elvin Hayes (16) .... .1256

This list passes the best test of the integrity of any all-time chart: Does it include players of all eras? This one does. Chamberlain and Russell remain at the top because they played higher minutes-per-game totals than the other players on the chart, but the margin of their advantage is smaller than on the other charts.

I want to note here that we are not attempting to deprive Chamberlain and Russell of their rightful place as great rebounders but rather to find a rating system that has a good common denominator, one that is fair for making comparison between players from all eras of professional basketball. The final list, that follows, does this best of all.

The final list compares players' rebounding totals with available rebounds during the minutes they spend on the court. Obviously, Chamberlain and Russell were the most valuable rebounders to their teams in pro basketball history because they played so many minutes and accumulated such big totals. But this final list is the one that should be used to settle the argument of who were indeed the greatest rebounders in terms of efficiency.

Two of the top three, Swen Nater and Moses Malone, had outstanding short-term and long-term credentials. In Nater's best season, 1974–75, he pulled down nearly 24 percent (.2373) of all rebounds during his minutes of playing time. The norm is 10 percent.

In Malone's best season, 1978–79, he snared .2347 of all rebounds during his minutes on the court. Malone played for five different teams in his first 12 professional seasons. His team outrebounded the opposition every one of those seasons.

The third member of the top three, Charles Oakley, is still in the prime of his career. His rebounding could decrease as he becomes older and loses some of his power and jumping ability. Another active player, Dennis Rodman, could enter the list in the top ten when he reaches the 5,000-rebound minimum.

REBOUNDING EFFICIENCY

1. Swen Nater (11) .... .2193
2. Charles Oakley (6) .... .2002
3. Moses Malone (17) .... .1999
4. Tom Boerwinkle (10) .... .1989
5. Mel Daniels (9) .... .1976
6. Larry Smith (11) .... .1952
7. Wilt Chamberlain (14) .... .1894
8. Hakeem Olajuwon (7) .... .1872
9. Wes Unseld (13) .... .1865
10. Bill Russell (13) .... .1859

11. Artis Gilmore (17) .... .1854	31. Otto Moore (9) .... .1612
12. George Mikan (7) .... .1853	32. Kareem Abdul-Jabbar (20) .... .1609
13. LaSalle Thompson (9) .... .1846	33. Elvin Hayes (16) .... .1608
14. Robert Parish (15) .... .1827	34. Sam Lacey (13) .... .1605
15. Buck Williams (10) .... .1816	35. Bob Lanier (14) .... .1600
16. Charles Barkley (7) .... .1792	36. Paul Silas (16) .... .1599
17. Bill Laimbeer (11) .... .1767	37. Willis Reed (10) .... .1564
18. Dave Cowens (11) .... .1765	38. Bob Pettit (11) .... .1527
19. Alton Lister (10) .... .1762	39. Bob McAdoo (14) .... .1526
20. Nate Thurmond (14) .... .1692	40. Walt Bellamy (14) .... .1523
21. Maurice Lucas (14) .... .1690	41. Red Robbins (8) .... .1517
22. Jerry Lucas (11) .... .1684	42. Harry Gallatin (10) .... .1510
23. Rich Kelley (11) .... .1673	43. Walter Dukes (8) .... .1500
24. Elmore Smith (8) .... .1670	44. Bill Bridges (13) .... .1487
25. Wayne Cooper (13) .... .1656	45. Larry Bird (12) .... .1472
26. Clyde Lee (10) .... .1656	46. Gus Johnson (10) .... .1467
27. George McGinnis (11) .... .1651	47. Johnny Green (14) .... .1459
28. Jack Sikma (14) .... .1643	48. Larry Foust (12) .... .1417
29. Dan Roundfield (12) .... .1643	49. Ray Felix (9) .... .1380
30. Karl Malone (6) .... .1641	50. Dolph Schayes (14) .... .1378

ABSTRACTION 2

An Offensive Statistic

One of the things that disturbs me about hoop statistical mania is the fixation on offensive rebounds. Some statisticians claim offensive rebounds are more valuable than defensive rebounds. They have the value figured down to the hundredth of a point.

I say baloney.

Show me a guy whose offensive rebounds are disproportionate to his defensive rebounds and I'll show you a guy who probably isn't a good team player, a guy who doesn't know how to box out, a guy who is more concerned about his own offensive stats than his team's success.

Boxing out—the technique in which a defender turns his body into the offensive player he is guarding and shields him away from the boards—is practically a lost art. The team that does a good job of boxing out on defense will not often be victimized by offensive rebounds. You can't get a rebound, even a deep rebound, with an opponent standing with his rear end against your belly, between you and the basket.

Let's say there are 100 rebounds available from missed shots in a game between the Philadelphia 76ers and Detroit Pistons. Let's say the 76ers front line consisting of Charles Barkley, Rick Mahorn, and Armon Gilliam pound the offensive boards relentlessly and accumulate the unusually high total of 20 offensive rebounds.

I can hear TV commentator Hubie Brown now, extolling the bruising play of these three monsters.

But somehow, when all the stats are totaled up at the end of the game, lo and behold, the Pistons win the game and wind up with 55 total rebounds to 45 for the 76ers.

This can mean one of two things: Either the 76ers did not play with as much enthusiasm on their defensive glass as they did on offense, or the Pistons did some offensive board pounding of their own.

There can be no real separation between offensive rebounds and defensive rebounds. There are rebounds at both ends of the court, but the offensive team can rebound only when there is a lapse by the defensive team in boxing out.

When I was statistician for the New York Knicks, one assignment I had was to keep track of the Knicks' failures to box out. If an opponent got an offensive rebound because of a Knick's failure to box him out, I was supposed to put a little X next to the offending player's name.

Want to know something? I made the rather elementary discovery that nearly every time a Knick opponent got an offensive rebound, it was a defensive player's fault. So it isn't really the offensive rebounder who should be receiving all the credit, but the inept defender who should get most of the blame.

With one exception, Dennis Rodman. Rodman plays an unusual role for the Pistons. He is the team's principal defensive player, but is not involved in the offense much, if at all.

Rodman's entire role at the offensive end of the court is to try to worm his way between defensive players for rebounds (which may have something to do with his nickname "worm"). He is difficult to box out because often the man assigned to him leaves him to double-team one of the more offensive-minded Pistons.

But Rodman is the exception that validates the rule: No offensive rebounds without defensive lapses. Even if a team accumulates big offensive-rebounding stats, these rebounds don't help if the bottom line shows them with less total rebounds than their opponents.

If half of those 100 rebounds in the Piston-76er game are at each end of the court, the only way the 76ers can get 20 offensive rebounds and come up 10 boards short of Detroit is if they allow the Pistons to get 25 offensive rebounds.

Go figure.

3
The Great Playmakers

The historical pattern of assists is the opposite of rebounds. The first NBA leader in assists, Ernie Calverley of Providence, averaged 3.4 per game. The 45th, John Stockton, averaged 14.2.

Through the years, assists totals have risen in direct proportion to shooting percentages, except for seasons when the standards of what constituted an assist were changed.

For the first two seasons, about the only pass that was deemed an assist was one that was caught within a few feet of the basket by a player who immediately took it in for a layup. Assists were awarded on only 26.2 percent of all baskets.

For the next eight seasons, it was almost as hard to score an unassisted basket in the NBA as it was to score an unassisted goal in the National Hockey League. The percent of assisted baskets for those seasons was 70.5.

Another change followed, dropping the rate of assisted baskets to about 50 percent. This pattern prevailed from the 1956–57 season through the 1967–68 season, a total of 12 seasons.

The next change was not a sudden one. It happened gradually over a period of six years, starting with the 1968–69 season. There were increases each season and, at the end of the 1973–74 season, the percent of assisted baskets was back up to 57.2.

It took another decade of very gradual increases to boost the percent to 60. It has hovered right around 60 since the 1983–84 season.

The radical fluctuations in standards for assisting baskets make it difficult to come up with a statistic that is fair to players of all eras in the NBA. The way to solve this problem is to adjust the final productivity and efficiency ratings on the basis of the standards of the era during which each player played.

For example, during the first nine seasons of Isiah Thomas' career, the standard was exactly 60 percent, so Thomas' efficiency and productivity ratings don't have to be adjusted at all. However, Guy Rodgers played during an era when the standard was considerably below the 60 percent norm of the 1980s. For Rodgers' 12-year career, the leaguewide percentage of assisted baskets was .511 or 51.1 percent. This was only 85.2 percent of the standard 60, so Rodgers' ratings need to be increased proportionately to make up for the fact that he played during a more difficult era than Thomas for receiving credit for assists.

The need to adjust the final productivity and efficiency ratings means that we will have seven lists of all-time greats in assists, two more than we had for rebounds or points. With 3,000-assist minimums for all lists, let's start with the basic three:

TOTAL ASSISTS

Player (Seasons)	Assists
1. Magic Johnson (12)	9,921
2. Oscar Robertson (14)	9,887
3. Isiah Thomas (10)	7,431
4. Len Wilkens (15)	7,211
5. Maurice Cheeks (13)	7,100
6. Bob Cousy (14)	6,955
7. Guy Rodgers (12)	6,917
8. Nate Archibald (13)	6,476
9. John Lucas (14)	6,454
10. Norm Nixon (10)	6,386

ASSISTS PER GAME

Player (Seasons)	
1. Magic Johnson (12)	11.35
2. John Stockton (7)	10.95
3. Kevin Johnson (4)	9.79
4. Isiah Thomas (10)	9.73
5. Oscar Robertson (14)	9.51
6. Norm Nixon (10)	8.32
7. Kevin Porter (10)	8.06
8. Terry Porter (6)	8.05
9. Guy Rodgers (12)	7.75
10. Bob Cousy (14)	7.53

ASSISTS PER MINUTE

Player (Seasons)	
1. John Stockton (7)	.3603
2. Magic Johnson (12)	.3073
3. Johnny Moore (9)	.2879
4. Kevin Johnson (4)	.2869
5. Nate McMillan (5)	.2799
6. Kevin Porter (10)	.2781
7. Isiah Thomas (10)	.2661
8. John Lucas (14)	.2525
9. Terry Porter (6)	.2514
10. Guy Rodgers (12)	.2413

Eight of the ten players on the assists-per-minute list played most of their careers during the 1980s when conditions were most advantageous for playmakers. Except for eight seasons during the 1940s and 1950s, the percentage of assisted baskets was the highest in NBA history during the 1980s and the all-time high field-goal percentages made it more likely that the shooter would follow a good pass with a successful shot. These two factors skew the all-time assists lists much to the favor of active and recently retired players.

The remaining four assists rating methods work toward elimination of this bias. The final method is the one that best shows the efficiency of playmakers in setting up teammates for baskets.

The first of the four compares players' total assists with their teams' total field goals, excluding the field goals they scored themselves. The formula is:

Player Assists/Team Field Goals –
Player Field Goals = Rating.

It is a productivity rating, favoring the players with the highest bulk totals. Since totals are related to minutes played, only players who play a high percentage of their team's minutes can be expected to make this list.

John Stockton, the all-time leader, has assisted on about 30 percent of all field goals made by Utah, excluding the ones he has scored himself, during his seven seasons with the Jazz. Here is the top ten:

Player (Seasons)	Productivity
1. John Stockton (7)	.2958
2. Magic Johnson (12)	.2554
3. Isiah Thomas (10)	.2501
4. Kevin Johnson (4)	.2488
5. Oscar Robertson (14)	.2367
6. Terry Porter (6)	.2021
7. Norm Nixon (10)	.1997
8. Bob Cousy (14)	.1949
9. Guy Rodgers (12)	.1787
10. Mo Cheeks (13)	.1764

This list still does not take care of the fact that during different eras assists were awarded on a greater or lower percentage of field goals.

The main reason so many active players are on this list is that during recent seasons assists have been credited on a high percentage of baskets. A secondary reason is that professional basketball has become more specialized than it was during the early 1950s, the only era in which the percentage of assisted baskets was higher. At that time, there wasn't such a clear distinction between point guards, shooting guards, and small forwards as there is today. Players other than the point guard did more handling of the basketball during that era than this one.

There is no statistical way to compensate for the second factor, which means we may expect to find a high percentage of active players on all of our assists lists. But we can make an adjustment to compensate for the fact that there have been different standards for awarding assists during different eras.

In order to do this, we have computed leaguewide the percentage of baskets each season for which assists were awarded. The norm is considered to be 60 percent, which it has been for the past eight years. If it is higher than this during the career of Player A, his ratings are decreased. If it is lower than this for Player B, his ratings are increased. This is similar to the game-pace factor in the TENDEX rating formula.

The top ten on the adjusted list below more accurately reflect the true productivity of the great playmakers than the list above:

Player (Seasons)	Adjusted Productivity
1. John Stockton (7)	.2943
2. Oscar Robertson (14)	.2690
3. Magic Johnson (12)	.2560
4. Isiah Thomas (10)	.2501
5. Kevin Johnson (4)	.2476
6. Guy Rodgers (12)	.2096
7. Norm Nixon (10)	.2024
8. Terry Porter (6)	.2009
9. Bob Cousy (14)	.1969
10. Norm Van Lier (10)	.1780

This list is much better balanced between active and retired players, as any all-time list should be. Robertson moves up from fourth to second place, Rodgers from tenth to sixth. It is doubtful whether Stockton will be able to stay ahead of Robertson when he hits the declining seasons of his career. Robertson played so many minutes for so many seasons at such a high level of skill that he probably was the most productive playmaker in NBA history.

Efficiency is a different matter. The player who plays too many minutes, as Robertson often did, is going to become tired and lose a little of his efficiency. The final two statistics do not necessarily show who were the greatest playmakers in NBA history. What they do show is the players who played at the highest levels of efficiency, in terms of assists per minute, for the time they spent on the court.

The next list is based on the percentage of all potential field goals each player assists on during his minutes on the court. Again, each player's own field goals are excluded from the potential. The formula for the first productivity list is used

Player Assists/Team Field Goals –
Player Field Goals = Rating

and the rating is then divided by the percentage of the team's minutes each player played.

Robertson, for example, played about 80 percent of his team's minutes for his 14-season career, the highest iron-man percentage of any backcourtman in NBA history. Some players on this list may not even have played half of their team's minutes, so long as they meet the minimum criterion of 3,000 assists for their careers.

Here is the first efficiency list:

Player (Seasons)	Efficiency
1. John Stockton (7)	.4783
2. Magic Johnson (12)	.3797
3. Kevin Johnson (4)	.3738
4. Isiah Thomas (10)	.3582
5. Kevin Porter (10)	.3416
6. Nate McMillan (5)	.3342
7. Johnny Moore (9)	.3374
8. Terry Porter (6)	.3136
9. John Lucas (14)	.3083
10. Dick McGuire (11)	.3034

Stockton's record of assisting on more than 47 percent of the field goals his team scores—excluding his own field goals—during his minutes on the court is one of the most remarkable statistics in the history of professional basketball.

The final list takes the efficiency list above and divides it by the same factor we used to adjust the productivity lists according to the different standards for awarding assists in different eras of play. We are counting ABA records, by the way, and a few ABA players show up on this list. This is probably the best method of judging the most efficient playmakers in professional basketball history, although, again, it does not necessarily mean these players were as great as the iron men on the productivity list.

As with the scoring and rebounding efficiency lists, we list the top fifty of all-time:

Player (Seasons)	Adjusted Efficiency
1. John Stockton (7)	.4759
2. Magic Johnson (12)	.3805
3. Kevin Johnson (4)	.3720
4. Isiah Thomas (10)	.3581
5. Kevin Porter (10)	.3574
6. Guy Rodgers (12)	.3510
7. Oscar Robertson (14)	.3391
8. Johnny Moore (9)	.3380
9. Nate McMillan (5)	.3321
10. John Lucas (14)	.3122
11. Terry Porter (6)	.3117
12. Bob Cousy (14)	.3051
13. Norm Nixon (10)	.2971
14. John Bagley (9)	.2918
15. Dick McGuire (11)	.2917
16. Glenn Rivers (8)	.2893
17. Nate Archibald (13)	.2855
18. Rickey Green (13)	.2816
19. Maurice Cheeks (13)	.2773
20. Len Wilkens (15)	.2753
21. Norm Van Lier (10)	.2720
22. Micheal Ray Richardson (8)	.2667
23. Eric Floyd (9)	.2662
24. Brad Davis (14)	.2622
25. Larry Drew (10)	.2596
26. Ray Williams (10)	.2586
27. Jerry West (14)	.2586
28. Derek Harper (8)	.2585
29. Richie Guerin (13)	.2578
30. Lafayette Lever (9)	.2574
31. Reggie Theus (13)	.2569
32. Walt Hazzard (10)	.2541
33. Jay Humphries (7)	.2540
34. Allen Leavell (10)	.2493
35. Rory Sparrow (11)	.2463
36. Dave Bing (12)	.2454
37. Andy Phillip (11)	.2430
38. Gus Williams (12)	.2425
39. Paul Pressey (9)	.2409
40. Darrell Walker (8)	.2349
41. Eddie Johnson (10)	.2348
42. Michael Jordan (7)	.2347
43. Mack Calvin (11)	.2317
44. Walt Frazier (13)	.2287
45. Quinn Buckner (10)	.2281
46. Paul Westphal (12)	.2264
47. Clyde Drexler (8)	.2239
48. Larry Bird (12)	.2234
49. Alvin Robertson (7)	.2209
50. Lou Dampier (12)	.2167

4
The Laker Assist-Maker

It was mentioned in Chapter 3 that the third change in standards for assisted baskets occurred gradually over a period of more than a decade, from the late 1960s until the early 1980s. It was not a sudden change based on a deliberate decision to change the definition of an assist, as had happened twice previously.

Why then did it happen?

Here's a theory. It's one man's idea, but statistical evidence lends support for it. The theory is this: The Los Angeles Lakers were responsible for the change.

During the early 1970s, professional basketball began to experience new popularity with improving television contracts that exposed the great players to the general public. By this time, the greatest backcourtman of the NBA's first 25 years, Oscar Robertson, had lost much of his skill. It was a good matchup between Robertson and Jerry West, who had lost less of his.

In Los Angeles, there had been envy of Robertson ever since he foiled an All-Star Game promotional gimmick. Robertson and Elgin Baylor both were 6-foot-5 and were generally considered to be the best players of that size in the world. The Lakers, believing Baylor was better, promoted a head-to-head matchup between the two players in the 1964 All-Star Game. They did not normally play against each other because Baylor was a forward and Robertson was a guard.

Robertson accepted the challenge and dominated Baylor so completely at both ends of the floor that the coach of the West team pulled Baylor off Robertson during the second quarter.

Seven years later, with Robertson's career in decline, comparisons began to be heard again from Los Angeles. This time the challenger was Jerry West. West's NBA career had started at the same time as Robertson's, and for the first ten seasons Robertson was indisputably the better of the two players. But by the early 1970s, Robertson's legs were showing wear-and-tear.

For their full 14-season careers, West played 7,295 fewer minutes than Robertson and so his legs were much fresher during the final few years. It was a good matchup between the two players, especially since Robertson had begun emphasizing defense with Kareem Abdul-Jabbar taking on most of the offensive load for Milwaukee. West was still the big offensive gun for the Lakers.

Robertson and West had been comparable scorers throughout their careers, but Robertson always had had big advantages in rebounds and assists. Especially assists.

Robertson was a pure point guard. Although West played the point much of the time, he was in style a shooting guard. Not until the 1970–71 season, the 11th of West's career, did he become a significant playmaker. He placed second in the NBA in assists that season and led the league the next season.

The trouble is, the career pattern of West's assists doesn't make sense. Here is a chart showing his percentage of assists per minute during the final nine seasons of his career:

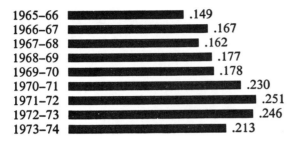

1965–66	.149
1966–67	.167
1967–68	.162
1968–69	.177
1969–70	.178
1970–71	.230
1971–72	.251
1972–73	.246
1973–74	.213

What this chart shows is that West, at age 32, suddenly went from being an average playmaker to an exceptional one, and that he further improved on his penetrating and passing abilities the following season, at age 33.

Or did he?

I remember a game televised from Los Angeles between Milwaukee and the Lakers during the 1970–71 season. It was a defensive struggle, a close game. Abdul-Jabbar was keeping the Bucks in the game with a remarkable display of hook shots and dunks. Robertson and West did not play particularly well in the first half.

Then the halftime statistics were announced. West had 12 points and 5 assists. Robertson had 8 points and 15 assists.

Fifteen assists! Robertson must have been the most surprised person in the arena. He had been credited with 15 assists and hadn't done much other than lob passes to Abdul-Jabbar. And they weren't alley-oops. Kareem was working for his points after receiving those passes.

It was the most liberal distribution of assists I had seen.

What had happened? In a spirit of overzealousness on behalf of West, in the Robertson comparison, had the Laker statistician relaxed the standard for assists? Or was this merely coincidental? The one certain thing was that

assists were being awarded for passes during that game in Los Angeles which were not normally considered to be assists.

The chart of West's assists above shows that he did experience a sudden increase during the 1970–71 season. If he played exactly as he had during the two previous seasons, in order for him to achieve the assist total he was credited with in 1970–71 he would have had to have his number at home inflated by 60 percent. In other words, he must have been credited with eight assists at home for every five he got from scorekeepers on the road, assuming the 16 guys on the road were still scoring them the same way as they always had and West was playing the same as before.

But if this is true, wouldn't it show up on the Lakers' assists totals as a team? If the scorekeeper in Los Angeles was being liberal with his awarding of assists, wouldn't the Lakers as a team have ranked among the league leaders?

For the three-year period from the 1970–71 through the 1972–73 seasons, West's three big playmaking years, the Lakers led the NBA in assists.

But let's assume that this is a contrived argument, that West did indeed suddenly become a great playmaker at age 32 and this was the reason the Lakers led the league. Well, then, this would mean the Lakers would slip far down in assists between the time of West's decline and the appearance of the next outstanding Laker playmaker, Magic Johnson, in 1979. And they wouldn't have ranked high in 1980–81, the season during which Johnson missed 45 games because of an injury.

The facts were otherwise. From 1973–74 through 1977–78, when the Lakers did not have a star playmaker, or even a good one, they still finished no lower than seventh in assists. They finished among the top 30 percent of the teams in the NBA in assists four of those five seasons.

In 1980–81, without Johnson most of the season, the Lakers finished No. 2 out of 23 teams in assists and had only six fewer assists than the top team, Philadelphia.

For the past 20 seasons, since that fateful one of 1970–71, the Lakers have led the NBA in assists 7 times and finished among the top three teams 15 times. They set an NBA record with 2,575 assists in 1984–85. For the 20-year period, they accumulated 2,053 assists more than the No. 2 team in that category, Boston, a team which always has been noted for a consummate passing game.

In 1969–70, the season before the Lakers started their remarkable run, they had almost the identical personnel they had from 1970–71 through 1972–73. But in 1969–70 they placed 9 out of 14 teams in assists.

Every statistic points to the conclusion that there was a sudden mysterious increase in the rate at which assists were awarded for Laker home games during the 1970–71 season and that this pattern continued during seasons after that. Following the Lakers' lead, perhaps, the leaguewide average of assists also increased, but didn't catch up to the rate of advance in Los Angeles.

This chart demonstrates the disparity between the Los Angeles Lakers' assists totals and the totals of other franchises that were in the NBA from 1970 through 1990. The question is: Were the Lakers really that much better than everybody else, or was there a different explanation for this phenomenon?

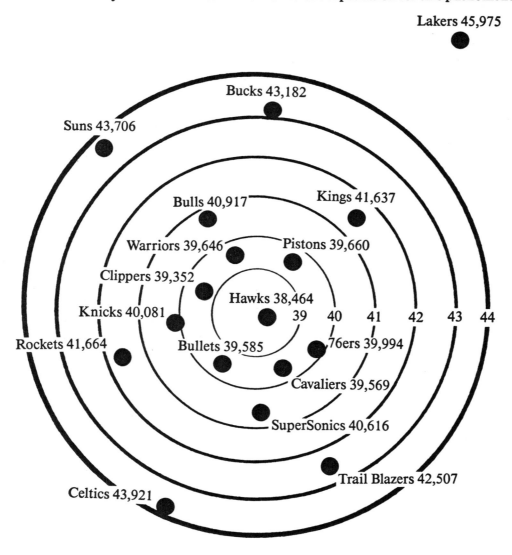

ABSTRACTION 3

Assisted Assists

Statistical theorist Dean Oliver has suggested that Hakeem Olajuwon and some of the other outstanding rebounders pad their statistics with "cheap" rebounds which their teammates would get if they didn't. The rebounding performances of Otis Thorpe and Larry Smith last season while Olajuwon was injured lend credence to this theory.

Oliver believes it's easier to rebound than score, but there can be cheap scoring statistics too. Some players will sacrifice defense to cheat toward midcourt so they can escape on fast breaks for easy baskets. And then, of course, there are the guys who never saw a shot they didn't like.

And may I suggest that there are cheap assists statistics also. Rules for crediting assists have become so liberalized in the NBA that it is possible now to receive credit for an assist for a pass that has very little to do with the scoring of a basket.

Case in point was the assist on which Magic Johnson broke Oscar Robertson's career assists record last season. Johnson tossed a lob pass to Terry Teagle who was closely guarded in the right corner of the frontcourt with his back to the basket. After receiving the pass, Teagle turned and launched a 20-foot jumpshot in the face of a defender. Johnson received his 9888th assist on the play—a debatable accreditation, to say the least, but not an unusual one.

This assist made a prophet of Robertson, who had ridiculed the liberality of assists statistics less than a year before Johnson broke his record. In a 1990 interview with a sportswriter for the Fort Lauderdale *News & Sun Sentinel,* Robertson said assists statistics are inflated in today's NBA game:

"Sometimes it gets out of hand. You read all the time now where a guy had 20 assists or more in a game, and that's ridiculous. When I played, you had to earn assists. Today they hand them out if you make a pass to a guy who then dribbles and shoots a 20-footer."

Sound familiar?

Robertson continued: "I wish someone would go back and look at a play-by-play of one of my games and record assists the way they do today. I'd probably have 25 a game. That would look good in the record book."

Not a bad idea. Maybe the NBA should pay a statistician to go through the archives and watch video tapes (if they exist) of every NBA game played before the 1973–74 season when steals and blocked shots began to be counted. Not only could they make the assists statistics uniform, but they could come up with exact blocked-shots totals for Bill Russell and Wilt Chamberlain, steals for Rick Barry and minutes played for everybody from 1946 through 1951.

It would be worth the effort and the expense.

5
The Blockers

The NBA was so slow to begin tabulating blocked shots, steals, and turnovers that it is impossible to rate the best players in these categories without doing estimations.

Two of the greatest shot-blockers, Bill Russell and Wilt Chamberlain, played their entire careers without having a block recorded to their names. The NBA did not start counting blocked shots until the 1973–74 season. Chamberlain retired in 1973, four years after Russell.

Many players had careers that overlapped the era when blocked shots were counted and the era when they weren't. These included Nate Thurmond, Kareem Abdul-Jabbar, Elvin Hayes, Julius Erving, Elmore Smith, Artis Gilmore, Billy Paultz, Bob Lanier, Sam Lacey, and Bob McAdoo.

All shot-blocking statistics listed in this book for these players are estimated, but they are careful estimations based on research and projections from statistical patterns during seasons in which their blocked shots were counted. Guesswork is kept to a minimum.

Here is an example. Blocked shots were counted during 16 of the 20 seasons Kareem Abdul-Jabbar played in the NBA. The missing seasons were his first four. Now, if we estimated Abdul-Jabbar's first four seasons on the basis of his final 16, we would attribute to

him about 200 blocks per season for those four because that is what he averaged for his final 16. That would give him a career total of about 4,000 blocks.

But Abdul-Jabbar was playing more minutes during those early seasons. His per-minute average was .07283 blocks for his final 16 seasons. Projecting that through his first four seasons would make his career total about 4,200 blocks.

The second method improves on the first, but the problem with both is that Abdul-Jabbar was a much stronger player during his first four seasons than his final four. A better way to estimate his blocked shots is to compare the missing early seasons with the ones that immediately followed, when he was still a dominant player.

From his fifth through his eighth season, his per-minute average of blocked shots was .08621. If he averaged the same for his first four seasons as he did for his second four, he would have blocked 1,178 shots in the first four and his total would have been 4,367. This is much closer to what his career number would have been, if the totals for his first four seasons were known.

Rebounds are associated with blocked shots in that agility and strength are necessary for both. They are more likely to be done well by young players. During Abdul-Jabbar's fifth through eighth NBA seasons, he totaled 1,094 blocks and 4,563 rebounds. The ratio was .2398 blocks for every rebound. If he did the same for his first four seasons, when he totaled 5,071 rebounds, his total of blocks for those seasons would have been 1,216 and his career total would have been 4,405. This is close to the estimation (4,367) based on his blocks for his fifth-through-eighth seasons. It now becomes clear that he blocked about 4,400 shots for his career. This is more than a guess. It is an estimation that is probably not off by more than 10 or 15.

For a player such as Nate Thurmond, whose blocked shots are known only for the final two seasons of his career, when he was a very weak player, estimations are much more difficult. The better methods result in a discrepancy of 400. One comes out to 3,500, the other to 3,100. We have split the difference, estimating that Thurmond collected 3,300 for his career. But it is a rough estimate indeed.

The most difficult of all players to estimate were Wilt Chamberlain and Bill Russell, neither of whom played a season when blocked shots were counted. For those two men, we have made even rougher estimates based on research assisted by Harvey Pollack of the Philadelphia 76ers. Pollack is the most experienced statistician, having served in that position for the Philadelphia franchise from the inception of the NBA.

Like scoring and rebounding, there is little resemblance between the charts naming the players with the most career blocked shots and the charts showing the most efficient shot-blockers of all-time.

Let's start with total career blocked shots, remembering that the totals are estimated for most of these players:

TOTAL BLOCKED SHOTS

Player (Seasons)	Blocks
1. Wilt Chamberlain (14)	5,000
2. Bill Russell (13)	4,500
3. Kareem Abdul-Jabbar (20)	4,400
4. Nate Thurmond (14)	3,300
5. Artis Gilmore (17)	3,025
6. Elvin Hayes (16)	2,950
7. Mark Eaton (9)	2,780
8. Tree Rollins (14)	2,394
9. Caldwell Jones (16)	2,270
10. George T. Johnson (13)	2,125

Notice the exceptional longevity of the players on this chart. All but Eaton have played at least 13 pro seasons, and Eaton is still active.

The next chart is similar to the one above, but there are a few differences based on the fact that it is not necessary to have played so many seasons to qualify. Here are the top ten players in average of blocked shots per game (minimum of 1,000 blocks):

BLOCKS PER GAME

1. Wilt Chamberlain (14)	4.78
2. Bill Russell (13)	4.67
3. Mark Eaton (9)	3.81
4. Manute Bol (6)	3.65
5. Elmore Smith (8)	3.56
6. Hakeem Olajuwon (7)	3.43
7. Nate Thurmond (14)	3.42
8. Patrick Ewing (6)	3.11
9. Kareem Abdul-Jabbar (20)	2.82
10. Benoit Benjamin (6)	2.68

Both total-blocks and blocks-per-game are bulk statistics, but only four players—Russell, Chamberlain, Thurmond, and Abdul-Jabbar—appear on both charts. Bol did not make the first, but trails only Chamberlain, Russell, and Mark Eaton on the second. Our third chart, blocks-per-minute, contains seven members who were also on the second one:

BLOCKS PER MINUTE

1. Manute Bol (6)	.1852
2. Mark Eaton (9)	.1261
3. George T. Johnson (12)	.1173
4. Elmore Smith (8)	.1119
5. Bill Russell (13)	.1104
6. Tree Rollins (14)	.1077
7. Wilt Chamberlain (14)	.1044
8. Hakeem Olajuwon (7)	.0938
9. Harvey Catchings (11)	.0931
10. Nate Thurmond (14)	.0920

Manute Bol is an interesting specimen, not only because of his physique, but also because of his statistics. If his career continues to follow its current pattern, he will become the first player in professional basketball history to accumulate more blocked shots than points.

I haven't done computations for every player, but there's a possibility that Bol is the worst scorer and ball-handler ever. If you're Manute's coach, you don't want the ball in his hands. When he does get it by blocking a shot or retrieving a rebound, you want him to get rid of it as quickly as possible to a teammate standing closeby. A handoff is fine, thank you.

But for pure shot-blocking ability, Bol is arguably the best player of all-time. His per-minute rate of blocking shots is about 40 percent better than No. 2 man Mark Eaton.

The blocked-shot statistic comparable to rebounds-per-available-rebounds or assists-per-field-goals-made is blocked-shots-per-opponents'-field-goals-attempted. This is the stat that shows a player's proficiency in blocking shots relative to his opportunities.

No matter how many minutes you spend on the court, you can't block a shot until your opponents attempt one. The more they try, the more you have a chance to block. The chart below bears a resemblance to the per-minute chart, but where there are differences the one below is more significant. It's blocked shots per opponents' field-goal attempts.

SHOT-BLOCKING PRODUCTIVITY

1. Wilt Chamberlain (14) .... .0438
2. Bill Russell (13) .... .0434
3. Mark Eaton (9) .... .0418
4. Manute Bol (6) .... .0383
5. Hakeem Olajuwon (7) .... .0351
6. Elmore Smith (8) .... .0324
7. Patrick Ewing (6) .... .0320
8. Nate Thurmond (14) .... .0292
9. Kareem Abdul-Jabbar (20) .... .0283
10. Benoit Benjamin (6) .... .0265

This is a productivity statistic because it is dominated by players who play most of the time. The more minutes a player spends on the court, the more shots he has a chance to block.

The final statistic gives equal opportunity to players who play fewer minutes. These players may have less value to their teams, since many of them play less time than the players on the productivity chart, but from a statistical standpoint they are more efficient shot-blockers.

For this final statistic the formula is:

Blocked Shots/Opponents' Field-Goal Attempts/ Player's Percentage of Team's Minutes Played = Shot-Blocking Efficiency.

Only the 38 players who have blocked at least 1,000 shots during their careers are eligible for this chart. Here are the all-time leaders:

SHOT-BLOCKING EFFICIENCY

1. Manute Bol (6) .... .0980
2. Mark Eaton (9) .... .0683
3. George T. Johnson (12) .... .0625
4. Tree Rollins (14) .... .0619
5. Elmore Smith (8) .... .0537
6. Bill Russell (13) .... .0527
7. Hakeem Olajuwon (7) .... .0512
8. Wilt Chamberlain (14) .... .0503
9. Harvey Catchings (11) .... .0499
10. Patrick Ewing (6) .... .0490
11. Benoit Benjamin (6) .... .0468
12. Nate Thurmond (14) .... .0452
13. Alton Lister (10) .... .0452
14. Bill Walton (10) .... .0421
15. Wayne Cooper (13) .... .0419
16. Kareem Abdul-Jabbar (20) .... .0395
17. Darryl Dawkins (14) .... .0351
18. Larry Nance (10) .... .0351
19. Caldwell Jones (16) .... .0350
20. Artis Gilmore (17) .... .0346
21. Billy Paultz (16) .... .0346
22. Terry Tyler (11) .... .0333
23. Herb Williams (10) .... .0322
24. Kevin McHale (11) .... .0314
25. Elvin Hayes (16) .... .0303

ABSTRACTION 4

Boxes & Blocks

On a radio show I said that Larry Nance was one of the best defensive forwards of all-time.

The show host disagreed, saying: "Nance is just a shot-blocker."

Which got me to thinking: What exactly constitutes great defense? Tight man-to-man? Blocking and altering shots? Forcing turnovers? Stealing the ball? Drawing offensive fouls? Playing good team defense? Boxing out on the boards?

All of these things are factors in good defense. Here's how I rate them in order of importance:

1. **MAN-TO-MAN**—Many basketball players think about scoring big, but there are too few who give thought to holding his opponent to little. Dennis Rodman is the best man-to-man defender in basketball and, yes, he is the best defensive player in basketball.

2. **SHOT-BLOCKING**—Not all shot-blockers are excellent man-to-man defenders, but the intimidation they cause is almost as important. Show me a team that holds its opponents to a low field-goal percentage and I'll show you a team with one or more shot-blockers. The best is Hakeem Olajuwon, who is also good in other aspects of defense. He's the second best defensive player in basketball.

3. **BOXING OUT**—A team that boxes out its opponents is a team that wins the defensive boards. This ranks just behind man-to-man and shot-blocking in order of importance. The Boston Celtics front line of Larry Bird, Robert Parish, and Kevin McHale are not great athletes, but they are good rebounders because they box out better than most.

4. **TEAM DEFENSE**—The Detroit Pistons, led by Rodman and Joe Dumars, play excellent man-to-man defense. The Los Angeles Lakers and Boston Celtics don't have expert man-to-man defenders, but they make up for individual deficiencies by double-teaming, switching and covering for each other.

5. **FORCING TURNOVERS**—Defenders don't receive credit for this, as they do for steals, but it's more important because it results from tough man-to-man defense, not from risk-taking. Alvin Robertson is good at both stealing the ball and forcing turnovers.

6. **DRAWING OFFENSIVE FOULS**—If this results from great defensive position, as it often does with Rodman, it's great defense. If it's a last-ditch effort to get a basket-saving whistle, it's poor defense and a good referee will ignore it. NBA referees generally are good on these no-calls, but college refs often are guilty of waving off baskets on questionable offensive fouls.

7. **STEALING THE BALL**—Too often, NBA defensive Players of the Year have been selected on the basis of their steals totals. Actually, this is the least important facet of defense because too often a defender will sacrifice good man-to-man position to go for a steal. If he makes the theft, he looks good and probably scores on a breakaway. If he misses, which happens more often than not, his opponent probably scores or sets up a teammate for an easy basket.

6
Steals & Turnovers

It is about as difficult to evaluate steals and turnovers as it is to catch snipes. The routine statistics—career totals, per-game and per-minute averages—are easy enough, but figuring ultimate stats is almost impossible.

The steals statistic comparable to rebounds-per-available-rebounds or assists-per-field-goals-made is steals-per-opponents-ball-possessions. The trouble is, it's impossible to compute ball possessions from available data.

Every ball possession ends with a shot or a turnover, so the total number of ball possessions for a team is the sum of its field-goal attempts, turnovers and trips to the free-throw line. To compute a player's ball-stealing proficiency means you must know the total ball possessions of his team's opponents, because every possession provides a chance for a steal. But it is not possible to make that computation.

The problem lies at the free-throw line. At one time there were single-shot fouls in the NBA, and even though those days are over, there are still three-point plays (field goal-free throw on the same play) to muddle the statistics. The best we could do would be to estimate, and we have to do enough of that already in tabulating steals.

Steals are the opposite of turnovers. About half of all turnovers result from an opponent stealing the ball. So instead of comparing steals with ball-possessions, let's compare them with turnovers. This is an equally valid comparison, and it has a second advantage in allowing us to combine these two elusive statistics.

But first, let's figure out who are the all-time steals leaders. Like blocked shots, this isn't easy. Steals were not counted before 1973–74 in the NBA or before 1972–73 in the ABA.

For players whose careers overlapped these transitional seasons, estimates are based on the same criteria as blocked shots . . . with one exception. Career patterns are used, with higher percentages of steals being accumulated during early and peak seasons of players' careers. Comparisons are made between steals and minutes played, taking these patterns into consideration.

Parallel statistics to steals are points and assists. It takes a quick player with good hands to pile up a lot of points, assists and steals. When the reflexes start to go the steals, assists, and points decline together. This gives us a second basis for estimation.

Players whose steals totals must be estimated include Julius Erving, Roland Taylor, Rick Barry, Joe Caldwell, Walt Frazier, Randy Smith, Len Wilkens, Billy Cunningham, Don Buse, John Havlicek, and Mike Gale. Using all factors in making estimations, here are the standard charts for steals:

CAREER STEALS

Player (Seasons)	Steals
1. Julius Erving (16)	2,475
2. Rick Barry (14)	2,380
3. Maurice Cheeks (13)	2,194
4. Don Buse (13)	1,925
5. Len Wilkens (15)	1,900
6. Joe Caldwell (11)	1,750
7. John Havlicek (16)	1,725
8. Magic Johnson (12)	1,698
9. Randy Smith (12)	1,675
10. Gus Williams (11)	1,638

STEALS PER GAME

1. Alvin Robertson (7)	2.87
2. Michael Jordan (7)	2.77
3. Micheal Ray Richardson (8)	2.63
4. John Stockton (7)	2.44
5. Roland Taylor (8)	2.39
6. Rick Barry (14)	.2.33
7. Lafayette Lever (9)	2.28
8. Joe Caldwell (11)	2.24
9. Clyde Drexler (8)	2.20
10. Maurice Cheeks (13)	2.17

STEALS PER MINUTE

1. Alvin Robertson (7)	.0892
2. Roland Taylor (8)	.0864
3. Quinn Buckner (10)	.0823
4. John Stockton (7)	.0802
5. Micheal Ray Richardson (8)	.0787
6. Johnny Moore (9)	.0757
7. Darwin Cook (8)	.0737
8. Don Buse (13)	.0736
9. Michael Jordan (7)	.0718
10. Mike Gale (11)	.0712

An overrated statistic is the ratio of assists to turnovers. It is overrated because only a point guard has much chance to excel in it. Even a point man who commits 300 or more turnovers in a season can have a "good" ratio because of the great potential for assists that they have. A big man, surrounded by ball-hawking defenders, with few chances for assists, has little hope of doing well in this category.

More significant than the ratio of steals to assists is that of steals to turnovers. Unlike steals and assists, steals and turnovers are related. A steal causes a turnover. Not all turnovers are caused by steals; the average is about 50 percent. But the two go together. A player who steals the ball more than half as often as he turns it over is a good ball-possession man. A player who steals the ball more often than he turns it over is a weapon.

During the 1987–88 through 1989–90 seasons, the Denver Nuggets were below-average in nearly every statistical category except ratio of steals to turnovers. The backcourt tandem of Lafayette Lever and Michael Adams was so good at stealing the ball on defense and avoiding turnovers on offense that the Nuggets obtained enough extra ball possessions to be respectable. Last season, when Lever was traded, that pattern was broken and the Nuggets sank into mediocrity.

Lever is one of only five players in NBA-ABA history to accumulate more steals than turnovers for his career, with a minimum of 1,000 steals. The all-time leaders are Don Buse and T. R. Dunn.

Buse played nine seasons in the NBA and four in the ABA. It is necessary to estimate his turnovers for one season and his steals for one, but he is clearly the best player of all-time in this category with a ratio of about 1.7 steals for every turnover. For 13 NBA seasons, defensive specialist Dunn averaged about 1.6 steals per turnover. Here are the all-time top ten (minimum 1,000 steals):

Player (Seasons)	Ratio
1. Don Buse (13)	1.695
2. T. R. Dunn (13)	1.614
3. Lafayette Lever (9)	1.085
4. Brian Taylor (10)	1.008
5. Alvin Robertson (7)	1.003
6. Maurice Cheeks (13)	.998
7. Mike Gale (11)	.980
8. Derek Harper (8)	.952
9. Darwin Cook (8)	.930
10. Chris Ford (10)	.893

Estimates had to be made for one of two seasons for Buse, Dunn, Taylor, Gale, and

Ford. But in each case statistical patterns gave enough evidence for us to make estimates that would keep the margin for potential error within a few percentage points.

Assists fit into this category in one way only. Players such as Lever, Cheeks, and Harper, who are excellent playmakers in addition to being great ball thieves, deserve extra credit for keeping their turnovers down considering the number of difficult passes they have to make. These three are among the most underrated backcourtmen in NBA history and deserve Hall of Fame consideration when they retire.

Lever should be a Hall of Famer if he recovers from the career-threatening knee injury he suffered last season and resumes piling up great totals of points, rebounds, assists and steals.

Harper and Cheeks, in addition to other assets, are two of the finest man-to-man defenders in the history of professional basketball. This does not show up on their TENDEX ratings.

The final adjustment for the steal-turnover ratio is based on the fact that liberalized crediting of steals through the years has resulted in almost annual increases in this ratio from 1973–74 to the present. For the 1973–74 season, this ratio was .4182 in the NBA and .4680 in the ABA. It increased to .4932 and .5105 for the final two seasons of the ABA, but did not climb above .500 in the NBA until the 1986–87 season. It has exceeded .500 for the past five seasons.

Our final statistic in this chapter is based on the ratio of steals to turnovers, adjusted according to league-wide averages for this statistic during all seasons of the careers of each player who totaled at least 1,000 steals. Players whose careers focused on the 1980s, when .500 was the approximate norm, won't experience much change in their ratios from the previous chart. Players who played during the 1970s, when it was more difficult to gain credit for steals, will experience slight increases. Estimates are made for players whose careers overlapped from the 1960s into the 1970s.

Rick Barry, Joe Caldwell, Billy Cunningham, Len Wilkens, and Walt Frazier are a few of the great ball thieves whose careers began in the 1960s. It was impossible to estimate Wilkens' career turnovers, so he doesn't make this chart. Other players, who probably belong on this chart, but aren't on it because of the difficulty of estimating their steals and turnovers, are Bob Cousy, Bill Russell, Andy Phillip, Dick McGuire, Richie Guerin, Tom Gola, Jerry West, and Oscar Robertson.

These were the all-time best ball-control players based on adjusted ratios of steals to turnovers:

BALL-CONTROL EFFICIENCY

Player (Seasons)	Ratio
1. Don Buse (13)	1.770
2. T. R. Dunn (13)	1.643
3. Lafayette Lever (9)	1.089
4. Brian Taylor (10)	1.049
5. Mike Gale (11)	1.019
6. Maurice Cheeks (13)	1.007
7. Alvin Robertson (7)	.980
8. Chris Ford (10)	.964
9. Darwin Cook (8)	.952
10. Derek Harper (8)	.939
11. Gus Williams (11)	.904
12. Johnny Moore (9)	.890
13. Glenn Rivers (8)	.886
14. Quinn Buckner (10)	.883
15. Rick Barry (14)	.879
16. Roland Taylor (8)	.875
17. Michael Jordan (7)	.863
18. Rickey Green (13)	.861
19. John Stockton (7)	.837
20. Walt Frazier (13)	.829
21. Calvin Murphy (13)	.827
22. Micheal Ray Richardson (8)	.824
23. Fred Brown (14)	.810
24. Clyde Drexler (8)	.766
25. Joe Caldwell (11)	.766
26. Bobby Jones (12)	.764
27. Michael Cooper (12)	.735
28. Norm Van Lier (10)	.726
29. Randy Smith (12)	.682
30. John Lucas (14)	.650
31. Lionel Hollins (10)	.648
32. Hakeem Olajuwon (7)	.612
33. Julius Erving (16)	.600
34. Ray Williams (10)	.593

35. Paul Westphal (12) .... .586
36. Dennis Johnson (14) .... .582
37. Dominique Wilkins (9) .... .572
38. Larry Bird (12) .... .565
39. Sam Lacey (13) .... .540
40. Magic Johnson (12) .... .535
41. Isiah Thomas (10) .... .527

42. George McGinnis (11) .... .526
43. Norm Nixon (10) .... .518
44. Billy Cunningham (11) .... .514
45. John Drew (11) .... .509
46. Dan Issel (15) .... .502
47. Alvan Adams (13) .... .502
48. Walter Davis (14) .... .495

7
Shootists

When it comes to winning basketball games, shooting is as important as scoring. That may sound simplistic, but give me a group of high-percentage shooters with balanced scoring and my team will hold its own against a team with two or three big scorers who shoot for a lower percentage. A player who calls himself a scorer, but has a low shooting percentage, probably shoots too much. The poorer shooters should distribute the ball to the better ones.

This chapter is about the better shooters. Again there are five charts. Let's start with the ten best two-point field-goal shooters of all time (minimum of 2,500 field goals made):

Player (Seasons)	Percent
1. Charles Barkley (7)	.617
2. Artis Gilmore (17)	.582
3. James Donaldson (11)	.576
4. Steve Johnson (10)	.573
5. Darryl Dawkins (14)	.573
6. Kevin McHale (11)	.565
7. Bobby Jones (12)	.561
8. Kareem Abdul-Jabbar (20)	.560
9. Buck Williams (10)	.555
10. James Worthy (9)	.553

This chart is not identical to the one listed in official records. Although the NBA did borrow a lot of progressive ideas from the ABA, it never has followed the defunct league's practice of separating two-point and three-point field-goal attempts. The NBA does keep a separate category for three-pointers, but it also includes them with two-pointers in a category it calls field-goal percentage. After inventing the three-point shot, the ABA always kept two-point records separate from three-pointers.

The reason for separating two and three-point field goals is that they are two radically different types of shots. A good three-point shooter exceeds 33 percent. A good two-point shooter exceeds 50 percent. If you combine the two, the men who launch a lot of three-pointers are made to appear to be poor shooters, in general, compared with those who attempt only higher percentage two-point shots. It is as illogical to combine two- and three-pointers as it would be to combine field goals and free throws.

On the official field-goal percentage list, Gilmore is the leader. Barkley's percentage decreases because he has attempted about 700 more three-pointers during his career than Gilmore did. Eliminating the three-pointers, so that we are comparing only the two-point shots of Barkley and Gilmore, Barkley assumes the all-time leadership in two-point field-goal percentage.

The NBA requires a minimum of 2,000 field goals made to qualify for this list. Jeff Ruland, who played only three full seasons before bad knees made him a part-time player, makes the official list with 2,080 field goals made. It wasn't Ruland's fault that the Washington Bullets asked him to play on a surgically-repaired knee that had not fully healed. But his career was too brief for him to be included on an all-time chart such as this one, so we have set the minimum requirement at 2,500 field goals made. It is doubtful that anyone playing less than five full seasons will make the top ten based on this criterion.

Here is a chart of the all-time leaders in three-point field-goal percentage (minimum 250 made):

Player (Seasons)	Percent
1. Mark Price (5)	.418
2. Hersey Hawkins (3)	.414
3. Trent Tucker (9)	.409
4. Craig Hodges (9)	.402
5. Dale Ellis (8)	.400
6. Danny Ainge (10)	.387
7. Reggie Miller (4)	.383
8. Byron Scott (8)	.380
9. Larry Bird (12)	.373
10. Terry Porter (6)	.370

Even though the NBA did not begin using the three-point shot until the 1979–80 season, it is remarkable that every player on this chart is still active. Players have begun practicing this shot more diligently and making it more proficiently during the past four or five seasons.

The NBA requires a minimum of 100 three-point field goals made, meaning that a player such as Dennis Scott could make this chart in his very first season. Much too easy. By setting the minimum at 250, we have eliminated Scott and Jon Sundvold from this chart. Sundvold's percentage is high enough to make it, but he is a part-time player and has not made 250 three-pointers, although he has been in the NBA for eight seasons.

The free-throw percentage chart, unlike three-pointers, contains players from all eras

of NBA and ABA history (minimum 1,500 made):

Player (Seasons)	Percent
1. Rick Barry (14)	.893
2. Calvin Murphy (13)	.892
3. Larry Bird (12)	.884
4. Bill Sharman (11)	.883
5. Chris Mullin (6)	.880
6. Jeff Malone (8)	.874
7. Reggie Miller (4)	.873
8. Kiki Vandeweghe (11)	.873
9. Mike Newlin (11)	.870
10. Ricky Pierce (9)	.866

Again we have made our minimum requirement a little stiffer than the official minimum (1,200 free throws made). Billy Keller makes the official list with his .872 percentage, but he sank only 1,202 free throws during his seven-season ABA career.

I have often wondered why players who have difficulty making free throws don't try to emulate Barry's rhythmical underhand style. The great Wilt Chamberlain didn't have too much pride to keep him from trying it. There are plenty of players in the NBA who could probably help themselves by taking a lesson or two from Barry.

The next list is an interesting one. It is compiled by taking the sum of all shots made by each player and dividing that number by his number of shots attempted (minimum 5,000 attempts):

Player (Seasons)	Percent
1. Cedric Maxwell (11)	.646
2. Charles Barkley (7)	.640
3. Adrian Dantley (1)	.639
4. James Donaldson (11)	.629
5. Magic Johnson (12)	.628
6. Kevin McHale (11)	.626
7. Artis Gilmore (11)	.623
8. Jeff Ruland (6)	.621
9. Bobby Jones (12)	.619
10. Bill Cartwright (11)	.619

Since this statistic represents the percentage of all shots made, players who take proportionately more of the easy free throws and less of the difficult three-pointers are going to dominate this list. Maxwell, the leader, had an extraordinarily high ratio of free throws to field goals attempted. For his career, he shot 6,293 times from the field and 4,592 times from the foul line. He tried only 19 three-pointers.

Ruland, who didn't make enough two-point field goals to qualify for that chart, makes this one because he shot a lot of free throws. Maxwell attempted 73 free throws for every 100 field goals. Ruland wasn't far behind with 58 free-throw attempts for every 100 from the field. The norm is about 1-to-4, or 25 free-throw attempts for every 100 field-goal attempts.

The best statistic for rating shooters is one I call shootist. It is the average of points per shot. This one statistic incorporates the three basic shooting categories. A player who makes all of his free throws, half of his two-point field-goal attempts, and one-third of his three-pointers will average a point a shot.

Of course, no one is perfect from the free-throw line, so even a good foul shooter will have to connect on slightly more than a third of his three-pointers or half of his two-pointers to attain a shootist rating of 1,000. But this is an excellent statistic that should receive widespread acceptance. Through the 1990–91 season, only 20 men had averaged at least one point per shot. Mark Price is only a few attempts short of making the list in the No. 3 or 4 position. Most of the players on this chart are still active. Here are the top 25 shootists (minimum 5,000 shots attempted):

Player (Seasons)	Shootist
1. Reggie Miller (4)	1.037
2. Kevin McHale (11)	1.036
3. James Worthy (9)	1.028
4. Kareem Abdul-Jabbar (20)	1.021
5. Kiki Vandeweghe (11)	1.020
6. Kyle Macy (7)	1.019
7. Bobby Jones (12)	1.017
8. Chris Mullin (6)	1.014
9. Charles Barkley (7)	1.013
10. Byron Scott (8)	1.013
11. James Donaldson (11)	1.011
12. Craig Hodges (9)	1.008
13. Darryl Dawkins (14)	1.007
14. Brad Davis (14)	1.007
15. Larry Nance (10)	1.007
16. Danny Ainge (10)	1.004
17. Walter Davis (14)	1.001
18. Dale Ellis (8)	1.001
19. Larry Bird (12)	1.000
20. Artis Gilmore (17)	1.000
21. Magic Johnson (12)	.996
22. Robert Parish (15)	.996
23. John Stockton (7)	.994
24. Maurice Cheeks (13)	.992
25. Ricky Pierce (9)	.992

8
Wilt & Larry

Six chapters. Thirty-two charts.

There are two extra charts in the chapter about assists, but so that playmaking won't count more than the other statistical categories, we are going to count only five assists charts in making overall player evaluations. The five are total career assists, assists per game, assists per minute, adjusted productivity, and adjusted efficiency.

Only one player in professional basketball history makes at least one chart in five of the six categories. That player, Larry Bird, ranks among the all-time greats in scoring, rebounding, playmaking, steals, and shooting. He missed out only in blocked shots.

Two players, Kareem Abdul-Jabbar and Hakeem Olajuwon, make four of the six. Abdul-Jabbar is ranked in scoring, rebounding, blocked shots, and shooting. Olajuwon excels in scoring, rebounding, blocked shots, and steals.

Players making it in three categories are Wilt Chamberlain, Elvin Hayes, Michael Jordan, Rick Barry, Charles Barkley, Paul Westphal, George McGinnis, Calvin Murphy, Artis Gilmore, Magic Johnson, Maurice Cheeks, John Stockton, and Walter Davis.

If statistics had been kept more efficiently in the early days of the NBA, Bill Russell, Oscar Robertson, and Jerry West would have

been listed in three categories instead of two. All three would have made at least one chart in steals. West might have made two or three steals charts.

Also, if adjustments had been made in shooting statistics to compensate for the norm of the era, Robertson and West probably would have been listed in the adjusted stats, putting them among the leaders in four of the six categories. Robertson was the best shooter of the 1960s, counting field-goal and free-throw percentages.

The reason we made no adjustments for shooting is that the basket always has been ten feet above the floor. Yes, it's true that more is known about the mechanics of good shooting now than was known during the 1940s and 1950s when two-handed set shots were bonking off backboards and ricocheting off rims. One-handed set shots were considered radical in those days. Jumpshots were more rare than underhand free throws.

Robertson and West should be ranked among the all-time great shooters. But we do not want to sacrifice the integrity of shooting statistics by comparing individual players to league-wide norms as we did in other categories such as steals and assists. If we did that, we would have 40 percent shooters from the 1940s and 1950s listed side-by-side with 55 percent shooters of the 1980s when in fact there was no comparison between the skill levels of the two. You don't want to make such radical adjustments that mediocre players are listed as equals with great ones.

Here is a chart showing the all-time leaders in both number of categories and number of total charts in all categories. Maximums are six categories and 30 charts. Players are listed according to total points based on number of categories plus number of charts:

Player	Category	Charts	Points
1. Wilt Chamberlain	3	14	17
2. Kareem Abdul-Jabbar	4	11	15
3. Larry Bird	5	7	12
4. Hakeem Olajuwon	4	8	12
5. Magic Johnson	3	9	12
6. Bill Russell	2	10	12
7. Michael Jordan	3	8	11
8. John Stockton	3	8	11
9. Artis Gilmore	3	8	11
10. Nate Thurmond	2	9	11
11. Rick Barry	3	6	9
12. Charles Barkley	3	6	9
13. Maurice Cheeks	3	6	9
14. Elvin Hayes	3	6	9
15. Oscar Robertson	2	7	9
16. Bob Pettit	2	7	9
17. Isiah Thomas	2	6	8
18. Julius Erving	2	5	7
19. Moses Malone	2	5	7
20. Dominique Wilkins	2	5	7
21. Karl Malone	2	5	7
22. George Mikan	2	5	7
23. Alvin Robertson	2	5	7
24. Terry Porter	2	5	7
25. Norm Nixon	2	5	7
26. Elmore Smith	2	5	7
27. Walter Davis	3	3	6
28. Paul Westphal	3	3	6
29. George McGinnis	3	3	6
30. Calvin Murphy	3	3	6
31. Jerry West	2	4	6
32. Patrick Ewing	2	4	6
33. Lafayette Lever	2	4	6
34. M.R. Richardson	2	4	6
35. Kevin McHale	2	4	6
36. Bobby Jones	2	4	6
37. John Lucas	2	4	6
38. Johnny Moore	2	4	6
39. Elgin Baylor	2	4	6
40. Wes Unseld	1	5	6
41. Guy Rodgers	1	5	6
42. Mark Eaton	1	5	6
43. Dan Issel	2	3	5
44. Buck Williams	2	3	5
45. Len Wilkens	2	3	5
46. Doc Rivers	2	3	5
47. Derek Harper	2	3	5
48. Gus Williams	2	3	5
49. Quinn Buckner	2	3	5
50. Clyde Drexler	2	3	5
51. Darryl Dawkins	2	3	5
52. Larry Nance	2	3	5
53. Kiki Vandeweghe	2	3	5
54. John Drew	2	3	5
55. George Gervin	1	4	5
56. Kevin Johnson	1	4	5
57. Bob Cousy	1	4	5
58. Jerry Lucas	1	4	5
59. Don Buse	1	4	5
60. Manute Bol	1	4	5

In this chart, whenever there is a tie in total points, the players with the most categories are listed ahead of those who earned most of their points from one specialty. In fact, the more versatile players usually are the better players. This method may not even go far enough. A player such as John Havlicek, Robert Parish, or Walt Frazier, who scored four points and qualified in two categories, is better than one such as Mark Eaton, Manute Bol, or Don Buse, who managed five or six points but got all of them from blocked shots or steals, which are not as significant statistics as the others.

Overall, however, this chart fairly represents some of the greatest players of all time. It fits in with the theme of this book, concerning players who qualify for the Hall of Fame. All of the players near the top of the list belong in the Hall, and most of those at the bottom probably do also. It is noteworthy that Maurice Cheeks is so high on the chart (tied for 11th). It will be interesting to see if he receives the kind of support he deserves when his name comes up for nomination.

There are some players who are listed too low on this chart because statistics were not adequately tabulated during the 1950s and

1960s. We have already mentioned that Oscar Robertson, Bill Russell, and Jerry West are three such players. Others are Elgin Baylor, Walt Frazier, and Bob Cousy.

Others didn't make this list at all, but are potential Hall of Famers. These include Adrian Dantley, John Havlicek, Bob McAdoo, Bob Lanier, Robert Parish, Walt Frazier, and Walt Bellamy. All of these guys accumulated four points, missing the chart by one.

And then there are some great players such as Bernard King, Paul Arizin, Pete Maravich, Neil Johnston, Spencer Haywood, Earl Monroe, Dave Cowens, Willis Reed, Harry Gallatin, Dolph Schayes, Larry Nance, Bill Walton, and Kevin McHale, who scored less than four points according to criteria of this chapter, but will do much better in the next few chapters.

9
Centers

A total of 184 players made at least one of the charts in the first eight chapters. It should be reasonably safe to assume that any candidates for the TENDEX Hall of Fame should have made at least one. But players who spent most of their careers in the NBA before the 1970s were at a disadvantage.

Steals, blocked shots, and turnovers were not counted until the 1970s, and no one during that era shot well enough to make any of the shooting charts except free-throw percentage. This means half of the six types of charts practically excluded players from that era.

There are 13 players in the Naismith Memorial Basketball Hall of Fame who did not earn a place on a single one of these charts. Of the 13, 12 played the majority of their careers before 1970. The only player from the 1970s or 1980s to have been elected to the Naismith Hall of Fame even though he did not stand out in a single statistical category was Bill Bradley.

Bradley may have been elected for what he did in college, not in the NBA. His career TENDEX rating of .403 for ten NBA seasons wasn't just short of being a Hall of Fame rating. It wasn't even an average rating for a small forward during his era.

The other 12 players in the chartless category were Al Cervi, Bob Davies, Joe Fulks,

Tom Gola, Hal Greer, Bob Houbregs, K.C. Jones, Ed Macauley, Slater Martin, Jim Pollard, Frank Ramsey, and Bobby Wanzer. The Hall of Fame qualifications of each of these men, and many others, will be considered in the next five chapters. In this chapter, the emphasis is on the great centers. Two of the 12, Macauley and Houbregs, were centers.

Although it is nice to be listed on a lot of all-time statistical charts, it is the all-around performance of a player that determines his excellence. TENDEX measures all-around performance. A player who had a career TENDEX rating 100 points above normal for his career, and played the equivalent of ten seasons as a regular, qualifies for the TENDEX Hall of Fame.

There have been a few players who played less than ten seasons, but who played enough minutes in those seasons to qualify. George Mikan was such a player.

But then there have been players who played ten or more seasons but did not play enough minutes to qualify. Bill Walton fits into this category, although he should be considered for the Hall of Fame primarily because of his collegiate performance. His credentials as a player, college and pro, were far superior to Bradley's.

Fifteen centers qualify for the Hall of Fame

with ease, according to TENDEX standards. One of the 15, Hakeem Olajuwon, is about 1,000 minutes short, but his TENDEX rating is so high that even if his rating for the deficient minutes is counted as .000, his overall rating still is high enough to make the Hall with 100 percentage points to spare.

However, four other centers—Dave Cowens, Alvan Adams, Neil Johnston, and Wes Unseld—have marginal qualifications. Let's discuss them.

Cowens had a career TENDEX rating of .668 for 11 seasons. The norm for his 11 seasons was .568, so he is exactly 100 percentage points above it, right on the edge as far as Hall of Fame credentials are concerned. He makes it because he was an outstanding clutch player, leading Boston to two NBA titles and winning one MVP award.

The norm for a player's position is determined by taking the average rating of all players at that position during each season of his career. In Cowens' 11 seasons, the average ratings for centers were .588, .551, .565, .571, .556, .568, .589, .570, .558, .568, and .566. The overall average for centers for these eleven seasons was .568.

Adams played 13 seasons. Unfortunately for him, all of it was in Phoenix when that city wasn't a hot TV market. His career TENDEX rating was .664, lower than Cowens'. But the norm for those seasons for centers was .555, so Adams was actually 109 percentage points above it, enough for Hall of Fame recognition.

We need to interject here that TENDEX doesn't care how actually famous a player is. The TENDEX Hall of Fame probably should be called the Hall of Ability, or the Hall of Performance, since actual fame often has little to do with playing proficiency. Adams was an unheralded player, but a great one who holds many Phoenix team records.

Johnston played eight seasons, but his minutes played (18,298) were high enough to surpass the ten-season equivalent of 17,250 for his era. His TENDEX rating was .651, also marginal.

A marginal rating can be good enough, as Cowens' is. But not when it is coupled with marginal minutes played. Johnston makes the TENDEX Hall because the average rating for centers during his era (the 1950s) was .503. He was 148 points above this norm, better than Cowens or Adams in that respect.

Unseld's TENDEX rating was .642 for 13 seasons. The center norm for those seasons was .573, so he falls 31 points short. In his favor, he was an iron-man, averaging 36 minutes per game for his full career. But that by itself is not enough to make up the difference. Unseld makes it because of his excellent coaching with an undermanned Washington team the past four seasons. He's an outstanding coach who should have a long career in that profession. His combination of excellent playing and excellent coaching is Hall of Fame caliber.

Here are short biographies of the centers who qualify for the TENDEX Hall of Fame:

1. WILT CHAMBERLAIN—Played 14 seasons, 47,859 minutes . . . Officially his TENDEX rating was an all-time record .897, but it should have been higher. According to best estimates of his blocked shots (5,000), steals (1,275) and turnovers (4,125), his actual TENDEX was .942 . . . NBA career record-holder in rebounds (23,924) . . . Led NBA in scoring seven times, rebounding 11 times and field goal percentage nine times . . . Four-time league MVP . . . Member of league champion teams in Los Angeles and Philadelphia . . . Ten-time TENDEX Player of the Year.

2. BILL RUSSELL—Played 13 seasons, 40,726 minutes . . . Unadjusted career TENDEX rating was .755, but with estimates for blocked shots (4,500), steals (1,925) and turnovers (2,900) it becomes .841, second to Chamberlain . . . Led NBA in rebounding four times . . . Five-time league MVP . . . TENDEX Player of the Year 1958 . . . Member of 11 league champion teams with Boston Celtics, the last two as player-coach.

3. KAREEM ABDUL-JABBAR—Played 20 seasons, 57,446 minutes . . . Three-time NCAA Tournament MVP, twice college Player of the Year . . . Holds NBA record for points (38,387) . . . Eleven-time TENDEX Player of the Year, most of any player . . . Six-time league MVP, another record . . . Member of six champion Los Angeles Laker teams and three NCAA champion teams at UCLA . . . Career TENDEX rating (adjusted for four seasons) .817.

4. HAKEEM OLAJUWON—Played 7 seasons, 19,176 minutes . . . NCAA Tournament MVP 1983 . . . Led NCAA in field-goal percentage, rebounds and blocked shots 1984 . . . Has led NBA in rebounding twice and blocked shots twice . . . The only player ever to register 200 blocked shots and 200 steals in the same season (1988–89) . . . Career TENDEX rating .795.

5. BOB LANIER—Played 14 seasons, 32,103 minutes . . . All-American college player for St. Bonaventure in 1970 . . . Averaged 20.1 points per game and field-goal percentage of .514 for his full NBA career . . . Won All-Star Game MVP honor in 1974 . . . Career TENDEX rating .746.

6. ARTIS GILMORE—Played in 17 seasons, 47,134 minutes . . . NCAA career rebounding leader (22.7) . . . Led ABA in rebounds four times, field-goal percentage twice, blocked shots once . . . Twice named ABA Most Valuable Player . . . Led Kentucky to ABA title in 1975 . . . Led NBA in field-goal percentage four times . . . Career field-goal percentage of .582 is best of all time . . . Career TENDEX rating .721.

7. MOSES MALONE—Played 17 seasons, 46,062 minutes . . . Eight times totaled more than 1,000 rebounds, four times had more than 2,000 points . . . Three-time NBA Most Valuable Player . . . Six-time league leader in rebounds . . . Playoff MVP in 1983 when he led Philadelphia to title . . . Career TENDEX rating .703.

8. GEORGE MIKAN—Played 9 seasons, 21,000 minutes (estimated) counting two seasons in National Basketball League . . . NCAA Player of the Year twice . . . Led NBA in scoring three times, rebounding once . . . Led Minneapolis Lakers to five NBA titles . . . TENDEX Player of the Year six times . . . Career TENDEX rating .700 (estimated).

9. WALT BELLAMY—Played 14 seasons, 38,940 minutes . . . Had career-high .928 TENDEX rating as rookie in 1961–62 when he averaged 31.6 points per game, led the NBA in field-goal percentage (.519) and was named Rookie of the Year . . . Career TENDEX rating .697.

10. WILLIS REED—Played 10 seasons, 23,073 minutes . . . NBA Rookie of the Year 1965 . . . Paced New York Knicks to league titles in 1970 and 1973 and was named playoff MVP both times . . . All-Star Game MVP 1970 . . . Career TENDEX rating .695.

11. ROBERT PARISH—Played 15 seasons, 36,442 minutes . . . Member of three champion teams with Boston Celtics . . . No. 16 on career list in rebounding efficiency . . . Career field-goal percentage ranks among top 15 of all time . . . Career TENDEX rating .688.

12. MEL DANIELS—Played 9 seasons, 22,466 minutes . . . ABA Rookie of the Year 1967–68 . . . MVP 1968–69 and 1970–71 . . . Led ABA in rebounding three times . . . Totaled more than 1,200 rebounds each of his first six seasons . . . No. 5 on all-time rebounding efficiency list . . . Career TENDEX rating .685.

13. CLYDE LOVELLETTE—Played 11 seasons, 19,075 minutes . . . MVP of NCAA champion Kansas team in 1952 . . . Member of three NBA champion teams . . . Best TENDEX rating was .828 in 1959–60 . . . TENDEX 700 Club member four times . . . Career TENDEX rating .685.

14. NATE THURMOND—Played 14 seasons, 35,875 minutes . . . Set NCAA Tournament record with 31 rebounds in one game . . . No. 4 player of all time in career blocked shots . . . First NBA player to register a quadruple-double with 22 points, 14 rebounds, 13 assists and 12 blocked shots in a game in 1974 . . . Estimated career TENDEX rating .678.

15. DAVE COWENS—Played 11 seasons, 29,565 minutes . . . Great rebounder, had at least 1,000 in six of 11 seasons . . . NBA Most Valuable Player 1973 . . . Member of two champion teams with Boston Celtics . . . All-Star Game MVP 1973 . . . Career TENDEX rating .668.

16. ALVAN ADAMS—Played 13 seasons, 27,203 minutes . . . Played his entire career in Phoenix and rewrote Suns' record book . . . A great ball-handling big man, he led all centers in average of assists per minute for full career . . . Career TENDEX rating .664.

17. NEIL JOHNSTON—Played 8 seasons, 18,298 minutes . . . Named to All-NBA First Team four times . . . Member of champion team in 1956 . . . Led league in scoring three times, rebounding once, field-goal percentage three times . . . Career TENDEX rating .651.

18. WES UNSELD—Played 13 seasons, 35,832 minutes . . . NBA Rookie of the Year and MVP 1969 . . . Led league in rebounding 1975, field-goal percentage 1976 . . . Member of champion team in 1978 and was named playoff MVP . . . TENDEX Coach of the Year 1989 . . . Career TENDEX rating .642.

The above 18 are the only centers who have qualified so far for the TENDEX Hall of Fame, but others deserve mention:

◇ David Robinson and Patrick Ewing who will make it sometime soon.

◇ Bill Walton and Ralph Sampson who should be considered on collegiate credentials even though injuries destroyed their professional careers.

◇ Ed Macauley and Bob Houbregs who somehow made the Naismith Hall of Fame, even though their careers were unexceptional. Houbregs played only 5 NBA seasons.

◇ Tom Boerwinkle and Swen Nater who had identical TENDEX ratings (.691), high enough to qualify, but who didn't play enough minutes.

◇ Zelmo Beaty and Jack Sikma who played enough minutes but came up a few points short on their TENDEX ratings.

◇ Jeff Ruland who looked like a Hall of Famer with a .708 TENDEX rating after three seasons, but sustained a career-shortening knee injury the next year.

Here is a chart of the TENDEX Hall of Fame centers, using ratings adjusted for estimated blocked shots, steals and turnovers for Chamberlain, Russell, Abdul-Jabbar, and Thurmond:

Player (Seasons)	TENDEX
1. Wilt Chamberlain (14)	.942
2. Bill Russell (13)	.841
3. Kareem Abdul-Jabbar (20)	.817
4. Hakeem Olajuwon (7)	.795
5. Bob Lanier (14)	.746
6. Artis Gilmore (17)	.721

 7. Moses Malone (17) .... .703
 8. George Mikan (9) .... .700
 9. Walt Bellamy (14) .... .697
10. Willis Reed (10) .... .695
11. Robert Parish (15) .... .688
12. Mel Daniels (9) .... .685

13. Clyde Lovellette (11) .... .685
14. Nate Thurmond (14) .... .678
15. Dave Cowens (11) .... .668
16. Alvan Adams (13) .... .664
17. Neil Johnston (8) .... .651
18. Wes Unseld (13) .... .642

ABSTRACTION 5

The Enigma of Dikembe

Disputing is not one of my favorite pastimes, but when the TENDEX rating system is criticized for no good reason I feel compelled to come to its defense.

Some criticism, either of the ignore-it-and-it-will-go-away variety or the more abrasive type, has come from my fellow sportswriters.

One of the most curious criticisms emanated from *The Basketball Times*. It was for *The Basketball Times* that I wrote my first TENDEX column, and I'll always be grateful to editor and publisher Larry Donald for being the first to recognize my system's potential.

The Basketball Times critiques nearly every basketball book that comes along, no matter how poorly written or hackneyed, but it ignored the first two editions of *The Basketball Abstract* and gave only one line of mention to the third. That was to ridicule my TENDEX-abetted evaluation of Dikembe Mutombo as potentially one of the best big men in basketball.

The Basketball Times pointed out (as if everybody was supposed to laugh) that I rated Mutombo ahead of Brad Daugherty and other standouts on my list of youthful big men in the 1990 edition of TBA. Actually, I rated Mutombo No. 6 last year. If I did another list this year, he'd be up to No. 5. The only big men ahead of him now are David Robinson, Hakeem Olajuwon, Shaquille O'Neal, and Patrick Ewing.

I repeat: Dikembe Mutombo is going to be a dominant NBA player.

So how does that fount of wisdom, *The Basketball Times,* rate Mutombo? It's hard to tell. Mutombo did not make the first, second, or third All-American teams announced by TBT last spring. Not among the top 15 players in college basketball.

Are they serious?

10
Power Forwards

During recent seasons, while centers have played to an average TENDEX rating of .550, the average for power forwards has been about .525. This means the TENDEX Hall of Fame minimum for power forwards is .625 at the present time, although it has fluctuated in the past.

The power-forward position is the only one not to have produced a single Naismith Hall of Famer who didn't make any of our statistical charts. This is not to say that there aren't some power forwards in the marginal zone where it is hard to say whether they belong in the Hall or not. What it does indicate is that never has a power forward been as absurdly overrated as a Bob Houbregs.

Here is a listing of the power forwards who have ratings and/or other credentials adequate to insure inclusion in the TENDEX Hall of Fame:

1. BOB PETTIT—Played 11 seasons, 30,690 minutes . . . Led NBA in scoring twice, rebounding once . . . Per-game rebounding average of 16.2 was third-best of all time . . . TENDEX Player of the Year three times, league MVP twice . . . Four-time All-Star Game MVP . . . Member of NBA champion team 1958 . . . All-NBA first team selection 10 straight seasons . . . Career TENDEX rating .818.

2. CHARLES BARKLEY—Played 7 seasons, 19,880 minutes . . . Career field-goal percentage of .580 is second-best of all time . . . Two-point field-goal percentage (excluding three-pointers) is .617, easily No. 1 . . . Four-time All-NBA selection . . . Led league in rebounding 1987 . . . Career TENDEX rating .783.

3. ELGIN BAYLOR—Played 14 seasons, 33,863 minutes . . . All-Star Game MVP in 1959 . . . Ten-time All-NBA choice . . . Scored Los Angeles Lakers team record 71 points in one game . . . Averaged 27.4 points for career, third best of all-time . . . Member of champion Laker team 1972 . . . Career TENDEX rating .753.

4. JERRY LUCAS—Played 11 seasons, 32,131 minutes . . . Two-time college Player of the Year, led Ohio State to NCAA title in 1960 . . . NBA All-Star seven times, All-Star Game MVP in 1965 . . . Led NBA in field-goal percentage 1964 . . . Averaged 15.6

rebounds per game, fourth best of all-time . . . Member of NBA champion team 1973 . . . Career TENDEX rating. 730.

5. KARL MALONE—Played 6 seasons, 18,080 minutes . . . Didn't enter the NBA as a superstar, but TENDEX ratings improved from .524 to .628 to .693 to .796 to .854 for his first 5 seasons, the most dramatic improvement of all-time . . . Three-time All-NBA selection . . . All-Star Game MVP 1989 . . . Career TENDEX Rating .726.

6. BOB McADOO—Played 14 seasons, 28,327 minutes . . . Led NBA in scoring three times, averaged 22.1 points per game for career . . . NBA Rookie of the Year 1973 . . . Led league in field-goal percentage 1974 . . . League MVP and TENDEX Player of the Year 1975 . . . Member of NBA champion teams 1982 and 1985 . . . Five-time TENDEX first-team All-NBA selection . . . Career TENDEX rating .692.

7. BILLY CUNNINGHAM—Played 11 seasons, 26,844 minutes . . . Three-time All-NBA selection, once in ABA . . . ABA Most Valuable Player 1973 . . . Led ABA in steals 1973 . . . Member of NBA champion team 1967, coach of champion team 1983 . . . Career TENDEX rating .674.

8. BAILEY HOWELL—Played 12 seasons, 30,427 minutes . . . Led NCAA in field-goal percentage 1957 . . . In NBA had career-best TENDEX rating of .804 in 1960–61, when he averaged 23.6 points and 14.4 rebounds per game . . . Member of NBA champion teams 1968 and 1969 . . . Career TENDEX rating .674.

9. KEVIN McHALE—Played 11 seasons, 27,064 minutes . . . Led NBA in field-goal percentage twice, has sixth best percentage of all-time

. . . Best Shootist in NBA-ABA history, averaging 1.0 points per shot . . . All-NBA selection 1987 . . . Two-time winner of Sixth Man award . . . Member of three NBA champion teams . . . Career TENDEX rating .654.

10. DOLPH SCHAYES—Played 13 seasons, 29,800 minutes . . . Averaged 24.9 points and 14.2 rebounds with a TENDEX rating of .718 in 1957–58 . . . All-NBA selection six times . . . Led league in free-throw percentage three times, rebounding once . . . Member of champion team 1955 . . . Coach of the Year 1966 . . . Career TENDEX rating .653.

11. GEORGE McGINNIS—Played 11 seasons, 28,179 minutes . . . All-ABA selection 1974 and 1975, All-NBA choice 1976 . . . ABA Co-Most Valuable Player 1975 . . . Member of ABA champion teams 1972 and 1973, playoff MVP 1973 . . . Led ABA in scoring 1975 . . . Career TENDEX rating .643.

12. DAN ISSEL—Played 15 seasons, 41,786 minutes . . . ABA Rookie of the Year 1971–72 when he led the league in scoring . . . ABA All-Star Game MVP 1972 . . . Set ABA scoring record with 2,538 points in 1972 . . . Member of ABA champion team 1975 . . . Averaged 20.4 points per game for 9 NBA seasons . . . Career TENDEX rating .637.

13. DAN ROUNDFIELD—Played 12 seasons, 24,208 minutes . . . A great defensive player, three times chosen for NBA All-Defensive team . . . Averaged 15.2 points, 9.7 rebounds and 1.5 blocked shots per game for his career . . . Career TENDEX rating of .636 was 128 points above the norm for power forwards during his era.

14. ELVIN HAYES—Played 16 seasons, 50,000 minutes . . . College Player of the Year 1968 . . . The first NBA

player to play 50,000 minutes and still ranks No. 2 on the all-time minutes-played list . . . Led NBA in scoring once, rebounding twice . . . All-NBA selection three times . . . TENDEX first-team choice seven times . . . Member of champion team 1978 . . . Career TENDEX rating .631.

15. SPENCER HAYWOOD—Played 13 seasons, 29,408 minutes . . . Led NCAA in rebounding 1969 . . . ABA Most Valuable Player and Rookie of the Year 1970 . . . Led ABA in scoring (30.0) and rebounding (19.5) in 1970 . . . ABA All-Star Game MVP 1970 . . . All-NBA selection in 1972 and 1973 . . . Career TENDEX rating .628, 120 points above normal for his era.

16. HARRY GALLATIN—Played 10 seasons, 21,500 minutes (estimated) . . . All-NBA first-team selection 1954 . . . Led NBA in rebounding 1954 . . . Began his career when few statistics were kept, but for 7 seasons his TENDEX rating was .613 . . . The power-forward average for those seasons was .452, so he was 161 points above the norm.

17. DAVE DeBUSSCHERE—Played 12 seasons, 31,202 minutes . . . Member of NBA champion teams 1970 and 1973 . . . Youngest coach (24) in NBA history . . . Six-time All-Defensive team selection . . . Career TENDEX rating of .577 was short of TENDEX Hall of Fame level, but great leadership and man-to-man defense more than make up the difference.

An interesting pattern has emerged: The ABA, in its brief 9-season existence, had many outstanding big men. In addition to TENDEX Hall of Fame centers Artis Gilmore, Swen Nater, Mel Daniels, and Moses Malone, we find Hall of Fame power forwards with ABA roots as well. McGinnis, Cunningham, Issel, Roundfield, and Haywood all played in the ABA before winding up their careers in the NBA.

Let's list ten other power forwards deserving of Hall of Fame consideration:

◇ Gus Johnson, Maurice Lucas, and Bobby Jones, three more ABA players (briefly), who had very good TENDEX ratings but were not quite Hall of Fame caliber.

◇ Harold (Happy) Hairston who didn't play in the ABA but had a creditable .605 TENDEX rating.

◇ Tom Heinsohn, a Naismith Hall of Famer, perhaps because of his Boston Celtic visibility, but who falls short of qualification by TENDEX standards.

◇ Maurice Stokes, a center-power forward, who was Hall-bound with a .718 rating for three seasons before being stopped by an illness that eventually took his life.

◇ Terry Cummings and Buck Williams, active veterans whose latter-career years will determine whether they belong in the Hall.

◇ Roy Tarpley, a young player who has the ability but maybe not the health to achieve Hall of Fame stature.

◇ Shawn Kemp, one of the NBA's youngest players, who has everything going for him to make it someday.

Here's a chart of TENDEX Hall of Fame power forwards:

Player (Seasons)	TENDEX
1. Bob Pettit (11)	.818
2. Charles Barkley (7)	.783
3. Elgin Baylor (14)	.753
4. Jerry Lucas (11)	.730
5. Karl Malone (6)	.726
6. Bob McAdoo (14)	.692
7. Billy Cunningham (11)	.674
8. Bailey Howell (12)	.674
9. Kevin McHale (11)	.654
10. Dolph Schayes (13)	.653
11. George McGinnis (11)	.643
12. Dan Issel (15)	.637
13. Dan Roundfield (12)	.636
14. Elvin Hayes (16)	.631
15. Spencer Haywood (13)	.628
16. Harry Gallatin (10)	.613
17. Dave DeBusschere (12)	.577

11
Small Forwards

The small-forward position has not produced as many outstanding players as center or power forward. It is equitably represented in the Naismith Hall of Fame only because of the selection of four players with questionable credentials.

A fifth Naismith honoree, Jack Twyman, also appears to fall short of TENDEX standards. But not when his statistics are carefully analyzed. Twyman's career TENDEX rating was .562, 93 percentage points above the norm for his era for small forwards (.469). The usual TENDEX Hall of Fame differential is 100 points or more.

But Twyman was a durable player. For his 11-season career he played about 64 percent of the potential minutes. A TENDEX qualifier should play at least 50 percent.

A good player who can play extra minutes is valuable to his team because for every extra minute he plays a less-skilled substitute is kept on the bench. Because of the importance of the iron-man factor, TENDEX All-NBA teams are selected on the basis of a statistic called positional rating instead of the pure TENDEX rating. A player's positional rating is the TENDEX rating of the position he plays, counting himself and substitutes.

If a small forward plays exactly 50 percent of the time and has a TENDEX rating of .600,

100 points above the present norm, his positional rating will be .550, 50 points above average. So a positional rating of 50 points above normal is as good a criterion for Hall of Fame selection as a TENDEX rating 100 points on the positive side. Actually it is a better one, for a player may have a TENDEX rating 100 points above normal even if he plays less than half of the potential minutes.

Twyman's career positional rating was 60 points above normal.

Let's take a look at the accomplishments of the small forwards who merit Hall of Fame induction:

1. LARRY BIRD—Played 12 seasons, 32,781 minutes . . . Probably the most versatile basketball player of all-time . . . The only player to earn positions on all-time charts in five of the six major statistical categories (points, rebounds, assists, steals and shooting) . . . College Player of the Year 1979 . . . NBA Rookie of the Year 1980 . . . Three-time league MVP, four-time TENDEX Player of the Year . . . Earned first-team All-NBA honors 9 straight seasons . . . Member of three champion teams, twice playoff MVP . . . All-Star Game MVP 1982 . . . Led NBA

in free-throw percentage four times . . . Career TENDEX rating .762.

2. JULIUS ERVING—Played 16 seasons, 45,227 minutes . . . Four-time All-ABA selection, three-time MVP . . . Won three ABA scoring titles . . . Member of two ABA champion teams, playoff MVP both times . . . Earned All-NBA honors five times . . . Member of NBA champion team 1983 . . . All-Star Game MVP 1977 and 1983 . . . All-time record-holder in steals . . . Career TENDEX rating .709.

3. RICK BARRY—Played 14 seasons, 38,153 minutes . . . NCAA scoring champion 1965 . . . NBA/ABA career record-holder in free-throw percentage (.893) . . . Second on all-time list of assists by a forward, trailing Bird . . . No. 2 player in career steals behind Erving . . . NBA Rookie of the Year 1966 . . . Led ABA in scoring 1969, led NBA in scoring 1967 . . . NBA All-Star Game MVP 1967 . . . Four-time All-ABA selection, five-time All-NBA choice . . . Playoff MVP and member of NBA champion team 1975 . . . Career TENDEX rating .626.

4. LARRY NANCE—Played 10 seasons, 24,155 minutes . . . One of the most underrated players of all-time, excellent offensively and defensively . . . Made NBA All-Defensive Team in 1989 . . . Most efficient shot-blocking forward in NBA history . . . Ranks No. 11 in NBA annals in field-goal percentage . . . Career TENDEX rating .661.

5. CLIFF HAGAN—Played 13 seasons, 24,074 minutes . . . Member of NCAA champion team 1951 . . . A great clutch player, averaged 20.4 points per game in NBA playoffs, 2.4 points higher than his career regular-season average . . . Member of NBA champion team 1958 . . . Career TENDEX rating .642.

6. CONNIE HAWKINS—Played 9 seasons, 22,232 minutes . . . Implication in gambling scandal caused him to lose four prime years out of his career, but he was reinstated and played two outstanding seasons in the ABA and seven in the NBA . . . ABA scoring champion 1968 . . . All-ABA selection 1968 and 1969 . . . League MVP 1968 . . . Career TENDEX rating .635.

7. MARQUES JOHNSON—Played 11 seasons, 23,694 minutes . . . Member of NCAA champion team 1975 . . . College Player of the Year 1977 . . . Averaged 20.1 points per game and shot .518 from the field for his full NBA career . . . All-NBA first-team choice 1979 . . . Comeback Player of the Year 1986 . . . Career TENDEX rating .624.

8. DOMINIQUE WILKINS—Played 9 seasons, 26,610 minutes . . . Twice has averaged over 30 points per game during his NBA career . . . Led the league in scoring 1986 (30.3) . . . No. 2 player of all-time in scoring efficiency, behind Michael Jordan . . . All-NBA choice 1986 . . . Still improving, had his best all-around season in 1990–91 . . . Career TENDEX rating .617.

9. BERNARD KING—Played 13 seasons, 28,987 minutes . . . Led NCAA in field-goal percentage 1975 . . . NBA Comeback Player of the Year 1981 . . . All-NBA selection 1984 and 1985 . . . Led league in scoring 1985 (32.9) . . . Career scoring average is 23.2 and field-goal percentage is .519 . . . Career TENDEX rating of .598 is 105 percentage points above the average for small forwards during his career.

10. ALEX ENGLISH—Played 15 seasons, 38,063 minutes . . . A great clutch player, his playoff scoring average for 68 games is 24.4, nearly three points better than his regular-season average

. . . Best was a 30.2 average in 14 games in 1985 playoffs . . . Led NBA in scoring 1983 . . . Only player in history to score at least 2,000 points in 8 straight seasons . . . Career TENDEX rating .584.

11. CHET WALKER—Played 11 seasons, 33,433 minutes . . . College All-American at Bradley in 1962 . . . Member of NBA champion team 1967 . . . Averaged 18.2 points per game in regular season and playoffs for full pro career . . . Career TENDEX rating of .576 was 101 points above average for small forwards during his era.

12. JACK TWYMAN—Played 11 seasons, 26,055 minutes . . . High-scoring forward averaged 31.2 points per game in 1961–62 season, second to Wilt Chamberlain's 37.6 . . . Scored 27 points in 1962 All-Star Game . . . Career scoring average was 19.2 . . . Led NBA in field-goal percentage 1958 . . . Career TENDEX rating .562.

13. PAUL ARIZIN—Played 10 seasons, 24,867 minutes . . . Led NCAA in scoring and won Player of the Year honors in 1950 . . . Led NBA in scoring and field-goal percentage in 1952 . . . All-Star Game MVP 1952 . . . Member of NBA champion team 1956 . . . All-NBA selection three times . . . Averaged 22.8 points per game for his career . . . Career TENDEX rating of .552 was 137 points above the norm for his era.

Barry is listed ahead of Nance, Hagan, and Hawkins—all of whom had higher TENDEX ratings—because of superior all-around credentials. Barry's career rating was an exceptional 155 points above the norm for his era (.471), which was 29 points below the small-forward average of today.

In addition to the 13 small forwards chosen for the TENDEX Hall of Fame, here are another 10 who were considered but came up short based on their careers as professionals; they are:

◇ Naismith Hall of Famer Frank Ramsey who came close but couldn't meet the TENDEX criteria.

◇ Naismith Hall of Famers Joe Fulks and Jim Pollard who did not come close.

◇ Naismith Hall of Famer Bill Bradley who missed by as much as Fulks and Pollard as a pro but will receive consideration for his collegiate exploits (see Chapter 15).

◇ James Worthy, an explosive scorer and outstanding clutch player, but a weak rebounder and defender whose TENDEX rating is 40 points too low.

◇ Rudy Tomjanovich and Bobby Dandridge, a couple of guys who were as good as Worthy but had the misfortune of not playing in the Laker limelight.

◇ Chris Mullin, a better player than Worthy, Tomjanovich or Dandridge, who could make it if he has 4 more good seasons.

◇ Adrian Dantley, a great scorer with a good TENDEX rating (.622); but he was traded six times and excelled only when the going was easy with a weak Utah team.

◇ Dennis Rodman, a non-scorer who is such an exceptional rebounder and defender that he belongs in the Hall if he can sustain his excellence for another five years.

Here is a full list of the small-forward qualifiers for the TENDEX Hall of Fame:

Player (Seasons)	TENDEX
1. Larry Bird (12)	.762
2. Julius Erving (16)	.709
3. Rick Barry (14)	.626
4. Larry Nance (10)	.661
5. Cliff Hagan (13)	.642
6. Connie Hawkins (9)	.635
7. Marques Johnson (11)	.624
8. Dominique Wilkins (9)	.617
9. Bernard King (13)	.597
10. Alex English (15)	.584
11. Chet Walker (13)	.576
12. Jack Twyman (11)	.562
13. Paul Arizin (11)	.552

12
Point Guards

Before listing the best point guards of all-time, let's discuss three players who, like Rick Barry among the small forwards, are listed out of TENDEX order.

The first is Bob Cousy who, if you just glance at his career TENDEX rating of .516, you wouldn't even think that he could be a Hall of Famer. The norm for a point guard these days is .475, but it was not always so. During Cousy's era, in the 1950s and early 1960s, when low shooting percentages held down assist totals, the point-guard average was .365. So Cousy's rating was 151 TENDEX points above average. That is a dominant rating and he deserves to be moved ahead of seven players from later eras who had higher ratings.

The second change was made for several reasons. Magic Johnson has the best career TENDEX rating of the point guards. His .758 rating is 20 points better than runnerup Oscar Robertson. But Robertson played during a much less productive era for backcourtmen. The point-guard norm for his era was 21 points below the norm during Johnson's, which more than makes up the difference between their ratings. And the swing is actually greater than that.

During Robertson's career, there were only about one-third as many NBA teams as there are now, which means one-third as many point guards. The significance of this is that Robertson's own rating pulled up the norm three times as much as Johnson's does.

During the 1963–64 season, for example, Robertson's rating was .860. The point-guard norm was .402, counting Robertson's rating. Not counting Robertson's rating it was .381, a difference of 21 points. In other words, Robertson's rating was 2.25 times as high as the league median for point guards excluding himself. That is a staggering statistic. No other player ever has come close to equaling it. And the 1963–64 season was not Robertson's best.

Also, Robertson's positional rating, which includes the iron-man factor, was 15 points higher than Johnson's.

And Robertson went through several "down" seasons at the end of his career. Johnson has not yet begun to slip, but all players do eventually. Johnson has played 12 seasons. After 12 seasons Robertson's rating was .771, 15 points higher than Johnson's is now.

These are all good reasons for rating Robertson ahead of Johnson at this point in Magic's career.

The third change pushes Jerry West ahead of higher-rated John Stockton for similar reasons.

Here are the qualifications of the TENDEX Hall of Fame point guards:

1. OSCAR ROBERTSON—Played 14 seasons, 43,866 minutes . . . Three-time college Player of the Year . . . Three-time NCAA scoring champion . . . NBA Rookie of the Year 1961 . . . As a pro averaged at least 30 points per game 6 seasons with a career average of 25.7 . . . Only player in history to average a triple-double for a full season with 30.8 points, 12.5 rebounds and 11.4 assists in 1961–62 . . . All-NBA selection nine straight seasons . . . League MVP 1964 . . . MVP in three All-Star Games . . . Member of champion team 1971 . . . Led NBA in assists per game seven times, free-throw percentage twice and scoring average once . . . Career TENDEX rating .738.

2. MAGIC JOHNSON—Played 12 seasons, 32,287 minutes . . . MVP of NCAA Tournament and member of champion team in 1979 . . . Member of five NBA champion teams, playoff MVP three times . . . Led NBA in assists four times, steals twice, free-throw percentage once . . . Broke Robertson's career record for total assists last season, becoming the first player to surpass 10,000 . . . Selected All-NBA the past nine seasons . . . Winner of three league MVP awards . . . Holds career playoff and All-Star Game records for assists . . . Career TENDEX rating .758.

3. JERRY WEST—Played 14 seasons, 36,571 minutes . . . NCAA Tournament MVP 1959 . . . Ten-time All-NBA selection . . . Four-time member of All-Defensive Team . . . Member of champion team and playoff MVP 1972 . . . Led NBA in scoring 1970, led in assists 1972 . . . All-Star Game MVP 1972 . . . Holds NBA record for most free throws in one season . . . Career scoring average of 27.0 is fourth best of all-time . . . Often thought of as a shooting guard, but played more at the point . . . Career TENDEX rating .688.

4. JOHN STOCKTON—Played 7 seasons, 17,314 minutes . . . Had fourth straight season with TENDEX rating higher than .700 in 1990–91; only other point guards to do that are Robertson and Johnson . . . Has led NBA in assists the last 4 seasons with four of the five highest season totals in history . . . Has averaged more than 14 assists per game the last two seasons; no one else has done it once . . . Second to Johnson in career assists per game . . . Led NBA in steals 1989 . . . Ranks among the top 25 players of all-time in ratio of points to shots (Shootist) . . . Career TENDEX rating .693.

5. WALT FRAZIER—Played 13 seasons, 30,965 minutes . . . Led Southern Illinois to NIT title in 1967 . . . Member of NBA champion teams 1970 and 1973 . . . Great clutch player, scored 36 points and had 19 assists in final game of 1970 playoffs . . . Averaged 18.9 points in 13 regular seasons, 20.7 in playoffs . . . Four-time All-NBA selection . . . Named to All-Defensive Team seven times . . . All-Star Game MVP 1975 . . . Career TENDEX rating .618.

6. BOB COUSY—Played 14 seasons, 30,165 minutes . . . Member of NCAA champion team 1947 . . . Three-time All-American at Holy Cross . . . All-NBA selection 10 straight seasons . . . League MVP 1957 . . . Member of six Boston Celtic champion teams . . . All-Star Game MVP 1954 and 1957 . . . Led NBA in assists eight straight seasons . . . Career TENDEX rating .516.

7. ISIAH THOMAS—Played 10 seasons, 27,926 minutes . . . MVP of Indiana's NCAA champion team in 1981 . . . Set NBA record (later broken by

Stockton) with 1,123 assists in 1985 . . . Member of NBA champion teams 1989 and 1990, playoff MVP 1990 . . . Three-time All-NBA selection . . . All-Star Game MVP 1984 and 1986 . . . Ranks No. 3 all-time in assists behind Johnson and Robertson . . . Career TENDEX rating .580.

8. PAUL WESTPHAL—Played 12 seasons, 20,947 minutes . . . Second-team All-American at USC in 1972 . . . All-NBA first-team 1977, 1979 and 1980 . . . Member of NBA champion team 1974 . . . Comeback Player of the Year 1983 . . . Had career highs of 25.2 points per game in 1978, 6.5 assists in 1979 and 2.6 steals in 1976 . . . Career TENDEX rating .584.

9. LAFAYETTE LEVER—Played 9 seasons, 20,983 minutes . . . One of the most versatile players in NBA history . . . For his career ranks among the all-time leading backcourtmen in rebounds (6.4), assists (6.8) and steals (2.3) per game . . . Third-ranked player of all-time in ratio of steals to turnovers, No. 7 in steals per game . . . Career TENDEX rating .585.

10. LEN WILKENS—Played 15 seasons, 38,064 minutes . . . Second-Team All-American at Providence College in 1960 . . . Career total of 7,211 assists is fourth-best in NBA history . . . Led league in assists 1970 . . . All-Star Game MVP 1971 . . . Coach of NBA champion team 1979 . . . Career TENDEX rating .541.

11. GUS WILLIAMS—Played 11 seasons, 25,645 minutes . . . Outstanding clutch scorer, averaged 19.5 points in 99 playoff games, 17.1 in regular season . . . Averaged 26.6 in playoffs for 1979 Seattle team that won NBA championship . . . All-NBA selection 1982 . . . Comeback Player of the Year 1982 . . . Rates among top ten players of all-time in steals . . . Career TENDEX rating .535.

12. NATE ARCHIBALD—Played 13 seasons, 31,159 minutes . . . One of five point guards to achieve a .700 TENDEX rating (.712 in 1972–73) . . . Led NBA in scoring and assists 1973 . . . Three-time All-NBA selection . . . All-Star Game MVP 1981 . . . Member of champion team 1981 . . . Career scoring average 18.8 . . . Ranks among the top ten of all-time in assists . . . Career TENDEX rating .532.

13. MAURICE CHEEKS—Played 13 seasons, 33,249 minutes . . . The Dave DeBusschere of point guards, with a TENDEX rating about 25 points too low to qualify for the Hall of Fame, but other credentials that make up the difference . . . Member of NBA champion team 1983 . . . All-Defensive Team selection four times . . . All-time NBA steals leader . . . No. 5 on all-time assists list . . . Career TENDEX rating .515.

14. DICK McGUIRE—Played 11 seasons, 21,000 minutes (estimated) . . . Second-Team All-American selection in 1944 for St. John's . . . TENDEX All-NBA selection 1952 and 1955 for New York Knicks . . . Led NBA in assists 1950 . . . No. 9 ranked player of all-time in assists efficiency . . . Career TENDEX rating .430.

Five of the 14 TENDEX Hall of Fame point guards would not have made it if we had maintained the requirement that a player's rating be 100 points above normal. Two others—Isiah Thomas and Lafayette Lever—could drop below this standard in latter years of their careers.

In evaluating the qualifications of these seven players, all of them seem to deserve Hall of Fame honors. It is apparent, therefore, that the 100-point requirement is too high for backcourtmen. Guards should have requirements proportionate to the standard ratings for their positions.

Percentagewise, a .525 rating is as much better than a .450 rating as a .700 rating is better than a .600 rating, so it did not seem inappropriate to reduce the backcourt requirement from 100 points to 75. This especially held true for early eras of the NBA when the TENDEX norm for guards was less than .400 and the average for centers was about .600.

During McGuire's career, in the 1950s, the median for point guards was .341. In achieving a TENDEX rating of .430, 89 points above the norm, he was proportionately better than several of the players who made the TENDEX Hall of Fame as centers, more than 100 points above normal. McGuire's rating was 26 percent above average for his position. A center who achieved a .650 career rating when .550 is average is just 18 percent above the norm.

The other point guards on this list whose ratings weren't quite 100 points above the median were Wilkens (plus-98), Williams (plus-90) and Archibald (plus-89). Williams was unheralded and sometimes unappreciated. He did not play for high-visibility teams but was an outstanding and durable player. There are few veteran NBA observers who would exclude Wilkens or Archibald from the Hall of Fame and few old-timers who would leave McGuire out.

Here are 10 other players who are difficult to omit:

⋄ Naismith Hall of Famers K.C. Jones, Andy Phillip, and Slater Martin who did not come close to meeting even the reduced TENDEX standards for backcourtmen.

⋄ Fred Brown whose rating of .540 was 96 points above the norm, but who was a sixth man most of his career for Seattle, playing only 47 percent of the potential minutes.

⋄ Mack Calvin, the ABA's best point guard, whose TENDEX rating was 103 points above normal, but whose minutes played were below 50 percent, like Brown's.

⋄ Micheal Ray Richardson, who was headed for the Hall but had his career shortened because of drug abuse.

⋄ Dennis Johnson, who may be selected for the Naismith Hall because of the Boston Celtic mystique, but who was overrated offensively and defensively (TENDEX rating. 464).

⋄ Kevin Johnson, Derek Harper, and Terry Porter, who have good credentials but need more longevity.

Here is a full chart of the point-guard honorees:

Player (Seasons)	TENDEX
1. Oscar Robertson (14)	.738
2. Magic Johnson (12)	.758
3. Jerry West (14)	.688
4. John Stockton (7)	.693
5. Walt Frazier (13)	.618
6. Bob Cousy (14)	.516
7. Isiah Thomas (10)	.580
8. Paul Westphal (12)	.584
9. Lafayette Lever (9)	.585
10. Len Wilkens (15)	.541
11. Gus Williams (11)	.535
12. Nate Archibald (13)	.532
13. Maurice Cheeks (13)	.515
14. Dick McGuire (11)	.430

ABSTRACTION 6

The Superstar Syndrome

The rationale you hear is this: Everybody wants to see the superstars play, and the referees don't want to spoil the fans' enjoyment of the game by making calls against them.

Now here's the truth: Some referees are intimidated by superstars and are afraid to make calls against them.

Fans are not going to go home disgusted if Magic Johnson is called once or twice for offensive fouls for hooking when he throws his elbows during a drive. They won't get despondent if Michael Jordan draws a whistle for traveling on an extra-long jaunt to the hoop. They won't become suicidal if a foul is called against Charles Barkley when he slugs a defender before slam-dunking the ball.

Let's face it, Magic, Michael, and Charles don't need that kind of advantage. They can do quite well on any man-to-man matchup without referees looking out for them as if they were vulnerable children.

But Magic, Michael, and Charles are smart enough to take advantage of any preferential treatment they can get. And they get plenty of it. Here are some other examples of the superstar syndrome:

⋄ I've seen Johnson get away with hooking, traveling, and flopping on the same play (flopping being defined as a graceful dive to the court with a mock cry of pain on a minimal-contact play).

⋄ The 275-pound Barkley often gets away with pushing opponents into the third row of seats, but he somehow gets "fouled" on uncontested layups. Opponents would be better off mugging him. He'd go to the free-throw line a dozen times a game even if they ignored him.

⋄ Patrick Ewing and David Robinson can do as much pushing and elbowing as they want to get offensive low-post position. Lesser players are called for offensive fouls for the same tactics.

⋄ Larry Bird gets away with shuffling his feet (traveling) sometimes when he shoots from long range.

⋄ In one televised game, I counted Scottie Pippen taking five distinct steps (not baby steps either), before consummating a drive with a dunk. Not only was there no traveling call, but on replay commentator Hubie Brown raved about the basket without mentioning the obvious violation.

What's the point of all this?

Well, maybe it's that superstars are not a vanishing species in need of protection. Or that Hubie Brown is myopic. Or that Scottie Pippen is about to join the Super Club.

Or all of the above.

13
Shooting Guards

A statistic that has played a prominent role in the selection of TENDEX Hall of Famers is percentage of performance above the average for a player's position. Of the players mentioned so far, only Oscar Robertson was able to achieve a TENDEX rating double the norm for his position. Robertson did it for the first eight years of his NBA career.

Despite having consistent TENDEX ratings in the neighborhood of 1.000, Wilt Chamberlain did not achieve this for a single season, let alone eight. The normal rating for a center during his era was about .600.

A third man is entering contention, along with Robertson and Chamberlain, as the outstanding player of all time. For the past four seasons, Michael Jordan has about doubled the TENDEX norm for shooting guards. Should he sustain such a pace for another four seasons and maintain a reasonable degree of skill during his latter-career seasons, he would rank right with Wilt and Oscar at the top of the list.

Jordan already holds a distinction neither Robertson nor Chamberlain can come close to equaling. His career TENDEX rating is about 200 points above that of the second-best rated shooting guard of all-time, Clyde Drexler. Chamberlain's rating was about 100 points higher than that of Bill Russell, but

there are a lot of old-timers who believe that Russell's superb man-to-man defense cut away most, if not all, of the difference.

Chamberlain also was an outstanding defensive player, but while Wilt will always face arguments from Russell and Abdul-Jabbar fans, and Robertson will face contention from Magic Johnson and Jerry West proponents, Jordan is practically unchallenged as the greatest shooting guard of all-time.

These are the TENDEX Hall of Fame shooting guards:

1. MICHAEL JORDAN—Played 7 seasons, 19,673 minutes . . . Member of NCAA champion North Carolina team 1982 . . . College Player of the Year 1984 . . . No. 1 NBA player of all-time in scoring average . . . Led NBA in scoring last five seasons . . . Led league in steals twice . . . League MVP in 1988 and 1991 . . . All-NBA selection five straight years . . . TENDEX Player of the Year last 5 seasons . . . All-Star Game MVP 1988 . . . Defensive Player of the Year 1988 . . . Career TENDEX rating .851.

2. CLYDE DREXLER—Played 8 seasons, 21,312 minutes . . . Versatile player, averaged 20.5 points, 6.0 rebounds, 5.6

assists and 2.3 steals per game for his career . . . Ranks No. 8 all-time in steals per game . . . Four-time TENDEX All-NBA Second Team selection . . . Career TENDEX rating .652.

3. GEORGE GERVIN—Played 14 seasons, 35,597 minutes . . . Five-time All-NBA selection, six-time choice by TENDEX . . . All-Star Game MVP 1980 . . . Led NBA in scoring four times, a feat accomplished by only two other players . . . No. 4 rated player of all-time in scoring efficiency . . . Career TENDEX rating .612.

4. ALVIN ROBERTSON—Played 7 seasons, 17,722 minutes . . . Top-rated NBA-ABA player of all-time in steals per game and steals per minute . . . Set NBA record for steals with 301 in 1985–86 . . . Has led NBA in steals three times . . . Defensive Player of the Year 1986 . . . Most Improved Player 1986 . . . Career TENDEX rating .584.

5. WALTER DAVIS—Played 14 seasons, 28,118 minutes . . . TENDEX rating of .720 in 1978–79 made him one of three shooting guards to surpass .700 for a season (others are Jordan and Drexler) . . . TENDEX All-NBA selection twice . . . Rookie of the Year 1978 . . . Career scoring average 19.5 . . . Career TENDEX rating .580.

6. SIDNEY MONCRIEF—Played 11 seasons, 23,150 minutes . . . Led NCAA in field-goal percentage 1976 . . . All-NBA selection 1983, TENDEX all-league selection 1983 and 1984 . . . Great defensive player, four times named to NBA's All-Defensive Team . . . Defensive Player of the Year 1983 and 1984 . . . Career TENDEX rating .578.

7. SAM JONES—Played 12 seasons, 24,285 minutes . . . Three-time All-NBA Second Team selection, four-time Second Team choice by TENDEX . . . Good clutch player, averaged 18.9

points for 154 playoff games, 1.2 points higher than regular-season average . . . Member of 10 NBA champion teams . . . Career TENDEX rating .573.

8. JOHN HAVLICEK—Played 16 seasons, 46,471 minutes . . . Member of NCAA champion Ohio State team 1960 . . . Career NBA scoring average was 20.8, boosted it to 22.0 in 172 playoff games . . . Member of eight NBA champion teams . . . Playoff MVP 1974 . . . Four-time All-NBA selection, seven-time second-team choice . . . Five-time All-Defensive Team selection . . . Career TENDEX rating .556.

9. RICHIE GUERIN—Played 13 seasons, 27,447 minutes . . . Three-time TENDEX All-NBA selection, two-time second-team choice . . . Averaged 29.5 points, 6.9 assists and 6.4 rebounds per game in 1961–62 season . . . Career marks were 17.3 points, 5.1 rebounds and 5.0 assists . . . NBA Coach of the Year 1968 . . . Career TENDEX rating .536.

10. JEFF MULLINS—Played 12 seasons, 24,574 minutes . . . Member of NBA champion team 1975 . . . Averaged more than 20 points per game four seasons in a row . . . Best season was 1972 with per-game averages of 21.5 points, 5.9 assists and 5.6 rebounds . . . Career TENDEX rating .518.

11. EARL MONROE—Played 13 seasons, 29,636 minutes . . . NCAA Division II record-holder for points in one season . . . NBA Rookie of the Year 1968 . . . All-NBA first-team choice 1969 . . . Member of NBA champion team 1973 . . . Career scoring average 18.8, six times averaged more than 20 points per game . . . Career TENDEX rating .505.

12. HAL GREER—Played 15 seasons, 39,788 minutes . . . Durable, had seven 3,000-minute seasons . . .

Averaged 20 points per game seven straight seasons, career average was 19.2 . . . Seven-time All-NBA Second Team choice . . . Member of champion team 1967 . . . All-Star Game MVP 1968 . . . Career TENDEX rating .501.

13. RON BOONE—Played 13 seasons, 32,381 minutes . . . Played an NBA-ABA record 1,041 consecutive games . . . The only player ever to play at least 10 seasons without missing a game from the first to the final game of his career . . . Member of ABA champion team 1971 . . . All-ABA First Team choice in 1975 when he averaged 25.2 points per game . . . Career TENDEX rating .490.

14. BILL SHARMAN—Played 11 seasons, 22,500 minutes (estimated) . . . All-NBA selection four times . . . All-Star Game MVP 1955 . . . Member of four champion teams . . . Led NBA in free-throw percentage seven times . . . NBA Coach of the Year 1972 . . . Coached champion teams in the NBA (1972), ABA (1971) and ABL (1962) . . . Career TENDEX rating of .457 was 91 points above the shooting-guard norm for his era.

Without the adjustment allowing a backcourtman to qualify for the TENDEX Hall of Fame with a rating 75 points above average, Mullins, Monroe, Greer, Boone, and Sharman would not have made it. All five of these men had excellent qualifications both in playing time and performance.

Three other shooting guards—David Thompson, Calvin Murphy, and Tom Gola—barely meet the adjusted qualifications. But these three men had better collegiate careers than professional careers and are included among the college honorees in Chapter 15.

Here are seven others who didn't quite make it:

◇ Gail Goodrich who came close.

◇ Naismith Hall of Famer Bobby Wanzer who didn't.

◇ Ray Williams who had the TENDEX rating (.557) but, like Adrian Dantley, lacked defense and commitment: Switched teams seven times in five years.

◇ Reggie Miller and Ron Harper who are good bets to make it someday if they stay healthy.

◇ Ricky Pierce and Joe Dumars who have an outside chance.

Here is a full list of the TENDEX Hall of Fame shooting guards:

Player (Seasons)	TENDEX
1. Michael Jordan (7)	.851
2. Clyde Drexler (8)	.652
3. George Gervin (14)	.612
4. Alvin Robertson (7)	.584
5. Walter Davis (14)	.580
6. Sidney Moncrief (11)	.578
7. Sam Jones (12)	.573
8. John Havlicek (16)	.556
9. Richie Guerin (13)	.536
10. Jeff Mullins (12)	.518
11. Earl Monroe (12)	.505
12. Hal Greer (15)	.501
13. Ron Boone (13)	.490
14. Bill Sharman (11)	.457

14
NBA-ABA Roster

More than 2,600 players have played in the National Basketball Association, the American Basketball Association, or both. Of these, 341 completed their careers before it was possible to do TENDEX ratings in 1951–52. More than 300 played less than 100 minutes, the minimum to qualify for rating by TENDEX. About 400 others are still active. Subtracting the unrated and active players from the total leaves about 1,600 players whose careers are finished and have been rated by TENDEX. The full list of these players appears at the end of this chapter.

In computing these ratings, some offbeat facts were disclosed that could become answers to trivia questions:

⋄ **BRICK-SHOOTERS:** In 1946–47, the NBA's first season, all 11 teams made less than 30 percent of their field-goal attempts. The league-low percentage was Detroit's .246. Every team averaged less than 75 points per game. There was only one 20-point scorer, Joe Fulks of Philadelphia.

⋄ **CONTRACTION DRAFTS:** The Boston Celtics got Bob Cousy and Bill Sharman from contraction (opposite of expansion). When the Chicago franchise disbanded in 1950, its players were raffled off. Boston drew Cousy's name out of a hat. In 1951, Fort Wayne drew Sharman's name from Washington's dispersed roster and traded him to the Celtics.

⋄ **PLAYER-COACHES:** Three of the great coaches played as substitutes for an NBA team in 1952–53. Rochester's 10-man roster that season included reserve forward Alex Hannum and guards Red Holzman and Jack McMahon.

⋄ **IRON-MAN TEAM:** The Minneapolis Lakers played the 1953–54 season with the skimpiest roster in NBA history, nine players. The Lakers won the league title with each of the nine men playing more than 1,000 minutes. George Mikan of Minneapolis became the first TENDEX 700 Club member that season with his rating of exactly .700.

⋄ **FRONT-RUNNERS:** The highest-rated frontcourt in NBA history belonged to the St. Louis Hawks of 1959–60. TENDEX ratings of the Hawk frontliners were center Clyde Lovellette .828, power forward Bob Pettit .827, and small forward Cliff Hagan .746. All three men are TENDEX Hall of Famers.

⋄ **GO WEST, YOUNG MEN:** In 1960–61 the Lakers were moved from Minneapolis to Los Angeles and showed immediately that they were destined for good fortune in their new city when they made Jerry West their No. 1 draft choice. In 31 seasons in Los Angeles, the Lakers have had at least one superstar every season but one, 1974–75, the year between West's retirement and Kareem Abdul-Jabbar's arrival.

◇ **AN ASSIST FOR THE BOOK:** No center ever has led the NBA in assists, although the official league record book lists Wilt Chamberlain as the champion in 1967–68. Chamberlain averaged 8.6 assists that season, but Oscar Robertson averaged 9.7. Under an antiquated system, Chamberlain was listed as the assists leader because Robertson missed 13 games due to injuries and had a lower total than Chamberlain. The record book has never been changed to reflect the modernized criteria based on per-game average instead of bulk total.

◇ **MORE THAN MAXIMUM:** In 1968–69, Walt Bellamy set an NBA record by playing in 88 regular-season games in an 82-game season. In 1973–74, Chuck Williams broke that record by playing 90 games in an 84-game ABA season. The two men managed to exceed the apparent maximum by being traded during the season from teams that had played six more games at that point than the teams they were traded to.

◇ **HEY, COACH:** Here's a classic case of poor coaching judgment. In 1974–75, the Chicago Bulls' best players, according to TENDEX, were center Tom Boerwinkle (.799), forward Mickey Johnson (.677), and guard Robert Wilson (.635). They totaled 1,891 minutes among them, less combined playing time than six lower-rated Bull players got individually that year.

◇ **SUB MVP:** The only player in NBA history to be voted MVP without playing half of his team's minutes was Bill Walton in 1977–78. Walton missed 24 games

because of injuries, played only 1,929 minutes, but had a TENDEX rating of .906 and led the Portland Trail Blazers to the league title.

◇ **SOARING WITH BIRD:** The Boston Celtics had a record of 29–53, second worst in the NBA, in 1978–79. Their only significant addition before the 1979–80 season was No. 1 draft choice Larry Bird. That season their record was 61–21, best in the league. Total improvement 32 games, a record. Coincidence? Well, the Celtics had a losing record in April of 1979, the final month of the last season before they signed Bird. The next time they had a losing record for a month was December of 1988, 10 seasons later. It was the next full month they played without Bird, who was sidelined because of foot injuries.

◇ **BLOCKS AND POINTS:** George Johnson became the first player to accumulate more blocked shots than points for a season. Playing for San Antonio, in 1981–82, Johnson blocked 234 shots and scored only 225 points. Johnson has been eclipsed by Manute Bol, who has had more blocks than points in all five of his NBA seasons.

◇ **BLOCKS AND STEALS:** In 1983–84, Bobby Jones of Philadelphia committed 101 turnovers. That same season he had 103 blocked shots and 107 steals. This is the only time a regular player has had more steals than turnovers and more blocked shots than turnovers in the same season.

◇ **HARD-WORKING AGENT:** Cut before the start of the 1985–86 season by Chicago, Rod Higgins signed in November with Seattle, but was waived after 12 games. Signed in January by San Antonio, he played 11 games with the Spurs before being released. He then signed with New Jersey in February and played two games before being cut. In March, he signed with Chicago and played five games before being released. Higgins played for four NBA teams under a total of seven contracts that season but was a free-agent when the campaign started and ended after being cut by the same team—Chicago. That same season he somehow found time to play 11 games for Tampa Bay in the Continental Basketball Association.

◇ **NAME GAME NO. 1:** Nearly half of the playing time for the Atlanta Hawks during the 1987–88 season was played by seven men whose last names started with the letter W: Dominique Wilkins (2,948 minutes), Kevin Willis (2,091), Randy Wittman (2,412), Spud Webb (1,347), Chris Washburn (174), Leon Wood (79), and Ennis Whatley (24). They totaled 9,075 of the team's 19,780 minutes. Wilkins, Willis, and Wittman were starters.

◇ **NAME GAME NO. 2:** All three retired players named Carr (Kenny, Austin, and M.L.) played 10 seasons in the NBA. A fourth Carr, Antoine, is on his way to equaling or surpassing the other three. He has played seven seasons and had his best season in 1990–91 with Sacramento. Even more durable were the three players named Lucas (Jerry, John, and Maurice), John and Maurice Lucas played 14 seasons each and Jerry played 11 and was a TENDEX Hall of Famer.

◇ **NAME GAME NO. 3:** When Hakeem Olajuwon changed his first name to Hakeem last season, he became the ninth player to change his name during his NBA or ABA career. The other eight were Jamaal Wilkes (from Keith Wilkes), Warren Jabali (from Warren Armstrong), Kareem Abdul-Jabbar (from Lew Alcindor), Mahdi Abdul-Rahman (from Walt Hazzard), Wali Jones (from Walter Jones), Stan Stutz (from Stan Modzelewski), Zaid Abdul-Aziz (from Don Smith), and World B Free (from Lloyd B. Free). All were outstanding players except Stutz, who later became a famous referee. Abdul-Jabbar

and Olajuwon are TENDEX Hall of Famers.

In the listings that follow, the ratings of five TENDEX Hall of Fame players are given with estimates included for steals, blocked shots, and turnovers for at least four seasons of their careers. These players are Wilt Chamberlain, Bill Russell, Nate Thurmond, Kareem Abdul-Jabbar, and Elvin Hayes.

The number in parenthesis after each player's name represents the seasons he played in the NBA and/or ABA. If two numbers are listed, the second number represents the number of TENDEX ratable seasons he played, beginning with the 1951–52 campaign when minutes were first tabulated.

Here are career TENDEX ratings of all retired NBA-ABA players who played at least 100 minutes:

Abdul-Aziz, Zaid (10)	.589
Abdul-Jabbar, Kareem (20)	.817
Abdul-Rahman, Mahdi (10)	.495
Abernethy, Tom (5)	.436
Ackerman, Buddy (1)	.087
Acton, Charles (1)	.410
Adams, Alvan (13)	.664
Adams, Don (7)	.403
Adams, George (3)	.487
Addison, Rafael (1)	.390
Adelman, Rick (7)	.381
Aitch, Mitch (1)	.431
Akin, Henry (3)	.353
Alcorn, Gary (2)	.397
Aleksinas, Chuck (1)	.387
Allen, Bill (1)	.472
Allen, Lucius (10)	.480
Allen, Bob (1)	.304
Allison, Odis (1)	.203
Allums, Darrell (1)	.322
Anderegg, Bob (1)	.324
Anderson, Andy (3)	.334
Anderson, Cliff (4)	.378
Anderson, Dan (2)	.615
Anderson, Danny (2)	.371
Anderson, Jerome (2)	.341
Anderson, Kim (1)	.201
Anderson, Michael (1)	.388
Anderson, Richard (6)	.447
Anderzunas, Wally (1)	.356

Arceneaux, Stacey (1)	.405	Becker, Art (6)	.547
Archibald, Nate (13)	.532	Bedell, Bob (4)	.562
Ard, Jim (8)	.450	Behagen, Ron (7)	.537
Arizin, Paul (10,9)	.552	Bell, Dennis (3)	.365
Armstrong, Robert (1)	.345	Bell, Whitey (2)	.377
Armstrong, Tate (2)	.314	Bellamy, Walt (14)	.697
Arnelle, Jesse (1)	.507	Bemoras, Irv (2)	.262
Arnette, Jay (3)	.304	Benbow, Leon (2)	.349
Arnzen, Bob (4)	.460	Bennett, Mel (5)	.381
Askew, Vincent (1)	.242	Bennett, Willis (1)	.364
Atha, Dick (2)	.362	Benson, Kent (11)	.519
Attles, Al (11)	.416	Bergh, Larry (1)	.471
Austin, John (2)	.348	Berry, Ricky (1)	.433
Averitt, Bird (5)	.364	Berry, Walter (3)	.528
Awtrey, Dennis (12)	.428	Beshore, Delmer (2)	.244
Bacon, Henry (1)	.346	Bialosuknia, Wes (1)	.337
Baechtold, Jim (5)	.336	Bianchi, Al (10)	.332
Bailey, Gus (5)	.374	Bibby, Henry (9)	.391
Bailey, James (9)	.515	Bigelow, Bob (4)	.297
Ballard, Greg (11)	.530	Billingy, Lionel (1)	.426
Banks, Gene (6)	.493	Bing, Dave (12)	.519
Banks, Walker (1)	.419	Birdsong, Otis (12)	.482
Bantom, Mike (9)	.495	Blab, Uwe (5)	.320
Barker, Cliff (3,1)	.292	Black, Charles (4,1)	.232
Barker, Tom (2)	.443	Black, Tom (1)	.433
Barksdale, Don (4)	.424	Blackwell, Cory (1)	.241
Barnes, Harry (1)	.170	Blackwell, Nate (1)	.234
Barnes, Jim (7)	.517	Blaney, George (1)	.286
Barnes, Marvin (6)	.624	Block, John (10)	.553
Barnett, Jim (11)	.460	Blume, Ray (1)	.321
Barnett, Dick (14)	.444	Bobb, Nelson (4,2)	.315
Barnhill, John (10)	.348	Bockhorn, Arlen (7)	.379
Barnhorst, Leo (5,3)	.351	Boerwinkle, Tom (10)	.691
Barr, Mike (5)	.352	Bolger, William (1)	.303
Barr, Moe (1)	.462	Bonham, Ron (3)	.559
Barrett, Ernie (2)	.321	Booker, Harold (1)	.589
Barrett, Mike (3)	.396	Boone, Ron (13)	.490
Barry, Rick (14)	.626	Boozer, Bob (11)	.574
Bartolome, Vic (1)	.322	Boryla, Vince (5,3)	.277
Baskerville, Jerry (1)	.365	Boston, Lawrence (1)	.484
Bassett, Tim (7)	.411	Boswell, Tom (6)	.517
Bates, Billy Ray (4)	.495	Boven, Don (3,2)	.320
Batton, Dave (2)	.413	Bowens, Tom (3)	.443
Baum, John (5)	.458	Bowie, Anthony (2)	.341
Baylor, Elgin (14)	.753	Bowman, Nate (6)	.515
Bayne, Howard (1)	.528	Boyd, Fred (6)	.297
Beard, Albert (1)	.552	Boynes, Winford (3)	.357
Beard, Butch (9)	.491	Bracey, Steve (3)	.393
Beasley, Charles (4)	.512	Bradds, Gary (6)	.581
Beasley, John (7)	.589	Bradley, Alex (1)	.409
Beaty, Zelmo (12)	.642	Bradley, Alonzo (3)	.303
Beck, Byron (10)	.550	Bradley, Bill (10)	.403
Beck, Ernie (7)	.367	Bradley, Bill (1)	.291

Bradley, Charlie (3)	.297	Butler, Al (4)	.429
Bradley, Dudley (9)	.397	Butler, Mike (4)	.370
Bradley, James (3)	.490	Byrd, Walt (1)	.214
Branch, Adrian (4)	.484	Byrnes, Marty (4)	.362
Brannum, Bob (6,4)	.384	Cable, Barney (6)	.450
Branson, Brad (2)	.465	Calabrese, Gerry (2,1)	.233
Branson, Jesse (2)	.570	Caldwell, Jim (3)	.572
Brasco, Jim (1)	.184	Caldwell, Joe (11)	.466
Bratz, Mike (9)	.394	Calhoun, Bill (8,4)	.279
Braun, Carl (13,10)	.413	Calhoun, Corky (8)	.341
Brennan, Pete (1)	.260	Calvin, Mack (11)	.518
Brewer, Jim (9)	.477	Cannon, Larry (4)	.432
Brewer, Ron (8)	.370	Card, Frank (5)	.449
Brian, Frank (9,5)	.331	Carl, Howie (1)	.317
Bridgeman, Junior (12)	.491	Carlisle, Rick (5)	.291
Bridges, Bill (13)	.591	Carlos, Don (1)	.464
Brisker, John (6)	.588	Carlson, Al (1)	.343
Bristow, Allan (10)	.499	Carney, Robert (1)	.285
Brittain, Mike (2)	.306	Carr, Austin (10)	.430
Brogan, James (2)	.423	Carr, Kenny (10)	.545
Brokaw, Gary (4)	.403	Carr, M. L. (10)	.465
Brooks, Michael (6)	.498	Carrier, Darel (6)	.431
Brown, Fred (13)	.540	Carrington, Bob (2)	.310
Brown, John (7)	.426	Carter, Butch (6)	.392
Brown, Larry (5)	.444	Carter, Fred (8)	.420
Brown, Rickey (5)	.421	Carter, George (8)	.470
Brown, Roger A. (8)	.522	Carter, Howard (2)	.320
Brown, W. Roger (5)	.429	Carter, Reggie (2)	.332
Brown, Stanley (2,1)	.211	Carter, Ron (2)	.294
Brundy, Stanley (1)	.375	Carty, Jay (1)	.462
Bruns, George (1)	.374	Catchings, Harvey (11)	.448
Bryant, Emmette (8)	.401	Cattage, Bobby (2)	.356
Bryant, Joe (8)	.431	Cavenall, Ron (2)	.308
Bryant, Wallace (3)	.404	Cervi, Al (4,2)	.496
Bucci, George (1)	.361	Chamberlain, Bill (2)	.420
Buckhalter, Joe (2)	.601	Chamberlain, Wilt (14)	.942
Buckner, Cleveland (2)	.603	Chambers, Jerry (6)	.464
Buckner, Quinn (10)	.457	Chaney, Don (12)	.411
Budd, Dave (5)	.481	Chapman, Wayne (4)	.357
Budko, Walter (4,1)	.346	Chappell, Len (10)	.545
Bunce, Larry (2)	.461	Charles, Ken (5)	.346
Bunt, Richard (1)	.154	Charles, Lorenzo (1)	.404
Buntin, Bill (1)	.535	Chenier, Phil (10)	.448
Bunting, Bill (3)	.396	Chones, Jim (10)	.529
Burden, Ticky (3)	.410	Christensen, Cal (5,4)	.372
Burleson, Tom (7)	.601	Christian, Bob (5)	.530
Burns, Jim (1)	.300	Chubin, Steve (3)	.553
Burris, Arthur (2,1)	.227	Clark, Archie (10)	.501
Burrow, Robert (2)	.421	Clark, Carlos (2)	.322
Burtt, Steve (2)	.288	Clark, Dick (2)	.252
Buse, Don (13)	.409	Clawson, John (1)	.381
Bustion, Dave (1)	.516	Cleamons, Jim (9)	.416
Butcher, Donnie (5)	.372	Clemens, Barry (11)	.464

Clifton, Nat (8,7)	.430	Cureton, Earl (9)	.418
Closs, William (3,1)	.291	Dahler, Ed (1)	.326
Clyde, Ben (1)	.462	Dailey, Quentin (8)	.453
Cofield, Fred (2)	.343	Dampier, Louie (12)	.433
Coleman, Ben (4)	.496	Dandridge, Bobby (13)	.554
Coleman, E. C. (6)	.395	Daniels, Mel (9)	.685
Coleman, Jack (9,7)	.476	Darden, Oliver (3)	.517
Coleman, Norris (1)	.255	Dark, Jesse (1)	.315
Collins, Art (1)	.168	Darnell, Rick (1)	.359
Collins, Don (6)	.474	Davies, Bob (7,4)	.379
Collins, Doug (8)	.468	Davis, Charlie (3)	.382
Collins, Jim (2)	.405	Davis, Dwight (5)	.471
Combs, Glenn (7)	.402	Davis, Harry (2)	.361
Combs, Leroy (1)	.423	Davis, Jim (8)	.565
Comeaux, John (1)	.384	Davis, Johnny (10)	.421
Comegys, Dallas (2)	.425	Davis, Lee (8)	.517
Congdon, Jeff (5)	.346	Davis, Mel (4)	.479
Conley, Gene (6)	.487	Davis, Mickey (6)	.489
Conlin, Ed (7)	.404	Davis, Mike (4)	.405
Cook, Bert (1)	.275	Davis, Ralph (2)	.327
Cook, Darwin (8)	.447	Davis, Ron (3)	.320
Cook, Jeff (8)	.444	Davis, Walter (5)	.377
Cook, Norm (2)	.338	Davis, Warren (6)	.571
Cooke, Joe (1)	.439	Dawkins, Darryl (14)	.602
Cooper, Chuck (6,5)	.353	Dawkins, Paul (1)	.407
Cooper, Joe (3)	.427	Dawson, Jim (1)	.244
Cooper, Michael (12)	.423	Daye, Darren (5)	.472
Copeland, Hollis (2)	.367	DeBusschere, Dave (12)	.577
Copeland, Lanard (1)	.323	Dee, Don (1)	.372
Costello, Larry (12)	.469	Dees, Archie (4)	.533
Coughran, John (1)	.230	Del Negro, Vinny (2)	.429
Counts, Mel (12)	.631	DeLong, Nate (1)	.625
Courtin, Steve (1)	.248	Demic, Larry (3)	.355
Cousy, Bob (14,13)	.516	Dempsey, George (5)	.409
Cowens, Dave (11)	.668	Dennard, Ken (3)	.383
Cox, John (1)	.383	Denton, Randy (6)	.610
Cox, Wesley (2)	.343	DePre, Joe (2)	.317
Crawford, Fred (5)	.419	Derline, Rod (2)	.330
Creighton, Jim (1)	.240	Devlin, Walter (3)	.327
Criss, Charlie (8)	.386	Dickerson, Henry (2)	.131
Critchfield, Russ (1)	.241	Dickey, Clyde (1)	.204
Crite, Winston (2)	.424	Dickey, Derrek (5)	.488
Crocker, Dillard (5,2)	.330	Dickey, Richard (1)	.298
Croft, Bob (1)	.373	Dickson, John (1)	.429
Crompton, Geoff (5)	.297	Dierking, Connie (10)	.531
Cross, Jeff (1)	.201	Dietrick, Coby (13)	.480
Cross, Pete (3)	.554	DiGregorio, Ernie (5)	.363
Cross, Russell (1)	.474	Dill, Craig (1)	.402
Crow, Mark (1)	.410	Dillard, Mickey (1)	.261
Cueto, Al (2)	.508	Dinwiddie, Bill (4)	.365
Cummings, Pat (11)	.514	Dischinger, Terry (9)	.547
Cunningham, Bill (11)	.674	Donham, Bob (4,3)	.359
Cunningham, Dick (7)	.490	Donovan, Billy (1)	.353

Dorsey, Jacky (3)	.399	Fendley, Jake (2)	.306
Douglas, John (2)	.384	Fernsten, Eric (6)	.432
Douglas, Leon (7)	.474	Ferrari, Al (6)	.340
Dove, Sonny (5)	.490	Ferrell, Duane (2)	.369
Downing, Steve (2)	.329	Ferry, Bob (10)	.500
Drew, John (11)	.630	Fields, Kenny (4)	.428
Driscoll, Terry (5)	.482	Fields, Bob (1)	.526
Duckett, Dick (1)	.317	Fillmore, Greg (2)	.473
Dudley, Charlie (6)	.484	Finch, Larry (2)	.305
Duerod, Terry (4)	.350	Finkel, Henry (9)	.530
Duffy, Bob (3)	.346	Finn, Daniel (3)	.345
Dukes, Walter (8)	.581	Fleishman, Jerry (5,1)	.342
Dunleavy, Mike (11)	.451	Fleming, Ed (5)	.452
Dunn, Pat (1)	.316	Flowers, Bruce (1)	.580
Duren, John (3)	.269	Flynn, Mike (3)	.362
Durrant, Devin (2)	.340	Fontaine, Levi (1)	.348
Durrett, Ken (4)	.375	Ford, Chris (10)	.387
DuVal, Dennis (2)	.363	Ford, Don (7)	.380
Dykema, Craig (1)	.426	Ford, Jake (2)	.369
Eakins, Jim (10)	.577	Ford, Phil (7)	.459
Eaves, Jerry (4)	.369	Forrest, Bayard (2)	.452
Eberhard, Al (4)	.370	Foster, Fred (8)	.351
Ebron, Roy (1)	.608	Foster, Jimmy (2)	.244
Eddleman, Dwight (4,2)	.266	Foster, Rod (3)	.367
Edelin, Kenton (1)	.265	Foust, Larry (12,11)	.601
Edge, Charles (2)	.557	Fowler, Calvin (1)	.362
Edmonds, Bobby Joe (2)	.494	Fox, Jim (10)	.593
Edmonson, Keith (2)	.369	Franklin, William (3)	.479
Edwards, Franklin (7)	.386	Franz, Ron (6)	.477
Egan, Jack (11)	.402	Frazier, Walt (13)	.618
Elliott, Bob (3)	.450	Frazier, Wilbert (3)	.544
Ellis, Bo (3)	.417	Frederick, Anthony (1)	.438
Ellis, Boo (2)	.497	Free, World B (13)	.502
Ellis, Joe (8)	.474	Freeman, Don (9)	.499
Ellis, LeRoy (14)	.517	Freeman, Gary (1)	.611
Elmore, Len (10)	.465	Freeman, Rod (1)	.357
Elston, Darrell (2)	.303	Friend, Larry (1)	.272
Embry, Wayne (11)	.577	Frink, Pat (1)	.312
Engler, Chris, (5)	.377	Fritsche, James (2)	.241
English, Scott (3)	.440	Fryer, Bernie (2)	.359
Erias, Bo (1)	.316	Fulks, Joe (8,3)	.297
Erickson, Keith (12)	.443	Fuller, Carl (2)	.453
Erving, Julius (16)	.709	Fuller, Tony (1)	.312
Evans, Earl (1)	.384	Furlow, Terry (4)	.463
Evans, Mike (9)	.382	Gabor, William (7,4)	.294
Evans, William (1)	.261	Gaines, Corey (2)	.318
Fairchild, John (4)	.439	Gale, Mike (11)	.407
Farley, Richard (3)	.357	Gallatin, Harry (10,7)	.612
Farmer, Jim (3)	.342	Gambee, Dave (12)	.554
Farmer, Mike (7)	.391	Gardner, Chuck (1)	.508
Feher, Butch (1)	.514	Gardner, Vernon (3,1)	.337
Feitl, Dave (3)	.428	Garland, Gary (1)	.339
Felix, Ray (9)	.561	Garmaker, Dick (6)	.414

Garner, Bill (1)	.249	Grunfeld, Ernie (9)	.444
Garnett, Bill (4)	.471	Guarilla, Gene (4)	.382
Garrett, Calvin (4)	.331	Gudmundsson, Petur (4)	.464
Garrett, Dick (5)	.384	Guerin, Richie (13)	.536
Garrett, Rowland (5)	.456	Guokas, Matt (10)	.346
Garris, John (1)	.642	Hackett, Rudy (2)	.354
George, Jack (8)	.343	Hadnot, Jim (1)	.584
Gerard, Gus (7)	.470	Haffner, Scott (1)	.319
Gervin, George (14)	.612	Hagan, Cliff (13)	.642
Gianelli, John (8)	.445	Hairston, Al (2)	.299
Gibbs, Dick (5)	.330	Hairston, Happy (11)	.605
Gibson, Mike (2)	.390	Hairston, Lindsay (1)	.492
Gilliam, Herm (8)	.461	Halbrook, Swede (2)	.535
Gilmore, Artis (17)	.721	Hale, Hal (1)	.274
Gilmore, Walt (1)	.358	Halimon, Shaler (5)	.445
Givens, Jack (2)	.394	Halliburton, Jeff (2)	.460
Glenn, Mike (10)	.464	Hamilton, Dennis (3)	.476
Glouchkov, Georgi (1)	.295	Hamilton, Joe (6)	.406
Glover, Clarence (1)	.556	Hamilton, Roy Lee (2)	.299
Gola, Tom (10)	.523	Hamilton, Steve (2)	.389
Gondrezick, Glen (6)	.480	Hammond, Julian (5)	.534
Gondrezick, Grant (2)	.392	Hamood, Joe (1)	.364
Goodrich, Gail (14)	.495	Hankinson, Phil (2)	.642
Gordon, Lancaster (4)	.307	Hannum, Alex (8,6)	.345
Govan, Gerald (9)	.471	Hanrahan, Don (1)	.440
Govedarica, Bato (1)	.193	Hans, Rollen (2)	.274
Graboski, Joe (13,11)	.419	Hansen, Glenn (3)	.373
Graham, Mal (2)	.332	Hansen, Lars (1)	.521
Grandison, Ron (1)	.353	Harding, Reggie (4)	.524
Granger, Stewart (3)	.410	Hardnett, Charles (3)	.599
Grant, Travis (4)	.562	Hardy, Alan (2)	.311
Gray, Gary (1)	.238	Hardy, Darrell (1)	.675
Gray, Leonard (3)	.453	Hardy, James (4)	.440
Gray, Sylvester (1)	.451	Harge, Ira (6)	.533
Greacen, Bob (3)	.366	Harkness, Jerry (3)	.424
Green, Johnny (14)	.635	Harlicka, Skip (1)	.481
Green, Kenny (2)	.288	Harper, Michael (2)	.414
Green, Lamar (6)	.485	Harris, Art (4)	.336
Green, Luther (3)	.439	Harris, Billy (1)	.309
Green, Mike (7)	.571	Harris, Chris (1)	.143
Green, Sihugo (9)	.395	Harris, Robert (5,3)	.368
Green, Steve (4)	.403	Harris, Steve (5)	.414
Greenspan, Jerry (2)	.404	Harrison, Robert (9,7)	.272
Greer, Hal (15)	.501	Haskins, Clem (9)	.480
Gregor, Gary (6)	.478	Hassett, Joey (6)	.381
Gregory, Claude (2)	.489	Hatton, Vern (4)	.290
Grevey, Kevin (10)	.384	Havlicek, John (16)	.556
Grey, Dennis (2)	.385	Hawes, Steve (10)	.547
Griffin, Greg (1)	.302	Hawkins, Connie (9)	.635
Griffin, Paul (7)	.474	Hawkins, Robert (4)	.514
Groat, Dick (1)	.404	Hawkins, Tom (10)	.426
Gross, Bob (8)	.514	Hawthorne, Nate (3)	.367
Grosso, Mike (1)	.442	Hayes, Elvin (16)	.631

Hayes, Steve (5)	.382	Horn, Ron (3)	.284
Haywood, Spencer (13)	.628	Horton, Ed (1)	.517
Heard, Gar (11)	.499	Hosket, Bill (4)	.544
Heinsohn, Tom (9)	.595	Houbregs, Bob (5)	.458
Hemric, Dixon (2)	.422	Howard, Greg (2)	.438
Henderson, David (1)	.253	Howard, Mo (1)	.466
Henderson, Gerald (11)	.433	Howard, Otis (1)	.498
Henderson, Kevin (2)	.260	Howell, Bailey (12)	.674
Henderson, Tom (9)	.385	Hubbard, Phil (10)	.484
Hennessy, Lawrence (2)	.244	Hudson, Lou (13)	.524
Henriksen, Don (2)	.377	Hughes, Alfredrick (1)	.267
Henry, Al (2)	.503	Hughes, Eddie (3)	.309
Henry, Carl (1)	.366	Hughes, Kim (6)	.484
Henry, Conner (2)	.328	Hummer, John (6)	.397
Hentz, Charlie (1)	.470	Hundley, Hot Rod (6)	.384
Herron, Keith (3)	.382	Hunter, Les (7)	.534
Hester, Dan (1)	.580	Huston, Geoff (8)	.401
Hetzel, Fred (6)	.540	Hutchins, Mel (7)	.430
Hewitt, Bill (6)	.429	Hutton, Joseph (2,1)	.246
Heyman, Art (6)	.496	Hyder, Greg (1)	.388
Hicks, Phil (2)	.441	Iavaroni, Marc (7)	.347
Higgins, Earle (1)	.518	Imhoff, Darrall (12)	.536
Higgins, William (1)	.232	Inglesby, Tom (3)	.333
Higgs, Kenny (3)	.391	Ingram, McCoy (1)	.412
High, Johnny (4)	.358	Inniger, Irv (2)	.409
Hightower, Wayne (10)	.461	Irvine, George (6)	.471
Hill, Armond (8)	.364	Issel, Dan (15)	.637
Hill, Cleo (1)	.357	Iverson, Willie (1)	.262
Hill, Gary (2)	.280	Ivory, Elvin (1)	.586
Hill, Simmie (4)	.464	Jabali, Warren (7)	.537
Hillman, Darnell (9)	.507	Jackson, Greg (1)	.245
Hilton, Fred (2)	.364	Jackson, Jaren (1)	.346
Hinson, Roy (7)	.518	Jackson, Lucious (8)	.523
Hitch, Lew (6)	.397	Jackson, Merv (5)	.393
Hoffman, Paul (6,3)	.349	Jackson, Michael (3)	.301
Hogsett, Bob (2)	.227	Jackson, Mike (4)	.514
Hogue, Paul (2)	.360	Jackson, Phil (12)	.504
Holland, John B. (3)	.310	Jackson, Tony (2)	.516
Holland, Joseph (3,1)	.326	Jackson, Tracy (3)	.370
Holland, Wilbur (4)	.427	Jackson, Wardell (1)	.223
Hollins, Lionel (10)	.408	James, Aaron (5)	.453
Hollis, Essie (1)	.444	Jarvis, Jim (2)	.371
Holman, Denny (1)	.352	Jeelani, Abdul (2)	.562
Holstein, James (4)	.281	Johnson, Andy (4)	.386
Holton, Michael (6)	.360	Johnson, Arnie (5,2)	.415
Holup, Joe (3)	.396	Johnson, Charles (7)	.377
Holzman, Red (6,3)	.192	Johnson, Clay (3)	.298
Hooper, Bob (1)	.343	Johnson, Clemon (10)	.483
Hooser, Carroll (1)	.525	Johnson, Dennis (14)	.464
Hoover, Tom (5)	.525	Johnson, Ed L. (3)	.541
Hopkins, Robert (4)	.480	Johnson, Eddie (10)	.486
Hordges, Cedrick (2)	.405	Johnson, Eric (1)	.265
Horford, Tito (2)	.256	Johnson, Frank (8)	.424

Johnson, George E. (4)	.439	Kauffman, Bob (7)	.601
Johnson, George L. (8)	.520	Kea, Clarence (2)	.523
Johnson, George T. (13)	.544	Keller, Bill (7)	.437
Johnson, Gus (10)	.625	Keller, Gary (2)	.508
Johnson, John (12)	.487	Kelley, Rich (11)	.607
Johnson, Ken (1)	.411	Kellogg, Clark (5)	.643
Johnson, Marques (11)	.624	Kelly, Arvesta (5)	.363
Johnson, Mickey (12)	.595	Kelser, Greg (6)	.489
Johnson, Neil (7)	.548	Kelso, Ben (1)	.191
Johnson, Ollie (10)	.433	Kempton, Tim (3)	.423
Johnson, Ralph (4,2)	.250	Kendrick, Frank (1)	.636
Johnson, Reggie (4)	.454	Kennedy, Eugene (6)	.556
Johnson, Rich (3)	.462	Kennedy, Joe (3)	.373
Johnson, Steffond (1)	.249	Kenon, Larry (10)	.567
Johnson, Stew (9)	.467	Kenville, Bill (6)	.393
Johnston, Neil (8)	.651	Kerr, John (12)	.593
Johnstone, Jim (1)	.264	Kerris, Jack (4,2)	.406
Joliff, Howie (3)	.438	Keye, Julius (6)	.445
Jones, Anthony (3)	.324	Kiffin, Irv (1)	.218
Jones, Caldwell (17)	.497	Kiley, Jack (2)	.123
Jones, Charles A. (4)	.455	Kimball, Toby (9)	.518
Jones, Collis (4)	.457	Kinch, Chad (1)	.259
Jones, Dwight (10)	.495	King, Albert (8)	.473
Jones, Edgar (6)	.537	King, Daniel (1)	.262
Jones, Jake (1)	.291	King, George (6)	.348
Jones, Jimmy (10)	.518	King, Jim (10)	.415
Jones, John (2)	.392	King, Loyd (2)	.311
Jones, K. C. (9)	.383	King, Maurice (2)	.337
Jones, Major (6)	.433	King, Reggie (6)	.413
Jones, Ozell (2)	.450	King, Ron (1)	.416
Jones, Rich (8)	.477	Kirk, Walton (3,1)	.239
Jones, Bobby (12)	.611	Kite, Greg (6)	.332
Jones, Robin (2)	.468	Knight, Billy (11)	.546
Jones, Ryan (5)	.374	Knight, Ron (2)	.408
Jones, Sam (12)	.573	Knight, Toby (4)	.502
Jones, Shelton (1)	.341	Kofoed, Bart (2)	.175
Jones, Steve (9)	.409	Kojis, Don (12)	.511
Jones, Wali (11)	.376	Komives, Howard (10)	.359
Jones, Wallace (3,1)	.359	Kondla, Tom (1)	.483
Jones, Walter (8)	.525	Koper, Bud (1)	.336
Jones, Wilbert (9)	.488	Kopicki, Joe (3)	.528
Jones, Willie (5)	.410	Kosmalski, Len (2)	.468
Jones, Willie (2)	.311	Kozelko, Tom (4)	.304
Jordan, Charles (1)	.398	Kozlicki, Ron (1)	.298
Jordan, Eddie (7)	.425	Kramer, Barry (2)	.361
Jordan, Walter Lee (1)	.326	Kramer, Joel (5)	.437
Jordon, Phil (7)	.493	Kramer, Steve (3)	.452
Jorgensen, Noble (5,2)	.362	Krebs, Jim (7)	.477
Joyce, Kevin (3)	.300	Kreklow, Wayne (1)	.051
Judkins, Jeff (5)	.424	Kron, Tom (4)	.461
Kaftan, George (5,2)	.362	Kropp, Tom (2)	.324
Kalafat, Ed (3)	.408	Krystkowiak, Larry (4)	.465
Karl, George (5)	.425	Kuberski, Steve (9)	.444

Martin, Whitey (1)	.285	McNeill, Bob (2)	.390
Martin, William (3)	.393	McNeill, Larry (6)	.594
Masino, Al (2)	.253	McWilliams, Eric (1)	.263
Mason, Anthony (1)	.385	Meely, Cliff (5)	.465
Mast, Eddie (3)	.429	Mehen, Richard (3,1)	.274
Mathis, John (1)	.427	Meineke, Don (5)	.423
Matthews, Wes (9)	.432	Melchionni, Gary (2)	.374
Maxwell, Cedric (11)	.546	Melchionni, Bill (8)	.446
May, Don (7)	.496	Meminger, Dean (6)	.388
May, Scott (7)	.467	Mencel, Charles (2)	.306
Mayes, Clyde (2)	.434	Mengelt, John (10)	.440
McAdoo, Bob (14)	.692	Menyard, DeWitt (1)	.508
McBride, Kenneth (1)	.231	Meriweather, Joe (10)	.490
McCann, Brendan (3)	.251	Meriweather, Porter (1)	.384
McCarter, Andre (3)	.326	Meschery, Tom (10)	.516
McCarter, Willie (3)	.290	Meyers, David (4)	.487
McCarthy, John (6)	.312	Miasek, Stanley (6,2)	.434
McClain, Dwayne (1)	.280	Micheaux, Larry (2)	.564
McClain, Ted (8)	.432	Mikan, Edward (6,3)	.352
McConathy, John (1)	.092	Mikan, George (7,4)	.700
McConnell, Bucky (1)	.302	Mikan, Larry (1)	.376
McCracken, Paul (3)	.368	Mikkelsen, Vern (10,8)	.529
McCray, Scooter (3)	.354	Miles, Eddie (9)	.414
McDaniels, Jim (5)	.605	Miller, Edwin (2)	.475
McDonald, Ben (4)	.324	Miller, Jay (4)	.389
McDonald, Glenn (3)	.325	Miller, Larry (7)	.415
McDonald, Rod (3)	.566	Minniefield, Dirk (3)	.423
McDowell, Hank (6)	.399	Minor, Davage (2)	.331
McElroy, Jim (7)	.387	Mitchell, Leland (1)	.299
McFarland, Pat (3)	.425	Mitchell, Mike (10)	.493
McGee, Mike (9)	.411	Mitchell, Todd (1)	.293
McGill, Bill (5)	.632	Mix, Steve (13)	.542
McGinnis, George (11)	.655	Mlkvy, Bill (1)	.251
McGlocklin, Jon (11)	.426	Moe, Doug (5)	.506
McGregor, Gil (1)	.385	Moffett, Larry (1)	.227
McGriff, Elton (2)	.478	Molinas, Jack (1)	.409
McGuire, Al (4)	.308	Molis, Wayne (2)	.430
McGuire, Dick (11,9)	.430	Moncrief, Sidney (10)	.588
McHartley, Maurice (3)	.396	Money, Eric (6)	.442
McIntosh, Kennedy (4)	.251	Monroe, Earl (13)	.505
McIntyre, Bob (2)	.349	Montgomery, Howard (1)	.363
McKenna, Kevin (6)	.355	Mooney, Jim (1)	.242
McKenzie, Stan (7)	.447	Moore, Gene (7)	.611
McKinney, Billy (7)	.423	Moore, Jack (3)	.424
McKinney, Bones (6,1)	.274	Moore, Johnny (9)	.530
McKinney, Carlton (1)	.108	Moore, Lowes (3)	.381
McLemore, McCoy (8)	.470	Moore, Otto (9)	.532
McMahon, Jack (8)	.270	Moore, Richie ()	.226
McMillen, Tom (11)	.446	Moreland, Jack (8)	.498
McMillian, Jim (9)	.438	Morgan, Rex (2)	.418
McMillon, Shellie (4)	.539	Morrison, Dwight (3)	.457
McNamee, Joseph (2,1)	.240	Morrison, Mike (1)	.195
McNealy, Chris (3)	.455	Mosley, Glenn (2)	.421

Moss, Perry (2)	.336	Ohl, Don (10)	.401
Mount, Rick (5)	.408	O'Koren, Mike (8)	.427
Mueller, Erwin (8)	.426	Olberding, Mark (12)	.462
Mullins, Jeff (12)	.518	Oldham, Jawann (9)	.455
Murphy, Allen (2)	.316	Oleynick, Frank (2)	.265
Murphy, Calvin (13)	.519	Olive, John (2)	.108
Murphy, Jay (4)	.287	Olsen, Bud (8)	.457
Murray, Kenneth (3,2)	.292	O'Malley, Grady (1)	.317
Murrell, Willie (3)	.503	Orms, Barry (2)	.263
Murrey, Dorie (6)	.531	Orr, Louis (8)	.439
Myers, Pete (4)	.380	Ortiz, Jose (2)	.361
Nash, Cotton (2)	.432	O'Shea, Kevin (3,2)	.274
Nash, Bob (5)	.392	Osterkorn, Wally (4)	.329
Nater, Swen (11)	.691	Otten, Don (4,2)	.482
Natt, Calvin (11)	.561	Overton, Claude (1)	.172
Natt, Kenneth (3)	.268	Owens, James (2,1)	.292
Naulls, Willie (10)	.569	Owens, Jim (2)	.313
Neal, Craig (1)	.305	Owens, Tom (12)	.601
Neal, Ebberle (2)	.294	Pace, Joe (2)	.542
Neal, Lloyd (7)	.561	Pack, Wayne (1)	.246
Nelson, Barry (1)	.357	Palazzi, Togo (6)	.457
Nelson, Don (14)	.569	Palmer, Errol (1)	.664
Nelson, Louie (5)	.360	Palmer, Jim (3)	.465
Nelson, Ron (1)	.330	Park, Medford (5)	.377
Nemelka, Dick (1)	.335	Parker, Sonny (6)	.488
Nessley, Martin (1)	.306	Parkhill, Barry (3)	.256
Netolicki, Bob (9)	.516	Parr, Jack (1)	.353
Neumann, John (7)	.452	Paspalj, Zarko (1)	.254
Neumann, Paul (6)	.456	Patterson, George (1)	.410
Nevitt, Chuck (7)	.452	Patterson, Steve (5)	.461
Newlin, Mike (11)	.475	Patterson, Tom (2)	.530
Newmark, Dave (3)	.524	Paulk, Charlie (3)	.403
Newton, Bill (2)	.489	Paultz, Billy (15)	.568
Nichols, Jack (9,6)	.410	Paxson, James (2)	.347
Nicks, Carl (3)	.329	Paxson, Jim (11)	.453
Niemann, Rich (5)	.630	Payak, John (2,1)	.274
Niles, Mike (1)	.276	Payne, Tom (1)	.563
Nimphius, Kurt (8)	.440	Payton, Mel (2)	.374
Nix, Dyron (1)	.339	Peck, Wiley (1)	.384
Nixon, Norm (10)	.466	Peek, Richard (1)	.430
Noble, Chuck (7)	.323	Peeples, George (6)	.506
Nordmann, Bob (4)	.488	Pellom, Sam (4)	.452
Norman, Coniel (3)	.376	Perry, Aulcie, (1)	.484
Norris, Audie (3)	.393	Perry, Curtis, (8)	.538
Norris, Sylvester (1)	.273	Perry, Ron (3)	.340
Norwood, Willie (7)	.494	Petersen, Loy (2)	.336
Nowell, Mel (2)	.428	Peterson, Mel (4)	.514
O'Brien, James (2)	.487	Peterson, Robert (3)	.430
O'Brien, Jimmy (4)	.365	Petrie, Geoff (6)	.438
O'Brien, Ralph (2)	.256	Pettit, Bob (11)	.818
Ogden, Bud (2)	.514	Pettway, Jerry (2)	.319
Ogden, Ralph (1)	.161	Phegley, Roger (6)	.427
O'Hanlon, Fran (1)	.204	Phelps, Michael (3)	.297

Phillip, Andy (7)	.366	Reed, Ron (2)	.488
Phillips, Eddie (1)	.326	Reed, Willis (10)	.695
Phillips, Gary (5)	.297	Regan, Richie (3)	.281
Phillips, Gene (2)	.342	Rehfeldt, Don (2,1)	.459
Piatkowski, Walt (3)	.384	Reid, Billy (1)	.270
Pietkiewicz, Stan (3)	.408	Reid, Robert (12)	.448
Piontek, Dave (7)	.395	Restani, Kevin (8)	.416
Pittman, Charles (4)	.413	Rhine, Kendall (2)	.532
Plummer, Gary (1)	.307	Rhodes, Eugene (1)	.227
Pollard, Jim (8,4)	.384	Richardson, Clint (8)	.375
Polson, Ralph (1)	.337	Richardson, Micheal (8)	.557
Pondexter, Cliff (3)	.415	Richter, John (1)	.412
Pope, David (2)	.217	Ricketts, Dick (3)	.386
Popson, Dave (1)	.343	Ridgle, Jackie (1)	.441
Poquette, Ben (10)	.483	Riedy, Bob (1)	.288
Porter, Howard (7)	.479	Riker, Tom (3)	.362
Porter, Kevin (10)	.508	Riley, Pat (9)	.356
Porter, Willie (2)	.608	Riley, Ron (4)	.445
Portman, Bob (4)	.488	Rinaldi, Rich (3)	.344
Powell, Cincy (8)	.537	Riordan, Mike (9)	.303
Pradd, Marlbert (2)	.574	Risen, Arnie (10,7)	.498
Pratt, Mike (2)	.430	Rivers, David (2)	.374
Pressley, Dominic (1)	.249	Robbins, Red (8)	.574
Previs, Steve (1)	.313	Roberson, Rick (7)	.525
Price, Jim (7)	.440	Roberts, Anthony (5)	.379
Price, Mike (3)	.354	Roberts, Joe (4)	.431
Priddy, Robert (1)	.311	Roberts, Marv (6)	.426
Quick, Bob (4)	.470	Robertson, Oscar (14)	.738
Rackley, Luther (5)	.505	Robertson, Tony (2)	.355
Radford, Mark (2)	.394	Robey, Rick (8)	.489
Radford, Wayne (1)	.324	Robinson, Cliff (10)	.588
Radovich, Frank (1)	.401	Robinson, Flynn (8)	.545
Ragelis, Ray (1)	.273	Robinson, Jackie (3)	.422
Rains, Ed (2)	.270	Robinson, Oliver (1)	.353
Ramsey, Cal (2)	.473	Robinson, Ronnie (2)	.401
Ramsey, Frank (9)	.509	Robinson, Sam (2)	.402
Rank, Wally (1)	.221	Robinson, Truck (11)	.542
Ransey, Kelvin (6)	.458	Robinson, Wayne (1)	.425
Ranzino, Sam (1)	.334	Robinson, Wilbert (1)	.353
Rascoe, Bobby (3)	.431	Robinzine, Bill (7)	.537
Ratkovicz, George (6,4)	.412	Robisch, Dave (13)	.534
Ratleff, Ed (5)	.426	Rocha, Red (9,5)	.388
Ratliff, Mike (2)	.429	Rodgers, Guy (12)	.470
Rautins, Leo (2)	.303	Rogers, Harry (1)	.573
Ray, Clifford (10)	.592	Rogers, Johnny (2)	.365
Ray, James (2)	.047	Rogers, Marshall (1)	.249
Ray, James (3)	.406	Rogers, Willie (1)	.253
Rayl, Jim (2)	.382	Roges, Albert (2)	.254
Raymond, Craig (5)	.513	Rollins, Kenneth (3,1)	.239
Rea, Connie (1)	.145	Rollins, Phil (3)	.400
Reaves, Joe (2)	.386	Romar, Lorenzo (5)	.432
Redmond, Marlon (2)	.373	Rook, Jerry (1)	.451
Reed, Hub (7)	.488	Rosenbluth, Lenny (1)	.356

Smith, Robert (7)	.378	Tart, Levern (4)	.508
Smith, Sam (4)	.441	Tatum, Earl (4)	.447
Smith, Sam (2)	.425	Taylor, Anthony (1)	.360
Smith, William (2)	.468	Taylor, Brian (10)	.448
Smith, Willie (4)	.415	Taylor, Fred (2)	.328
Smrek, Mike (5)	.368	Taylor, Jay (1)	.290
Smyth, Joseph (1)	.310	Taylor, Jeff (2)	.311
Snyder, Dick (13)	.457	Taylor, Ollie (4)	.428
Sobers, Ricky (11)	.447	Taylor, Roland (8)	.372
Sobie, Ron (4)	.433	Taylor, Ron (3)	.509
Sojourner, Mike (3)	.509	Taylor, Vince (1)	.308
Sojourner, Willie (4)	.542	Temple, Collis (1)	.552
Somerset, Willie (3)	.506	Terrell, Ira (2)	.434
Sorensen, Dave (3)	.540	Terry, Carlos (3)	.446
Spain, Ken (1)	.349	Terry, Chuck (5)	.321
Spanarkel, Jim (5)	.486	Terry, Claude (6)	.389
Sparks, Dan (2)	.396	Thacker, Tom (7)	.377
Sparrow, Guy (3)	.394	Theard, Floyd (1)	.252
Spears, Marion (8,6)	.386	Thibeaux, Peter (2)	.352
Spoelstra, Art (4)	.415	Thieben, William (2)	.365
Spriggs, Larry (5)	.416	Thigpen, Justus (3)	.226
Stacom, Kevin (6)	.331	Thirdkill, David (5)	.289
Staggs, Erv (1)	.312	Thomas, Jim (3)	.411
Stallworth, Bud (5)	.324	Thomas, Joe (1)	.200
Stallworth, Dave (8)	.523	Thomas, Ron (4)	.472
Stansbury, Terence (3)	.365	Thomas, Terry (1)	.515
Starks, John (1)	.320	Thomas, Willis (1)	.398
Staverman, Larry (5)	.559	Thompson, Bernard (5)	.355
Steele, Larry (9)	.415	Thompson, Corny (1)	.291
Stephens, Everette (1)	.262	Thompson, David (9)	.557
Stephens, Jack (1)	.377	Thompson, George (6)	.468
Steppe, Brook (5)	.410	Thompson, John (2)	.471
Stipanovich, Steve (5)	.551	Thompson, Paul (3)	.461
Stith, Sam (1)	.309	Thoren, Skip (3)	.658
Stith, Tom (1)	.261	Thorn, Rod (8)	.450
Stokes, Greg (2)	.341	Thornton, Dallas (2)	.393
Stokes, Maurice (3)	.718	Thurmond, Nate (14)	.678
Stoll, Randy (1)	.405	Tieman, Dave (1)	.193
Stone, George (4)	.478	Tillis, Darren (2)	.439
Stovall, Paul (2)	.454	Tinsley, George (2)	.398
Strawder, Joe (3)	.522	Tolbert, Ray (5)	.396
Stroeder, John (2)	.399	Tolson, Dean (3)	.656
Suiter, Gary (1)	.336	Tomjanovich, Rudy (11)	.555
Sunderlage, Don (2)	.274	Toney, Andrew (8)	.491
Surhoff, Richard (2)	.284	Toney, Sedric (4)	.303
Sutor, George (3)	.475	Toone, Bernard (1)	.410
Suttle, Dane (2)	.471	Tormohlen, Gene (6)	.549
Swagerty, Keith (2)	.499	Tosheff, William (3)	.267
Swain, Ben (1)	.497	Towe, Monte (2)	.337
Swanson, Norman (1)	.184	Townes, Lonton (3)	.376
Swartz, Dan (1)	.537	Townsend, Raymond (3)	.322
Swift, Harlee (5)	.413	Trapp, George (6)	.467
Szczerbiak, Walt (1)	.609	Trapp, John (5)	.452

Tresvant, John (9)	.551	Walther, Paul (6,4)	.319
Tschogl, John (3)	.262	Walton, Bill (10)	.755
Tsioropoulos, Lou (3)	.329	Walton, Lloyd (5)	.374
Tucker, Al (5)	.463	Wanzer, Bobby (9,6)	.405
Tucker, James (3)	.384	Ward, Gerry (4)	.312
Turner, Andre (3)	.300	Ward, Henry (2)	.390
Turner, Elston (8)	.342	Ware, Jim (3)	.356
Turner, Henry (1)	.441	Warley, Ben (8)	.524
Turner, Herschell (1)	.249	Warlick, Bob (5)	.415
Turner, Jack (1)	.327	Warner, Cornell (7)	.477
Turner, John (1)	.332	Warren, Bob (8)	.447
Turner, William (6)	.441	Warren, John (5)	.417
Turpin, Melvin (5)	.524	Warrick, Bryan (4)	.361
Twardzik, Dave (8)	.459	Washburn, Chris (2)	.321
Twyman, Jack (11)	.562	Washington, Bob (3)	.521
Tyler, Terry (11)	.481	Washington, Donald (2)	.399
Tyra, Charlie (5)	.477	Washington, Duane (1)	.568
Unseld, Wes (13)	.642	Washington, Jim (11)	.493
Uplinger, Hal (1)	.290	Washington, Kermit (10)	.593
Upshaw, Kelvin (2)	.386	Washington, Pearl (3)	.428
Vacendak, Steve (3)	.402	Washington, Richard (6)	.516
Valentine, Darnell (8)	.451	Washington, Tom (6)	.585
Valentine, Ron (1)	.327	Washington, Wilson (2)	.506
Vallely, John (2)	.307	Watson, Robert (1)	.263
Van Arsdale, Dick (12)	.444	Watts, Sam (1)	.320
Van Arsdale, Tom (12)	.404	Watts, Slick (6)	.498
Van Breda Kolff, Jan (9)	.409	Weatherspoon, Nick (7)	.457
Vance, Gene (5,1)	.211	Webb, Jeff (2)	.258
Vandeweghe, Ernie (6,4)	.433	Webster, Elnardo (1)	.469
Van Lier, Norm (10)	.481	Webster, Marvin (10)	.548
Vanos, Nick (2)	.367	Wedman, Scott (13)	.465
Vaughn, Charles (8)	.355	Weiss, Bob (12)	.411
Vaughn, David (2)	.567	Wells, Owen (1)	.420
Verga, Bob (6)	.496	Welp, Chris (3)	.387
Verhoeven, Peter (6)	.402	Wesley, Walt (10)	.533
Vincent, Jay (9)	.505	West, Jerry (14)	.688
Virden, Claude (1)	.374	Westbrook, Dexter (1)	.437
Volkov, Aleksandr (1)	.390	Westphal, Paul (12)	.584
Vranes, Danny (7)	.367	Wetzel, John (7)	.359
Wade, Mark (2)	.270	Whatley, Ennis (6)	.465
Wagner, Phil (1)	.205	Wheeler, Clinton (2)	.403
Waiters, Granville (5)	.382	White, Eric (2)	.418
Wakefield, Andre (2)	.210	White, Hubie (4)	.345
Walk, Neal (8)	.631	White, Jo Jo (12)	.444
Walker, Andy (1)	.441	White, Rory (5)	.384
Walker, Brady (4,1)	.425	White, Rudy (5)	.291
Walker, Chet (13)	.576	White, Tony (1)	.294
Walker, Foots (10)	.464	White, Willie (2)	.414
Walker, Horace (1)	.490	Whitehead, Jerome (11)	.468
Walker, Jimmy (9)	.415	Whitney, Hank (3)	.591
Walker, Phil (1)	.276	Whitney, Hawkeye (2)	.406
Walker, Wally (8)	.408	Wicks, Sidney (10)	.552
Waller, Dwight (3)	.444	Widby, Ron (1)	.455

Wiesenhahn, Bob (1) .... .392
Wiggins, Mitchell (5) .... .454
Wilburn, Ken (3) .... .570
Wiley, Gene (5) .... .458
Wiley, Michael (2)....................... .533
Wiley, Morlon (2) .... .384
Wilfong, Win (4) .... .402
Wilkens, Len (15) .... .541
Wilkerson, Bob (7) .... .383
Wilkes, Jamaal (12) .... .507
Wilkes, James (3) .... .400
Wilkins, Jeff (6).......................... .428
Williams, Art (8) .... .532
Williams, Bernie (5) .... .369
Williams, Charles (6) .... .356
Williams, Chuck (8) .... .405
Williams, Donald (1) .... .281
Williams, Earl (4) .... .623
Williams, Freeman (6) .... .472
Williams, Gus (11) .... .535
Williams, Guy (2) .... .479
Williams, Hank (1) .... .412
Williams, James (1) .... .393
Williams, Kevin (5) .... .393
Williams, Michael (2).................... .435
Williams, Milt (3) .... .392
Williams, Nate (8)....................... .481
Williams, Pete (2) .... .441
Williams, Ray (10) .... .557
Williams, Rickey (1)..................... .309
Williams, Rob (2) .... .404
Williams, Robert (2)..................... .429
Williams, Ron (8) .... .445
Williams, Sam (2) .... .302
Williams, Sam (4) .... .505
Williams, Sly (7) .... .520
Williams, Willie (1) .... .183
Williamson, John (8) .... .418
Williford, Vann (1) .... .451
Willoughby, Bill (8) .... .430
Wilson, Bobby (4) .... .400
Wilson, Bobby (1) .... .436
Wilson, Bubba (1) .... .129
Wilson, George (7) .... .507
Wilson, Isaiah (2) .... .429

Wilson, Jasper (2) .... .387
Wilson, Mike (3) .... .355
Wilson, Othell (2) .... .396
Wilson, Rick (2) .... .313
Wilson, Ricky (1) .... .315
Wilson, Robert (1) .... .259
Wilson, Steve (2) .... .357
Windis, Tony (1) .... .364
Winfield, Lee (7)........................ .423
Wingate, David (4) .... .328
Wingo, Harthorne (4) .... .509
Winkler, Marvin (2) .... .172
Winters, Brian (9) .... .459
Wise, Willie (9) .... .558
Witte, Luke (3) .... .510
Wittman, Greg (2) .... .308
Witts, Garry (1).......................... .376
Wohl, Dave (7) .... .353
Wood, Al (6) .... .444
Wood, Howard (1) .... .375
Wood, Leon (5) .... .376
Woods, Thomas (1)...................... .418
Woollard, Bob (1) .... .452
Workman, Mark (2) .... .248
Workman, Tom (4) .... .550
Worsley, Willie (1) .... .250
Worthen, Sam (2) .... .342
Wright, Brad (2) .... .400
Wright, Howard (2) .... .312
Wright, Joby (3)......................... .371
Wright, Larry (6)........................ .418
Wright, Leroy (2)........................ .383
Wright, Lonnie (5) .... .322
Wuycik, Dennis (3) .... .409
Yardley, George (7)...................... .577
Yates, Barry (1) .... .403
Yates, Wayne (1) .... .369
Yelverton, Charlie (1).................... .360
Young, Michael (1) .... .507
Zaslofsky, Max (10,5).................... .287
Zawoluk, Robert (3) .... .391
Zeller, Dave (1) .... .361
Zeller, Gary (2) .... .199
Zopf, Bill (1) .... .340

ABSTRACTION 7

Things I'd Like to See

Wilt Chamberlain did not foul out of a single game during his 14-season career, and that's the way it should be: Nobody—superstar or ordinary player—should be disqualified from a game for the routine accumulation of personal fouls.

No team should be able to devise and execute a game plan predicated on influencing an official into disqualifying the opposing teams's best player. Sports contests should not be decided by whistles but by performance.

Nobody should foul out of a basketball game.

Disqualification isn't done in any other sport for reasons other than flagrant misconduct, and it shouldn't happen in basketball either. The foul-out rule is archaic and should be abolished, whether ultraconservative traditionalists like it or not.

Here are a few other things I'd like to see:

⬦ Extend the three-point line in college basketball to the compromise distance of 22 feet. The current 19-foot, 6-inch distance makes for too easy a shot. The NBA's distance of 23-feet, 9-inches would be too difficult for collegians.

⬦ Eliminate college basketball's three-foul-shot rule on three-point field-goal attempts. It enhances the already excessive rewards for shots that aren't all that difficult.

⬦ Eliminate the two-shot rule for all fouls after 10 in a half. If this rule had been in effect in 1983, there would have been no chance for North Carolina State to make its historic comeback against Houston. This rule is a great lead-preserver that takes virtually all of the excitement out of games at the end.

⬦ Call a foul (just once) on a player under six-feet tall who runs helter-skelter into a stationary seven-footer.

⬦ Reduce the 45-second clock in college basketball to a 30-second clock.

⬦ Award first prize in the NBA's slam-dunk contest to the best dunker instead of the smallest.

⬦ Eliminate all charging calls on players who run into defenders stationed directly under the basket where they can do nothing defensively except try for a charging call.

⬦ Call fouls on offensive players who initiate contact by jumping forward into defenders, whether the defenders leave their feet or not.

⬦ After one miserable experience, CBS should forget about trying to do blanket coverage of the NCAA Tournament and let ESPN go back to covering all but prime-time games.

⬦ Bill Raftery should be hired as somebody's No. 1 color commentator. His intelligent analysis and light-hearted disposition makes him the best on TV.

⬦ Either the traveling rule should be liberalized to allow three steps, or the existing rule should be enforced. It is violated with such impunity that it has become a joke.

⬦ When a player drives the baseline and is forced out of bounds by physical contact with a defender, it is usually called a turnover. It should be called a foul.

⬦ The rule allowing a team to advance the ball to midcourt on a timeout should be eliminated. At no time should a team gain an offensive advantage while the ball is not in play.

⬦ When a player injures another player by punching, elbowing, kicking, or making any kind of flagrantly vicious contact with him, the guilty player should be suspended, without pay, for as long as the injured player cannot play. Would Bill Cartwright have thrown that dangerous elbow into Hakeem Olajuwon's face last season if this rule had been on the books?

Isn't it ironic that a player can "foul out" on a ticky-tack, but he can remain in a game, as Cartwright did, after causing potential permanent injury to an opponent?

15
College Players

There are a few players who could have been selected for the TENDEX Hall of Fame based on NBA exploits, but were left out so they could be included among the collegians where they really belong. A few others had great college careers but did not perform to the same standards as pros. And then there are some young players whose college credentials are so exceptional that they should be placed in the Hall of Fame regardless of their future performance as professionals.

Based on these three criteria, a dozen players have been selected for the TENDEX Hall of Fame based on collegiate performances (listed in alphabetical order):

1. BILL BRADLEY—Princeton University, 1964–67 . . . Scored 2,503 points in 3 seasons at Princeton, ninth best of all-time for three-year players . . . One of 16 players averaging at least 30 points per game for college career (30.2) . . . Career free-throw percentage of .876 is No. 19 on the NCAA list . . . Led Division I players in free-throw percentage in 1965 . . . Set NCAA Tournament records for scoring (177 points) and scoring average (35.4) for five games in 1965 . . . Scoring record stood until Glen Rice

scored 184 points in six games in 1989 . . . Scoring average remains the best ever for players playing at least five games in the tournament . . . Career scoring average of 33.7 for tournament games is second best of all-time . . . College Player of the Year 1965 . . . Played 10 seasons in NBA, two as a member of champion teams.

2. AUSTIN CARR—University of Notre Dame, 1968–71 . . . Sensational clutch scorer, holds three NCAA Tournament scoring records: Career scoring average (41.3), scoring average for one tournament (52.7 in 1970), most points in one game (61) . . . Played in seven NCAA Tournament games, scoring 61, 52, 52, 47 and 45 points in five of them; all five games rank among the top dozen individual scoring efforts in tournament history . . . Scored 2,560 points, No. 6 among players who played three seasons . . . Career scoring average (34.6) is No. 2 of all-time . . . Averaged 38.1 points per game in 1970 and 38.0 in 1971 . . . Twice totaled more than 1,100 points in a season, which has been done only seven other times . . . College Player of the

Year 1971 . . . Played 10 seasons in NBA.

3. PATRICK EWING—Georgetown University, 1981–85 . . . Yes, he is going to make the TENDEX Hall of Fame soon anyway for his NBA accomplishments, but why wait? . . . College Player of the Year 1985 . . . NCAA Tournament MVP in 1984 as member of champion team . . . Career TENDEX rating of .849 is second-best since it became possible to compute ratings for college players . . . Scored 2,184 points and pulled down 1,316 rebounds in four seasons . . . NBA Rookie of the Year 1986 . . . All-NBA First Team selection 1990 . . . TENDEX rating of .742 for 6 seasons is third best among active NBA centers.

4. TOM GOLA—LaSalle College, 1951–55 . . . His TENDEX rating of .523 for 10 NBA seasons as a shooting guard was good enough for the Hall of Fame, but he was even better as a collegian . . . Holds the NCAA record with 2,201 rebounds in 118 games (18.7 average) . . . Had 652 rebounds in 1954, third-best one-season total of all-time . . . One of two players to total more than 2,000 points and 2,000 rebounds for his career . . . Career scoring average was 20.9 . . . Player of the Year in 1955 . . . NCAA Tournament scoring leader and MVP as member of champion team in 1954.

5. DANNY MANNING—Kansas University, 1984–88 . . . Iron-man Dan played 147 games in 4 seasons, an NCAA record . . . Scored 2,951 points, seventh best of all-time . . . Scoring average was 20.1 . . . Pulled down 1,187 rebounds . . . Sensational play helped Kansas win NCAA Tournament in 1988; he was the tournament leader in scoring (163 points), scoring average (27.2) and rebounding (56) . . . NCAA Tournament MVP and consensus Player of the Year

1988 . . . Ranks No. 2 in NCAA Tournament career scoring with 328 points . . . Has played three injury-marred seasons in the NBA.

6. PETE MARAVICH—Louisiana State University, 1967–70 . . . Greatest scorer in collegiate history, averaging over 43 points per game for 3 straight seasons . . . NCAA scoring records include career points (3,667), one-season points (1,381), career average (44.2), one-season average (44.5) and single-game scoring against a Division I opponent (69 points) . . . Season averages of 44.5, 44.2 and 43.8 rank No. 1, No. 2 and No. 3 on the all-time list . . . Great long-range shooter, he probably could have averaged 50 points per game if the three-point shot had been in existence when he played . . . College Player of the Year 1970 . . . Excelled for 10 NBA seasons, averaging 24.2 points and 5.4 assists per game . . . Led league in scoring 1977 . . . All-NBA selection twice . . . NBA career TENDEX rating .539.

7. CALVIN MURPHY—Niagara University, 1966–70 . . . Scored 68 points in a game, the second highest total ever against a Division I opponent . . . Scoring average of 38.2 in 1968 was the eighth best of all-time . . . Career average of 33.1 ranks No. 4 . . . NBA Rookie of the Year 1968 . . . Played 13 professional seasons, winning TENDEX All-NBA honors twice . . . Set NBA records with .958 free-throw percentage and 78 consecutive free throws made in 1980–81 season . . . Twice led league in free-throw percentage . . . Career TENDEX rating .519.

8. DAVID ROBINSON—U.S. Naval Academy, 1983–87 . . . Career TENDEX rating for 4 collegiate seasons was .781, fourth best of all-time . . . Led NCAA in rebounding and blocked shots in 1986 . . . Led in blocked shots again in 1987 . . . Set NCAA

records for blocked shots with 14 in one game, 207 in one season, a season average of 5.9 per game and a career average of 5.2 . . . Scored 2,669 points (21.0 average) and pulled down 1,314 rebounds (10.3) for his career . . . College Player of the Year 1987 . . . Had highest scoring average in 1986 NCAA Tournament (27.5) . . . NBA Rookie of the Year 1990 . . . All-NBA First Team selection 1991.

9. RALPH SAMPSON—University of Virginia, 1979–83 . . . One of only three college players to win three consensus Player of the Year awards . . . Totaled 2,228 points and 1,511 rebounds in 4 seasons . . . His 381 rebounds in 1980 was the fourth best total ever by a freshman . . . Career rebound total is the second best by a college player since 1973 . . . Career TENDEX rating of .869 is the best by a college player since 1980 when ratings were begun . . . NBA Rookie of the Year in 1984 with a .706 TENDEX rating . . . All-Star Game MVP 1985 . . . Ill-advised position change from center to power forward and subsequent knee injuries destroyed his professional career.

10. LIONEL SIMMONS—LaSalle College, 1986–90 . . . He's here despite youthful age (22) because his name threads through the NCAA record book . . . Holds the record for most consecutive games scoring in double figures (115) . . . No. 3 on the career scoring list with 3,217 points . . . No. 4 in rebounds with 1,429 since 1973 . . . One of two men in NCAA history with more than 3,000 points and 1,000 rebounds; he had more points and rebounds than No. 2 man Harry Kelly . . . College Player of the Year 1990 . . . Made the NBA All-Rookie Team in 1991.

11. DAVID THOMPSON—North Carolina State University, 1972–75 . . .

Thompson's career TENDEX rating as a shooting guard in pro basketball was .557, good enough to make the TENDEX Hall of Fame . . . He scored 73 points in an NBA game in 1978, more than any player other than Wilt Chamberlain . . . Averaged 22.7 points per game in the regular season, boosted that to 24.1 in playoffs and was a standout in five All-Star Games (20.8) . . . But he was even better as a collegiate player, averaging 26.8 points per game for three varsity seasons . . . Best season was 1974–75 when he averaged 29.9 and won Player of the Year honors . . . Averaged 24.3 points and won NCAA Tournament MVP honors in 1974 while leading North Carolina State to upset victory over UCLA for the title . . . ABA Rookie of the Year 1975–76.

12. BILL WALTON—UCLA, 1971–74 . . . Injuries prevented him from meeting Hall of Fame qualifications as a pro, even though he led Portland to an NBA title in 1978 and was the league's MVP that season . . . As a collegian, he matched the feats of Oscar Robertson and Ralph Sampson as a three-time Player of the Year . . . Paced UCLA to national titles in 1972 and 1973 and was the NCAA Tournament MVP both times . . . His performance of scoring 44 points on 21 of 22 shooting from the floor in the 1973 championship game is generally considered to be the greatest in NCAA Tournament history . . . Averaged 20.3 points and 15.7 rebounds for his college career . . . Was an outstanding defensive player and probably the greatest passing big man of all-time in college basketball.

Most NCAA Players of the Year are in the TENDEX Hall of Fame, but here is a list of men who were either consensus or co-consensus players of the year without having good enough careers to be cited. In other words, these guys narrowly missed making it:

⋄ 1957—Chet Forte, Columbia University

⋄ 1963—Art Heyman, Duke University

⋄ 1964—Gary Bradds, Ohio State University

⋄ 1966—Cazzie Russell, University of Michigan

⋄ 1976—Scott May, Indiana University

⋄ 1978—Butch Lee, Marquette University Phil Ford, University of North Carolina

⋄ 1985—Chris Mullin, St. John's University

⋄ 1986—Walter Berry, St. John's University

⋄ 1988—Hersey Hawkins, Bradley University

⋄ 1989—Danny Ferry, Duke University Sean Elliott, University of Arizona

Hawkins and Elliott have a chance to make it in the future. Mullin probably will.

Here is an alphabetized chart of the players selected for the TENDEX Hall of Fame based primarily on collegiate achievements:

Player, School	Scoring
1. Bill Bradley, Princeton	30.2
2. Austin Carr, Notre Dame	34.6
3. Patrick Ewing, Georgetown	15.3
4. Tom Gola, LaSalle	20.9
5. Danny Manning, Kansas	20.1
6. Pete Maravich, LSU	44.2
7. Calvin Murphy, Niagara	33.1
8. David Robinson, Navy	21.0
9. Ralph Sampson, Virginia	16.9
10. Lionel Simmons, LaSalle	24.6
11. David Thompson, NC State	26.8
12. Bill Walton, UCLA	20.3

16
Coaches

Differences in the nature of college and professional basketball bring about differences in the Hall of Fame selection process. For players, it is easier to make it as pros with careers of 10 to 15 seasons. The limit for a college career is 4 seasons and for Pete Maravich, Oscar Robertson, and many other great college players, it was 3.

In coaching, it is easier to sustain longevity at the college level than as a pro. The pressures on a pro coach are greater and there is a higher percentage of firings. About half of the "superstars" of college basketball are coaches.

So, while the TENDEX Hall of Fame player listings were dominated by pros at a ratio of more than six to one, the reverse is true of coaches. Of the 20 coaches cited in this chapter, 14 made their marks at the college or university level.

This is not to say that there are only 20 coaches in the TENDEX Hall of Fame. Not so. Many of the 93 men honored as players also coached. Four of them—Billy Cunningham, Len Wilkens, Bill Sharman, and Bill Russell—probably did enough to be selected for their coaching accomplishments alone.

Here are the TENDEX Hall of Fame coaches (in alphabetical order):

1. PHOG ALLEN—48 college seasons, 39 with Kansas . . . During an era when teams played only about two-thirds as many games as they do today, Allen led his team to 746 victories and only 264 losses . . . Victory total is No. 4 on the all-time NCAA Division I list . . . Career winning percentage of .739 is tied for 14th place . . . One of eight college coaches to coach in more than 1,000 games . . . Holds record for most seasons as head coach (48).

2. RED AUERBACH—20 pro seasons, 16 with Boston . . . Won more games (1,037), more titles (nine) and more consecutive titles (eight) than any professional coach in history . . . Career winning percentage of .654 is the best of all NBA coaches with at least 10 years of experience . . . NBA Coach of the Year 1965.

3. DENNY CRUM—20 college seasons, all at Louisville . . . Ranks No. 7 among active coaches with winning percentage of .735, No. 17 of all-time . . . Averages 24 victories per season . . . No. 10 in number of seasons with current school . . . TENDEX

Coach of the Decade for the 1980s, leading Louisville to four Final Fours and two NCAA Tournament championships (1980 and 1986).

4. CHUCK DALEY—Has coached 17 seasons, 8 with Detroit in NBA . . . Coached 8 seasons of college basketball, compiling 151–62 record (.709) with Pennsylvania and Boston College . . . In 9 pro seasons has a percentage of .614, winning NBA titles in 1989 and 1990 with Detroit Pistons . . . Combined college/professional record is 579–331 (.636).

5. ED DIDDLE—42 college seasons, all at Western Kentucky . . . Won 759 games, third best of all-time . . . Winning percentage of .715 ranks No. 27 of coaches with at least ten seasons in Division I . . . Coached in 1,061 games, fifth best of all-time . . . Longevity of 42 seasons is tied for second behind Allen . . . Tied for first with Ray Meyer in most seasons at a single Division I school.

6. CLARENCE GAINES—45 college seasons, all at Winston-Salem . . . Greatest NCAA Division II coach of all-time . . . Still active, closing in an Adolph Rupp's record of 875 career coaching victories . . . Has coached more games (1,230) than any other college coach . . . Is more than 200 victories ahead of the second-best active Division II coach . . . Career record is 818–412 (.665).

7. MARV HARSHMAN—40 college seasons, 14 at Washington . . . Unlike other great college coaches, who spent most of their careers at one school, Harshman divided his career into three parts—13 years at Pacific Lutheran, 13 at Washington State and 14 at Washington . . . Victory total of 642 is No. 9 on the all-time list in Division I . . . Coached in 1,090 games to rank No. 2 . . . Winning percentage was .589.

8. RED HOLZMAN—18 pro seasons, 14 with New York . . . All-American guard at City College of New York . . . Played 9 seasons as a pro . . . Member of two champion Rochester teams . . . All-National Basketball League First Team selection twice . . . Won 696 games as NBA head coach . . . Coach of the Year 1970 . . . Coached New York Knicks to championships in 1970 and 1973.

9. HENRY IBA—41 college seasons, 36 with Oklahoma State . . . Ranks No. 2 on the all-time list of Division I coaches with 767 victories, trailing Adolph Rupp . . . Coached in more games (1,105) than any other Division I coach . . . Tied for fourth in longevity with 41 seasons . . . Tied for seventh with 36 seasons at the same school . . . Winning percentage .684.

10. BOBBY KNIGHT—26 college seasons, 20 at Indiana . . . Has won three NCAA titles, more than any other active coach . . . Ranks No. 7 on the list of active coaches with 561 victories . . . No. 8 among active coaches in winning percentage (.734), No. 18 of all-time . . . NCAA Division I Coach of the Year 1975, 1976, and 1989.

11. JOE LAPCHICK—29 seasons, 20 with St. John's University, 9 with the New York Knicks . . . Played 19 seasons as a professional from 1917 through 1936 . . . Won 334 games and lost 130 (.720) in two stints as St. John's coach between 1936 and 1965 . . . Won 326 games and lost 247 (.569) with the Knicks from 1947 through 1956, including two divisional titles . . . Had only one losing season in 29 years of coaching.

12. FRANK McGUIRE—30 college seasons, including 16 with South Carolina . . . Won 550 games and lost 235 for a winning percentage of .701 . . . He was the first coach to win 100

games at three schools: 103 at St. John's, 164 at North Carolina and 283 at South Carolina . . . Three-time Coach of the Year . . . Guided North Carolina to undefeated season and NCAA title in 1957.

13. RAY MEYER—42 college seasons, all at DePaul . . . No. 5 on NCAA Division I victory list with 724 . . . No. 3 in games coached with 1,078 . . . Tied for second place in most seasons coached at the Division I level . . . Tied for first in most seasons at the same school . . . Career record was 724–354 for a winning percentage of .672 . . . NCAA Coach of the Year 1980 and 1984.

14. RALPH MILLER—38 college seasons, including 19 at Oregon State . . . Won 657 games to rank No. 8 on the all-time Division I list . . . No. 6 in games coached with 1,039 . . . Tied for No. 8 with 38 seasons as a college coach . . . Coached 13 seasons at Wichita State and six at Iowa before taking the Oregon State job in 1971 . . . NCAA Coach of the Year 1981.

15. DOUG MOE—14 pro seasons, including 10 with Denver . . . Averaged 20.4 points as a senior at the University of North Carolina in 1961 . . . Second-Team All-American selection twice . . . Named to All-ABA First Team in 1968 when he averaged 24.2 points per game . . . Member of ABA champion team 1969 . . . Coached San Antonio from 1977 through 1980 and Denver from 1981 through 1990 . . . NBA Coach of the Year 1988 . . . Career coaching record 609–492 (.549) . . . Won four divisional titles.

16. DON NELSON—Has coached 15 pro seasons, including 11 with Milwaukee . . . Played 14 NBA seasons, 11 with Boston . . . Career TENDEX rating .569 . . . Member of five NBA champion teams . . . Led league in field-goal percentage 1975 . . . Won

seven consecutive divisional titles as Milwaukee coach from 1980 through 1986 . . . Coach of the Year 1983 and 1985 . . . Career record as NBA coach 664–466 for a percentage of .588.

17. JACK RAMSAY—32 total seasons, 21 in NBA . . . Ranks with Lapchick as coach achieving the most success with college and professional teams . . . Record in 11 college seasons at St. Joseph's was 234–72 . . . Percentage of .765 ranks No. 7 on the all-time NCAA list . . . Counting 864 wins in 21 NBA seasons, he won a combined college/pro record 1,098 games . . . Coached Portland to the NBA title in 1977.

18. ADOLPH RUPP—41 college seasons, all with Kentucky . . . Perhaps the greatest college coach of all-time . . . Leader in career victories with 875 . . . Ranks No. 3 in winning percentage (.822) . . . No. 4 in games coached (1,065) . . . Tied for third in most games at the same school . . . Coach of the Year 1959 and 1966 . . . Directed Kentucky teams to NCAA Tournament titles in 1948, 1949, 1951 and 1958.

19. DEAN SMITH—30 college seasons, all with North Carolina . . . No. 1 among NCAA Division I active coaches with 717 victories, sixth best of all-time . . . Second-best active coach in winning percentage (.774), fifth best of all-time . . . National Association of Basketball Coaches Coach of the Year 1977, U.S. Basketball Writers Association Coach of the Year 1979 . . . Coached Tar Heels to NCAA Tournament title in 1982.

20. JOHN WOODEN—29 college seasons, including 27 with UCLA . . . If Rupp wasn't the greatest college coach of all-time, Wooden was . . . Record of 10 NCAA Tournament championships in 12 seasons with UCLA, from 1964 through 1975, may never be

challenged . . . Winning percentage of .804 is the fourth-best of all-time . . . Victory total of 664 is No. 7 of Division I coaches . . . Six-time NCAA Coach of the Year (1964, 1967, 1969, 1970, 1972, 1973).

Here are a dozen coaches in the just-missed category:

◇ Pat Riley, who led the Los Angeles Lakers to four NBA titles in 9 seasons, but didn't stick around long enough.

◇ K.C. Jones, who coached Boston to NBA titles in 1984 and 1986 during the Bird-McHale-Parish heyday, but needs to prove he can win with less talent somewhere else.

◇ Dick Motta, Gene Shue, Bill Fitch, Cotton Fitzsimmons, and John MacLeod—the Nos. 3, 4, 5, 7, and 8 coaches on the NBA's victory list—whose winning percentages are hovering around .500.

◇ Phil Woolpert and Ed Jucker, who won two NCAA Tournament titles apiece but did not have long distinguished careers.

◇ Al McGuire, who had 405 career victories, 1 NCAA title and 1 Coach of the Year Award.

◇ Norm Sloan, who won 627 games and one NCAA title, but got in trouble with the NCAA for rules violations at Florida.

◇ Jerry Tarkanian, who has one NCAA title, 600 victories, and a career-record percentage: but who also has set records for conniving, cheating, and (in the 1991 NCAA Tournament) choking.

Here's a full list of the coaches in the TEN-DEX Hall of Fame:

Coach, Principal Team	Seasons
1. Phog Allen, Kansas	39
2. Red Auerbach, Boston Celtics	20
3. Denny Crum, Louisville	20
4. Chuck Daley, Detroit Pistons	17
5. Ed Diddle, Western Kentucky	42
6. Clarence Gaines, Winston-Salem	45
7. Marv Harshman, Washington	40
8. Red Holzman, New York Knicks	18
9. Henry Iba, Oklahoma State	41
10. Bobby Knight, Indiana	26
11. Joe Lapchick, St. John's	29
12. Frank McGuire, South Carolina	30
13. Ray Meyer, DePaul	42
14. Ralph Miller, Oregon State	38
15. Doug Moe, Denver Nuggets	14
16. Don Nelson, Milwaukee	14
17. Jack Ramsay, St. Joseph's	32
18. Adolph Rupp, Kentucky	41
19. Dean Smith, North Carolina	30
20. John Wooden, UCLA	29

17
Professional Teams

There are only four teams in the Naismith Hall of Fame. All of them, including the "first team" and the Original Celtics, had historical significance. None of them were particularly outstanding teams by today's standards.

This is not to say that these teams don't belong in the Hall of Fame, but it is the purpose of the TENDEX Hall of Fame to designate the greatest teams instead of the oldest. This chapter is about the greatest professional teams. Chapter 18 is about the greatest college teams.

Any team can be rated by the TENDEX system. The way it is done is to plug the team's full-season statistical totals into the basic TENDEX formula. Then do the same thing using statistical totals for the team's composite opponents, subtract the opponents' rating from the team's rating and add the difference to the base number 100. Any rating above 100 is good.

The difference between a team's TENDEX rating and its opponents' rating usually will be similar to the difference between the team's points scored and points allowed. Not until the 1970s did the NBA keep enough statistics to make it possible to rate teams effectively according to the TENDEX system, so in our computations in this chapter to determine the best team of all time, point differential will be used for team ratings before the 1970–71 season. TENDEX ratings will be used from 1970–71 on.

None of the 10 teams selected for the all-time list played before the era when superstars began to dominate professional basketball. Teams that did not win both regular-season and playoff titles are excluded from consideration. Here are the nominees:

1. BOSTON (1959–60)—With a regular-season record of 59–16, the Celtics won their division by 10 games. They captured the league championship by beating Philadelphia four games to two, and St. Louis 4–3. Top Celtic players were center Bill Russell .798 (TENDEX), forward Tom Heinsohn .624, and guards Sam Jones .570, Bob Cousy .565, and Bill Sharman .536. Team rating 108.3.

2. BOSTON (1964–65)—The Celtics (62–18) won their division by 14 games. In the playoffs they beat Philadelphia 4–3, and Los Angeles 4–1, to take the title. Russell again led the team with a .781 rating. The other players were consistent, but only one, Sam Jones, achieved a TENDEX rating of better than .500. Jones, a shooting guard, rated .569. Team rating 108.3.

3. PHILADELPHIA (1966–67)—The 76ers (68–13) finished eight games ahead of runner-up Boston. They breezed through the playoffs, defeating Cincinnati 3–1, Boston 4–1, and San Francisco 4–2. The 76ers were led by center Wilt Chamberlain with a .977 TENDEX, and forwards Bill Cunningham .656 and Chet Walker .612. Guards Hal Greer, Larry Costello, and Wally Jones were solid. Team rating 109.4.

4. NEW YORK (1969–70)—The Knicks (60–22) had three outstanding starters and an excellent bench. Paced by center Willis Reed .769, guard Walt Frazier .698, and forward Dave DeBusschere .588, they won their division by four games over Milwaukee. Reserves included forwards Cazzie Russell .569 and Dave Stallworth .553. In playoffs, the Knicks defeated Baltimore 4–3, Milwaukee 4–1, and Los Angeles 4–3. Team rating 109.1.

5. MILWAUKEE (1970–71)—The Bucks (66–16) depended on Kareem Abdul-Jabbar's offense, Oscar Robertson's all-court play and respectable depth in registering the NBA's best record, 14 games better than runnerup New York. In playoffs, the Bucks' record was 12–2. They routed San Francisco 4–1, Los Angeles 4–1, and Baltimore 4–0. Best-rated Milwaukee players were Abdul-Jabbar .971, Robertson .636, Bob Dandridge .586, and Greg Smith .541. Team rating 112.8.

6. LOS ANGELES (1971–72)—The Lakers (69–13) broke the NBA victory record set by Philadelphia in 1966–67. They finished six games better than runnerup Milwaukee during the regular season, and in the playoffs swept past Chicago 4–0, Milwaukee 4–2 and New York 4–1. Top players were Wilt Chamberlain .704, Jerry West .690, Happy Hairston .617, and Gail Goodrich .579. Team rating 107.0.

7. LOS ANGELES (1979–80)—The Lakers (60–22) finished just one game better than runner-up Boston during the regular season, but had an easy time in the playoffs, beating Phoenix 4–1, Seattle 4–1, and Philadelphia 4–2. Top Laker players were center Kareem Abdul-Jabbar .801, point guard Magic Johnson .647, and forward Jamaal Wilkes .523. Team rating 107.0.

8. PHILADELPHIA (1982–83)—The 76ers (65–17) won seven more games than the second-place Los Angeles Lakers during the regular season and breezed through three playoff series, losing only one game. Best players were center Moses Malone .801, forwards Julius Erving .690 and Bobby Jones .551, and guards Mo Cheeks .558, and Andrew Toney .526. These five probably constituted the greatest starting unit in NBA history. Team rating 106.8.

9. BOSTON (1985–86)—The Celtics (67–15) finished five games better than the Los Angeles Lakers during the regular season. In the playoffs, Boston defeated Atlanta 4–1, Milwaukee 4–0 and Houston 4–2. The team was paced by forwards Larry Bird .801, and Kevin McHale .682, and centers Bill Walton .672 and Robert Parish .638. This was the best four-player frontline ever in the NBA. Team rating 110.8.

10. LOS ANGELES (1986–87)—The Lakers (65–17) outplayed Boston by six games during the regular season and took six games to beat the Celtics in the playoff championship series after routing Denver 3–0, Golden State 4–1 and Seattle 4–0. Top Laker players were guard Magic Johnson .811, center Kareem Abdul-Jabbar .577, and forwards James Worthy .544 and A.C. Green .523. Team rating 109.0.

WHICH WAS THE GREATEST?

Before making our choice of the best team of all time, let's break down the 10 nominees into four other lists of 10. Only the nominated 10 teams will be listed, although in some cases, teams not included may have had better ratings than one or more of the nominated teams. In no cases will excluded teams have better overall ratings than any of the nominated teams. These were indeed the 10 greatest NBA teams of all time.

Let's start by placing the teams in order of regular-season records:

Team, Season	Percentage
1. Los Angeles, 1971–72	.841
2. Philadelphia, 1966–67	.840
3. Boston, 1985–86	.817
4. Milwaukee, 1970–71	.805
5. Philadelphia, 1982–83	.793
6. Los Angeles, 1986–87	.793
7. Boston, 1959–60	.787
8. Boston, 1964–65	.775
9. New York, 1969–70	.732
10. Los Angeles, 1979–80	.732

In some seasons, there is more overall balance in the NBA than others, so the regular-season champion's margin of victory over the runner-up team is as significant a statistic as the champion team's percentage. Here is the way the great teams line up in order of victory margin:

Team, Season	Games Ahead
1. Boston, 1964–65	14
2. Milwaukee, 1970–71	14
3. Boston, 1959–60	10
4. Philadelphia, 1966–67	8
5. Philadelphia, 1982–83	7
6. Los Angeles, 1971–72	6
7. Los Angeles, 1986–87	6
8. Boston, 1985–86	5
9. New York, 1969–70	4
10. Los Angeles, 1979–80	1

Another important measure of a great team is playoff performance. All 10 of the listed teams won NBA championships. This is how they rate in order of playoff records:

Team, Season	Percentage
1. Philadelphia, 1982–83	.923
2. Milwaukee, 1970–71	.875

3. Los Angeles, 1986–87	.833
4. Los Angeles, 1971–72	.800
5. Boston, 1985–86	.800
6. Los Angeles, 1979–80	.750
7. Philadelphia, 1966–67	.733
8. Boston, 1964–65	.667
9. New York, 1969–70	.632
10. Boston, 1959–60	.615

Now here is the way they stand in order of TENDEX ratings:

Team, Season	TENDEX
1. Milwaukee, 1970–71	112.8
2. Boston, 1985–86	110.8
3. Los Angeles, 1971–72	110.3
4. Philadelphia, 1966–67	109.4
5. New York, 1969–70	109.1
6. Los Angeles, 1986–87	109.0
7. Boston, 1959–60	108.3
8. Boston, 1964–65	108.3
9. Los Angeles, 1979–80	107.0
10. Philadelphia, 1982–83	106.8

Now let's compile the ratings from all four lists and see which team comes out on top. Take the 1959–60 Boston Celtics, for example. They placed No. 7, No. 3, No. 10, and tied for No. 7 on the four lists for a total of 27½ points. Since the lower ratings are better than the higher ones (No. 1 is better than No. 10), we shall list these teams in order, from the one with the lowest point total to the one with the highest total:

Team, Season	Total
1. Milwaukee, 1970–71	8.5
2. Los Angeles, 1971–72	15.0
3. Philadelphia, 1966–67	17.0
4. Boston, 1985–86	17.5
5. Los Angeles, 1986–87	21.0
6. Philadelphia, 1982–83	21.5
7. Boston, 1964–65	24.5
8. Boston, 1959–60	27.5
9. New York, 1969–70	32.5
10. Los Angeles, 1979–80	34.5

First-place Milwaukee's 6.5-point margin makes it evident that the 1970–71 Bucks were the best team in NBA history. The Bucks' rating in the four categories were No. 4, No. 1 (tie), No. 2, and No. 1.

It is interesting that of the four rating methods, the one which proved truest to the overall listing was TENDEX. TENDEX had the top four teams listed No. 1, No. 3, No. 4, and No. 2 and was accurate for most of the other teams. According to TENDEX, the 1970–71 Milwaukee team was the best of all time with a rating of 112.8, a full two points better than the runnerup Boston team of 1985–86.

18
College Teams

There are no clearcut standards for rating college teams because of the variables of schedule strength and player talent. There has been a general escalation of basketball talent over the years, particularly during the decades of the 1950s and 1960s.

It's not necessarily true that there are better individual players today than Oscar Robertson, Wilt Chamberlain, and Bill Russell. But there are more of them, so many more that the NBA is probably as strong today, top to bottom, with 27 teams, as it was during the 1950s and 1960s with nine. Three times as many teams means three times as many players, and there seem to be enough to go around. Even the recent expansion teams are stocked with developing young talent.

The feeder system for professional basketball is college basketball, and here again there is evidence of improving depth. There are more quality teams than ever before and more good players entering the NBA each season as rookies than there were during the 1950s, 1960s, and even the 1970s.

The number of colleges and universities playing basketball has expanded gradually until now there are about 300 of them at the Division I level alone. The NCAA has expanded its championship tournament accordingly, from seven teams in the inaugural 1939 season to 64 today. Because of these differences, it is not easy to compare the great teams of today with those of the past.

Let's start with the unbeatens. There have been seven undefeated NCAA Division I champions in 53 years. Listing them according to number of victories, they are:

Team, Season	Record
1. North Carolina, 1957	32–0
2. Indiana, 1976	32–0
3. UCLA, 1964	30–0
4. UCLA, 1967	30–0
5. UCLA, 1972	30–0
6. UCLA, 1973	30–0
7. San Francisco, 1956	29–0

Five other teams completed undefeated regular seasons, but for one reason or another did not participate in the NCAA Tournament. One of these teams, LIU in 1939, won the National Invitation Tournament (NIT), which at that time was probably more prestigious than the NCAA Tournament. 1939 was the NCAA Tournament's inaugural year. The other undefeateds that did not compete in the NCAA Tournament: Seton Hall, 19–0, 1940; Army, 15–0, 1944; Kentucky, 25–0, 1954; and North Carolina State, 27–0, 1973.

In a computerized tournament held in March of 1991, involving the seven undefeated

NCAA champions, plus the Nevada-Las Vegas team which was undefeated at the time and favored to win its second straight NCAA title, the order of finish was:

Team, Season
1. UCLA, 1967
2. UCLA, 1973
3. UCLA, 1972
   UNLV, 1991
5. UCLA, 1964
   San Francisco, 1956
   Indiana, 1976
   North Carolina, 1957

A computer is no better than its inputted data, but this imaginary tournament is not to be lightly regarded. It's quite possible that the 1967 UCLA team, starring Lew Alcindor, was the best of all time. Incidentally, the UCLA teams of 1972 and 1973, led by Bill Walton, finished right behind Alcindor's Bruins.

The only way TENDEX can enter into this evaluation is by following these players from college on into the pros and determining their TENDEX ratings at the higher level. This has drawbacks, not the least being that many a great college player is not able to adapt to the pro game. But, for the sake of argument, let's compare these teams on the basis of their player talent, taking them in chronological order, with the addition of four other talented teams:

1. SAN FRANCISCO (1956)—This team actually won two NCAA titles, in 1955 and 1956. It won because center Bill Russell was a decade ahead of his time as a defensive rebounder and intimidator. This team also had one good guard, K.C. Jones. Russell and Jones later would be elected to the Naismith Hall of Fame. The other players were just ordinary.

2. NORTH CAROLINA (1957)—Probably the least talented of the 12 listed teams, the Tar Heels were built around the scoring of forward Lenny Rosenbluth, who played one unimpressive season in the NBA. No other name on this roster would be recognizable to the average fan today.

3. OHIO STATE (1960)—Hall of Famers Jerry Lucas and John Havlicek were complemented by other fine players on this NCAA champion team. Guard Larry Siegfried was the third player drafted in 1963 and went on to play nine NBA seasons. Guard Mel Nowell and forward Joe Roberts also had NBA careers.

4. UCLA (1964)—This was the team, more than any other, that proved what a great coach John Wooden was. It had two excellent guards, Gail Goodrich and Walt Hazzard, and one pretty good small forward, Keith Erickson. No big man. Not the kind of team you would expect to go undefeated.

5. UCLA (1967)—Alcindor was the big guy, but he had frontcourt and backcourt help. Forward Lynn Shackelford was good and so was guard Lucius Allen. Alcindor (Kareem Abdul-Jabbar) went on to play 20 seasons in the NBA, Allen 10, and Shackelford 1.

6. UCLA (1972)—This team is a candidate for most talented. In addition to the great Walton, it had Swen Nater, a standout reserve center who went on to have a longer pro career than Walton. Other NBA players on this team were guard Henry Bibby and forward Keith (Jamaal) Wilkes. These four players totaled 42 NBA seasons.

7. UCLA (1973)—The line-up of this team was almost identical to the 1972 UCLA team, except for the addition of forward Dave Meyers and guard Greg Lee, both of whom played briefly in the NBA. Gone was Bibby, a nine-season NBA player, but this team was probably better than the 1972 team because the key players had one more season of experience.

8. INDIANA (1976)—All five starters on this team went on to have NBA careers,

although none of them starred. They were center Kent Benson (11 seasons), forwards Tom Abernethy (5) and Scott May (7), and guards Quinn Buckner (10) and Bob Wilkerson (7). Reserve Wayne Radford also spent a season in the NBA. A well-balanced team, no weaknesses, but no superstars. Total NBA experience: 41 seasons.

9. MICHIGAN STATE (1979)—This was the famous Magic Johnson team that defeated Larry Bird's team for the NCAA Tournament title. Unlike Bird, who was basically a lone ranger for Indiana State, Magic had plenty of help from forwards Greg Kelser and Jay Vincent. Kelser showed NBA star potential before being injured. Vincent was a good NBA player for nine seasons.

10. HOUSTON (1983)—One of the three best teams not to win an NCAA title. The Cougars had North Carolina State blown out by 14 points midway through the second half before coach Guy Lewis did the one thing that could make a loss possible: He slowed down the game and stymied the talents of his own great players, Akeem Olajuwon and Clyde Drexler. Other NBA players on this team were guard Michael Young and forward Larry Micheaux.

11. GEORGETOWN (1984)—Another heralded NCAA final loser. Villanova had to shoot an NCAA record 79 percent from the field to beat this team. Superstar Patrick Ewing was surrounded by good players. Cornermen Bill Martin and Reggie Williams, and guards David Wingate and Michael Jackson all played in the NBA, although only Ewing has excelled at the professional level.

12. NEVADA-LAS VEGAS (1991)—It is speculation at this point about the professional future of the Rebel players. Just guessing, though, it looks as if this team has one NBA superstar—Larry Johnson—plus several others who could excel. Forward Stacey Augmon and guard Greg Anthony appear to have long NBA careers ahead of them. There is a good chance that centers George Ackles and Elmore Spencer, guard Anderson Hunt, and reserve forward Evric Gray will be NBA players also.

Considering pure talent, the 1991 UNLV team was probably the greatest of all time. It got a lousy coaching job against Duke by Jerry Tarkanian, similar to the job Guy Lewis did on his Houston team in 1983. UNLV had one superstar, one less than the 1960 Ohio State team and the 1983 Houston team. But it was the deepest of the 12 teams.

Here are ratings of the top 12 college teams of all time in terms of player talent. The number of NBA players or, in UNLV's case, potential NBA players, are listed on the right:

Team, Season	Players
1. UNLV, 1991	7
2. Ohio State, 1960	5
3. Houston, 1983	4
4. UCLA, 1973	5
5. UCLA, 1972	4
6. Michigan State, 1979	3
7. UCLA, 1967	3
8. Georgetown, 1984	5
9. Indiana, 1976	6
10. San Francisco, 1956	2
11. UCLA, 1964	3
12. North Carolina, 1957	1

19
Oldies & Goodies

They meet once a week for breakfast at a bagel shop in Sunrise, Florida, these men who were legendary basketball players, coaches, and referees.

"This is just a group of kids," said Abe Gerchick, organizer of some of their get-togethers. The catch is that these "kids" did most of their playing between 1925 and 1950, before the so-called modern era of the sport. They call themselves The Basketball Fraternity.

Gerchick calls them kids because his memories remain vivid of the days when they grew up together, playing basketball in New York schoolyards, settlement houses, and dance halls.

"Most of the games were played in dance halls," said Irv Lipman, who was a youth league teammate of Gerchick's in 1932. "The big feature was a basketball game and a dance. But they tried to avoid conflicts with fights at the St. Nick's Arena. Fights were very big in those days."

New York City was the hub of sports, but basketball was only a small spoke in the wheel. There was little money to be made in the sport. Some of the best players represented labor unions, industrial firms, defense plants, and the Jewish Welfare Board. They tried to land good jobs at places where they could also play basketball.

There were also barnstormers, traveling from city to city, playing for $5 to $15 a game. Many of the better players played for the great college teams in the New York City area during the 1930s and 1940s. Some played for professional leagues that became defunct during the 1940s. A few went on to play in the National Basketball Association.

Ossie Schectman, a member of the fraternity, was the first captain of the New York Knicks and scored the first basket during the NBA's inaugural 1946–47 season. Leo Gottlieb, uncle of former Miami Heat coach Ron Rothstein, was credited with an assist on that basket. Rothstein's father, Howie Rothstein of Lauderhill, a former industrial league star, is also a fraternity member. So is Jerry Fleishman, a member of the NBA's first champion team, Philadelphia, in 1946–47.

The pro game was different in those days. The Knicks did not have a single player average double-figure scoring in 1946–47, but still managed to post a winning record. Only one player in the league that season averaged more than 17 points per game. The league leader averaged 3.4 assists and Schectman was third with his 2.0-assists average.

But that wasn't only because of differences in playing style: Statisticians were much stingier then, especially when it came to doling out assists. There were some outstanding playmakers in those days, the best of whom was the late Bob Davies.

Another notable player was Irv Torgoff, the first sixth man in NBA history. Torgoff played for the Washington Capitals team coached by Red Auerbach during the NBA's first season. Beginning with Torgoff it became a tradition for Auerbach to use sixth men in prominent roles, a tradition he continued for many years as coach of the Boston Celtics.

Hy Gotkin was one-half of the famous "twins" who led St. John's University teams to prominence. Gotkin was the small half of the Little Hy-Big Harry (Boykoff) combination.

Two notable coaches of that era, Roy Rubin of Long Island University and Harry Litwack of Temple, are fraternity members. Both men live in Miami Beach.

In a way, it is a misnomer to refer to this group of men as a fraternity. There is no formal organization, no initiation, no membership card. It started in 1977 when three men who remembered playing basketball against each other, met by chance. The three were Moe Goldman, Lovey Brown, and Eddie Gottlieb.

They decided to have a dinner for former basketball players from the New York City area. Sixteen men showed up for the dinner.

The dinners are now annual events with hundreds of men in attendance.

NEW YORK, NEW YORK

In a sense, this isn't really a Hall of Fame chapter, because it is based on a poll of members of The Basketball Fraternity, most of whom are from the New York City area. So any catalogue of names gleaned from these men is bound to have a Gotham glimmer.

The voters admitted their era, from 1925 to 1950, had two things against it: First, the athletes weren't as big, fast, or talented as they are today; second, the point-shaving scandals of the 1940s implicated many of the best players. So not all of the players mentioned in this chapter were great ones. Certainly, they weren't players of the caliber of a Wilt Chamberlain or an Oscar Robertson, or a David

Robinson or a Michael Jordan. But they were some of the best players in the world when they played.

Nearly all of these men agree, however, that one coach from their era would have been among the greatest of any era. They'll tell you almost to a man that Nat Holman was not only the greatest coach of their era, but the greatest of all-time. Holman is a member of the Naismith Hall of Fame as a player, but it is as a coach that he is remembered by his peers.

Milt Trupin played for a Holman-coached City College of New York team that had only one player on its roster who had been a starter on a high school team.

"I was a substitute in high school, but I developed under Holman," Trupin said. "He was a great teacher. I remember one season Nat was still teaching and we were in the last week of the season. I said to him, 'Coach, we've got to get ready for NYU.' We played NYU in the last game of the season. It was our big rivalry."

Because of the emphasis on academics, Holman did not have much latitude to recruit great players at City College, but he always had great teams. His teams won 423 games and lost 190 in 37 years for a winning percentage of .690.

Holman was a perfectionist. "If you made a mistake, you didn't make it twice," Trupin said. "In my opinion, Nat Holman was head and shoulders above all the greats, even the great John Wooden. Wooden got the great players. Holman developed players who had average talent."

Next to Holman, the man from this era who received the greatest acclaim was another coach, Clair Bee. Bee was to recruiting what Holman was to teaching. He tirelessly scouted metropolitan-area high schools to find the best talent and talked many of the best players into attending Long Island University.

Butch Schwartz said he didn't have the grades to attend CCNY, so he joined Bee at LIU with the promise of a summer job at Manhattan Beach. In those days, that wasn't against NCAA rules. The NCAA was a paper tiger. It didn't conduct its first championship tournament until 1939, Schwartz's second season at LIU. LIU won two NIT titles under Bee's tutelage when the NIT was *the* national tournament.

"Clair Bee gave jobs to the top players," Schwartz said. "I got $45 a week and in those days that was a lot of money."

In 21 seasons of coaching, Bee won 410 games and lost 86. His winning percentage was .827. He was an innovator who originated the 3-second and 24-second rules.

A third man who had the respect of his peers was Eddie Gottlieb, one of basketball's first entrepreneurs. In 1918, at age 20, Gottlieb became coach of the legendary Philadelphia Sphas. In 1946, he founded the Basketball Association of America, which later had its name changed to the National Basketball Association.

Gottlieb coached the Philadelphia Warriors of the NBA and was in charge of scheduling games for the NBA during its early years. He carried pieces of paper in his pocket on which he had written scheduling notes. Maybe it was a slipshod way to run a league, but during an era when the NBA couldn't afford big salaries, it worked.

Other outstanding coaches who received votes from fraternity members included Harry Litwack of Temple, Howard Cann of NYU, Honey Russell of Seton Hall, Branch McCracken of Indiana, and Buck Freeman of St. John's.

Fraternity members cast many votes for Joe Lapchick of St. John's, and Red Holzman of the New York Knicks, two men cited for the TENDEX Hall of Fame for accomplishments that carried on into the 1950s, 1960s and, in Holzman's case, the 1970s.

THE COACH-PLAYER

Another votegetter was John Chaney, but he is remembered by fraternity members more for his playing talent than his coaching. Chaney set scoring records at Bethune-Cookman College and was an outstanding playmaker.

"He was as good as Bob Cousy," said Hal Blitman.

Blitman was a pretty good coach himself. He coached successfully at the collegiate level and later coached the Floridians of the American Basketball Association.

A player who received a lot of support was Hank Luisetti of Stanford, the first one-handed shooter. Stanford won an NCAA title in 1942 and on an eastern road trip stunned New York City teams with a wide-open style of play. Stanford predated Loyola Marymount by nearly 50 years in perfecting the technique of fast-breaking after an opponent's basket.

"We were used to having a center jump after every basket," said Milt Perkel, who played for Brooklyn College. "Stanford caught us not getting back on defense."

Another great one was Bob Davies, who played at Seton Hall from 1938 to 1942 and had enough endurance to play 10 professional seasons in spite of spending three years in military service during World War II.

Two men who went on to have excellent baseball careers started out as All-American basketball players at midwestern schools—Lou Boudreau of Illinois and Frankie Baumholtz of Ohio University.

Seven-footers Alex Groza of Kentucky and Bob Kurland of Oklahoma A&M, who paced their teams to two NCAA titles apiece during the 1940s, received acclaim from their fraternal contemporaries.

So did Irv Torgoff, who played for LIU and went on to become the first sixth-man in the NBA. Torgoff played for a Washington team coached by Red Auerbach in 1947 before Auerbach became famous for his great sixth men with the champion Boston Celtic teams of the 1950s and 1960s.

Ossie Schectman, who scored the first NBA basket, is remembered by his peers, as is Pop Gates, one of the first great black players.

Others ensconced in memory are Willie Rubenstein, Harry Boykoff, Kenny Sailors, Rip Kaplinsky, Bobby McDermott, Moe Spahn, Bernie Fliegel, Butch Schwartz, Julie Bender, Andy Phillip, Ed Sadowski, Ernie Calverley, Jerry Fleishman, Hy Gotkin, Moe Goldman, and finally Dutch Lancaster, whose brother Burt went on to fame in Hollywood.

TEAM TRIO

Three teams from the era between 1925 and 1950 stand out in the minds of fraternity members: The Original Celtics, the St. John's "Wonder Five," and the Philadelphia Sphas.

Holman and Lapchick both were members of the Original Celtics, not to be confused with the Boston Celtics. The Original Celtics are generally acknowledged as the first excellent basketball team of all-time. They developed techniques of team basketball that set standards for eras to come.

The St. John's team, known as the Wonder Five, was led by Davie Banks. Other members of this team were Mac Kinsbruner, Matty Begovich, Rip Kaplinsky, Allie Schechtman, Rip Gerson, and Hy Gotkin. This team was notable not only for what it accomplished at the college level, but also for turning professional as a unit and playing winning basketball as the New York Jewels.

The Philadelphia Sphas were organized by Eddie Gottlieb. The team's roster included Shikey Gothoeffer, Red Rosen, Inky Lautman, Cy Castleman, Moe Goldman, Red Wolfe, Irv Torgoff, Ossie Schectman, and Petey Rosenberg. Several of these players received Hall of Fame votes for individual excellence.

It's difficult to single out players, coaches, and teams from this era and certify them as Hall of Famers, but we can do so with at least these ten:

- ◇ Nat Holman, the first great teaching coach
- ◇ Clair Bee, the first great recruiting coach
- ◇ John Chaney, a good coach who began as an excellent player
- ◇ Pop Gates, who along with Chaney were two of the first outstanding black players
- ◇ Bob Davies, whose magical handling of the basketball gave Bob Cousy some ideas
- ◇ Hank Luisetti, the first great one-handed shotmaker
- ◇ Bob Kurland, the first prominent seven-footer
- ◇ The Original Celtics
- ◇ The St. John's Wonder Five—New York Jewels
- ◇ The Philadelphia Sphas.

20
One-Hundred-Forty
Hall of Famers

The Boston Celtics' mystique has been mentioned several times in this book. Here's a clear example of it: There are 11 former Boston Celtic players in the Naismith Hall of Fame, only six of whom are in the TENDEX Hall of Fame.

A basketball player who puts on a Boston Celtic uniform can be practically assured of being overrated. No question but that great Celtic players such as Bill Russell, John Havlicek, Dave Cowens, Bob Cousy, Bill Sharman, and Sam Jones belong in the Hall of Fame.

Tom Heinsohn and Frank Ramsey didn't quite make the TENDEX Hall, but they were good players whose selection into the Naismith Hall won't be disputed by many basketball historians.

But what about Chuck Cooper, Ed Macauley, and K.C. Jones?

Jones is in the Naismith Hall as a player, but if he is considered at all, it should be as a coach. He was an ordinary player with a career TENDEX rating of .383 for 9 seasons. Cooper's rating was even worse (.353 for 6 seasons). Macauley's was .495 for 10 seasons, a lot better except when you consider he was a center. As centers go, .495 was below average, even when Macauley played.

The next overrated Celtic to receive Hall of Fame support probably will be Dennis Johnson. It will be argued that he played a long time (14 seasons) and that he was a good defensive player and a clutch scorer. Those are at best lukewarm qualifications.

Johnson's career TENDEX rating was only .464, below the .475 norm for point guards. No one belongs in the Hall of Fame if he is basically an average player.

Much of the Celtics' improvement last season was based on the fact that Johnson had retired and Brian Shaw, a superior defensive player, was the starting point guard. The fact that Johnson often was the guy who took big shots for the Celtics was not because he was a great shooter. He was in fact the worst Celtic shooter for most of his career with teammates Larry Bird, Kevin McHale, Robert Parish, and Dan Ainge. He was put in the position of taking big shots—some of which he made and more of which he missed—because opponents deliberately left him open in their zeal to cover the more dangerous Celtics.

Bird, Parish, and McHale belong in the Hall of Fame and are already in the TENDEX Hall. They'll make the Naismith Hall, too. But I seriously question the selection of guys like Cooper, Jones, Macauley, and even Heinsohn and Ramsey, and the possible future consideration of Johnson, especially when there are some deserving players who haven't been selected as yet.

Here's a chart showing the combined number of players, coaches and teams represented by each NBA franchise in the TENDEX Hall of Fame:

1. Boston 13
2. Philadelphia 10
3. Minneapolis-Los Angeles 9
4. New York 8
5. Phoenix 5
   Detroit 5
7. Cincinnati-Kansas City 4
   Denver 4
   Milwaukee 4
10. Chicago 3
    San Francisco-Golden St. 3
    St. Louis 3
    Washington 3
    Utah 3
16. Indiana 2
    Houston 2
    Seattle 2
    San Antonio 2
20. Buffalo 1
    Syracuse 1
    Portland 1

TOTALS 91

The combination of 76 players, 10 teams, and 5 coaches results in the total of 91 NBA entities in the TENDEX Hall of Fame. Representing colleges, there are 12 players, 15 coaches, and 12 teams for a total of 39. Here are the colleges and universities represented by at least two players, coaches and/or teams:

1. UCLA 6
2. LaSalle 2
   Kansas 2
   North Carolina 2
   Georgetown 2
   Indiana 2

The colleges with one TENDEX Hall of Fame representative are Princeton, Notre Dame, LSU, Niagara, Navy, Virginia, North Carolina State, Louisville, Western Kentucky, Washington, Winston-Salem, Oklahoma State, St. John's, South Carolina, DePaul, Oregon State, St. Joseph's, Kentucky, Nevada-Las Vegas, Ohio State, Houston, Michigan State, and San Francisco.

Old-timers are placed in a separate category, not necessarily college or pro. Altogether, counting pros, collegians and old-timers, there are 140 entities in the TENDEX Hall of Fame: 93 players, 25 teams, and 22 coaches.

Here's an alphabetized list of the TENDEX Hall of Famers, categorized by pros, collegians, and old-timers:

PROFESSIONALS

Name (Seasons)	TENDEX
1. Abdul-Jabbar, Kareem (20)	.817
2. Adams, Alvan (13)	.664
3. Archibald, Nate (13)	.532
4. Arizin, Paul (10)	.552
5. Auerbach, Red (20)	COACH
6. Barkley, Charles (7)	.783
7. Barry, Rick (14)	.626
8. Baylor, Elgin (14)	.753
9. Bellamy, Walt (14)	.697
10. Bird, Larry (12)	.762
11. Boone, Ron (13)	.490
12. BOSTON CELTICS	1959–60
13. BOSTON CELTICS	1964–65
14. BOSTON CELTICS	1985–86
15. Chamberlain, Wilt (14)	.942
16. Cheeks, Maurice (13)	.515
17. Cousy, Bob (14)	.516
18. Cowens, Dave (11)	.668
19. Cunningham, Bill (11)	.677
20. Daley, Chuck (9)	COACH
21. Daniels, Mel (9)	.685
22. Davis, Walter (14)	.580
23. DeBusschere, Dave (12)	.577
24. Drexler, Clyde (8)	.652
25. English, Alex (15)	.584
26. Erving, Julius (16)	.709
27. Frazier, Walt (13)	.618
28. Gallatin, Harry (10)	.612
29. Gervin, George (14)	.612
30. Gilmore, Artis (17)	.721
31. Greer, Hal (15)	.501
32. Guerin, Richie (13)	.536

33. Hagan, Cliff (13)	.642	85. Unseld, Wes (13)	.642
34. Havlicek, John (16)	.556	86. Walker, Chet (13)	.576
35. Hawkins, Connie (9)	.635	87. West, Jerry (14)	.688
36. Hayes, Elvin (16)	.631	88. Westphal, Paul (12)	.584
37. Haywood, Spencer (13)	.628	89. Wilkens, Len (15)	.541
38. Holzman, Red (18)	COACH	90. Wilkins, Dominique (9)	.617
39. Howell, Bailey (12)	.674	91. Williams, Gus (11)	.535
40. Issel, Dan (15)	.637		
41. Johnson, Magic (12)	.758		
42. Johnson, Marques (11)	.624		
43. Johnston, Neil (8)	.651		
44. Jones, Sam (12)	.573		
45. Jordan, Michael (7)	.851		
46. King, Bernard (13)	.597		
47. Lanier, Bob (14)	.746		
48. Lever, Lafayette (9)	.585		
49. LOS ANGELES LAKERS	1971–72		
50. LOS ANGELES LAKERS	1979–80		
51. LOS ANGELES LAKERS	1986–87		
52. Lovellete, Clyde (11)	.685		
53. Lucas, Jerry (11)	.730		
54. Malone, Karl (6)	.726		
55. Malone, Moses (17)	.703		
56. McAdoo, Bob (14)	.692		
57. McGinnis, George (11)	.655		
58. McGuire, Dick (11)	.430		
59. McHale, Kevin (11)	.654		
60. Mikan, George (9)	.663		
61. MILWAUKEE BUCKS	1970–71		
62. Moe, Doug (14)	COACH		
63. Moncrief, Sidney (11)	.578		
64. Monroe, Earl (13)	.505		
65. Mullins, Jeff (12)	.518		
66. Nance, Larry (10)	.661		
67. Nelson, Don (14)	COACH		
68. NEW YORK KNICKS	1969–70		
69. Olajuwon, Hakeem (7)	.795		
70. Parish, Robert (15)	.688		
71. Pettit, Bob (11)	.818		
72. PHILADELPHIA 76ERS	1966–67		
73. PHILADELPHIA 76ERS	1982–83		
74. Reed, Willis (10)	.695		
75. Robertson, Alvin (7)	.584		
76. Robertson, Oscar (14)	.738		
77. Roundfield, Dan (12)	.636		
78. Russell, Bill (13)	.841		
79. Schayes, Dolph (15)	.653		
80. Sharman, Bill (11)	.457		
81. Stockton, John (7)	.693		
82. Thomas, Isiah (10)	.580		
83. Thurmond, Nate (14)	.678		
84. Twyman, Jack (11)	.562		

COLLEGIANS

Name	Seasons
1. Allen, Phog	COACH–48
2. Bradley, Bill	1964–67
3. Carr, Austin	1968–71
4. Crum, Denny	COACH–20
5. Diddle, Ed	COACH–42
6. Ewing, Patrick	1981–85
7. Gaines, Clarence	COACH–45
8. GEORGETOWN	1983–84
9. Gola, Tom	1951–55
10. Harshman, Marv	COACH–40
11. HOUSTON	1982–83
12. Iba, Hank	COACH–41
13. INDIANA	1975–76
14. Knight, Bobby	COACH–26
15. Lapchick, Joe	COACH–29*
16. Manning, Danny	1984–88
17. Maravich, Pete	1967–70
18. McGuire, Frank	COACH–30
19. Meyer, Ray	COACH–42
20. MICHIGAN STATE	1978–79
21. Miller, Ralph	COACH–38
22. Murphy, Calvin	1966–70
23. NEVADA-LAS VEGAS	1990–91
24. NORTH CAROLINA	1956–57
25. OHIO STATE	1959–60
26. Ramsay, Jack	COACH–32*
27. Robinson, David	1983–87
28. Rupp, Adolph	COACH–41
29. Sampson, Ralph	1979–83
30. SAN FRANCISCO	1955–56
31. Simmons, Lionel	1986–90
32. Smith, Dean	COACH–30
33. Thompson, David	1972–75
34. UCLA	1963–64
35. UCLA	1966–67
36. UCLA	1971–72
37. UCLA	1972–73
38. Walton, Bill	1971–74
39. Wooden, John	COACH–29

* Includes NBA coaching career.

OLD-TIMERS

Name	Category
1. Bee, Clair	Coach
2. Chaney, John	Player
3. Davies, Bob	Player
4. Gates, Pop	Player
5. Holman, Nat	Coach
6. Kurland, Bob	Player
7. Luisetti, Hank	Player
8. ORIGINAL CELTICS	Team
9. PHILADELPHIA SPHAS	Team
10. ST. JOHN'S WONDER FIVE	Team

ABSTRACTION 8

Future Famers

This is about potential only. It's a projection of the likelihood of future Hall of Fame induction for players who haven't played a minute yet in the NBA.

Let's start with five players who are almost certain future famers, barring injury, of course:

1. SHAQUILLE O'NEAL—Do-it-all big man in the genre of Wilt Chamberlain. TENDEX rating .946 last season as LSU sophomore.
2. LARRY JOHNSON—Charles Barkley look-alike had .828 TENDEX rating for UNLV team that lost only one game.
3. DIKEMBE MUTOMBO—Plays defense like Bill Russell, and is five inches taller. TENDEX rating .841 for Georgetown.
4. BILLY OWENS—Versatile cornerman could play any position except center in NBA. TENDEX rating .633 for Syracuse.
5. KENNY ANDERSON—Still young and lacks durability, but ball-handling talent is unexcelled. TENDEX .514 for Georgia Tech.

And then there are five players who are probable Hall of Famers, but not quite as certain as the first five:

6. ALONZO MOURNING—Forget his injury-plagued 1990–91 season. He can be a Hall of Famer as either a center or a power forward. TENDEX .696 for Georgetown.
7. SHAWN BRADLEY—The only negatives for this shot-blocking machine are a thin body and a two-year Mormon missionary commitment. TENDEX .652 for Brigham Young.
8. JIM JACKSON—Great all-court player who puts team ahead of personal achievements. TENDEX .589 for Ohio State.
9. STEVE SMITH—Ditto what was just said about Jackson, but Smith is older without being better. TENDEX .583 for Michigan State.
10. CALBERT CHEANEY—Only difference between Cheaney and Jackson or Smith is Cheaney might not be able to switch from forward to guard in the NBA. TENDEX .657 for Indiana.

And now five more who are in the category of possible future Hall of Famers:

11. TONI KUKOC—Best player in the world outside of the United States and would be one of the 10 best in the NBA. But will he ever play in the NBA? Chicago Bulls have draft rights but don't seem to want him.
12. HAROLD MINER—It's said he's a Michael Jordan clone, but I don't see it yet. TENDEX rating .472 for USC.
13. CHRISTIAN LAETTNER—Does many things like Kevin McHale. TENDEX rating .695 for NCAA champion Duke team.
14. BYRON HOUSTON—If he learns to face the basket and handle the ball better, he'll be compared with Charles Barkley and Larry Johnson. TENDEX rating .768 for Oklahoma State.
15. JOSH GRANT—The closest thing to Larry Bird in college basketball. Led Utah in nearly all statistical categories last season, the most important being a 30–4 team record. TENDEX .728.

SECTION II

THE 1990–91 AND
1991–92 SEASONS

Introduction

This is more of a statistical code than an introduction. It should help to explain some of the statistics in the second half of this book which otherwise might be confusing.

All statistics listed for teams at the beginning of Chapters 4–30 are based on per-game averages. Here are explanations of a few of them that might be confusing:

◇ **REBOUNDS:** Unlike any other statistic, rebounds are an either-or proposition. Either one team gets the ball off the glass or the other does. Therefore, the ratings for rebounds are based on the difference between a team's total of rebounds and its opponents' total. If we just used team totals, those that played fast game-paces would have the advantage. Instead of being rated No. 23 in rebounding, Denver would be No. 1.

◇ **TWO-POINT FIELD-GOAL PERCENTAGE:** This is not identical to the field-goal percentages listed in official NBA records. For some mystifying reason, the NBA has chosen to combine two and three-point percentages in one statistic, called field-goal percentage. The NBA then lists three-point percentage separately without doing the same for two-point percentage.

◇ **SHOOTIST:** This is a simple TENDEX statistic showing the overall proficiency of a shooter. It is figured by dividing a team's point total by the total number of shots of all kinds taken by all members of the team.

◇ **PAR:** Another TENDEX statistic, it is the combination of a team's points, assists, and rebounds, compared to the sum of its opponents' PAR statistics. If the listed team has more than its opponents, this statistic will be plus. If not, minus.

◇ **BEST:** Another TENDEX statistic, this one involves the three ball-control statistics—blocked shots, steals, and turnovers. It is the team's sum of blocks and steals, minus its total of turnovers.

◇ **TURNOVERS:** This is the only statistic for which inverse ratings are used. For all the other stats, most is best. For turnovers, most is worst.

◇ **COACHES:** These ratings are based on a comparison of team records with team ratings. Good coaches are the ones (with plus ratings) who are able to get more victories out of their teams than the player personnel warrants.

Concerning the individual player ratings at the end of Chapters 4–30, the ages are listed according to calendar years. So it is possible you might read this book in October or November before certain players actually reach the birthdays making them the age they are listed.

Only players who played at least 2,000 minutes during the 1990–91 season have complete statistical biographies. This means there are some glaring omissions—Isiah Thomas, Moses Malone, Michael Williams, Kendall Gill, and Pervis Ellison, to name a few. Where important players must be omitted, there are commentaries about them in the text of the chapters about their teams.

For individual statistics, per-game and per-minute averages are listed. The ratings are based on the per-minute averages because

TENDEX is a per-minute system. It is inequitable to make per-game comparisons between players who average 25 minutes of playing time and those who average 35 minutes. Players are placed on an equal basis only when per-minute comparisons are made.

One new category has been added to the individual player biographies: Positional Rating. This is the player's rating in comparison with all others who played at least 2,000 minutes at the same position during the 1990–91 season.

Because of trades made after this book went to publication, some players may be listed with the teams they played for in 1990–91, instead of the ones with whom they will open the 1991–92 season.

1
Game-Pace & Strength-of-Schedule

The theory of the TENDEX formula is simple enough for any basketball fan to understand. Few fans question the reason for awarding TENDEX points for rebounds, assists, steals, blocked shots, and points scored. Or for subtracting TENDEX points for shots missed and turnovers. Or for dividing the total by minutes played. It's like batting average in baseball. The more times at bat, the more hits a baseball player can accumulate; the more minutes played, the more TENDEX points a basketball player can compile.

But when it comes to the computations of game-pace and strength-of-schedule, there is less understanding. For it is certainly true that these two things must enter into the final formula for a player's TENDEX rating to be accurate.

GAME-PACE

The faster the pace of play, the more ball-possessions. Increasing the number of ball-possessions will increase the ratings of all players on a team. Players on slow-paced teams will have their ratings negatively affected. Balance needs to be restored.

Were it not for game-pace, Michael Adams of the Denver Nuggets would have had a TENDEX rating of .720 for the 1990–91 season.

With it, his rating was .617. Adams had his best season as a pro, and his rating was the fifth-best of all point guards. But despite his averages of 26.5 points, 10.5 assists and 2.23 steals per game (all among the NBA leaders), no one was about to classify him as a superstar, which is what he would be with a rating over .700.

Game-pace is vitally important to the computation of TENDEX ratings. Here's how it works, using Adams' team, Denver, for our example.

The formula for game-pace is identical to the TENDEX formula, except that it must be calculated for a team and its opponents, instead of for an individual player. Once again, here's the basic TENDEX formula: Points + Assists + Rebounds + Steals + Blocked Shots – Turnovers – Missed Shots (field goals and free throws) / Minutes Played = TENDEX Rating.

In order to determine a team's game-pace, the composite TENDEX ratings for all its players is computed and then added to the composite ratings of its opponents.

Denver totaled 9,828 points, 4,050 rebounds, 2,005 assists, 856 steals, and 406 blocked shots for a positive total of 17,145 TENDEX points. The Nuggets missed 4,967 field-goal attempts, 537 free-throw attempts and committed 1,332 turnovers for a negative total of 6,836. Subtracting 6,836 from 17,145 yields a total of 10,309 TENDEX points. Dividing 10,309 by 19,730 (the Nuggets' total of minutes played) gives a team TENDEX rating of .5225.

Inserting the numbers of Denver's opponents for all 82 games of the season gives a TENDEX rating of .6438. Adding the two numbers results in a sum of 1.1663, which is the Nuggets' game-pace.

Adams' .720 rating, divided by 1.1663, gives his final TENDEX rating of .617.

The Nuggets' game-pace (1.1663) for the 1990–91 season was one of the highest in professional basketball history. They raced up and down the floor at such a rapid pace that they set records for most points allowed (130.8 per game) and for most total points by a team and its opponents (250.7 per game).

The difference between a team's TENDEX rating and the rating of its opponents gives the team's TENDEX power rating. In Denver's case, subtracting its opponents' rating (.6438) from its own rating (.5225) gives a result of minus −.1213. Using 100 instead of 1.000 as the basic statistic, moving the decimal two places and subtracting 12.13 (instead of .1213) gives a team rating of 87.87, worst in the NBA for the 1990–91 season and one of the worst ever.

The team with the best regular-season TENDEX power rating for the 1990–91 season was Chicago with a mark of 109.04. This means that on a neutral court, with both teams playing a normal game, and no "garbage time" at the end, the Bulls could have been expected to defeat Denver by 21 points (109.04 − 87.87 = 21.17).

STRENGTH-OF-SCHEDULE

There were no strength-of-schedule computations for the NBA last season. During the decade of the 1980s the Eastern Conference so dominated the Western Conference that we would have been justified to do strength-of-schedule ratings for every team, and the schedules of the Eastern teams would have been considerably more difficult than those in

the West. Had we done this, all players in the East would have had 10 or more points added to their TENDEX ratings and those in the West would have lost the same number to compensate for their easier schedules.

During the 1989–90 season, there was a power swing and, for one year at least, the West became the dominant conference. But what about last season? These were the TENDEX ratings for all NBA teams for the 1990–91 campaign:

EASTERN CONFERENCE

Team	TENDEX
1. Chicago	109.04
2. Boston	108.15
3. Detroit	103.30
4. Milwaukee	101.65
5. New York	100.95
6. Indiana	100.77
7. Cleveland	98.32
8. Philadelphia	97.93
9. Atlanta	97.70
10. Washington	96.88
11. New Jersey	96.36
12. Charlotte	94.24
13. Miami	94.11
AVERAGE	99.95

WESTERN CONFERENCE

Team	TENDEX
1. Portland	107.77
2. Phoenix	107.11
3. San Antonio	105.99
4. LA Lakers	105.79
5. Utah	104.93
6. Houston	102.48
7. Seattle	102.38
8. Golden State	99.32
9. LA Clippers	98.38
10. Dallas	95.58
11. Minnesota	95.38
12. Sacramento	94.86
13. Orlando	92.76
14. Denver	87.87
AVERAGE	100.04

The difference between the strengths of the two conferences last season was minuscule, not worth taking the trouble to factor into the TENDEX ratings of teams or players. As a matter of fact, it was so small that it would not have changed the TENDEX ratings of most players by as much as one percentage point.

Such was not the case in college basketball. Calculations were made for all player and team ratings in college ball as for the NBA, with one exception: An additional division was made based on strength-of-schedule.

Each season I do careful research to determine the strength of all NCAA Division I teams. I have learned that for most seasons the shadings of difference are such that all teams can be placed in one of ten categories. For the 1990–91 season there were four conferences rated at the strongest (No. 1) level: Big East, Atlantic Coast, Big Eight, and Big Ten.

Here's a listing of the 33 conferences, placed at the levels befitting their strength:

- ◇ **LEVEL ONE**—Big East, Atlantic Coast, Big Eight, Big Ten
- ◇ **LEVEL TWO**—Pacific-Ten, Southeastern
- ◇ **LEVEL THREE**—Southwest, Metro
- ◇ **LEVEL FOUR**—Western Athletic, Atlantic Ten, Big West, Missouri Valley
- ◇ **LEVEL FIVE**—American South, Sun Belt, Midwestern Collegiate, Mid-American
- ◇ **LEVEL SIX**—Colonial Athletic, West Coast, Metro Atlantic, Ohio Valley
- ◇ **LEVEL SEVEN**—Southern, Mid-Continent, Trans America, Big Sky
- ◇ **LEVEL EIGHT**—Patriot, Northeast, Southwestern Athletic
- ◇ **LEVEL NINE**—North Atlantic, Ivy, Mid-Eastern
- ◇ **LEVEL TEN**—Southland, Big South, East Coast.

This does not mean that every conference at the first level is exactly equal in overall strength to every other. The Big East was slightly stronger than the Atlantic Coast, which in turn was slightly stronger than the Big Eight, etc. Nor does it mean that every team in each conference was exactly the same in strength. Certain teams were assigned strengths different from the levels of their conferences. For example, Nevada-Las Vegas played in a Level Four conference (the Big West) but was assigned a team strength of One. Northwestern, playing in a Level One conference (the Big Ten), was assigned a team strength of Three.

Assigning numbers ranging from One to Ten to Division I teams, and Eleven for non-Division I teams, each team's strength-of-schedule was computed. With a base number of 1.000 for teams with Level One ratings, 25 percentage points are added for each level of difference. This yields a potential range from 1.000 for a team playing only Level One opponents, to 1.250 for a team playing only non-Division I foes.

Indiana played only one team weaker than a Three and had the strongest overall schedule, 1.017. These were the top 10 teams in terms of strength-of-schedule:

Team	Schedule
1. Indiana	1.017
2. Iowa State	1.022
3. North Carolina	1.027
4. Purdue	1.028
5. Michigan State	1.029
6. Stanford	1.033
7. St. John's	1.034
8. Iowa	1.036
Michigan	1.036
Oregon State	1.036

In college basketball, the average TENDEX rating is about .400 for players on the top 100 teams and lower than that for players on weaker teams. Since we include only the top 100 teams in our listings, .400 is cited as the average player rating, 100 percentage points below the average for a pro.

Now, let's compute the TENDEX rating of a player chosen at random from the first team, Alabama, on our alphabetized list of the top 100 teams.

Versatile forward Robert Horry totaled 381 points, 38 steals, 77 blocked shots, 56 assists and 260 rebounds for a positive total of 812. He missed 163 field-goal attempts, 20 free-throw attempts, and turned the ball over 74 times for a negative total of 257. Subtracting 257 form 812 yielded a total of 555. Horry played 959 minutes, so in order to get his basic TENDEX rating we have to divide 555 by 959, which results in a rating of .579.

But we aren't finished. Next we have to divide by Alabama's team game-pace (1.022).

That changes the rating to .566. And finally we must divide by Alabama's strength-of-schedule (1.045), which yields Horry's final TENDEX rating of .542.

This is an excellent rating, best on the Alabama team and good enough to make the best 100 players in the country, as listed in the next chapter.

2
College Players & Teams

There seems to be a trend in the United States to pity the poor sleaze-bag. Maybe it has something to do with our media, books, and movies, most of the time portraying the criminal element as not all bad.

No matter what a man has done, no matter what heinous crime he has committed, we are assured of hearing a neighbor or family member saying on TV what a wonderful, gentle person he is. I suspect this kind of mindset had something to do with the nauseating public disclaimers we were subjected to last season in support of Jerry Tarkanian and against his old adversary, the NCAA.

Now, I am not a big NCAA booster. Through the years there have been some astounding decisions by that enigmatic organization, doling out the severest penalties to schools guilty of only meager rules violations and letting politically powerful universities off practically penalty-free despite a multitude of major offenses (e.g., the University of Florida).

But in the Tarkanian case, the NCAA didn't deserve to be portrayed as the bad guy. This was a case that hung around for 10 years through no fault of the NCAA's, but because Tarkanian stubbornly pursued it through the courts. Let's face it: Tarkanian has run a dirty program at UNLV. Miami Herald columnist

Edwin Pope described Tarkanian as "old lizard eyes." Perfect description.

Few salamander tears were shed for Tarkanian when, with help from vested TV interests, he managed to get his televisually-popular team out of the NCAA's doghouse and into its 1991 Tournament, only to be upset by Duke. If ever there was justice, this was it.

The Duke game showed what a really average coach Tarkanian is. UNLV was a team which, some basketball enthusiasts believed, could have played the NBA's Denver Nuggets to a standoff. And yet it was upset by an unexceptional team in a game that required some preparation and coaching adjustments by Tarkanian that he simply couldn't figure out.

How good was the 1990–91 UNLV team in terms of player personnel? Here is a listing of the TENDEX ratings of the top college teams based on a formula similar to the one described for pro teams in the previous chapter:

Team	Rating
1. Nevada-Las Vegas	111.84
2. Indiana	95.21
3. Arkansas	94.81
4. Ohio State	93.68
5. Arizona	93.38
6. Duke	92.75
7. UCLA	90.43

107

8.	Kansas	89.87
9.	Louisiana State	89.40
10.	Nebraska	89.08
	Oklahoma State	89.08
12.	Syracuse	88.50
13.	Missouri	86.60
14.	Georgia	85.97
15.	Stanford	85.91
16.	East Tennessee State	84.46
17.	Connecticut	84.23
18.	Kentucky	83.60
19.	Purdue	83.39
20.	Seton Hall	83.37
21.	St. John's	83.25
22.	New Mexico	83.17
23.	Georgetown	82.96
24.	Utah	82.49
25.	Brigham Young	81.91

Notice that there is a 16.63-point difference between No. 1 UNLV and No. 2 Indiana. From No. 2 to No. 25 the increments are small, so that there is only a 13.30-point difference between Indiana and No. 25 BYU—less than the difference between No. 1 and No. 2. What we have here are two levels of player strength— UNLV and everybody else. And yet, somehow, UNLV managed to lose to Duke, a team it should have overpowered by 19 points, according to man-to-man matchups.

The formula for computing the strength of college teams is:

◇ Calculate the TENDEX ratings of the team and its composite opponents.

◇ Subtract from the team's rating the rating of its opponents and add the difference to 80.

◇ Divide by the team's strength-of-schedule factor.

This differs from the professional team ratings in two respects. First, it includes a strength-of-schedule factor, something that was unnecessary in the NBA during the 1990–91 season. Second, it uses 80 as the base number instead of 100. This is in order to keep the proportions correct, because the average player rating in the NBA is .500, compared to .400 for a collegian.

This does not mean that UNLV, with its 111.84 rating, was a superior team to the Chicago Bulls, the NBA's best team with a 109.04 rating. UNLV probably was not as good as Denver, the NBA's worst team with an 87.87 rating. These ratings should be compared only within their correct contexts— college teams with college teams and pro teams with pro teams.

TENDEX did not overrate UNLV. This team's personnel was so strong that it probably had seven future NBA players.

The abilities of its coach, however, are often overrated.

For TENDEX Coach of the Year, it's Mike Krzyzewski of Duke. The Blue Devils not only pulled off the impossible upset, beating UNLV in the NCAA Tournament semi-finals, but they went on to win the title with only the sixth-best player personnel in the nation, according to TENDEX.

Concerning individual players, all the propensities that had been shown in the past by TENDEX showed up again in the 1991 ratings:

◇ TENDEX picks out the greatest players, so they are plainly identifiable.

◇ It points out players who aren't quite as good as their reputations.

◇ It overrates some big men, especially those who star for unexceptional teams.

Overrated players for last season included Chris Gatling of Old Dominion (No. 4 overall, TENDEX rating .773), Popeye Jones of Murray State (No. 6, .739), Larry Stewart of Coppin State (No. 7, .730), Victor Alexander of Iowa State (No. 10, .709), Ervin (not Magic) Johnson of New Orleans (No. 14, .683), and Damon Lopez of Fordham (No. 15, .682).

Don't misunderstand: We are not talking about TENDEX being inaccurate. These guys, all of them space-eaters, were featured low-post players. They earned their ratings with excellent play but are too short, and in some cases not athletic enough, to be NBA centers.

But now look at the positive side of what TENDEX can do with college ratings. Let's talk about five players:

1. SHAQUILLE O'NEAL—The LSU sophomore set a record with a TENDEX rating of .946. His performance was reminiscent of what Wilt Chamberlain did at Kansas during the 1950s. In those days not enough statistics were compiled to do TENDEX ratings, but Chamberlain's career rating in the NBA was .941.

2. DIKEMBE MUTOMBO—The Georgetown senior is underrated because, despite the supposed sophistication of basketball experts today, stifling defense still is not given as much attention as awesome offense. Mutombo's TENDEX rating of .841 was similar to Bill Russell's ratings when he made defensive rebounding, intimidation and shot-blocking essential elements of basketball. Those just happen to be the three strongest parts of the 7-foot-2 Mutombo's game.

3. LARRY JOHNSON—UNLV's best player had a TENDEX rating of .828. Johnson is about the same height (listed at 6-7 but actually about 6-4) as Charles Barkley, and if his game doesn't remind you of Barkley's, it should. Barkley's rating in the NBA last season was .833.

4. JOSH GRANT—If you are looking for TENDEX to pick out an underrated player who can become an NBA star, look no further than Grant. He is the same height (6-9) as Larry Bird, plays in obscurity for a little-known school (Utah) just as Bird did (Indiana State) and has versatility similar to Bird's. He led Utah to a 30-4 record last season, and I mean he led Utah. He paced the team in scoring, rebounding, assists, steals, blocked shots, free-throw percentage, and two-point field-goal percentage. TENDEX rating .728.

5. KENNY ANDERSON—It was suggested in some quarters that Anderson was the best player in the 1991 draft.

TENDEX doesn't think so, at least, not yet. A late-season slump during his sophomore season may have indicated that Anderson does not yet have the strength in his body to endure the pounding of an 82-game NBA schedule. His TENDEX rating was .514, good enough for the TENDEX All-American Third Team, but not outstanding enough to indicate that he will be dominant in the NBA in his rookie season.

Here are the first five TENDEX All-American teams, based on the TENDEX productivity rating that includes the basic TENDEX rating plus a durability factor, giving advantage to players who play a lot of minutes over those who don't play as much:

FIRST TEAM

Position—Player, Team	Rating
C —Shaquille O'Neal, LSU	.801
F —Larry Johnson, UNLV	.740
F —Byron Houston, Oklahoma State	.706
G —Keith Jennings, E. Tennessee St	.593
G —Steve Smith, Michigan State	.570

SECOND TEAM

C —Dikembe Mutomgo, Georgetown	.774
F —Larry Stewart, Coppin State	.702
F —Josh Grant, Utah	.641
G —Eric Murdock, Providence	.550
G —Tony Bennett, Wis.-Green Bay	.549

THIRD TEAM

C —Chris Gatling, Old Dominion	.688
F —Doug Smith, Missouri	.634
F —Billy Owens, Syracuse	.619
G —Terrell Brandon, Oregon	.528
G —Kenny Anderson, Georgia Tech	.509

FOURTH TEAM

C —Popeye Jones, Murray State	.669
F —Calbert Cheaney, Indiana	.593
F —Clarence Weatherspoon, Sou. Miss	.590
G —Terrell Lowery, Loyola Marymount	.492
G —Kevin Lynch, Minnesota	.487

FIFTH TEAM

C —Victor Alexander, Iowa State .... .653
F —Dale Davis, Clemson .... .587
F —Malik Sealy, St. John's .... .578
G —John Taft, Marshall .... .484
G —Darelle Porter, Pittsburg .... .478

PLAYER OF THE YEAR: Shaquille O'Neal

Byron Houston is a talented player who resembles Larry Johnson in body-type and style of play, although he does not as yet have as much diversification to his game. He'll have another season to develop under the excellent tutelage of Eddie Sutton at Oklahoma State.

Three underrated guards to watch when they become professionals are Lynch, a Jeff Hornacek look-alike; Lowery, who runs like TENDEX Hall of Famer Gus Williams; and Brandon, who reminds of Tim Hardaway.

The toughest omissions from the All-America teams were a pair of swing-men, Jim Jackson of Ohio State and Doug Christie of Pepperdine. Jackson and Christie both are 6-foot-6 and probably will be guards in the NBA, but for these All-American teams it would have been unfair to list them as guards since they actually played a lot more minutes at the forward position, which is more advantageous for producing high ratings in the college style of play. If they had been counted as guards, Jackson would have qualified for the Second Team and Christie for the Fourth Team.

In the NBA, the average rating for centers is .550, followed by .525 for power forwards, .500 for small forwards, .475 for point guards and .450 for shooting guards. In the college ranks, there are greater discrepancies between the positions. The average ratings for players on the top 100 teams are: Centers .470, power forwards .450, small forwards .390, point guards .355, and shooting guards .340.

The difference between collegiate power and small forwards is 60 points. This makes the accomplishment of Cheaney in making the third All-American TENDEX team seem more noteworthy. Although some of the forwards on the five TENDEX teams will play the small forward position in the NBA, Cheaney is the only one who played that position during the 1990–91 college season.

North Carolina was omitted from the top 25 teams in the college ratings early in this chapter. It was impossible to compute Tar Heel ratings, team or individual, because they did not include minutes-played totals with their official statistics. Since North Carolina was the only team omitting minutes played, there is no reason to feel any great loss concerning the omission of their players from the ratings that follow. Here are the top 100 college players, based on TENDEX ratings:

Player, Team	TENDEX
1. Shaquille O'Neal, Louisiana St	.946
2. Dikembe Mutombo, Georgetown ..	.841
3. Larry Johnson, UNLV	.828
4. Chris Gatling, Old Dominion	.773
5. Byron Houston, Oklahoma State ...	.768
6. Popeye Jones, Murray State	.739
7. Larry Stewart, Coppin State	.730
8. Josh Grant, Utah	.728
9. Oliver Miller, Arkansas	.724
10. Victor Alexander, Iowa State	.709
11. Alonzo Mourning, Georgetown	.696
12. Christian Laettner, Duke	.695
13. Ervin Johnson, New Orleans	.683
14. Damon Lopez, Fordham	.682
15. Doug Smith, Missouri	.667
16. Calbert Cheaney, Indiana	.657
17. Luc Longley, New Mexico	.656
18. Shawn Bradley, Brigham Young	.652
19. Chuckie White, Purdue	.633
20. Billy Owens, Syracuse	.633
21. Shaun Vandiver, Colorado	.632
22. Keith Jennings, E. Tennessee St	.631
23. Dwayne Davis, Florida	.629
24. Stacey Augmon, UNLV	.629
25. P.J. Brown, Louisiana Tech	.628
26. Dale Davis, Clemson	.618
27. Brian Williams, Arizona	.617
28. Clarence Weatherspoon, S. Miss ...	.617
29. Anthony Avent, Seton Hall	.615
30. Harper Williams, Massachusetts ...	.613
31. Rich King, Nebraska	.611
32. Donnell Thomas, Northern Ill	.599
33. Malik Sealy, St. John's	.592
34. George Hendrick, California	.591
35. Jim Jackson, Ohio State	.589

36. Tanoka Beard, Boise State .... .584
37. Adam Keefe, Stanford .... .583
38. Steve Smith, Michigan State .... .583
39. Joe Wylie, Miami .... .581
40. Rodney Rogers, Wake Forest ...... .579
41. Isaac Austin, Arizona State .... .576
42. Eric Murdock, Providence .... .575
43. Kit Mueller, Princeton .... .574
44. Ron Ellis, Louisiana Tech .... .572
45. Chad Gallagher, Creighton .... .571
46. Alonzo Jamison, Kansas .... .567
47. Tony Bennett, Wis.-Green Bay ..... .567
48. Don MacLean, UCLA .... .563
49. Acie Earl, Iowa .... .560
50. Chancellor Nichols, James Mad .... .560
51. Kendrick Warren, Va. Common .... .557
52. Reggie Slater, Wyoming .... .555
53. Rodney English, E. Tennessee St ... .555
54. Andrew Wells, Northern Illinois ... .555
55. Patrick Tompkins, Wisconsin ...... .555
56. Brent Scott, Rice .... .553
57. Walter Watts, Utah .... .550
58. Mike Peplowski, Michigan State.... .547
59. Tracy Murray, UCLA .... .546
60. Jimmy Oliver, Purdue .... .544
61. Mark Randall, Kansas .... .543
62. Robert Horry, Alabama .... .542
63. Scott Burrell, Connecticut .... .540
64. Chris Collier, Georgia State .... .539
65. Chris Brooks, West Virginia .... .539
66. Jamal Mashburn, Kentucky .... .539
67. Steve Carney, Northeastern .... .536
68. Reggie Hanson, Kentucky .... .534
69. James Barnes, Penn State .... .534
70. David Booth, DePaul .... .534
71. Greg Carter, Mississippi State...... .533
72. Terrell Brandon, Oregon .... .532
73. Doug Christie, Pepperdine .... .530
74. Herbert Jones, Cincinnati .... .528
75. Cornelius Holden, Louisville ...... .524
76. Marcell Gordon, Tulsa .... .524
77. Richard Petruska, Loyola Mary .... .524
78. LeRon Ellis, Syracuse .... .524
79. Jeff Roulston, South Carolina ...... .522
80. Sean Rooks, Arizona .... .521
81. Darelle Porter, Pittsburgh .... .519
82. Eric Riley, Michigan .... .518
83. Ronnie Coleman, Southern Cal .... .517
84. Geoff Lear, Pepperdine .... .515
85. Bryant Stith, West Virginia .... .514
86. Kenny Anderson, Georgia Tech .... .514
87. Anthony Peeler, Missouri .... .513
88. Tyrone Phillips, Marshall .... .512

89. Fred Shepherd, Arkansas State ..... .512
90. Darin Archbold, Butler .... .511
91. Dion Brown, Washington .... .511
92. Stephen Howard, DePaul .... .510
93. Robert Werdann, St. John's .... .510
94. Terrell Lowery, Loyola Mary ...... .509
95. Dewayne McCray, Arkansas State .. .508
96. Perry Carter, Ohio State .... .508
97. Deon Thomas, Illinois .... .506
98. Mike Iuzzolino, St. Francis .... .505
99. Kevin Lynch, Minnesota .... .502
100. Alvaro Teheran, Houston .... .501

Here are the ratings of all regular players, plus all other players averaging at least 20 minutes per game, for the top 100 college teams:

Player	TENDEX
ALABAMA (23-10)	
Robert Horry	.542
Melvin Cheatum	.440
James Robinson	.419
Latrell Sprewell	.415
Gary Waites	.379
ALABAMA-BIRMINGHAM (18-13)	
Andy Kennedy	.465
Elbert Rogers	.462
Stanley Jackson	.428
Stan Rose	.343
Jack Kramer	.313
ARIZONA (28-7)	
Brian Williams	.617
Sean Rooks	.521
Chris Mills	.499
Khalid Reeves	.425
Matt Muehlebach	.390
Matt Othick	.378
ARIZONA STATE (20-10)	
Isaac Austin	.576
Jamal Faulkner	.478
Tarence Wheeler	.387
Dwayne Fontana	.381
Stevin Smith	.336
Lynn Collins	.304
ARKANSAS (34-4)	
Oliver Miller	.724
Todd Day	.499

Ron Huery .... .498
Lee Mayberry .... .391
Arlyn Bowers .... .342

ARKANSAS STATE (23-9)
Fred Shepherd .... .512
Dewayne McCray .... .508
Bobby Gross .... .349
Philip McKellar .... .345
Brian Reaves .... .260

AUBURN (13-16)
Wesley Person .... .460
Robert McKie .... .443
John Caylor .... .416
Ronnie Battle .... .306
Reggie Gallon .... .299

BALL STATE (21-10)
Chandler Thompson .... .470
Keith Stalling .... .435
Emanuel Cross .... .403
Mike Spicer .... .317
Rodney Holmes .... .252

BAYLOR (12-15)
Kelvin Chalmers .... .451
David Wesley .... .416
Willie Sublett .... .391
Melvin Hunt .... .363
Joey Fatta .... .321

BOSTON COLLEGE (11-19)
Bill Curley .... .481
Doug Able .... .464
Bobby Moran .... .376
Gerrod Abram .... .338
Malcolm Huckaby .... .243
Howard Eisley .... .242

BRIGHAM YOUNG (21-13)
Shawn Bradley .... .652
Steve Schreiner .... .448
Kenneth Roberts .... .339
Mark Heslop .... .329
Scott Moon .... .300
Nathan Call .... .251

BUTLER (18-11)
Darin Archbold .... .511
J.P. Brens .... .435
Brett Etherington .... .426

John Karaffa .... .328
Jermaine Guice .... .323
Tim Bowen .... .293

CALIFORNIA (13-15)
Brian Hendrick .... .591
Roy Fisher .... .486
Billy Dreher .... .351
Bill Elleby .... .323
Sean Harrell .... .239

CINCINNATI (18-12)
Herbert Jones .... .528
Keith Starks .... .470
Louis Banks .... .413
Lavertis Robinson .... .362
Allen Jackson .... .319

CLEMSON (11-17)
Dale Davis .... .618
Ricky Jones .... .426
David Young .... .392
Eric Burks .... .251
Steve Harris .... .228

CONNECTICUT (20-11)
Scott Burrell .... .540
Rod Sellers .... .501
Chris Smith .... .415
Toraino Walker .... .385
John Gwynn .... .369

COLORADO (19-14)
Shaun Vandiver .... .632
Stevie Wise .... .363
Billy Law .... .350
House Guest .... .343
James Hunter .... .257

CREIGHTON (24-8)
Chad Gallagher .... .571
Bob Harstad .... .475
Duan Cole .... .374
Darin Plautz .... .342
Matt Petty .... .313

DE PAUL (20-9)
David Booth .... .534
Stephen Howard .... .510
Melvon Foster .... .321
Joe Daughrity .... .282
Terry Davis .... .265

DUKE (32-7)
Christian Laettner .... .695
Thomas Hill .... .478
Grant Hill .... .464
Brian Davis .... .340
Billy McCaffrey .... .332
Bobby Hurley .... .326

EAST TENNESSEE STATE (28-5)
Keith Jennings .... .631
Rodney English .... .555
Calvin Talford .... .392
Marty Story .... .336
Alvin West .... .318

FLORIDA STATE (21-11)
Doug Edwards .... .484
Michael Polite .... .440
Rodney Dobard .... .427
Charlie Ward .... .410
Chuck Graham .... .338
Aubry Boyd .... .288

FORDHAM (25-8)
Damon Lopez .... .682
Sanford Jenkins .... .403
Fred Herzog .... .365
Jean Prioleau .... .342
Dave Buckner .... .311
Jay Fazande .... .234

GEORGETOWN (19-13)
Dikembe Mutombo .... .841
Alonzo Mourning .... .696
Joey Brown .... .301
Robert Churchwell .... .279
Charles Harrison .... .250
Lamont Morgan .... .244

GEORGIA (17-13)
Litterial Green .... .489
Marshall Wilson .... .456
Antonio Harvey .... .405
Rod Cole .... .388
Neville Austin .... .327

GEORGIA TECH (17-13)
Kenny Anderson .... .514
Malcolm Mackey .... .498
Matt Geiger .... .426
Jon Barry .... .359

Ivano Newbill .... .314
Bryan Hill .... .257

HOUSTON (18-14)
Alvaro Teheran .... .501
Derrick Smith .... .433
Darrell Mickens .... .425
Byron Smith .... .315
Roger Fernandes .... .298
Derrick Daniels .... .293

ILLINOIS (21-10)
Deon Thomas .... .506
Andy Kaufmann .... .489
Larry Smith .... .442
Andy Kpedi .... .354
Rennie Clemons .... .302

INDIANA (29-5)
Calbert Cheaney .... .657
Eric Anderson .... .497
Damon Bailey .... .430
Jamal Meeks .... .387
Matt Nover .... .372

IOWA (21-11)
Acie Earl .... .560
James Moses .... .391
Troy Skinner .... .366
Val Barnes .... .300
Kevin Smith .... .282

IOWA STATE (12-19)
Victor Alexander .... .709
Doug Collins .... .429
Paul Doerrfeld .... .345
Justus Thigpen .... .278
Brian Pearson .... .158

JAMES MADISON (19-10)
Chancellor Nichols .... .560
Jeff Chambers .... .382
Steve Hood .... .364
Billy Coles .... .346
Fess Irvin .... .283

KANSAS (27-8)
Alonzo Jamison .... .567
Mark Randall .... .543
Terry Brown .... .453
Adonis Jordan .... .444
Mike Maddox .... .361

KANSAS STATE (13-15)
Wylie Howard .... .487
Jeff Wires .... .454
Maurice Brittian .... .441
Keith Amerson .... .404
Jean Derouillere .... .373
Marcus Zeigler .... .282

KENTUCKY (22-6)
Jamal Mashburn .... .539
Reggie Hanson .... .534
Deron Feldhaus .... .468
John Pelphrey .... .404
Jeff Brassow .... .338
Richie Farmer .... .330
Sean Woods .... .325

LA SALLE (19-10)
Randy Woods .... .436
Doug Overton .... .413
Jack Hurd .... .394
Milko Lieverst .... .337
Broderick President .... .324

LOUISIANA STATE (20-10)
Shaquille O'Neal .... .946
Shawn Griggs .... .418
Vernel Singleton .... .398
Harold Boudreaux .... .357
T.J. Pugh .... .329
Mike Hansen .... .262

LOUISIANA TECH (21-10)
P.J. Brown .... .628
Ron Ellis .... .572
Anthony Dade .... .444
Eric Brown .... .292
Reni Mason .... .257

LOUISVILLE (14-16)
Cornelius Holden .... .524
LaBradford Smith .... .436
Everick Sullivan .... .378
Troy Smith .... .354
Derwin Webb .... .350
James Brewer .... .327

LOYOLA MARYMOUNT (16-15)
Richard Petruska .... .524
Terrell Lowery .... .509
Craig Holt .... .346

John O'Connell .... .290
Christian Scott .... .243

MARSHALL (14-14)
Tyrone Phillips .... .512
John Taft .... .490
Brett Vincent .... .259
Andre Cunningham .... .255
Eric Clay .... .247

MARYLAND (16-12)
Walt Williams .... .496
Cedric Lewis .... .460
Garfield Smith .... .429
Matt Roe .... .365
Vince Broadnax .... .320
Kevin McLinton .... .287

MASSACHUSETTS (20-13)
Harper Williams .... .613
William Herndon .... .493
Tony Barbee .... .394
Rafer Giles .... .351
John Tate .... .307
Anton Brown .... .296
Jim McCoy .... .295

MEMPHIS STATE (17-15)
Kelvin Allen .... .498
Elliot Perry .... .470
Ernest Smith .... .381
Todd Mundt .... .357
Tony Madlock .... .340

MICHIGAN (14-15)
Eric Riley .... .518
Demetrius Calip .... .440
Kirk Taylor .... .422
Michael Talley .... .330
Sam Mitchell .... .315

MICHIGAN STATE (19-11)
Steve Smith .... .583
Mike Peplowski .... .547
Matt Steigenga .... .465
Mark Montgomery .... .353
Parish Hickman .... .298
Dwayne Stephens .... .255

MINNESOTA (12-16)
Kevin Lynch .... .502
Dana Jackson .... .410

Randy Carter .... .389
Walter Bond .... .386
Arriel McDonald .... .349

MISSISSIPPI STATE (20-9)
Greg Carter .... .533
Tony Watts .... .490
Cameron Burns .... .435
Todd Merritt .... .370
Doug Hartsfield .... .308

MISSOURI (20-10)
Doug Smith .... .667
Anthony Peeler .... .513
Jamal Coleman .... .407
Jeff Warren .... .321
Melvin Booker .... .238

MURRAY STATE (24-9)
Popeye Jones .... .739
John Jackson .... .461
Greg Coble .... .358
Paul King .... .304
Frank Allen .... .247

NEBRASKA (26-8)
Rich King .... .611
Tony Farmer .... .492
Eric Piatkowski .... .483
Carl Hayes .... .452
Beau Reid .... .323
Clifford Scales .... .323

NEVADA-LAS VEGAS (34-1)
Larry Johnson .... .828
Stacey Augmon .... .629
Greg Anthony .... .483
George Ackles .... .438
Anderson Hunt .... .395

NEW MEXICO (20-10)
Luc Longley .... .656
Willie Banks .... .403
Rob Robbins .... .351
Jimmy Taylor .... .314
Ike Williams .... .257

NEW MEXICO STATE (23-6)
Reggie Jordan .... .492
Tracey Ware .... .455
Randy Brown .... .407

William Benjamin .... .384
Michael New .... .362

NEW ORLEANS (23-8)
Ervin Johnson .... .683
Tank Collins .... .468
Melvin Simon .... .428
Dwight Myvett .... .366
Louweegi Dyer .... .305
Cass Clarke .... .270

NORTH CAROLINA STATE (20-11)
Tom Gugliotta .... .438
Rodney Monroe .... .420
Chris Corchiani .... .416
Kevin Thompson .... .375
Bryant Feggins .... .341

NORTHERN ILLINOIS (25-6)
Donnell Thomas .... .599
Andrew Wells .... .555
Antwon Harmon .... .377
Mike Lipnisky .... .350
Donald Whiteside .... .316
Mike Hidden .... .311

OHIO STATE (27-4)
Jim Jackson .... .589
Treg Lee .... .535
Perry Carter .... .508
Chris Jent .... .425
Mark Baker .... .395
Jamaal Brown .... .378

OKLAHOMA (20-15)
Jeff Webster .... .495
Roland Ware .... .453
Kermit Holmes .... .439
Brent Price .... .401
Terrence Mullins .... .284
Terry Evans .... .247

OKLAHOMA STATE (24-8)
Byron Houston .... .768
Johnny Pittman .... .412
John Potter .... .404
Corey Williams .... .386
Sean Sutton .... .372

OLD DOMINION (14-18)
Chris Gatling .... .773
Ricardo Leonard .... .406

Keith Jackson .... .385
John Robinson .... .257
Donald Anderson .... .244

OREGON (13-15)
Terrell Brandon .... .532
Richard Lucas .... .442
Bob Fife .... .375
Jordy Lyden .... .293
Kevin Mixon .... .263

OREGON STATE (14-14)
Chad Scott .... .454
Mario Jackson .... .439
Teo Alibegovic...................... .436
Will Brantley .... .418
Charles McKinney .... .302

PENN STATE (21-11)
James Barnes .... .534
Monroe Brown .... .394
DeRon Hayes........................ .393
Freddie Barnes .... .351
Dave Degitz .... .297

PEPPERDINE (22-9)
Doug Christie .... .530
Geoff Lear .... .515
Dana Jones .... .481
Steve Guild .... .249
Rick Welch .... .239

PITTSBURGH (21-12)
Darelle Porter .... .519
Bobby Martin .... .468
Brian Shorter .... .459
Jason Matthews..................... .414
Sean Miller......................... .341

PRINCETON (24-3)
Kit Mueller .... .574
Chris Marquardt .... .533
Sean Jackson .... .382
George Leftwich .... .283
Chris Mooney .... .271

PROVIDENCE (19-13)
Eric Murdock .... .575
Marques Bragg...................... .500
Dickie Simpkins .... .448
Marvin Saddler .... .388
Chris Watts .... .232

PURDUE (17-12)
Chuckie White .... .633
Jimmy Oliver .... .544
Matt Painter .... .305
Linc Darner .... .261
Dave Barrett .... .225

RICE (16-14)
Brent Scott .... .553
Kenneth Rourke .... .404
Dana Hardy .... .322
Chase Maag .... .308
Marvin Moore .... .295

RUTGERS (19-10)
Keith Hughes .... .488
Brent Dabbs .... .404
Daryl Smith .... .346
Mike Jones .... .339
Earl Duncan .... .332
Craig Carter .... .248

ST. JOHN'S (23-9)
Malik Sealy .... .592
Robert Werdann .... .510
Jason Buchanan..................... .426
Billy Singleton .... .337
Chucky Sproling .... .224

ST. PETER'S (24-7)
Tony Walker........................ .496
Marvin Andrews .... .414
Jasper Walker .... .408
John Connell .... .318
Antoine Allen .... .272

SETON HALL (25-9)
Anthony Avent .... .615
Terry Dehere .... .433
Jerry Walker .... .404
Arturas Karnishovas .... .386
Oliver Taylor .... .356
Gordon Winchester .... .332

SIENA (25-10)
Marc Brown .... .469
Lee Matthews .... .426
Steve Downey .... .393
Mike Brown .... .374
Bruce Schroeder .... .335
Tom Huerter .... .285

SOUTH ALABAMA (22-9)
Kevin McDaniels .... .406
Marvin Eackles .... .403
Bobby Curtis .... .388
Cesar Portillo........................ .378
Cedric Yelding........................ .282

SOUTH CAROLINA (20-13)
Jeff Roulston .... .522
Joe Rhett .... .460
Jo Jo English .... .421
Barry Manning .... .379
Michael Glover .... .317

SOUTHERN CALIFORNIA (19-10)
Ronnie Coleman .... .517
Harold Miner......................... .472
Robert Pack .... .414
Mark Boyd .... .327
Duane Cooper .... .303

SOUTHERN MISSISSIPPI (21-8)
Clarence Weatherspoon .... .617
Daron Jenkins .... .425
Darrin Chancellor .... .327
Russell Johnson...................... .316
Bernard Haslett .... .314

SOUTH FLORIDA (19-11)
Gary Alexander .... .495
Fred Lewis .... .448
Radenko Dobras .... .331
Tony Armstrong .... .275
Bobby Russell .... .231

STANFORD (20-13)
Adam Keefe .... .583
Andrew Vlahov .... .497
Deshon Wingate .... .416
Kenny Ammann .... .397
John Patrick......................... .359

SYRACUSE (26-6)
Billy Owens .... .633
LeRon Ellis .... .524
Dave Johnson........................ .458
Adrian Autry .... .265
Michael Edwards..................... .190

TEMPLE (24-10)
Mark Macon .... .481
Donald Hodge .... .421

Mik Kilgore .... .411
Mark Strickland .... .367
Vic Carstarphen .... .318

TENNESSEE (12-22)
Allan Houston .... .469
Ronnie Reese .... .411
Carius Groves .... .395
Jay Price .... .346
Lang Wiseman........................ .340
Steve Rivers .... .322

TEXAS (23-9)
Locksley Collie .... .501
Dexter Cambridge.................... .488
Guillermo Myers .... .433
Joey Wright .... .388
Benford Williams .... .383
Teyon McCoy .... .299
Courtney Jeans .... .260

TEXAS-EL PASO (16-13)
Von Bennett .... .432
David Van Dyke .... .430
Johnny Melvin....................... .373
Mark McCall .... .302
Henry Hall .... .281
Gym Bico .... .249

TULSA (18-12)
Marcell Gordon .... .524
Reggie Shields .... .422
Alyn Thomsen .... .395
Michael Scott .... .378
Wade Jenkins .... .371

UCLA (23-9)
Don MacLean .... .563
Tracy Murray........................ .546
Keith Owens .... .448
Mitchell Butler .... .372
Darrick Martin .... .360
Gerald Madkins .... .333

UTAH (30-4)
Josh Grant .... .728
Walter Watts .... .550
Byron Wilson........................ .373
Jimmy Soto .... .320
Tyrone Tate .... .246

VANDERBILT (17-13)
Todd Milholland .... .466
Bruce Elder .... .464
Steve Grant .... .444
Scott Draud .... .429
Kevin Anglin .... .400
Charles Mayes .... .352

VILLANOVA (17-15)
Lance Miller .... .448
Aron Bain .... .388
Marc Dowdell .... .380
Greg Woodard .... .341
Chris Walker .... .312

VIRGINIA (21-12)
Bryant Stith .... .514
Kenny Turner .... .497
John Crotty .... .399
Ted Jeffries .... .342
Matt Blundin .... .240

WAKE FOREST (19-11)
Rodney Rogers .... .579
Robert Siler .... .439
Randolph Childress .... .436
Chris King .... .427
Anthony Tucker .... .390
Derrick McQueen .... .315

WASHINGTON (14-14)
Dion Brown .... .511
Doug Meekins .... .497
Brent Merritt .... .444
Mike Hayward .... .366
James French .... .184

WASHINGTON STATE (16-12)
Bennie Seltzer .... .429
Terrence Lewis .... .418

Ken Critton .... .399
Rob Corkrum .... .399
Neil Derrick .... .325

WEST VIRGINIA (16-13)
Chris Brooks .... .539
Mike Boyd .... .440
Pervires Greene .... .418
Chris Leonard .... .377
Charles Becton .... .366
Jeremy Bodkin .... .348

WISCONSIN (15-15)
Patrick Tompkins .... .555
Willie Simms .... .470
Tim Locum .... .378
John Ellenson .... .318
Larry Hisle .... .297

WISCONSIN-GREEN BAY (24-7)
Tony Bennett .... .567
Dean Vander Plas .... .369
John Martinez .... .338
Dean Rondorf .... .325
Ben Johnson .... .285

WYOMING (20-12)
Reggie Slater .... .555
Reggie Page .... .405
Mo Alexander .... .357
Paris Bryant .... .323
Tim Breaux .... .322

XAVIER (22-10)
Brian Grant .... .459
Aaron Williams .... .387
Jamal Walker .... .384
Michael Davenport .... .364
Jamie Gladden .... .346

ABSTRACTION 9

Born in the U.S.A.

When Shaquille O'Neal turns professional, he will become a rarity in the National Basketball Association—an American-born big man.

Nearly all of the other highly regarded 7-footers who could be entering the NBA in 1991, 1992, or 1993 have made it by round-about routes. The top ones are:

1. DIKEMBE MUTOMBO of Zaire, one of the top prospects in the college draft of 1991. The 7-foot-2 Mutombo started out at Georgetown as a clumsy backup to Alonzo Mourning, but surpassed Mourning as a pro prospect during the past year.

2. LUC LONGLEY of Australia, a lottery selection in 1991 from New Mexico. Longley has been compared with Bill Walton. He isn't as quick or skilled as Walton was, but he is an agile big man who handles the ball well and is an excellent shot-blocker.

3. ALVARO TEHERAN of Colombia, a fast-developing 7-footer with grace and talent who played college ball at Houston. With experience, he could become a good NBA center. But he's probably three years away.

4. CHARLES CLAXTON of the Virgin Islands. This is a young man you may not have heard much about, but you will this season if he makes his grades. He's a 7-foot-1 sophomore at the University of Georgia.

5. ARVIDAS SABONIS of the Soviet Union. Someday an NBA team that lacks a 7-footer is going to get smart and make a deal with the Portland Trail Blazers for his draft rights. The Trail Blazers have shown little interest in signing the 7-foot-3 Sabonis, who is the best big man in the world outside of the United States.

These are the best of the potential future NBA big men, but they are by no means the only good foreign-born 7-footers. Most of the top big men already in the NBA are from exotic places:

◇ HAKEEM OLAJUWON, the NBA's best rebounding and shot-blocking center, from Nigeria.

◇ PATRICK EWING, the 7-footer with the best low-post moves in the NBA, from Jamaica.

◇ RONY SEIKALY of Greece, one of the quickest young centers in the NBA.

◇ VLADE DIVAC of Yugoslavia, a developing third-year player with star potential.

◇ RIK SMITS of Holland, who may never be a star, but should be a better-than-average big man during the 1990's.

And then there is David Robinson, the world's best all-around center. Robinson is from Key West. That's a suburb of Havana, Cuba, isn't it?

3
NBA Award Winners

For only the third time in NBA history, TENDEX had difficulty selecting the outstanding player for the 1990–91 NBA season. It happened in 1957–58 that Bill Russell was chosen as the league's top player even though Bob Pettit had a higher basic TENDEX rating. And in 1974–75, Bob McAdoo got the nod over Kareem Abdul-Jabbar under similar circumstances. This came about because Russell and McAdoo played more minutes and this made their overall productivity, based on performance and durability, superior to Pettit and Abdul-Jabbar, even though the latter had better TENDEX ratings.

The circumstances last season were different, although the situation was no less confused. David Robinson had the highest TENDEX rating in the NBA (.904) and also the highest productivity rating. So what's the big problem?

Just this: Michael Jordan's .881 TENDEX rating exceeded the norm for his position by much more than Robinson's .904.

Let me explain. The average rating for a center is .550, for a power forward .525, for a small forward .500, for a point guard .475, for a shooting guard .450. In other words, although Robinson had the highest rating in the league, his was 354 percentage points above average for his position whereas Jordan's was 431 above average for his position. The Bulls got more productivity out of the shooting guard position than the Spurs got out of the center position compared to the league norms. By this standard, Jordan was more valuable. And it didn't hurt his value that the Bulls had a much more successful season than the Spurs.

What we have here is two winners:

- ◇ DAVID ROBINSON—TENDEX Player of the Year.
- ◇ MICHAEL JORDAN—TENDEX Most Valuable Player.

The productivity rating, which includes the factors of performance and minutes played, has been used to select All-NBA players for each season. It is better in this respect than the pure TENDEX (performance only) rating because a player who plays 3,000 minutes deserves more credit than one who plays 2,000. Just by keeping himself on the court he is making himself more valuable to his team. The All-NBA teams are affected by only one player change using this method: Patrick Ewing, who had a lower TENDEX rating than Hakeem Olajuwon, makes the Second Team over Olajuwon because Hakeem was injured and played fewer minutes.

Here are the first three All-NBA teams for 1990–91 based on the TENDEX productivity rating:

FIRST TEAM

Position—Player, Team	Rating
C—DAVID ROBINSON, San Antonio	.813
F—KARL MALONE, Utah	.754
F—CHARLES BARKLEY, Philadelphia	.708
G—MICHAEL JORDAN, Chicago	.789
G—MAGIC JOHNSON, LA Lakers	.733

SECOND TEAM

C—PATRICK EWING, New York	.727
F—DENNIS RODMAN, Detroit	.565
F—LARRY NANCE, Cleveland	.629
F—JOHN STOCKTON, Utah	.685
G—CLYDE DREXLER, Portland	.633

THIRD TEAM

C—HAKEEM OLAJUWON, Houston	.686
F—DOMINIQUE WILKINS, Atlanta	.626
F—SCOTTIE PIPPEN, Chicago	.614
G—KEVIN JOHNSON, Phoenix	.638
G—TERRY PORTER, Portland	.606

Player of the Year: DAVID ROBINSON

Most Valuable Player: MICHAEL JORDAN

There are two players who appear to be out of place on the three teams. Drexler is listed on the Second Team even though his rating is five points lower than that of Kevin Johnson, a Third Team choice. But, remember, we are taking positions into consideration. The normal TENDEX rating for a shooting guard (.450) is 25 points lower than for a point guard (.475), so Drexler's rating is actually higher than Johnson's when it is considered that Clyde is a shooting guard and Kevin is a point man.

The other case is not so simple. Dennis Rodman's .565 rating is not nearly good enough for Second Team or even Third Team honors. In addition to the other five forwards listed here, he trails Chris Mullin, Detlef Schrempf, Larry Bird, and Kevin McHale. However, these are All-NBA teams. The best players should be selected for these teams, counting *all* aspects of play.

For the first time this past season, I thought of a way to compute the defensive play of a player such as Rodman. It isn't possible to keep track of how he does against every opponent through an 82-game season, but the NBA keeps track of playoff series totals, meaning it is possible to figure out how Rodman did against his principal playoff opponents— Wilkins, Pippen, and Bird.

It's particularly significant that in these series Rodman was matched against all-star caliber forwards. Overall, he held his opponents far below normal.

Wilkins, who had a .664 rating during the regular season, was held to .509 in the playoffs, mostly because of Rodman's defense. Rodman held Bird 221 points below his regular-season rating. Pippen played slightly better than his normal level. Adding a point total to Rodman's rating equal to the average of the number of points he held his opponents below normal makes him the third best forward in the NBA.

Here are the top ten players in the NBA for last season based on TENDEX ratings (minimum 2,000 minutes played):

Player, Team	Rating
1. David Robinson, San Antonio	.904
2. Michael Jordan, Chicago	.881
3. Hakeem Olajuwon, Houston	.867
4. Charles Barkley, Philadelphia	.833
5. Magic Johnson, LA Lakers	.818
6. Karl Malone, Utah	.808
7. Patrick Ewing, New York	.793
8. John Stockton, Utah	.739
9. Kevin Johnson, Phoenix	.699
10. Clyde Drexler, Portland	.686

All other factors being equal, these players—and Rodman who, counting defense, has a rating slightly below Stockton's—are the best in the NBA. Olajuwon is a better player than Ewing, but lost two months of playing time because of a misdirected elbow to the temple by Chicago's Bill Cartwright. It is arguable that Olajuwon remains a better center than Robinson for the same reason that Rodman is better than Wilkins, Nance, Pippen, Mullin, etc: Defense. In head-to-head matchups against Ewing and Robinson, Olajuwon usually comes out on top simply because he plays better defense than his two principal opponents, who are better offensive players than he is.

Most players refuse to compare their opponents—not wanting to get anyone angry at them. But Rony Seikaly has never been known for this kind of tact. You may recall he managed to insult the entire city of Charlotte when the Hornets drafted Rex Chapman, leaving Seikaly to be selected by the Miami Heat. During the 1990–91 season, Seikaly brazenly stated that Olajuwon was the best center in the NBA.

Last season was not a great one for rookies, but there were two who stood out, Derrick Coleman and Lionel Simmons. These two clearly were the best of the rookies. They played the most minutes and performed with the best efficiency and skill. This was the TENDEX All-Rookie team (minimum of 1,500 minutes played):

Position—Player, Team	Rating
C—FELTON SPENCER, Minnesota	.540
F—DERRICK COLEMAN, New Jersey	.614
F—LIONEL SIMMONS, Sacramento	.549
G—KENDALL GILL, Charlotte	.501
G—GARY PAYTON, Seattle	.467

Rookie of the Year: DERRICK COLEMAN

There is no Second Team because there were no other rookies worthy of recognition. Yes, I know that Dennis Scott and Travis Mays and Chris Jackson scored more points than Gill and Payton, but as balanced players they were not in the same class. Other than score, they did little for their teams' positive good and much on the negative side. Ratings for these players were Mays .384, Scott .381, and Jackson .349.

This is one time when I say, "Thank goodness for TENDEX." It seems to be the only way to separate the real players from the hotshots. Willie Burton (TENDEX .402) and Dee

Brown (.419) played a little better than Scott, Mays, and Jackson, but not exceptionally well. With the exception of Jackson, however, all of these players do have potential to be successful in the NBA. In Jackson's case, it would take a miraculous turn-around, especially at the defensive end of the court.

The 1991–92 group of rookies will be better than the 1990–91 group, both in quality and quantity. Headed by Larry Johnson and Dikembe Mutombo, both of whom would have been selected ahead of Coleman if they had been in last year's draft, here are the top ten:

1. LARRY JOHNSON—A Charles Barkley clone, probably the best draftee since David Robinson in 1987.

2. DIKEMBE MUTOMBO—An inexperienced player, but someday he may be compared with Bill Russell and Dennis Rodman in the category of best-defensive-players-of-all-time.

3. BILLY OWENS—The latest, and perhaps the best, of a succession of recent Syracuse players including Coleman, Rony Seikaly, and Sherman Douglas.

4. KENNY ANDERSON—He's leaving school prematurely, after his sophomore season, so his durability is questionable; but in three or four years he'll be compared with the Magic Johnsons and Isiah Thomases of the NBA.

5. LUC LONGLEY—Handles the ball well for a 7-2 player, but isn't a wimp. He'll intimidate and block shots better than most NBA centers.

6. STEVE SMITH—At 6-7 he's a prototype NBA shooting guard. Lacks the explosiveness of a Clyde Drexler, but should be an excellent NBA player for a decade.

7. DOUG SMITH—He can run the floor and score better than most 6-9 players, but needs to become more aggressive on the boards to excel in the NBA.

8. ERIC MURDOCK—The second coming of Alvin Robertson. Despite his

25.6 scoring average as a college senior, he won't be a big scorer in the NBA. What he will do is drive opposing guards crazy with his defense and score off steals and forced turnovers.

9. DALE DAVIS—Had a great season as a college junior, slumped as a double-teamed senior. He isn't quick enough to be an offensive star, but could become one of the NBA's better rebounding and defensive power forwards.

10. TERRELL BRANDON—Don't be surprised if he has a better rookie season than Anderson. He's a strong 6-footer who will drive fearlessly against 7-footers. Does a lot of things like Tim Hardaway.

In the competition for the Sixth Man Award, these were the top players, according to TENDEX (minimum of 1,500 minutes played):

Player, Team	Rating
1. Kevin McHale, Boston	.665
2. Detlef Schrempf, Indiana	.617
3. Moses Malone, Atlanta	.601
4. Ricky Pierce, Seattle	.590
5. Mark Aguirre, Detroit	.555
6. Danny Ainge, Portland	.553
7. Dan Majerle, Phoenix	.515

Good cases could be made for McHale, Schrempf, Pierce, Ainge, and Majerle. Majerle is a defensive specialist. If you think his defense is as good as Rodman's, you might vote for him. Pierce played the shooting guard position, so his TENDEX rating was actually the most above the positional standard (140 points) of all seven candidates. Ainge was second in this category, 103 points above the shooting-guard norm. McHale had the highest TENDEX rating, and Schrempf played the most minutes and was right behind McHale in the ratings.

I have seen no evidence, statistical or otherwise, that Majerle's defense is good enough to overcome the kind of deficit that he has in comparative ratings with these players, so

that narrows it down to a choice among Pierce (who was clearly better than Ainge, playing the same position), Schrempf, and McHale. My suspicion is that Schrempf was given the official NBA award because McHale and Pierce had won it in the past. It's a very tough choice among these three, but on the basis of productivity, combining performance and durability, Pierce comes out with a slight edge over McHale and Schrempf. Pierce's productivity rating of .549 is 99 points above the average for his position. McHale comes out at .585 (plus-60) and Schrempf at .577 (plus-52).

Ricky Pierce is the TENDEX Sixth Man of the Year.

There also was good competition for the TENDEX Most Improved Award. Eight players improved their TENDEX ratings by more than 100 points while also increasing their minutes played. These were the eight, in order of TENDEX ratings:

Player, Team	Rating
1. Scottie Pippen, Chicago	.651
2. Pervis Ellison, Washington	.618
3. Michael Adams, Denver	.617
4. Tim Hardaway, Golden State	.612
5. Scott Skiles, Orlando	.559
6. Kenny Smith, Houston	.556
7. Harvey Grant, Washington	.555
8. Kevin Gamble, Boston	.483

These ratings mean little in themselves, because improvement must be determined by comparing these ratings with ratings for the 1989–90 season. Pippen gained 123 points (from .528 to .651), Ellison 176 points (from .442 to .618), Adams 168 (from .449 to .617), Smith 141 (from .415 to .556), Grant 134 (from .421 to .555), Skiles 115 (from .444 to .559), Hardaway 102 (from .510 to .612) and Gamble 101 (from .382 to .483).

Of the eight players, Pippen and Hardaway were by far the most productive in 1990–91. They played the most minutes and had the best productivity ratings. But this award goes to the most improved player, and neither Pippen nor Hardaway was the most improved.

The most improved was Ellison, who had a terrible rookie season after being drafted No. 1 by Sacramento in 1989—so bad that the Kings traded him to the Bullets. He not only increased his TENDEX rating by 176 points last season, with excellent shot-blocking and rebounding, but also more than doubled his minutes played from his rookie season.

Pervis Ellison is the TENDEX Most Improved Player.

Maybe the Kings should rehire Bill Russell, whom they fired at least in part for drafting Ellison, and fire whoever was responsible for trading Pervis. Trading a potentially outstanding player without giving him more than one season to prove himself is not the wisest move an NBA executive can make.

During recent seasons, there has been a steady increase in the number of players playing more than 3,000 minutes. During the playoffs last spring, Commissioner David Stern said he had been discussing this as a potential problem for the league because a tired player is an injury-prone player.

"And," said Stern, "these players are our league."

Stern is right. The best players are singled out for heavy playing duty. And it's true not only that tired players are susceptible to injury, but also that they do not perform up to their best ability. Golden State and Minnesota both had three players with more than 3,000 minutes last season. Here's a full list of the 3,000-minute players:

Player, Team	Minutes
1. Chris Mullin, Golden State	3315
2. Karl Malone, Utah	3302
3. Tim Hardaway, Golden State	3215
4. Tyrone Corbin, Minnesota	3196
5. Pooh Richardson, Minnesota	3154
6. Sam Mitchell, Minnesota	3121
7. Hersey Hawkins, Philadelphia	3110
8. Patrick Ewing, New York	3104
9. John Stockton, Utah	3103
10. David Robinson, San Antonio	3095
11. Dominique Wilkins, Atlanta	3078
12. Joe Dumars, Detroit	3046

Player, Team	Minutes
13. Sean Elliott, San Antonio	3044
14. Otis Thorpe, Houston	3039
15. Michael Jordan, Chicago	3034
16. Mitch Richmond, Golden State	3027
17. James Worthy, LA Lakers	3008

The TENDEX system is based on minutes played rather than games played. It is much better to determine statistical champions based on what they do per minute of playing time than to figure it per-game. Provided, of course, that the qualifying minimum of 2,000 minutes played is met. These were the outstanding players for the 1990-91 season in major statistical categories:

Category	Player, Team	Per-Minute
2FG%:	Charles Barkley, Philadelphia	.614
3FG%:	Jim Les, Sacramento	.461
FT%:	Reggie Miller, Indiana	.918
Rebounds:	Dennis Rodman, Detroit	.373
Assists:	John Stockton, Utah	.375
Steals:	Alvin Robertson, Milwaukee	.095
Turnovers:	Rod Higgins, Golden State	.032
Blocks:	Hakeem Olajuwon, Houston	.107
Points:	Michael Jordan, Chicago	.850

Les did not play 2,000 minutes, but met the minimum requirement by attempting more than 100 three-point shots. There were close races in several categories, the closest being rebounds, in which Rodman edged Olajuwon by .0001; and turnovers, in which Higgins finished ahead of Byron Scott by .0002.

Manute Bol averaged .162 blocked shots per minute, but played only 1,522 minutes. The only categories in which a minimum of playing time was not required were the shooting categories, in which there were minimums for shot attempts.

The TENDEX method for selecting the Coach of the Year is to compare each team's TENDEX rating with its won-loss record. The team with the record which most exceeds the composite ratings of its players is the one that has over-achieved the most, thanks primarily to excellent coaching. These were the top coaches of the 1990–91 season, according to this standard:

Coach, Team	Rating
1. Paul Westhead, Denver	+9
2. Jim Lynam, Philadelphia	+8
Matt Guokas, Orlando	+8
Bob Weiss, Atlanta	+8
5. Don Nelson, Golden State	+5
Don Chaney, Houston	+5
7. Del Harris, Milwaukee	+3
8. Mike Dunleavy, LA Lakers	+2.5
Rick Adelman, Portland	+2.5
10. Chuck Daley, Detroit	+1
11. Jerry Sloan, Utah	+1

Although there are ties listed for several positions on this list, there are actually shadings of difference between the ratings. For example, the rating for Lynam is actually 8.2, while Guokas is 8.0 and Weiss is 7.8, although they are listed as exactly tied. The reason rounded-off numbers are used is that it isn't easy to explain how a team can win 8.2 games. The exception is one-half, because in this case it isn't easy to tell whether the higher or lower whole number should be used.

The shadings of difference in the ratings of Guokas, Weiss, and Lynam are important because, even though Denver did win 20 games while its player talent merited only 11 wins, the Nuggets still wound up with the league's worst record. And for every bit of good strategy employed by Westhead to win these extra games, he made worse mistakes in player personnel decisions. He had a hand in deciding what the Nuggets' final roster looked like and, if it resembled his previous college team, Loyola Marymount, in having an abundance of offensively-minded players who couldn't play much defense, that was Westhead's fault. He doesn't belong on the list of top coaches at all.

Jim Lynam is the TENDEX Coach of the Year for directing a below-average Philadelphia team to 44 victories, including a record-tying eight in overtime, plus a first-round playoff upset over Milwaukee.

About 400 players played for the 27 NBA teams during the 1990–91 season. These were the top 100, according to TENDEX ratings, who played at least 2,000 minutes:

Player, Team	TENDEX
1. David Robinson, San Antonio	.904
2. Michael Jordan, Chicago	.881
3. Hakeem Olajuwon, Houston	.867
4. Charles Barkley, Philadelphia	.833
5. Magic Johnson, LA Lakers	.818
6. Karl Malone, Utah	.808
7. Patrick Ewing, New York	.793
8. John Stockton, Utah	.739
9. Kevin Johnson, Phoenix	.699
10. Clyde Drexler, Portland	.686
11. Robert Parish, Boston	.686
12. Larry Nance, Cleveland	.676
13. Brad Daugherty, Cleveland	.668
14. Kevin McHale, Boston	.665
15. Dominique Wilkins, Atlanta	.664
16. Terry Porter, Portland	.659
17. Scottie Pippen, Chicago	.651
18. Larry Bird, Boston	.635
19. Vlade Divac, LA Lakers	.632
20. Michael Adams, Denver	.617
21. Detlef Schrempf, Indiana	.617
22. Derrick Coleman, New Jersey	.614
23. Tim Hardaway, Golden State	.612
24. Chris Mullin, Golden State	.609
25. Antoine Carr, Sacramento	.609
26. Shawn Kemp, Seattle	.609
27. Otis Thorpe, Houston	.605
28. Benoit Benjamin, Seattle	.601
29. Alvin Robertson, Milwaukee	.598
30. Dennis Rodman, Detroit	.595
31. Ricky Pierce, Seattle	.590
32. Charles Smith, LA Clippers	.590
33. Reggie Miller, Indiana	.585
34. Bernard King, Washington	.583
35. Danny Manning, LA Clippers	.580
36. Rony Seikaly, Miami	.579
37. Buck Williams, Portland	.576
38. Bill Laimbeer, Detroit	.573
39. Sherman Douglas, Miami	.567
40. Horace Grant, Chicago	.565
41. Scott Skiles, Orlando	.559
42. Charles Oakley, New York	.559
43. Terry Cummings, San Antonio	.557
44. Kenny Smith, Houston	.556
45. Harvey Grant, Washington	.555
46. Mark Aguirre, Detroit	.555
47. Derek Harper, Dallas	.554
48. Ken Norman, LA Clippers	.549

49. Lionel Simmons, Sacramento ...... .549
50. Jeff Hornacek, Phoenix .... .544
51. Felton Spencer, Minnesota .... .540
52. Jay Humphries, Milwaukee .... .536
53. Pooh Richardson, Minnesota ...... .535
54. Joe Dumars, Detroit .... .534
55. Hersey Hawkins, Philadelphia ..... .534
56. Tyrone Corbin, Minnesota .... .533
57. Dan Schayes, Milwaukee .... .531
58. Jerome Kersey, Portland .... .529
59. Eddie Johnson, Seattle .... .526
60. James Worthy, LA Lakers .... .525
61. Rod Strickland, San Antonio ...... .522
62. Mitch Richmond, Golden State .... .522
63. Kevin Willis, Atlanta .... .522
64. Rodney McCray, Dallas .... .520
65. Tom Chambers, Phoenix .... .520
66. Sam Perkins, LA Lakers .... .515
67. Dan Majerle, Phoenix .... .515
68. Tyrone Bogues, Charlotte .... .514
69. Derrick McKey, Seattle .... .513
70. Xavier McDaniel, Phoenix .... .512
71. Armon Gilliam, Philadelphia ...... .504
72. Chuck Person, Indiana .... .503
73. Chris Morris, New Jersey .... .502
74. Darrell Walker, Washington .... .497
75. Brian Shaw, Boston .... .496
76. Olden Polynice, LA Clippers ...... .493
77. Mike Gminski, Charlotte .... .483
78. Kevin Gamble, Boston .... .483
79. Reggie Lewis, Boston .... .481
80. Spud Webb, Atlanta .... .480
81. Grant Long, Miami .... .479
82. Rolando Blackman, Dallas .... .476
83. Glen Rice, Miami .... .472
84. Gary Payton, Seattle .... .467
85. Michael Cage, Seattle .... .467
86. Ron Anderson, Philadelphia .... .467
87. Tony Campbell, Minnesota .... .466
88. James Donaldson, Dallas .... .465
89. Sedale Threatt, Seattle .... .465
90. Doc Rivers, Atlanta .... .464
91. Maurice Cheeks, New York .... .462
92. A.C. Green, LA Lakers .... .459
93. Rick Mahorn, Philadelphia .... .459
94. Sean Elliott, San Antonio .... .458
95. Willie Anderson, San Antonio ..... .458
96. Gary Grant, LA Clippers .... .458
97. Johnny Newman, Charlotte .... .454
98. Rex Chapman, Charlotte .... .454
99. Kevin Duckworth, Portland .... .452
100. Reggie Theus, New Jersey .... .448

ABSTRACTION 10

Corporate Absurdities

Let's see if I can remember all the NBA awards.

There is the Schick Pivotal Player of the Year, Master Lock Defensive Player of the Year, Edge Most Valuable Player, Digital Coach of the Year, Minute Maid Orange Soda Rookie of the Year, All-state Good Hands Award, American Airlines Most Improved Player, and Miller Lite Sixth Man Award.

Some of the awards are as ridiculous as you might expect from the basketball expertise of the corporations awarding them.

For example, one of the statistics included in the good-hands award is rebounding. Now, anybody with a grain of basketball savvy knows that the best rebounders often have the worst hands. Do you think any point guard would want to trade hands with Swen Nater or Moses Malone or Charles Oakley?

Then there is the muddled Schick award, which is pivotal only in the frequency with which it turns on its own axis. For years Schick has been trying to come up with a "computer formula" that actually works. Trouble is, if you feed junk into a computer, you get you-know-what back out.

The latest Schick formula includes something silly called team-wins-times-10. It includes field goals attempted, but not free-throws attempted. It has personal fouls on both sides of the equation. The whole formula is multiplied by 250 (Is that a magic number?).

No wonder Schick has come up with players like Darrell Walker, Michael Cage and Buck Williams among its leaders during the past few seasons.

It might help if Schick would compare players on a league-wide scale instead of comparing teammates with each other. But maybe the "computer" isn't smart enough to do that.

One of the most amusing computer systems appeared in *The Sporting News,* purporting to evaluate the best players in the 1990 NBA draft. No criteria were given other than the nebulous ones of "offensive rating," "defensive rating," "rebound rating" and "player rating."

To begin with, why rebounding? Why not scoring? Playmaking? Ball-handling? Shooting?

The ratings were arbitrary. They represented only the opinion of whoever was inputting the computer. In the final ratings, Derrick Coleman was listed behind Dennis Scott, Gerald Glass, Anthony Bonner and Bo Kimble. Chris Jackson was ahead of Lionel Simmons.

I suspect, though, that we haven't seen the end of "computer" ratings and awards. Here are a few we could see in the near future:

◇ Mr. Clean Award to the player with the fewest technical fouls

◇ Damper Pampers Award to the biggest crybaby

◇ Henry Fonda Award to the worst actor

◇ Boris Karloff Award to the meanest player

◇ Quasimodo Award to the ugliest player

◇ Burger King Whopper Award to the fattest player

◇ Energizer Award to the player who keeps going . . . and going . . . and going

4
Atlanta Hawks

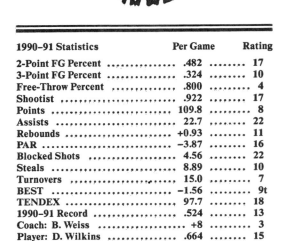

1990–91 Statistics	Per Game	Rating
2-Point FG Percent	.482	17
3-Point FG Percent	.324	10
Free-Throw Percent	.800	4
Shootist	.922	17
Points	109.8	8
Assists	22.7	22
Rebounds	+0.93	11
PAR	−3.87	16
Blocked Shots	4.56	22
Steals	8.89	10
Turnovers	15.0	7
BEST	−1.56	9t
TENDEX	97.7	18
1990–91 Record	.524	13
Coach: B. Weiss	+8	3
Player: D. Wilkins	.664	15
Rookie: S. Augmon	.629	12

For years there has been dissatisfaction in Atlanta over the performance of the Hawks. During the 1990–91 season, there came a new realization: The Hawks don't win because they are just not a very good team.

It took an excellent job by Bob Weiss, ranked by TENDEX as one of the top three coaches in the NBA, to produce a record (43-39) just over .500. But the player personnel isn't this good.

There is still Dominique Wilkins (can you believe he is starting his 10th season in the NBA?), better than ever at age 31. His TEN-DEX rating of .654 last season—second best

of his career—did not tell the full story. Wilkins sacrificed scoring for improvement in other aspects of play. He rebounded, passed, and defended better than at any other time in his career, but in the NBA a single player cannot do it alone.

Weiss got the most possible out of 36-year-old Moses Malone by using him as a sixth man playing about half of the time. Malone (TEN-DEX .601) was one of the better sixth men in the league.

A TENDEX Hall of Famer, Malone broke two NBA records last season, surpassing Oscar Robertson's NBA career mark of 7,694 free throws and Wilt Chamberlain's record of not fouling out in 1,045 consecutive games. Early this season, Moses should become the fourth player to score 28,000 points as a pro. He needs 92 points to join Kareem Abdul-Jabbar, Wilt Chamberlain, and Julius Erving in the 28,000-point club. Moses is the No. 3 active center with a career TENDEX rating of .707.

The other Hawks had below-average 1990–91 seasons. At 5-foot-7, Spud Webb needs to be an offensive force like Michael Adams or a defensive pest like Tyrone Bogues in order to justify his starting role. Last season he was neither. At critical moments of important games he seemed unable to make good decisions about distributing the ball. Too often he held onto it and tried to shoot over 7-footers instead of passing to open teammates. But Webb had to start because rookie Rumeal Robinson wasn't ready. The Hawks need dramatic improvement by Robinson or a new starting point guard.

Doc Rivers adapted well to playing the shooting guard position with Webb at the point. But there was another problem: Rivers is not a good shooter. Neither his scoring average (15.2) nor his field-goal percentage (.435) were impressive by shooting-guard standards. His TENDEX rating of .464 wasn't as good as 14 other starters at his position.

At power forward, Kevin Willis was just ordinary (TENDEX .522) and at center Jon Koncak's woeful .354 rating must have made Weiss wish Malone still had the durability he once had when he was playing 3,000-plus minutes per season.

Except for Malone, John Battle (TENDEX .456), and Sidney Moncrief (.366), there wasn't much bench depth. And it didn't help that Battle and Moncrief both were shooting guards, and aging ones at that.

This is a team in need of improvement at four positions and on the bench. Have patience, Hawk fans: With Rivers and Malone gone, your team is probably going to get a lot worse before it develops enough young talent to replace the elderly veterans.

Atlanta was fortunate to finish with the 13th best record in the NBA last season because its team TENDEX rating was only the 18th best in the league. Don't look for any repeat of this good fortune in 1991–92.

Probable finish: Seventh in Central Division.

DOMINIQUE WILKINS

AGE: 31
HEIGHT: 6-8
WEIGHT: 200
POSITION: Small Forward
EXPERIENCE: 9 Seasons
COLLEGE: Georgia
BIRTHPLACE: Sorbonne, France
1990–91 TENDEX: .664
POSITIONAL RATING: 2 of 30
CAREER TENDEX: .617

With consistency and durability, Wilkins has developed into one of the greatest scorers in professional basketball history. His career scoring average of 26.1 is No. 6 on the all-time NBA-ABA list and he should surpass the 20,000-point mark this season . . . if he scores 2,000 points in 1991–92 he'll tie Alex English for the record of eight straight seasons with at least 2,000 . . . seventh in the NBA in scoring last season (25.9) . . . a fine rebounder for a small forward, he had a career-best 732 rebounds last season and his average of 9.0 per game was 15th best in the league . . . also set personal career highs with 265 assists and 85 successful three-point shots . . . ranked second behind Charles Barkley among small forwards with a TENDEX rating of .664; career rating of .617 is No. 3 on the list of active small forwards . . . TENDEX All-NBA Third Team selection . . . TENDEX Hall of Famer.

SPUD WEBB

AGE: 28
HEIGHT: 5-7
WEIGHT: 135
POSITION: Point Guard
EXPERIENCE: 6 Seasons
COLLEGE: North Carolina State
BIRTHPLACE: Dallas
1990–91 TENDEX: .480
POSITIONAL RATING: 17 of 23
CAREER TENDEX: .504

Webb was forced into the role of starting point guard when Rivers was injured in 1989–90, won the job on his own last season . . . led Hawks in assists, but his average of 5.6 per game wasn't close to making the top 20 in the NBA . . . led Hawks in free-throw percentage (.868), ranking No. 17 in the league . . . although his TENDEX rating of .480 was five points above the norm for a point guard, it didn't compare well with other regular point men: Spud's rating was No. 17 out of 23 point guards.

WILKINS

1990–91	2PFG	3PFG	F.T.	REB.	AST.	STL.	T.O.	BLK.	PTS.
Per Game	.493	.341	.829	9.04	3.27	1.52	2.48	0.80	25.9
Per Minute	.493	.341	.829	.238	.086	.040	.065	.021	.683
Rating	19	5t	7	3	15t	10t	18	10t	3

WEBB

1990–91	2PFG	3PFG	F.T.	REB.	AST.	STL.	T.O.	BLK.	PTS.
Per Game	.480	.321	.868	2.32	5.56	1.57	1.95	0.08	13.4
Per Minute	.480	.321	.868	.079	.190	.054	.067	.003	.457
Rating	14t	11	4	19	19t	11	8	17	10

KEVIN WILLIS

AGE: 29
HEIGHT: 7-0
WEIGHT: 235
POSITION: Power Forward
EXPERIENCE: 6 Seasons
COLLEGE: Michigan State
BIRTHPLACE: Los Angeles
1990–91 TENDEX: .522
POSITIONAL RATING: 15 of 22
CAREER TENDEX: .533

Willis did not have a big season for the Hawks in 1990–91, at least he kept healthy enough to give them 2,373 minutes, his highest total in four years . . . averaged 8.8 rebounds per game, second behind Wilkins on the Hawks and 19th in the NBA . . . led Hawks in field-goal percentage (.504) . . . compared with 22 other regular power forwards, Willis is good in only one category, rebounding; he ranked second behind Charles Oakley last season, averaging .297 rebounds per minute . . . worst rankings were No. 21 in free-throw percentage, No. 19 in assists, No. 18 in blocked shots and No. 15 in TENDEX rating.

WILLIS

1990–91	2PFG	3PFG	F.T.	REB.	AST.	STL.	T.O.	BLK.	PTS.
Per Game	.505	.400	.668	8.80	1.24	0.75	1.91	0.50	13.1
Per Minute	.505	.400	.668	.297	.042	.025	.065	.017	.443
Rating	13	3	21	2	19	14	12	18	14

ABSTRACTION 11

The Two-Thousand Club

Dominique Wilkins scored 2,000 points for the seventh straight season in 1990–91, heading a list of six NBA players to score 2,000, including:

Player, Team	Points
1. Michael Jordan, Chicago	2,580
2. Karl Malone, Utah	2,382
3. Patrick Ewing, New York	2,154
4. Chris Mullin, Golden State	2,107
5. Dominique Wilkins, Atlanta	2,101
6. David Robinson, San Antonio	2,101

If Wilkins scores 2,000 points during the 1991–92 season, he'll tie a record set by Alex English with eight straight between 1982 and 1989.

By scoring 2,000 seven straight times, Wilkins tied the feats of Wilt Chamberlain and Oscar Robertson.

Jordan also is within striking distance of English's record with five straight seasons of 2,000 or more points.

But nobody is likely to touch the one-season scoring records of Wilt Chamberlain. Chamberlain is the only player ever to score 4,000 points. He did it in 1962 with a scoring average of 50.4. Chamberlain also holds the record of three seasons with more than 3,000 points.

The only other player to score 3,000 in a season, in the NBA or the ABA, was Jordan with 3,041 in 1986–87.

The record-holder for most seasons scoring at least 2,000 points is Kareem Abdul-Jabbar with nine. That record also could be challenged by Wilkins, who has seven, and Jordan, who has six.

Here's one for trivia buffs: Who was the first player to score 2,000 points in a season? Answer: George Yardley with 2,001 points in 1957–58.

Since that season there have been about five 2,000-point scorers per season in the NBA for a total of 159.

For those who would scoff at records set in the ABA, think again. Despite an 84-game schedule—two more games than the NBA—there were only 32 2,000-point scorers in the nine-year history of the ABA, an average of less than four per season. Julius Erving led the way with five 2,000-point seasons in the ABA.

Here is a list of all players who managed at least three 2,000-point seasons in the NBA and/or the ABA:

Player, League	Seasons
1. Kareem Abdul-Jabbar, NBA	9
2. Alex English, NBA	8
3. Dominique Wilkins, NBA	7
4. Wilt Chamberlain, NBA	7
5. Oscar Robertson, NBA	7
6. Julius Erving, ABA-NBA	7
7. Michael Jordan, NBA	6
8. George Gervin, NBA	6
9. Rick Barry, NBA-ABA	5
10. Jerry West, NBA	5
11. Bob Pettit, NBA	5
12. Elgin Baylor, NBA	5
13. Karl Malone, NBA	4
14. Elvin Hayes, NBA	4
15. Moses Malone, NBA	4
16. Bob McAdoo, NBA	4
17. Dan Issel, ABA	4
18. Adrian Dantley, NBA	4
19. Larry Bird, NBA	4
20. Mark Aguirre, NBA	3
21. George McGinnis, ABA	3
22. Bill Cunningham, NBA-ABA	3
23. David Thompson, NBA-ABA	3
24. Kiki Vandeweghe, NBA	3
25. Walt Bellamy, NBA	3
26. Lou Hudson, NBA	3
27. Pete Maravich, NBA	3
28. Nate Archibald, NBA	3

5
Boston Celtics

1990–91 Statistics	Per Game	Rating
2-Point FG Percent	.522	1
3-Point FG Percent	.315	17
Free-Throw Percent	.824	1
Shootist	.993	1
Points	111.5	6
Assists	26.3	8
Rebounds	+4.74	2
PAR	+11.9	5
Blocked Shots	6.89	3
Steals	8.20	16
Turnovers	16.1	14
BEST	−1.01	7
TENDEX	108.2	2
1990–91 Record	.683	4
Coach: C. Ford	−5	23t
Player: R. Parish	.686	10t
Rookie: R. Fox	NR	NR

It's a simple fact of life: With a healthy Larry Bird the Boston Celtics still can win 75 percent of their games. Without him they have to struggle to win 50 percent.

Another fact of life: Bird's days of being healthy are down to a precious few, if they aren't over.

Playing injured most of the 1990–91 season, Bird had a .635 TENDEX rating, lowest of his career. Two Celtics—Robert Parish (.686) and Kevin McHale (.665)—did better than that. But when Bird went out of the lineup it was as if the Celtics were missing an .800 player: They simply fell apart.

Why is Bird so important to the Celtics—as important perhaps as any player to any other team in the NBA? Intensity has something to do with it. So does versatility. Bird is probably the most intense and versatile player in NBA history. But most of all, it's leadership. With Bird out of the lineup, the Celtics can't seem to find anyone capable of running the team, and it has been that way for the past 12 years.

Yes, I know the point guard is supposed to be the man who runs the team, but the Celtics haven't had a good point guard since Bob Cousy. Dennis Johnson was the Celtics' nominal point guard for seven seasons. Holding that position now is the combination of Brian Shaw (TENDEX .496) and Dee Brown (.419). Both men are good defenders, but neither does a good job of directing an offense. Bird actually directs the team as the "point forward."

In Kevin Gamble (.483) and Reggie Lewis (.481), the Celtics have two respectable swing men, and Ed Pinckney is a good reserve power forward (.565), but this team sinks without Bird.

With Bird in the lineup for most of last season, the Celtics challenged Chicago for the best record in the Eastern Conference and played so well offensively that they almost became the first team in history to average one point for every shot taken—a statistic I call Shootist. They wound up averaging 0.9928 points per shot, which was still an NBA record, but the shooting of everyone except Parish fell off when Bird's injured back misbehaved late in the season.

Let me pretend I'm Red Auerbach for a moment. Eleven years ago, Auerbach swung an amazing trade with Golden State, obtaining Parish and draft rights to McHale without giving up anyone or anything of importance. Twenty-four years before that he obtained draft rights to Bill Russell in exchange for Cliff Hagan and Ed Macauley.

It could be time for the old redhead to strike again for a rookie draftee such as Larry Johnson or Dikembe Mutombo. If he can't swing a deal of this magnitude, he might do it for another available big man. The best players in this category are John Williams and Patrick Ewing. And don't forget about Arvidas Sabonis, the 7-foot-3 Lithuanian who has been playing professionally in Europe since outplaying David Robinson in the 1988 Olympic Games.

I'd be surprised if at least one of these five players does not wind up in a Celtic uniform within the near future. It wouldn't shock me to see a Ewing-Johnson-Williams starting Celtic frontcourt by the beginning of the 1992–93 season.

Rookie coach Chris Ford did not have a good TENDEX rating as the Celts won five fewer games than their player personnel indicated they should have won last season, but that may not have been all his fault. He was at the mercy of Bird's deteriorating physical condition. Even with Bird out, the Celtics' talent showed up as better than average. But they just couldn't play that way without their missing leader.

Don't expect them to do any better this season. They should once again win the weak Atlantic Division, but not with as many victories (56) as they had last season.

Probable finish: First in Atlantic Division.

LARRY BIRD

AGE: 35
HEIGHT: 6-9
WEIGHT: 220
POSITION: Small Forward
EXPERIENCE: 12 Seasons
COLLEGE: Indiana State
BIRTHPLACE: West Baden, IN
1990–91 TENDEX: .635
POSITIONAL RATING: 4 of 30
CAREER TENDEX: .762

The best small forward in professional basketball history had the lowest TENDEX rating of his career last season . . . still a fine player, the four-time TENDEX Player of the Year led the Celtics in scoring (19.4), steals (1.8) and three-point field-goal shooting (.389), making 70 percent of the team total of three-pointers . . . he was second on the team in rebounds (8.5) and second in assists (7.2), making him the only PAR-7 player in the NBA averaging more than seven points, rebounds and assists . . . had three triple-double games . . . the only player in history to make all-time lists in five of the six major categories (points, rebounds, assists, steals, and shooting percentages) . . . when Larry reached the 20,000-point and 5,000-assist plateaus last season, he became the fourth player in NBA history to total more than 20,000 points, 8,000 rebounds, and 5,000 assists for his career. Bird did it in 12 seasons. The other three players all needed 16 or 17 seasons.

KEVIN McHALE

AGE: 34
HEIGHT: 6-10
WEIGHT: 225
POSITION: Power Forward
EXPERIENCE: 11 Seasons
COLLEGE: Minnesota
BIRTHPLACE: Hibbing, MN
1990–91 TENDEX: .665
POSITIONAL RATING: 3 of 22
CAREER TENDEX: .654

McHale is still one of the best sixth men in the NBA, but the onus of not being able to play big minutes is still with him. Despite an assortment of injuries, teammate Larry Bird averaged 38 minutes per game when he was able to play at all last season. Typical of McHale, he averaged only 30 . . . but his efficiency continued to be excellent in his 11th NBA season . . . ranked eighth in the NBA in field-goal percentage (.553) . . . No. 1 among power forwards in blocked shots and free-throw percentage, No. 2 in two- and three-point field-goal percentages, No. 3 in TENDEX rating, and No. 4 in scoring . . . scored his 15,000th point during the 1990–91 season . . . career TENDEX rating of .654 is third among active power forwards . . . TENDEX Hall of Famer.

BIRD

1990–91	2PFG	3PFG	F.T.	REB.	AST.	STL.	T.O.	BLK.	PTS.
Per Game	.470	.341	.891	8.48	7.18	1.80	3.12	0.97	19.4
Per Minute	.470	.341	.891	.224	.189	.047	.082	.025	.511
Rating	25	5t	2t	5	1	6	27	8	15

McHALE

1990–91	2PFG	3PFG	F.T.	REB.	AST.	STL.	T.O.	BLK.	PTS.
Per Game	.559	.405	.829	7.06	1.85	0.37	2.06	2.15	18.4
Per Minute	.559	.405	.829	.232	.061	.012	.068	.071	.605
Rating	2	2	1	12	13	22	15t	1	4

ROBERT PARISH

AGE: 38
HEIGHT: 7-0
WEIGHT: 230
POSITION: Center
EXPERIENCE: 15 Seasons
COLLEGE: Centenary
BIRTHPLACE: Shreveport, LA
1990–91 TENDEX: .686
POSITIONAL RATING: 4 of 21
CAREER TENDEX: .688

Parish played amazingly well during his 15th NBA season, nearly matching his career TENDEX rating of .688. He has never been a 40-minute man, but he also nearly matched his career average of 31 minutes per game with his 30-minute average of last season . . . still an excellent shooter, he ranked No. 2 in the NBA in field-goal percentage (.598) . . . No. 1 among regular NBA centers in two-point field-goal percentage (.599) and No. 2 in rebounds per minute, behind Hakeem Olajuwon and ahead of David Robinson . . . No. 4 among centers in TENDEX rating . . . career rating is No. 4 among active centers with at least five years of experience . . . should score his 20,000th point this season . . . TENDEX Hall of Famer.

REGGIE LEWIS

AGE: 26
HEIGHT: 6-7
WEIGHT: 195
POSITION: Shooting Guard
EXPERIENCE: 4 Seasons
COLLEGE: Northeastern
BIRTHPLACE: Baltimore
1990–91 TENDEX: .481
POSITIONAL RATING: 10 of 27
CAREER TENDEX: .498

One of the surprises of the 1990–91 season for the Boston Celtics was that Reggie Lewis led the team in minutes played with 2,878 . . . the minutes may have taken a toll on Lewis, because his TENDEX rating of .481 was not up to the level of the two previous seasons, .523 and .501 . . . scoring average of 18.7 was second best on the Celts . . . ranked No. 1 out of 27 regular shooting guards in blocked shots, No. 6 in rebounds, No. 10 in two-point field-goal percentage, No. 10 in TENDEX rating, and No. 12 in scoring . . . needs to improve long-range shooting because he was last in three-point percentage (.077) and three-pointers made (one).

PARISH

1990–91	2PFG	3PFG	F.T.	REB.	AST.	STL.	T.O.	BLK.	PTS.
Per Game	.599	.000	.767	10.6	0.82	0.82	1.89	1.27	14.9
Per Minute	.599	.000	.767	.351	.027	.027	.063	.042	.494
Rating	1	12t	7	2	16	6	13	10	6

LEWIS

1990–91	2PFG	3PFG	F.T.	REB.	AST.	STL.	T.O.	BLK.	PTS.
Per Game	.495	.077	.826	5.19	2.54	1.24	1.86	1.08	18.7
Per Minute	.495	.077	.826	.142	.070	.034	.051	.030	.514
Rating	10	27	13	6	25	20	6	1	12

KEVIN GAMBLE

AGE: 26
HEIGHT: 6-5
WEIGHT: 215
POSITION: Small Forward
EXPERIENCE: 4 Seasons
COLLEGE: Iowa
BIRTHPLACE: Springfield, IL
1990–91 TENDEX: .483
POSITIONAL RATING: 22 of 30
CAREER TENDEX: .455

Gamble was one of eight regular players in the NBA who improved their TENDEX ratings by at least 100 points last season and he did it the hard way while playing nearly three times as many minutes as the season before. In fact, Gamble's total of 2,706 minutes nearly doubled his combined total (1,384) for the three previous seasons . . . finished second on the Celtics last season with a .587 field-goal percentage and third best in the NBA . . . at 6-5 he is very small for a forward, would perhaps be better suited to the shooting-guard position where he wouldn't be overmatched . . . TENDEX rating ranked No. 22 out of 30 small forwards, but the same rating would have placed him No. 10 among shooting guards.

GAMBLE

1990–91	2PFG	3PFG	F.T.	REB.	AST.	STL.	T.O.	BLK.	PTS.
Per Game	.592	.000	.815	3.26	3.12	1.22	1.80	0.42	15.6
Per Minute	.592	.000	.815	.099	.095	.037	.055	.013	.473
Rating	2	29	8	29	10t	13	11	19t	19

ABSTRACTION 12

Cornered Markets

The NBA may have 27 franchises, but most of them have little if any hope of winning a league title. Economics dictate that the league be dominated by about a half-dozen major commercial markets. The other cities will never have the broad TV exposure or economic base necessary to become powerhouses in the league.

Unless population statistics have changed radically during the past few years, the six biggest markets in the United States are the metropolitan areas of New York, Los Angeles, Chicago, Philadelphia, Detroit, and Boston.

Boston finally may have slipped behind Atlanta or Houston, but for most of the past 32 years, since the NBA began commanding national interest and generating television money in the 1959–60 season, the cities listed above have been the top six.

In those 32 years, these six cities have had 27 of the 32 champion teams. All except Chicago have won at least two titles. No other team has won more than once.

Here's a breakdown of the last 32 league champions:

Franchise	Titles
1. Boston Celtics	14
2. Los Angeles Lakers	6
3. Philadelphia 76ers	2
4. Detroit Pistons	2
5. New York Knicks	2
6. Portland Trail Blazers	1
7. Golden State Warriors	1
8. Washington Bullets	1
9. Seattle Supersonics	1
10. Milwaukee Bucks	1
11. Chicago Bulls	1

Portland, Washington, and Seattle won in successive seasons following the 1976 merger between the NBA and the ABA, when players from the ABA were distributed in such a way as to make the NBA a more balanced league. No non-major market franchise has won a title since 1979.

In Milwaukee's title season of 1970–71, the Bucks' key player was Kareem Abdul-Jabbar. Four years after winning a title with the Bucks, Abdul-Jabbar bluntly ordered them to trade him. Continuing to play in such an obscure city as Milwaukee was beneath the dignity of this man who had spent all of his life amid the glitter of New York and Los Angeles.

Golden State's MVP in 1974–75 was Rick Barry, a temperamental player who once had sat out a season rather than signing with the low-visibility Warriors, and then defected for four years to the ABA before grudgingly returning to the Warriors, who had stubbornly refused to relinquish their rights to him.

Want more proof? How much more often did you see the mediocre New York Knicks and Philadelphia 76ers on TV last season than superior teams from cities like Phoenix, Milwaukee, and Salt Lake City?

Here are the 10 best players in the NBA:

Player, Team	1991 TENDEX
1. David Robinson, San Antonio	.904
2. Michael Jordan, Chicago	.881
3. Hakeem Olajuwon, Houston	.867
4. Charles Barkley, Philadelphia	.833
5. Magic Johnson, LA Lakers	.818
6. Karl Malone, Utah	.808
7. Patrick Ewing, New York	.793
8. John Stockton, Utah	.739
9. Kevin Johnson, Phoenix	.699
10. Clyde Drexler, Portland	.686

Why do you suppose it is that David Robinson, Michael Jordan, Charles Barkley, Magic Johnson, and Patrick Ewing are among the best-known athletes in the world?

But ask the person on the street to identify Hakeem Olajuwon, Karl Malone, John Stockton, Kevin Johnson, and Clyde Drexler and what you are likely to get is a blank stare.

Why so much difference?

Look at the markets: Los Angeles, Chicago, New York, Philadelphia. The exception is Robinson, who has achieved fame despite low exposure in San Antonio. He's done it through national publicity of his U.S. Navy service and "Mr. Robinson's Neighborhood" commercials. He is the exception, but he does not disprove the rule.

6
Charlotte Hornets

1990–91 Statistics	Per Game	Rating
2-Point FG Percent	.477	19
3-Point FG Percent	.314	18
Free-Throw Percent	.779	9
Shootist	.911	18
Points	102.8	20
Assists	24.6	15
Rebounds	−5.34	26
PAR	−12.1	26
Blocked Shots	3.71	27
Steals	9.26	7
Turnovers	15.7	10
BEST	−2.77	21
TENDEX	94.2	24
1990–91 Record	.317	23t
Coach: G. Littles	0	12t
Player: T. Bogues	.514	68
Rookie: L. Johnson	.828	1

Of the four expansion teams, the Hornets have done the poorest job of stocking themselves with players for the future.

They have a respectable backcourt, with point guards Tyrone Bogues (TENDEX .514) and Kendall Gill (.501) and shooting guards Dell Curry (.529) and Rex Chapman (.454). Gill, a TENDEX All-Rookie selection, has a chance with normal improvement to become a legitimate star. But of all NBA teams, this one has the weakest frontcourt.

J.R. Reid (.404) seems to be regressing rather than progressing after two NBA seasons. The other principal frontcourt players of 1990–91—Johnny Newman (.454), Mike Gminski (.483), and Kelly Tripucka (.463)—are either on their way down or already out.

It might help a little to give more playing time to rugged power forward Kenny Gattison. The 27-year-old Gattison never has been given an opportunity to start, but has done well off the bench with TENDEX ratings of .491 and .514 the past two seasons.

But what the Hornets really need is a whole new front line. Their 1991 draft choice, Larry Johnson should fill one of the three positions.

It might help to settle on Curry as the regular shooting guard. He is better than Chapman in every phase of play, but especially defense. The delight of any NBA shooting guard is to know he is going to spend most of a game being guarded by Rex Chapman.

Statistically, the Hornets did about as well last season as they should have been expected to do. They won precisely the number of games (26) that were projected by their team TENDEX rating of 94.24 (100.00 is average). So coach Gene Littles neither helped nor hindered this team by his leadership.

Without intimidating big men, and with shooting guards running wild against them, the Hornets ranked ahead of only Denver and Atlanta in opponents' field-goal percentage. They were last in blocked shots and next to last in rebounding—two other big men's statistics.

Thanks to the quickness of point guards Bogues and Gill, they placed seventh in steals, but, other than a seven-game improvement in the standings, this was about the only positive statistic for this team. Don't expect the Hornets to improve much this season, either, unless rookie Larry Johnson is a miracle-worker.

Probable finish: Sixth in Central Division.

TYRONE BOGUES

AGE: 26
HEIGHT: 5-3
WEIGHT: 140
POSITION: Point Guard
EXPERIENCE: 4 Seasons
COLLEGE: Wake Forest
BIRTHPLACE: Baltimore
1990–91 TENDEX: .514
POSITIONAL RATING: 14 of 23
CAREER TENDEX: .515

Bogues is to point guards what Manute Bol is to centers, and it isn't because they are at opposite extremes of the height scale or because their names are side by side in the alphabetized listings of players. Both men are bidding to set unique career records. Bol is on his way to becoming the first player ever to accumulate more blocked shots than points for his career while Bogues is on a pace to become the first to compile more assists than points and more steals than turnovers; a few players have done one or the other, but none has done both . . . Muggsy ranked ninth in the NBA in assists last season (8.3), 20th in steals (1.7) and fourth in ratio of steals to turnovers (1.14) . . . best ratings among point guards were No. 3 in turnovers, No. 4 in assists, and No. 6 in steals . . . led the Hornets in these three categories.

REX CHAPMAN

AGE: 24
HEIGHT: 6-4
WEIGHT: 185
POSITION: Shooting Guard
EXPERIENCE: 3 Seasons
COLLEGE: Kentucky
BIRTHPLACE: Bowling Green, KY
1990–91 TENDEX: .454
POSITIONAL RATING: 17 of 27
CAREER TENDEX: .394

Although Chapman is one of the weakest defensive players in the NBA, he has two things going for him: He is improving and he's only 24 years old. Since he left college after his sophomore year, he's the equivalent of a second-year pro even though he has played three seasons . . . improved his TENDEX rating from .357 to .454 last season and the Hornets are hoping for more improvement from his this year . . . very weak 1990–91 stats compared with other shooting guards, with no ratings higher than No. 10 in scoring . . . low ratings were No. 21 in two-point field-goal percentage, No. 19 in rebounds, and No. 19 in steals.

BOGUES

1990–91	2PFG	3PFG	F.T.	REB.	AST.	STL.	T.O.	BLK.	PTS.
Per Game	.471	.000	.796	2.67	8.26	1.69	1.48	0.04	7.0
Per Minute	.471	.000	.796	.094	.291	.060	.052	.001	.247
Rating	17	23	14	13	4	6t	3	23	22

CHAPMAN

1990–91	2PFG	3PFG	F.T.	REB.	AST.	STL.	T.O.	BLK.	PTS.
Per Game	.468	.324	.830	2.73	3.57	1.04	1.87	0.23	15.7
Per Minute	.468	.324	.830	.091	.119	.035	.062	.008	.525
Rating	21	14	12	19	14	19	11t	15	10

JOHNNY NEWMAN

AGE: 28
HEIGHT: 6-7
WEIGHT: 190
POSITION: Small Forward
EXPERIENCE: 5 Seasons
COLLEGE: Richmond
BIRTHPLACE: Danville, VA
1990–91 TENDEX: .454
POSITIONAL RATING: 25 of 30
CAREER TENDEX: .414

Newman had the best season of his career in 1990–91 but still was only the 25th best regular small forward in the NBA. With all of the flaws in his game, it is remarkable that he has been able to win starting jobs for the past three seasons, the first two with New York and last year with Charlotte . . . led the Hornets in scoring (16.9) and ranked No. 8 among small forwards in this category . . . multitude of weaknesses included two-point field-goal shooting (No. 22), rebounds (No. 27), assists (No. 18), turnovers (No. 24), blocked shots (No. 25), and TENDEX (No. 25).

MIKE GMINSKI

AGE: 32
HEIGHT: 6-11
WEIGHT: 260
POSITION: Center
EXPERIENCE: 11 Seasons
COLLEGE: Duke
BIRTHPLACE: Monroe, CT
1990–91 TENDEX: .483
POSITIONAL RATING: 13 of 21
CAREER TENDEX: .562

The 11th NBA season for Gminski was his worst, and the Philadelphia 76ers, perhaps noticing that, traded him to the Hornets for Armon Gilliam, who is five years younger and, right now, a better player. Hornets got stung again . . . Mike did score his 10,000th career point last season, but the rest of the news was mostly bad . . . out of 21 regular centers, he ranked last in two-point field-goal percentage and 13th in TENDEX rating . . . best rankings were No. 3 in free-throw percentage, No. 5 in three-point field-goal percentage and No. 5 in turnovers.

NEWMAN

1990–91	2PFG	3PFG	F.T.	REB.	AST.	STL.	T.O.	BLK.	PTS.
Per Game	.480	.357	.809	3.14	2.32	1.23	2.33	.210	16.9
Per Minute	.480	.357	.809	.103	.076	.040	.076	.007	.553
Rating	22	3	10	27	18	10t	24	25	8

GMINSKI

1990–91	2PFG	3PFG	F.T.	REB.	AST.	STL.	T.O.	BLK.	PTS.
Per Game	.447	.143	.810	7.28	1.16	0.50	1.06	0.70	10.6
Per Minute	.447	.143	.810	.265	.042	.018	.039	.026	.384
Rating	21	5t	3	12	11	15	5	15	11

J. R. REID

=========================

AGE: 23
HEIGHT: 6-9
WEIGHT: 255
POSITION: Power Forward
EXPERIENCE: 2 Seasons
COLLEGE: North Carolina
BIRTHPLACE: Virginia Beach, VA
1990–91 TENDEX: .404
POSITIONAL RATING: 22 of 22
CAREER TENDEX: .410

A disappointment in his rookie season, Reid was even a bigger disappointment in his second season. After his weak TENDEX rating of .417 in his initial season, improvement was expected. Instead, he got even worse with a .404 rating last season. This could be his last chance to improve before the Hornets relegate him to the bench or trade him . . . his best rating among power forwards last season was No. 3 in steals . . . had very poor ratings in two-point field-goal percentage (No. 20), free-throw percentage (No. 18), rebounds (No. 17), assists (No. 22), points (No. 19), and TENDEX (No. 22, last place.).

REID

1990–91	2PFG	3PFG	F.T.	REB.	AST.	STL.	T.O.	BLK.	PTS.
Per Game	.467	.000	.703	6.28	1.11	1.09	1.91	0.59	11.3
Per Minute	.467	.000	.703	.203	.036	.035	.062	.019	.366
Rating	20	17t	18	17	22	3	10	13	19

7
Chicago Bulls

1990–91 Statistics	Per Game	Rating
2-Point FG Percent	.519	2
3-Point FG Percent	.366	3
Free-Throw Percent	.760	17
Shootist	.977	2
Points	110.0	7
Assists	27.0	4
Rebounds	+3.24	5
PAR	+14.7	2
Blocked Shots	5.34	12
Steals	10.0	4
Turnovers	14.4	3
BEST	+0.93	2
TENDEX	109.0	1
1990–91 Record	.744	2
Coach: P. Jackson	−1.5	15
Player: M. Jordan	.881	2
Rookie: M. Randall	.543	17

Chicago made the final leap from a very good team to the top-rated team in the NBA (TENDEX 109.04) last season because Michael Jordan no longer had to carry the team by himself.

Small forward Scottie Pippen graduated to the star category with a TENDEX rating of .651, good for All-NBA Third Team honors. And power forward Horace Grant (.565) continued his steady progress and became a real force on the boards.

But this is a team that cannot afford to relax. No team as weak in backup strength as the Bulls can afford to stand pat. What would happen if Jordan were injured? Or if Pippen or Grant missed a lot of action?

The Bulls were fortunate last season that all three of these players stayed healthy. Jordan and Pippen played every game. Grant missed only four. They couldn't get very good odds on this happening two seasons in a row.

The name Toni Kukoc comes up. Kukoc is the best player in the world, outside of the United States, not yet to have signed with an NBA team, and the Bulls have the good fortune of holding draft rights to him. Their bad fortune is that he recently signed a multi-year contract to play in Italy. The Bulls' bad news is good news for the rest of the NBA because the Chicago team, with Kukoc, would be good enough to run off and hide from everybody else.

Led by TENDEX Most Valuable Player Jordan, the Bulls finished near the top of the NBA last season in nearly every statistical category. They were second in two-point field-goal percentage, third in three-pointers, second in Shootist (combining all three shooting categories), seventh in points, fourth in assists, fifth in rebounds, second in PAR (combining points, assists and rebounds), fourth in steals, third in turnovers, second in BEST (combining blocked shots, steals and turnovers), and first in ratio of steals to turnovers.

On paper, this is a team that has few needs. But on the roster it has nine spots that should be up for grabs.

Other than the big three, all of the top-minute players are replaceable, beginning with 34-year-old center Bill Cartwright (TENDEX .404, 146 points below the league average). The others are forwards Stacey King (.369) and Cliff Levingston (.423), guards B.J. Armstrong (.458) and John Paxson (.418), and center Will Perdue (.416).

Coach Phil Jackson had an uncomplicated job last season and did it well, making sure that all the Bulls knew the exact pecking order— No. 1 Jordan, No. 2 Pippen, No. 3 Grant, No. 4 . . . we're in big trouble.

If Chicago is healthy again this season— and that's a big if—championships of the Central Division, Eastern Conference, and NBA playoffs all are possible, if not probable.

Probable finish: First in Central Division.

MICHAEL JORDAN

AGE: 28
HEIGHT: 6-6
WEIGHT: 198
POSITION: Shooting Guard
EXPERIENCE: 7 Seasons
COLLEGE: North Carolina
BIRTHPLACE: Brooklyn, NY
1990–91 TENDEX: .881
POSITIONAL RATING: 1 of 27
CAREER TENDEX: .851

NBA's best active player already has 16,596 points in 509 NBA games. Scoring average of 32.6 is best in league history . . . career TENDEX rating of .851 is second best in league annals, better by 199 percentage points than Clyde Drexler, who ranks second to Jordan on the all-time shooting guard list . . . Michael led the league last season in scoring (31.5), was No. 3 in steals (2.72), No. 12 in field-goal percentage (.539) and No. 6 in ratio of steals to turnovers (1.10) . . . led shooting guards in scoring and TENDEX rating; No. 2 in two-point field-goal percentage, steals and blocked shots; No. 3 in rebounds . . . TENDEX rating of .881 was second best in the NBA to David Robinson's .904, breaking Jordan's string of four straight seasons leading the league . . . but Michael was the best player in the NBA with a rating .431 percentage points above the norm for his position . . . TENDEX Hall of Famer.

SCOTTIE PIPPEN

AGE: 26
HEIGHT: 6-8
WEIGHT: 210
POSITION: Small Forward
EXPERIENCE: 4 Seasons
COLLEGE: Central Arkansas
BIRTHPLACE: Hamburg, AR
1990–91 TENDEX: .651
POSITIONAL RATING: 3 of 30
CAREER TENDEX: .544

Pippen was one of the most improved players in the NBA last season. He improved his TENDEX rating by 123 percentage points over the previous season, mostly on the strength of superior playmaking and rebounding . . . became a PAR-6 player, averaging more than six points (17.8), assists (6.2) and rebounds (7.3) per game, one of five players to do this . . . ranked fifth in the NBA in steals (2.35) . . . led the Bulls in steals and assists . . . out of 30 rated small forwards he was No. 1 in steals, No. 2 in assists, No. 3 in TENDEX rating, No. 4 in blocked shots, and No. 6 in two-point field-goal percentage . . . led the Bulls with three triple-double games (10 or more points, assists, and rebounds) . . . emerging NBA superstar.

JORDAN

1990–91	2PFG	3PFG	F.T.	REB.	AST.	STL.	T.O.	BLK.	PTS.
Per Game	.551	.312	.851	6.00	5.52	2.72	2.46	1.01	31.5
Per Minute	.551	.312	.851	.162	.149	.074	.067	.027	.850
Rating	2	18	9	3	5	2	16t	2	1

PIPPEN

1990–91	2PFG	3PFG	F.T.	REB.	AST.	STL.	T.O.	BLK.	PTS.
Per Game	.534	.309	.706	7.26	6.23	2.35	2.83	1.13	17.8
Per Minute	.534	.309	.706	.197	.170	.064	.077	.031	.485
Rating	6	11	28	11	2	1	25t	4	17

HORACE GRANT

AGE: 26
HEIGHT: 6-10
WEIGHT: 215
POSITION: Power Forward
EXPERIENCE: 4 Seasons
COLLEGE: Clemson
BIRTHPLACE: Augusta, GA
1990–91 TENDEX: .565
POSITIONAL RATING: 11 of 22
CAREER TENDEX: .521

TENDEX chart shows him making steady improvement for his first four NBA seasons. Rookie rating was .478, followed by .491, .539, and career-high .565 in 1990–91 . . . Bulls' best rebounder and strongest defender from the power-forward position . . . No. 11 player in the league in field-goal percentage (.547), No. 7 in ratio of steals to turnovers (1.03) . . . except for scoring (No. 18), he had consistently good ratings among the NBA's power forwards last season: No. 4 in two-point field-goal percentage, No. 9 in rebounds, No. 10 in assists, No. 2 in steals, No. 3 in turnovers, No. 8 in blocked shots, No. 11 in TENDEX rating.

BILL CARTWRIGHT

AGE: 34
HEIGHT: 7-1
WEIGHT: 245
POSITION: Center
EXPERIENCE: 11 Seasons
COLLEGE: San Francisco
BIRTHPLACE: Lodi, CA
1990–91 TENDEX: .404
POSITIONAL RATING: 20 of 21
CAREER TENDEX: .556

Mr. Bill made more impact in 1990–91 with an elbow that knocked Hakeem Olajuwon out of action for two months than he did with his basketball skills . . . last season was the worst in Cartwright's 11-year career: His TENDEX rating of .404 was 20th out of 21 centers who played at least 2,000 minutes and worst of the Bulls' starting five players . . . weakness was emphasized by the fact that the 7-1 Cartwright ranked only No. 4 on the Bulls in rebounds and No. 7 in blocked shots . . . worst shot-blocking center in NBA, second-worst rebounding center.

GRANT

1990–91	2PFG	3PFG	F.T.	REB.	AST.	STL.	T.O.	BLK.	PTS.
Per Game	.550	.167	.711	8.45	2.28	1.22	1.18	0.89	12.8
Per Minute	.550	.167	.711	.250	.067	.036	.035	.062	.019
Rating	4	12t	16	9	10	2	3	8	18

CARTWRIGHT

1990–91	2PFG	3PFG	F.T.	REB.	AST.	STL.	T.O.	BLK.	PTS.
Per Game	.490	.000	.697	6.15	1.59	0.41	1.43	0.19	9.6
Per Minute	.490	.000	.697	.214	.055	.014	.050	.007	.334
Rating	16	7t	15	20	6	18	10	21	15

ABSTRACTION 13

The All-Mean Team

Bill Cartwright holds the unofficial record for most opposing players injured, including his infamous elbow shot that knocked Hakeem Olajuwon out of action for two months during the 1990–91 season.

Charles Barkley is the annual leader in technical fouls and fines and did not enhance his ugly reputation by spitting at a spectator and throwing a tray full of Gatorade into a crowd last season.

The Cleveland Cavaliers were in first place in March of 1989 when Rick Mahorn dealt such a savage forearm to the face of Mark Price that it put him out of action until the playoffs. Mahorn's Detroit team went on to win the NBA title. Mahorn has learned his lesson well: Since then he has flattened anybody foolish enough to come within arm's distance.

In a game during the 1988–89 season, 6-foot-9, 250-pound Armon Gilliam pursued 6-foot-2, 190-pound Pearl Washington into a locker room with the intention of assaulting him.

Cartwright, Barkley, Mahorn, and Gilliam are members of the TENDEX All-Mean Team. The other player on the starting five is LaSalle Thompson, who hasn't done anything particularly notorious, but does a lot of nasty little things.

Here is the All-Mean Team, which, coincidentally, includes the entire frontcourt of the Philadelphia 76ers:

Player, Height, Weight	Team
Bill Cartwright, 7-0, 245	Chi
Charles Barkley, 6-5, 260	Pha
Rick Mahorn, 6-10, 265	Pha
Armon Gilliam, 6-9, 245	Pha
LaSalle Thompson, 6-10, 260	Ind

The omission of Bill Laimbeer might be questioned, but although Laimbeer certainly will never win friends or influence people, he actually does more whining than slugging.

All five players on this team are big men, but that doesn't mean the little guys can't be vicious. They just can't do as much damage as the big guys.

Here's an All Teenie-Mean Team:

Player, Height, Weight	Team
Joe Dumars, 6-3, 190	Det
Danny Ainge, 6-5, 185	Por
Dan Majerle, 6-6, 220	Pho
Drazen Petrovic, 6-5, 195	NJ
Travis Mays, 6-2, 190	Sac

8
Cleveland Cavaliers

1990–91 Statistics	Per Game	Rating
2-Point FG Percent	.486	15
3-Point FG Percent	.334	7
Free-Throw Percent	.765	13
Shootist	.924	14
Points	101.7	22
Assists	27.3	2
Rebounds	−1.89	20
PAR	−3.26	15
Blocked Shots	5.49	10
Steals	7.84	20
Turnovers	15.6	9
BEST	−2.29	15
TENDEX	98.3	16
1990–91 Record	.402	17
Coach: L. Wilkens	−4	21t
Player: L. Nance	.676	12
Rookie: T. Brandon	.532	10

In 1988–89, the Cavaliers won 57 games. Then they traded Ron Harper and won 42 games in 1989–90. Then Mark Price got hurt and they won 33 games in 1990–91.

The problem with the Cavaliers is that they believe Brad Daugherty is their best player. Daugherty looks good in TENDEX ratings, but the trouble with him is that he builds his stats in the categories where a small forward or a shooting guard would build them. He scores and passes exceptionally well for a center. What he does not do well is the one thing you need from a big man because you aren't going to get it from a shooting guard: He doesn't play intimidating defense. He hardly plays any defense.

Could this be why the Cavs seemed so much worse off when Mark Price missed games the past couple of seasons because of injuries than when Daugherty was out?

In the absence of defense from Daugherty, the Cavaliers have gotten some good low-post defense from shot-blocking forwards Larry Nance and John Williams.

But now that Nance is nearly 33 years old and Williams is on the trading block and flat-footed Danny Ferry (obtained in the Harper trade) is in line of succession to replace

Williams in the starting lineup, Cavalier fans should not expect a miraculous turn-around even if Price returns to 100 percent strength this season.

Price was off to his greatest start as a pro (TENDEX rating .654) when he blew out his knee in the 16th game of the 1990–91 season. Most players come back to play again after reconstructive knee surgery such as Price had, but few come back to 100 percent mobility. The Cavaliers desperately need a healthy Price, the No. 5 active point guard in career TENDEX rating (.556).

A telltale statistic in Cleveland's disfavor is opponents' field-goal percentage. None of the teams at or near the bottom in this statistic have good defensive centers. The Cavs ranked 21st in the NBA in this stat last season.

Another negative stat, which may or may not have reflected on the coaching of Lenny Wilkens, was that the Cavs were 14–18 in games decided by six points or less. Wilkens was the No. 21 coach in the league based on the comparison between team record and the performance of players.

On the positive side, the Cavaliers were the No. 2 team in the NBA in assists and Daugherty ranked No. 1 among the league's centers in assists.

If Price can't come back, maybe the Cavs should convert Daugherty into a point guard.

Probable finish: Fourth in Central Division.

LARRY NANCE

AGE: 32
HEIGHT: 6-10
WEIGHT: 215
POSITION: Power Forward
EXPERIENCE: 10 Seasons
COLLEGE: Clemson
BIRTHPLACE: Anderson, SC
1990–91 TENDEX: .676
POSITIONAL RATING: 2 of 22
CAREER TENDEX: .661

One of the most underrated players in the NBA, Nance is a perennial TENDEX Second or Third Team choice . . . played power forward last season but is usually a small forward . . . TENDEX rates him the second-best active small forward (behind Larry Bird) and No. 3 of all-time (behind Bird and Julius Erving) . . . blocked 200 shots last season, fifth-best total in the NBA . . . No. 19 in field-goal percentage (.524) . . . career field-goal percentage (.549) is 11th best of all-time . . . in power forward rankings last season was among the top half of players in nine of 10 basic statistical categories: No. 8 in two-point field-goal percentage, No. 7 in free-throw percentage, No. 3 in assists, No. 6 in turnovers, No. 2 in blocked shots, No. 7 in scoring, No. 10 in three-point field-goal percentage, No. 11 in rebounds, and No. 2 in TENDEX . . . he's a TENDEX Hall of Famer.

BRAD DAUGHERTY

AGE: 26
HEIGHT: 7-1
WEIGHT: 263
POSITION: Center
EXPERIENCE: 5 Seasons
COLLEGE: North Carolina
BIRTHPLACE: Black Mountain, NC
1990–91 TENDEX: .668
POSITIONAL RATING: 5 of 21
CAREER TENDEX: .604

Daugherty is an excellent offensive center, who had his best all-around season in 1990–91 . . . led Cavaliers in scoring (21.6) and rebounding (10.9) . . . No. 8 in the NBA in rebounds per game, No. 10 out of 21 regular centers in rebounds per minute . . . led centers in assists, had good ratings of No. 7 in two-point field-goal percentage, No. 9 in free-throw percentage, No. 8 in steals, No. 4 in scoring, No. 5 in TENDEX . . . set personal career highs in points, rebounds, free-throw percentage, and TENDEX rating . . . career TENDEX rating of .604 is sixth-best of active centers with at least five seasons of experience.

NANCE

1990–91	2PFG	3PFG	F.T.	REB.	AST.	STL.	T.O.	BLK.	PTS.
Per Game	.526	.250	.803	8.58	2.96	0.83	1.64	2.50	19.2
Per Minute	.526	.250	.803	.234	.081	.023	.045	.068	.525
Rating	8	10	7	11	3	17	6	2	7

DAUGHERTY

1990–91	2PFG	3PFG	F.T.	REB.	AST.	STL.	T.O.	BLK.	PTS.
Per Game	.525	.000	.751	10.9	3.33	0.97	2.78	0.61	21.6
Per Minute	.525	.000	.751	.282	.086	.025	.072	.016	.558
Rating	7	16t	9	10	1	8	15	18	4

CRAIG EHLO

AGE: 30
HEIGHT: 6-7
WEIGHT: 200
POSITION: Shooting Guard
EXPERIENCE: 8 Seasons
COLLEGE: Washington State
BIRTHPLACE: Lubbock, TX
1990–91 TENDEX: .409
POSITIONAL RATING: 25 of 27
CAREER TENDEX: .447

Two years ago, after Ron Harper was traded, Craig Ehlo played well enough as his replacement to keep second-guessers off the backs of Cleveland management. Last season, however, was a disaster for the shooting guard. His TENDEX rating of .409 was 65 points lower than the season before. It was his worst rating since his rookie season (1983–84) . . . Ehlo led the Cavaliers in assists (4.7) and steals (1.5), but ranked No. 26 out of 27 shooting guards in scoring and No. 25 in TENDEX.

EHLO

1990–91	2PFG	3PFG	F.T.	REB.	AST.	STL.	T.O.	BLK.	PTS.
Per Game	.473	.329	.679	4.73	4.59	1.48	1.95	0.42	10.1
Per Minute	.473	.329	.679	.140	.136	.043	.058	.012	.301
Rating	19	13	26	7	8	9t	9	9t	26

ABSTRACTION 14

We Missed You

I wish TENDEX ratings could tell everything there is about basketball players, but they can't. They can't measure intangibles that determine how much a player is really worth to his team.

Case in point: Larry Bird.

According to TENDEX, Bird had the worst season of his NBA career in 1990–91, with limited mobility caused by a back injury.

According to Boston Celtic records, he was still the NBA's Most Valuable Player. The Celtics were within one percentage point of Portland for the best winning percentage in the NBA with Bird in the lineup. With him sidelined, they were the No. 17 team in a 27-team league.

In the 60 games Bird played, Boston won 46 for a winning percentage of .767. In the 22 games he missed, the Celtics went 10-12 for a percentage of .455. That's a difference of 312 percentage points.

Was it coincidence? Well, in 1988–89, Boston played nearly the entire season without Bird. He struggled to play in six games on two injured feet, but in effect missed the whole season. Boston finished with a 42-40 record, barely over .500. The year before, the Celtics had played .695 basketball.

In 1978–79, the year before Bird entered the NBA, Boston went 29-53 for the season (.354). The next season, with Bird, they were 61-21 (.744).

Three other star players joined Bird on the sidelines for much of the 1990–91 season. Hakeem Olajuwon missed 25 games in a row at midseason, Isiah Thomas missed a total of 34, and Mark Price missed the final 66 games.

With Price in the lineup Cleveland was 9–7 (.563). Without him the Cavs were 24–42 (.364). That's a difference of 199 percentage points, and the difference is the more remarkable when it is considered that power forward John Williams missed the 16 games Price played, but was in the lineup for most of the rest of the season.

Price's value becomes even more obvious when a comparison is made with how the Cavaliers did in the absence of center Brad Daugherty the season before. With Daugherty Cleveland was 24–19, without him 18–23. Daugherty was a five-game player, meaning the Cavs lost five games in the standings because of his absence. They lost 17 games because of Price's injury.

With Thomas in the lineup last season, Detroit was 31–17 (.646). Without him, the Pistons struggled to exceed the .500 mark with a 19–15 record (.559).

The one who is not so easy to figure is Olajuwon. Before his injury, Houston was 17–13 (.567). During the 25 consecutive games he missed, the Rockets were 15–10 (.600). Which means they're better off without Olajuwon, right?

Wrong.

When he returned, the Rockets launched a 13-game winning streak and won 20 of their last 27 games (.741).

9
Dallas Mavericks

1990–91 Statistics	Per Game	Rating
2-Point FG Percent	.485	16
3-Point FG Percent	.322	12
Free-Throw Percent	.761	16
Shootist	.923	15
Points	99.9	25
Assists	22.2	25
Rebounds	−3.18	24
PAR	−10.2	24
Blocked Shots	4.84	17
Steals	7.09	26
Turnovers	14.5	4
BEST	−2.54	20
TENDEX	95.6	21
1990–91 Record	.341	22
Coach: R. Adubato	−2	17t
Player: D. Harper	.554	47
Rookie: D. Smith	.667	7

For five seasons the Mavericks have been trying to build an NBA champion team around Roy Tarpley. All of a sudden it's time to rebuild practically the entire team.

Tarpley has just about thrown away his final chance to be what he should have been in the NBA—a superstar. A succession of substance-abuse offenses and violations of law have branded him as a player on whom no team, not even Dallas, is likely to take another chance.

While Tarpley has been getting himself in trouble, the rest of the Mavericks have been getting old. Guards Derek Harper and Rolando Blackman haven't shown their age yet. They averaged 40 points between them last season and are probably the best tandem of defensive backcourtmen in the NBA. Individually, Harper could be the best defensive guard in the NBA. But Blackman is 32 and Harper is 30.

Add to that twosome Lafayette (Fat) Lever, a TENDEX Hall of Famer with a lifetime rating of .585, and the backcourt is still in good hands. Lever ranks among the all-time leaders in steals and assists and is perhaps the greatest of all rebounding guards. TENDEX rates him as the ninth-best point guard in history.

But Lever missed nearly all of last season after injuring his knee and being reinstated in the lineup before it had healed. The result was predictable: Recurrence of knee problems, out for the season. In many cases—Ralph Sampson, Jeff Ruland, and Derek Smith, to name three—when a player comes back too soon after a knee injury and is reinjured, he never again is the same player that he was before. So at age 31, Lever could be near the end.

The outlook is poor in frontcourt. Center James Donaldson is 34 and had his worst-rated season (.465) in 1990–91. Power forward Herb Williams (.476) is 33. Small forward Rodney McCray (.520) is 30.

Mostly because of season-ending injuries to Tarpley and Lever, Dallas had the most disappointing season in franchise history in 1990–91. The Mavs' decline of 19 victories, from 47 in 1989–90 to 28 in 1990–91, was the second biggest drop-off last season in the NBA.

Dallas was rated among the worst teams in the league in points (No. 25), assists (No. 25), rebounds (No. 24), steals (No. 26), winning percentage (No. 22), and TENDEX rating (No. 21).

Coach Richie Adubato was the victim rather than the cause of the problems. With the player personnel the Mavericks had, they were projected to win 30 games. They practically matched that with 28.

This is one of the most unpredictable teams for the 1991–92 season. A return to pre-injury form by Lever could make the Mavs a .500 team. A miraculous return by Tarpley could make them a champion contender. A return by neither could push them past a few expansion teams, ever closer to the bottom of the league standings.

In anticipation of a comeback by Lever, but not a complete recovery, and of some help from rookie Doug Smith but no help at all from Tarpley, expect the Mavericks to have a 1991–92 season similar to 1990–91.

Probable finish: Fifth in Midwest Division.

DEREK HARPER

AGE: 30
HEIGHT: 6-4
WEIGHT: 203
POSITION: Point Guard
EXPERIENCE: 8 Seasons
COLLEGE: Illinois
BIRTHPLACE: Elberton, GA
1990–91 TENDEX: .554
POSITIONAL RATING: 10 of 23
CAREER TENDEX: .522

Harper is the Dennis Rodman of guards, but receives much less recognition for his man-to-man defense because he gets so little national television exposure . . . received some acclaim last season for becoming the first player in history to improve his scoring average in each of his first eight NBA seasons. His progressive averages are 5.7, 9.6, 12.2, 16.0, 17.0, 17.3, 18.0, 19.7. Maybe he'll hit the 20-point mark in 1991–92 to make it nine in a row . . . ranks No. 6 among active point guards in career TENDEX rating . . . one of the all-time leaders in ratio of steals to turnovers, he had a ratio of 0.831 last year with 147 steals and 177 turnovers . . . led Dallas in steals (1.9) and assists (7.1) . . . ranked No. 15 in the NBA in steals and No. 16 in assists . . . should score his 10,000th point this season.

ROLANDO BLACKMAN

AGE: 32
HEIGHT: 6-6
WEIGHT: 194
POSITION: Shooting Guard
EXPERIENCE: 10 Seasons
COLLEGE: Kansas State
BIRTHPLACE: Panama City, Panama
1990–91 TENDEX: .476
POSITIONAL RATING: 11 of 27
CAREER TENDEX: .487

Like Harper, Blackman is one of the truly excellent, underrated players in the NBA. For 10 seasons, he has averaged 34.3 minutes and 19.4 points per game. His 19.9 scoring average last season, at the age of 32, led the Mavericks and was the fourth best of his career . . . a fine shooter, he has a career field-goal percentage of .500, including three-pointers . . . set a personal high with 40 successful three-point shots and a .351 percentage last season . . . free-throw percentage of .865 was the third-best of his career, career percentage is .836 . . . great clutch shooter who takes (and makes) many game-winning shots . . . outstanding man-to-man defender . . . scored his 15,000th point last season . . . good shooting-guard ratings were No. 8 in three-point field-goal percentage, No. 7 in free-throw percentage, No. 7 in turnovers, and No. 8 in points.

HARPER

1990–91	2PFG	3PFG	F.T.	REB.	AST.	STL.	T.O.	BLK.	PTS.
Per Game	.493	.362	.731	3.03	7.12	1.91	2.30	0.18	19.7
Per Minute	.493	.362	.731	.081	.190	.051	.062	.005	.528
Rating	11	7	17	16	19t	12	7	10	4t

BLACKMAN

1990–91	2PFG	3PFG	F.T.	REB.	AST.	STL.	T.O.	BLK.	PTS.
Per Game	.494	.351	.865	3.20	3.76	0.86	1.99	0.24	19.9
Per Minute	.494	.351	.865	.086	.102	.023	.054	.006	.536
Rating	11	8	7	21	19	26	7	16	8

RODNEY McCRAY

AGE: 30
HEIGHT: 6-8
WEIGHT: 235
POSITION: Small Forward
EXPERIENCE: 8 Seasons
COLLEGE: Louisville
BIRTHPLACE: Mount Vernon, NY
1990–91 TENDEX: .520
POSITIONAL RATING: 16 of 30
CAREER TENDEX: .512

McCray isn't really underrated or over-rated. He's the epitome of a quietly average NBA player, always ranking near the middle of the pack. The 1990–91 season was no exception: His TENDEX rating of .520 was 16th best out of 30 small forwards . . . good rebounder and passer, he ranked third on the Mavericks in both categories . . . in the small-forward ratings he was No. 6 in rebounds and No. 7 in assists . . . very weak scorer, averaged 11.4 points per game, next to last among small forwards.

JAMES DONALDSON

AGE: 34
HEIGHT: 7-2
WEIGHT: 278
POSITION: Center
EXPERIENCE: 11 Seasons
COLLEGE: Washington State
BIRTHPLACE: Heacham, England
1990–91 TENDEX: .465
POSITIONAL RATING: 15 of 21
CAREER TENDEX: .521

At age 34, Donaldson could be near the end after 11 NBA seasons. TENDEX rating of .465 in 1990–91 was the worst of his career . . . led Dallas in rebounds and field-goal percentage, No. 2 on the team in minutes played . . . field-goal percentage of .532 was 15th best in NBA but not up to his usual standards . . . Donaldson led the NBA in field-goal percentage with .637 in 1985 and ranks No. 3 on the all-time list with a .576 career average, behind Charles Barkley and Artis Gilmore . . . career Shootist percentage (points per shot) of 1.011 is No. 10 on the all-time list.

McCRAY

1990–91	2PFG	3PFG	F.T.	REB.	AST.	STL.	T.O.	BLK.	PTS.
Per Game	.505	.333	.803	7.57	3.50	0.95	1.74	0.69	11.4
Per Minute	.505	.333	.803	.219	.101	.027	.050	.020	.330
Rating	12t	8	13	6	7	21t	6t	12t	29

DONALDSON

1990–91	2PFG	3PFG	F.T.	REB.	AST.	STL.	T.O.	BLK.	PTS.
Per Game	.532	.000	.721	8.87	0.84	0.42	1.78	1.13	10.0
Per Minute	.532	.000	.721	.260	.025	.012	.052	.033	.293
Rating	6	7t	12	16	18	20	11t	13	16

10
Denver Nuggets

1990–91 Statistics	Per Game	Rating
2-Point FG Percent	.461	24
3-Point FG Percent	.283	23
Free-Throw Percent	.763	14
Shootist	.883	25
Points	119.9	1
Assists	24.5	16
Rebounds	−3.16	23
PAR	−20.0	27
Blocked Shots	4.95	16
Steals	10.4	3
Turnovers	16.2	16
BEST	−0.85	3
TENDEX	87.9	27
1990–91 Record	.244	27
Coach: P. Westhead	+9	NR
Player: M. Adams	.617	20t
Rookie: D. Mutombo	.841	2

What can we say to the Nuggets except: Told you so.

In the 1990–91 edition of *The Basketball Abstract,* Chris Jackson was rated as the No. 29 prospect from the 1990 college draft. Analysis was: "He's just a scorer, with very little awareness of teammates and no interest in defense."

The Nuggets made Jackson the No. 3 selection in the draft.

It wasn't only the Loyola-Marymount style of play introduced by rookie coach Paul Westhead that made the Nuggets the worst defensive team in professional basketball history last season. To a large extent, it was the work of Jackson (TENDEX rating .349).

Jackson missed the first 10 days of the season. In his first game in the starting lineup, Phoenix scored 173 points against Denver, including an NBA-record 107 points in the first half. In successive games, later in the season, Jackson gave up 36 points to Travis Mays of Sacramento (season average 14.3) and 42 to Sherman Douglas of Miami (average 18.5). The next time out after facing Jackson, Mays was held to four points by Dallas' Rolando

Blackman on 2-for-12 shooting. Mays' TEN-DEX rating for the Dallas game was a minus number. For the Denver game, it was close to 1.000.

All season long, in games Jackson played the minutes of a regular, Denver gave up astronomical numbers of points. In games he played sparingly or not at all, the Nuggets' defensive yield wasn't nearly as large.

The combined circumstances of losing TENDEX Hall of Fame player Lafayette Lever and TENDEX Hall of Fame coach Doug Moe, and having them replaced by Jackson and Westhead, resulted in the Nuggets falling from a team that won 43 games in 1989–90 to one that could win only 20 in 1990–91. It was the worst dropoff in the NBA.

In fairness to Westhead, TENDEX showed that he was a good game strategist. The Nuggets, based on personnel strength, should have won only 11 times last season. They had terrible players.

Orlando Woolridge, obtained from the Los Angeles Lakers, did his part by averaging 25.1 points on a .549 TENDEX rating, but injuries caused Woolridge to miss 29 games.

Point guard Michael Adams took up some of the slack after Lever was traded to Dallas, averaging 26.5 points and 10.5 assists. The cat-quick Adams was rated by TENDEX as the No. 5 point guard in the NBA behind Magic Johnson, John Stockton, Kevin Johnson and Terry Porter. But Adams missed 16 games because of injuries.

The rest of the team could have missed the entire season because of injuries and Denver could have brought in players just as good from the Continental Basketball Association.

Not only did the Nuggets give up a record-setting number of points (130.8 per game) to opponents, but they proved this was no fluke by allowing opponents to shoot .512 against them from the field. No other team gave up a field-goal percentage higher than .500 to its opponents.

The Nuggets finished last in the league in PAR (a statistic combining points, assists and rebounds), last in winning percentage (.244) and last in TENDEX with one of the worst ratings (87.87) in NBA history.

They led the league in scoring (119.9) but gave up a league-leading 10.9 points per game more than they scored.

Does this prove that the wild Westhead system can't work in the NBA? I don't think it does. Give him the Golden State Warriors foursome of Mullin-Hardaway-Richmond-Marciulionis and it might. But for a talentless team, forget it.

Even with standout rookie Dikembe Mutombo, the Nuggets' probable 1991–92 finish is sixth in the Midwest Division.

BLAIR RASMUSSEN

AGE: 29
HEIGHT: 7-0
WEIGHT: 260
POSITION: Center
EXPERIENCE: 6 Seasons
COLLEGE: Oregon
BIRTHPLACE: Auburn, WA
1990–91 TENDEX: .448
POSITIONAL RATING: 18 of 21
CAREER TENDEX: .516

Rasmussen played the most minutes of his career, 2,325, last season, but did not adapt well to Paul Westhead's run-and-gun system. His TENDEX rating of .448 represented a decline of 152 points from the 1989–90 season, one of the biggest decreases in the NBA . . . led Denver in blocked shots (1.9) and rebounds (9.7) . . . No. 13 in the league in rebounds and No. 16 in blocks . . . out of 21 regular centers he ranked No. 7 in blocked shots and rebounds, but was far down the list in two-point field-goal percentage (No. 20), assists (No. 15), free-throw percentage (No. 16), points (No. 12), and TENDEX rating (No. 18).

RASMUSSEN

1990–91	2PFG	3PFG	F.T.	REB.	AST.	STL.	T.O.	BLK.	PTS.
Per Game	.458	.400	.677	9.69	1.00	0.74	1.16	1.89	12.5
Per Minute	.458	.400	.677	.292	.030	.022	.035	.057	.376
Rating	20	1	16	7t	15	13	1	7	12

11
Detroit Pistons

1990–91 Statistics	Per Game	Rating
2-Point FG Percent	.476	21
3-Point FG Percent	.298	21
Free-Throw Percent	.763	15
Shootist	.903	19
Points	100.1	24
Assists	22.3	23
Rebounds	+4.66	3
PAR	+9.01	7
Blocked Shots	4.48	23
Steals	5.94	27
Turnovers	14.4	2
BEST	−3.99	24
TENDEX	103.3	8
Winning Percentage	.610	9
Coach: C. Daly	+1	10t
Player: D. Rodman	.595	30
Rookie: D. Overton	.413	NR

The Pistons had their run—two straight NBA titles and an Isiah Thomas injury that cost them a third—but now they are growing old.

Detroit was the best defensive team in the NBA for the second season in a row in 1990–91, mostly because of Dennis Rodman. The Pistons have been no worse than No. 3 in the league in defense since Rodman became a regular in 1987–88 and have progressed from No. 3 to No. 2 to No. 1 as Rodman's minutes have increased.

Rodman is the best defender in the NBA since Bill Russell, one of the best rebounders, and probably the third-best active forward, behind Karl Malone and Charles Barkley.

The bad news is that Rodman, with five years experience in the NBA, already is 30 years old. Five other key Piston players are older than that.

Center Bill Laimbeer has been durable, playing at least 80 games in every one of his 11 NBA seasons. He's 34. His reserve, James Edwards, a 14-year veteran, is 36.

Forward Mark Aguirre and guard Isiah Thomas are 10-year veterans. Aguirre is 32, Thomas is 30.

Guard Vinnie Johnson, a 12-year man, is 35.

The team's "youngsters" are guard Joe Dumars, a six-year veteran at age 28, and forward John Salley, a five-year man at 27.

The age showed last season. Thomas missed 34 games and part of the playoffs because of injuries, and with him out of the lineup the Pistons fared almost as badly as the Celtics without Bird. Dumars and Johnson picked up the scoring slack, but did not distribute the ball to the big men nearly as well as Thomas, and the Pistons became a jump-shooting team in the absence of Isiah (TENDEX .579).

Despite the injuries, Thomas ranked sixth in the NBA last season in assists (9.3) and moved into third place on the all-time assists list with 7,431. He trails only Magic Johnson and Oscar Robertson. Isiah is No. 3 among active point guards in career TENDEX rating.

Isiah is expected to start this season healthy, but with so many players over 30, can the Pistons get through the season without two or three guys missing a lot of games? Since they have virtually no bench after the eighth man, any injuries to the top eight would be crucial.

TENDEX Hall of Fame coach Chuck Daly has assembled and carefully molded the Pistons into one of the most cohesive units since the great Boston Celtic teams, coached by Red Auerbach.

Daly managed to squeeze one more victory out of his team last season than TENDEX showed its player personnel warranted. Detroit needed that win to reach 50—a minimum number for a team to consider itself a championship contender.

Detroit's victory total was nine fewer than its total the previous season and was lower than six other teams last season.

Tell-tale weaknesses for the Pistons last season were shooting (No. 21 in field-goal percentage), scoring (No. 24), assists (No. 23), blocked shots (No. 23) and steals (No. 24). The only reason they remained a winning team was the Rodman-led defense.

Expect some more erosion in 1991–92. Probable finish: Third in Central Division.

DENNIS RODMAN

AGE: 30
HEIGHT: 6-8
WEIGHT: 210
POSITION: Small Forward
EXPERIENCE: 5 Seasons
COLLEGE: Southeastern Oklahoma State
BIRTHPLACE: Trenton, NJ
1990–91 TENDEX: .595
POSITIONAL RATING: 6 of 30
CAREER TENDEX: .607

The NBA's Defensive Player of the Year, Rodman also contributed enough statistically to rank as one of the top three forwards overall in the NBA last season as he played a heavy load of minutes for the first time in his five-year career . . . ranked No. 3 in the NBA in rebounds-per-game, but No. 1 in the more significant statistic of rebounds-per-minute . . . held Dominque Wilkins and Larry Bird more than 150 points below their regular-season TENDEX ratings in playoffs . . . out of 30 small forwards ranked No. 1 in rebounds, No. 1 in turnovers and No. 6 in TENDEX . . . last-place ratings in assists and points didn't mean much because in Chuck Daly's system his only role on offense is rebounding . . . No. 4 among active small forwards in career TENDEX rating.

JOE DUMARS

AGE: 28
HEIGHT: 6-3
WEIGHT: 190
POSITION: Shooting Guard
EXPERIENCE: 5 Seasons
COLLEGE: McNeese State
BIRTHPLACE: Shreveport, LA
1990–91 TENDEX: .529
POSITIONAL RATING: 7 of 27
CAREER TENDEX: .464

Dumars had a career season in 1990–91. Set personal highs with 3,046 minutes, 443 assists, 89 steals, and 1,629 points . . . led Pistons in scoring average (20.4) . . . won MVP honors in the 1989 championship series against the Los Angeles Lakers when the Pistons won their first NBA title . . . out of 27 shooting guards, had good 1990–91 rankings of No. 5 in free-throw percentage, No. 6 in assists, No. 9 in points and No. 7 in TENDEX rating . . . eleventh in the league in free-throw percentage (.890) . . . often makes NBA All-Defensive teams, but isn't as consistent as Rodman . . . gave up 21.4 points per game to Boston's Reggie Lewis in the playoffs, 4.2 points above Lewis' regular-season average.

RODMAN

1990–91	2PFG	3PFG	F.T.	REB.	AST.	STL.	T.O.	BLK.	PTS.
Per Game	.509	.200	.631	12.5	10.4	0.79	1.15	0.67	8.2
Per Minute	.509	.200	.631	.373	.031	.024	.034	.020	.244
Rating	11	22t	29	1	30	24	1	12t	30

DUMARS

1990–91	2PFG	3PFG	F.T.	REB.	AST.	STL.	T.O.	BLK.	PTS.
Per Game	.488	.311	.890	2.34	5.54	1.11	2.36	0.09	20.4
Per Minute	.488	.311	.890	.061	.145	.029	.062	.002	.535
Rating	14	19	5	26	6	23t	11t	27	9

MARK AGUIRRE

AGE: 32
HEIGHT: 6-6
WEIGHT: 235
POSITION: Small Forward
EXPERIENCE: 10 Seasons
COLLEGE: DePaul
BIRTHPLACE: Chicago
1990–91 TENDEX: .555
POSITIONAL RATING: 9 of 30
CAREER TENDEX: .579

Acquired by Detroit in a trade for Adrian Dantley during the 1988–89 season, Aguirre finally paid dividends to the Pistons last season. Had his best TENDEX rating in three years (.555) . . . played some excellent basketball in the playoffs, including a 34-point game against the Boston Celtics . . . averaged 14.2 points per game for Detroit last season and has a career average of 22.0 for 10 NBA seasons . . . best ratings out of 30 small forwards last year were No. 9 in points and No. 9 in TENDEX . . . not so good in two-point field-goal percentage (No. 24), assists (No. 20), steals (No. 25), and blocked shots (No. 24) . . . ranks No. 8 among active small forwards in career TENDEX rating.

BILL LAIMBEER

AGE: 34
HEIGHT: 6-11
WEIGHT: 260
POSITION: Center
EXPERIENCE: 11 Seasons
COLLEGE: Notre Dame
BIRTHPLACE: Boston
1990–91 TENDEX: .573
POSITIONAL RATING: 9 of 21
CAREER TENDEX: .616

Age may finally be catching up to Laimbeer, who has been a rock of consistency and durability for 11 years in the NBA. He had his lowest TENDEX rating in 10 years last season and only his second rating below .600 since 1981–82 . . . rebounding declined slightly, but his 9.0 average per game still was good enough to tie for 15th in the league . . . a steady player, he had ratings among the top 10 regular centers in two-point field-goal percentage (No. 9), three-point field-goal percentage (No. 4), free-throw percentage (No. 1), assists (No. 5), turnovers (No. 2), and TENDEX (No. 9) . . . should pull down his 10,000th rebound this season . . . ranks No. 5 among active centers in career TENDEX rating.

AGUIRRE

1990–91	2PFG	3PFG	F.T.	REB.	AST.	STL.	T.O.	BLK.	PTS.
Per Game	.477	.308	.757	4.79	1.78	0.60	1.64	0.26	14.2
Per Minute	.477	.308	.757	.186	.069	.023	.064	.010	.550
Rating	24	12t	18	13	20t	25	16t	24	9t

LAIMBEER

1990–91	2PFG	3PFG	F.T.	REB.	AST.	STL.	T.O.	BLK.	PTS.
Per Game	.513	.296	.837	8.99	1.91	0.46	1.20	0.68	11.0
Per Minute	.513	.296	.837	.276	.059	.014	.037	.021	.339
Rating	9t	4	1	11	5	17	2t	17	14

VINNIE JOHNSON

AGE: 35
HEIGHT: 6-2
WEIGHT: 200
POSITION: Shooting Guard
EXPERIENCE: 12 Seasons
COLLEGE: Baylor
BIRTHPLACE: Brooklyn, NY
1990–91 TENDEX: .412
POSITIONAL RATING: 24 of 27
CAREER TENDEX: .476

With Johnson's decline in performance the past two seasons, it becomes too easy to forget what an exceptional career he has had. But the memory comes back quickly when his career record is compared with teammate Joe Dumars. In 12 seasons, twice as long as Dumars has played, Johnson's career TENDEX rating is still 12 points higher . . . but the deterioration has become obvious: last season's .412 rating was the lowest of Johnson's career, 144 points below his career high of .556 in 1980–81 . . . out of 27 small forwards, he had low ratings of No. 25 in two-point field-goal percentage, No. 27 in free-throw percentage, No. 21 in steals, No. 25 in points, and No. 24 in TENDEX.

JOHNSON

1990–91	2PFG	3PFG	F.T.	REB.	AST.	STL.	T.O.	BLK.	PTS.
Per Game	.438	.324	.646	3.41	3.30	0.92	1.44	0.18	11.7
Per Minute	.438	.324	.646	.117	.113	.031	.049	.006	.401
Rating	25	16	27	12	16	21	5	17	25

ABSTRACTION 15

The New Olympians

It's being said in some quarters that even if the United States puts together a collection of its best NBA players, a good European team from Russia or Yugoslavia that has been playing together for years will win the Gold Medal in the 1992 Olympic Games.

Forget it.

There are certainly benefits to playing as an experienced unit, but that goes only so far. Point guards like Magic Johnson, John Stockton, and Kevin Johnson could quickly develop quite good chemistry with big guys like Karl Malone, David Robinson, and Hakeem Olajuwon.

About 30 years ago, a collection of NBA stars toured Europe playing national teams. The European teams wanted to learn what they could from the American players to prepare for the Olympic Games. They figured the tour would be a lark for the American pros: They wouldn't be too intense, nor would they be unified because they were selected from different NBA teams.

The tour went to several countries before the Soviet Union. But after the Americans won most of the games by more than 50 points, the Russians canceled their part of the tour. They reasoned that losing by embarrassing scores would not be worth the little they could learn that might help them.

The key player for the American team was Oscar Robertson. He had a fine surrounding cast, including Jerry West, but the Europeans couldn't cope with the great point guard at all. Robertson quickly developed the team into a unit, scoring and distributing the ball in a way

the Europeans hadn't seen before and haven't seen since.

What do you think will happen when they see Magic Johnson . . . and John Stockton . . . and Kevin Johnson . . . coming at them in waves?

And this American team should be better at other positions than the one back in the 1960s.

The team has not been selected yet, but Chuck Daly of the Detroit Pistons has been named head coach and there is an "understanding," according to the NBA office, that there will be one or two college players on the team.

Here's the team I'd like to see represent the U.S.A. in the 1992 Olympic Games, assuming it must have two collegians:

Position—Player	Source
C —HAKEEM OLAJUWON	NBA
C —DAVID ROBINSON	NBA
C —SHAQUILLE O'NEAL	NCAA
PF—KARL MALONE	NBA
PF—CHARLES BARKLEY	NBA
SF—DENNIS RODMAN	NBA
SF—JOSH GRANT	NCAA
PG—MAGIC JOHNSON	NBA
PG—JOHN STOCKTON	NBA
PG—KEVIN JOHNSON	NBA
SG—MICHAEL JORDAN	NBA
SG—CLYDE DREXLER	NBA

If Olajuwon decided to play for his native Nigeria instead of the United States, the United States wouldn't lose much with Patrick Ewing as his replacement.

Drexler could play small forward, if necessary. Rodman could be inserted in the lineup at any position to defend an opposing player who was hot. He'd be the designated Toni Kukoc stopper.

If 11 NBA players could be selected instead of 10, Dominque Wilkins would replace Josh Grant on the roster.

This team could name the score against an all-star team representing the rest of the world.

12
Golden State Warriors

1990–91 Statistics	Per Game	Rating
2-Point FG Percent	.504	7
3-Point FG Percent	.337	6
Free-Throw Percent	.783	8
Shootist	.946	8
Points	116.6	2
Assists	23.8	18
Rebounds	−4.31	25
PAR	−5.23	19
Blocked Shots	4.61	21
Steals	9.79	5
Turnovers	16.6	18
BEST	−2.17	14
TENDEX	99.3	14
Winning Percentage	.537	11t
Coach: D. Nelson	+5	4t
Player: T. Hardaway	.612	23
Rookie: G. Gatling	.773	13

Coach Don Nelson has the Warriors over-achieving, but the question is: Over the long haul, will it be worth it?

The Warriors pulled off a major upset by defeating the San Antonio Spurs in the first round of the playoffs last spring, but then a knee injury to Chris Mullin made them help-less victims against the Los Angeles Lakers in the second round.

Possibly the most significant game of the season for the Warriors was the only one they won against the Lakers. After taking a game off to rest the knee, a refreshed Mullin came out and scored 44 points to spark the upset. It was the first rest of the season for Mullin, who led the league with 3,315 minutes played, av-eraging 40.4 minutes per game while playing all 82 regular-season games.

Mullin got no more chance to rest his in-jured knee in the Laker series and showed it, with 9- and 13-point games. James Worthy was given credit for stopping Mullin, but what was Worthy doing in the game Mullin scored 44? This was clearly a case of exhaus-tion, compounded by injury: In the final three games, playing on the gimpy knee, Mullin missed many open shots he normally makes.

Mullin's tiredness also showed in his TEN-DEX rating, which for most of the season was around .650, but plummeted in April to .609. Mullin is not old, but at 28 he is the oldest of the Warriors' three key players and should not be expected to play so many minutes. Nobody on any team should be expected to play that many minutes.

The other two Warrior stars—Tim Hard-away and Mitch Richmond—also took on a heavy load of minutes, averaging 39 per game. They are younger than Mullin but could show signs of the strain prematurely if continually asked to play that much over the next few seasons.

Nelson is one of the best in the NBA, but his contention, quoted by a television commentator, that he has to play those three players all those minutes, because he has no replacements for them, simply doesn't make sense. He has Sarunas Marciulionis, an excellent player who could fill in for all three. Marciulionis played only 987 minutes last season. He could easily play 2,500 this season.

Chicago does not have a Marciulionis to fill in for Michael Jordan, but Phil Jackson played Jordan about 300 fewer minutes than Nelson played Mullin last season. There is no sub for Magic Johnson, but Magic played about 400 minutes less than Mullin.

Michael and Magic were tired by playoff time. Mullin was exhausted. If Nelson thinks he has no replacement for Mullin now, what will he think when Mullin's legs go and he has no Mullin?

Nelson's ability as a coach is not being questioned, only his distribution of minutes. His ability is made clear by the fact that the Warriors won five more games than their player personnel warranted, placing him among the top five coaches in the NBA last season.

Golden State's biggest strength was shooting. The Warriors ranked No. 7 in two-point field-goal percentage, No. 6 in three-point field-goal percentage, No. 8 in free-throw percentage and No. 2 in scoring. With their multiguard offense, they also did well in steals (No. 5).

They did poorly in the categories in which big men excel—No. 21 in blocked shots and No. 25 in rebounding.

Overall, their TENDEX rating was 14th best in the NBA, but the clever Nelson steered them to the 11th best record.

An important player for the Warriors this season could be Tyrone Hill, who as a rookie last season showed a lot of rebounding potential. If he improves and plays more minutes this season, the Warriors could hold their ground in the standings of the tough Pacific Division. If not, they'll probably drop down a notch.

Probable finish: Fifth in Pacific Division.

TIM HARDAWAY

AGE: 25
HEIGHT: 6-0
WEIGHT: 175
POSITION: Point Guard
EXPERIENCE: 2 Seasons
COLLEGE: Texas-El Paso
BIRTHPLACE: Chicago
1990–91 TENDEX: .612
POSITIONAL RATING: 6 of 23
CAREER TENDEX: .566

Hardaway was one of eight NBA players who improved their TENDEX ratings by at least 100 points last season. He was the Warriors' best player in the playoffs as they upset San Antonio in the opening round before losing to the Los Angeles Lakers . . . tremendously strong and needed all his strength to play 3,215 minutes last season, the most by a guard in the NBA and third most overall . . . placed 11th in the league in scoring (22.9), fifth in assists (9.7), fourth in steals (2.61) and 10th in three-point field-goal percentage (.385) . . . led Golden State in steals, assists, and three-point shooting . . . had excellent point-guard ratings of No. 10 in two-point field-goal percentage, No. 4 in three-point percentage, No. 8 in rebounds, No. 7 in assists, No. 3 in steals, No. 3 in points, and No. 6 in TENDEX . . . Rick Barry said of Hardaway: "Nobody thought he'd be this good." But somebody did. He had the best TENDEX rating of all backcourtmen in the 1989 college draft.

CHRIS MULLIN

AGE: 28
HEIGHT: 6-7
WEIGHT: 220
POSITION: Small Forward
EXPERIENCE: 6 Seasons
COLLEGE: St. John's
BIRTHPLACE: New York City
1990–91 TENDEX: .609
POSITIONAL RATING: 5 of 30
CAREER TENDEX: .580

Mullin showed signs of wear-and-tear last spring, injuring a knee during the playoffs after leading the league with 3,315 minutes played . . . was on his way to his greatest season before fatigue set in and his TENDEX rating wound up at .609, his worst rating in three years . . . placed eighth in the NBA in scoring (25.7), 12th in free-throw percentage (.884), 10th in steals (2.11), 12th in free-throw percentage (.884), 10th in steals (2.11), and 13th in field-goal percentage (.536) . . . led Warriors in scoring, field-goal percentage, and free-throw percentage . . . out of 30 small forwards, he had top-10 ratings: No. 3 in two-point field-goal percentage, No. 4 in free-throw percentage, No. 8 in assists, No. 4 in steals, No. 5 in points, and No. 5 in TENDEX . . . career TENDEX rating of .580 ranks No. 7 among active small forwards . . . should score his 10,000th point this season.

HARDAWAY

1990–91	2PFG	3PFG	F.T.	REB.	AST.	STL.	T.O.	BLK.	PTS.
Per Game	.494	.385	.803	4.05	9.67	2.61	3.29	0.15	22.9
Per Minute	.494	.385	.803	.103	.247	.067	.084	.004	.585
Rating	10	4	12	8	7	3	14	16	3

MULLIN

1990–91	2PFG	3PFG	F.T.	REB.	AST.	STL.	T.O.	BLK.	PTS.
Per Game	.560	.301	.884	5.40	4.01	2.11	2.99	.768	25.7
Per Minute	.560	.301	.884	.134	.099	.052	.074	.019	.636
Rating	3	14	4	22	8	4	23	14	5

MITCH RICHMOND

AGE: 26
HEIGHT: 6-5
WEIGHT: 225
POSITION: Shooting Guard
EXPERIENCE: 3 Seasons
COLLEGE: Kansas State
BIRTHPLACE: Fort Lauderdale, FL
1990–91 TENDEX: .522
POSITIONAL RATING: 9 of 27
CAREER TENDEX: .513

Richmond reached the 5,000-point mark in this third season. Among active players, only Michael Jordan, Mark Aguirre, Terry Cummings, and Walter Davis did it in fewer games . . . set personal highs last season in minutes played (3,027), steals (126), blocked shots (34) and points (1,840) . . . has averaged at least 22 points per game each of his three NBA seasons, with a career mark of 22.7 . . . in shooting guard ratings, Richmond was among the best in two-point field-goal percentage (No. 8), rebounds (No. 4), and scoring (No. 5), but among the worst in assists (No. 21) and turnovers (No. 23) . . . No. 9 in TENDEX rating.

ROD HIGGINS

AGE: 31
HEIGHT: 6-7
WEIGHT: 205
POSITION: Power Forward
EXPERIENCE: 9 Seasons
COLLEGE: Fresno State
BIRTHPLACE: Monroe, LA
1990–91 TENDEX: .434
POSITIONAL RATING: 20 of 22
CAREER TENDEX: .445

At 6-foot-7 and 205 pounds, Higgins really isn't a power forward but played more minutes at the position than any other Warrior last season . . . out of 22 power forwards, Higgins had excellent ratings of No. 5 in two-point field-goal percentage, No. 6 in three-point field-goal percentage, No. 4 in free-throw percentage, and No. 1 in turnovers . . . had the lowest turnover ratio in the league . . . on the negative side he was No. 20 among power forwards in rebounds, No. 17 in points, and No. 20 in TENDEX rating . . . could be challenged for a starting job this season by Tyrone Hill.

RICHMOND

1990–91	2PFG	3PFG	F.T.	REB.	AST.	STL.	T.O.	BLK.	PTS.
Per Game	.506	.348	.847	5.87	3.09	1.64	2.99	0.44	23.9
Per Minute	.506	.348	.847	.149	.079	.042	.076	.011	.608
Rating	8	9t	10	4	21	11t	23	11t	5

HIGGINS

1990–91	2PFG	3PFG	F.T.	REB.	AST.	STL.	T.O.	BLK.	PTS.
Per Game	.549	.332	.819	4.32	1.38	0.63	0.79	0.45	9.5
Per Minute	.549	.332	.819	.175	.056	.026	.032	.018	.383
Rating	5	6	4	20	15	12	1	14t	17

13
Houston Rockets

1990–91 Statistics	Per Game	Rating
2-Point FG Percent	.490	 14
3-Point FG Percent	.320	 13
Free-Throw Percent	.741	 21
Shootist	.923	 16
Points	106.7	 10
Assists	23.2	 19
Rebounds	+1.34	 10
PAR	+4.12	 10
Blocked Shots	4.99	 15
Steals	9.71	 6
Turnovers	17.3	 23
BEST	−2.40	 16
TENDEX	102.5	 9
Winning Percentage	.634	 8
Coach: D. Chaney	+5	.... 4t
Player: H. Olajuwon	.867	 3
Rookie: J. Turner	NR	 25

First the Houston Rockets discovered they had more than just Hakeem Olajuwon. Then they learned that Olajuwon was a better team player than they had thought. Finally they found out that, with or without Olajuwon, they still did not have enough.

Understand one thing: There is no better center in the NBA than Hakeem Olajuwon. Fitting the right players around him is the problem the Rockets have had for seven years. They found one, Otis Thorpe, three years ago, and added a second, Kenny Smith, last year.

During Hakeem's two-month absence from the lineup last season due to a head injury, Buck Johnson, Vernon Maxwell, Sleepy Floyd, and Larry Smith all had their moments. But when it came down to crunch time, these guys showed up for what they are—quality bench players, but no more.

There was a period of euphoria, after Olajuwon's return, when the Rockets came within one game of going through the month of March undefeated. But they awakened from the dream month to the reality of April—a third-place finish in the Midwest Division and a first-round kayo from the playoffs by the Los Angeles Lakers.

The Rockets still need a quality small

forward and a quality shooting guard. Even if they just had one or the other—a top-shooting perimeter player of any description to pull the double-team off Olajuwon—that might be enough. But they haven't had such a player since Hakeem entered the NBA in 1984.

Olajuwon does not have the shooting touch of David Robinson or Patrick Ewing, but is a better rebounder and defensive player than either of them. This becomes evident in head-to-head matchups, which Olajuwon usually wins.

Thorpe is an excellent power forward and Smith became an outstanding point guard in the Houston system last season. But neither of those two players is a good outside shooter and—despite his own beliefs to the contrary—neither is Vernon Maxwell. Maxwell is a gunner in need of a sight adjustment, shown by his below-average percentages (.450 on two-pointers, .337 on three-pointers, and .733 on free throws).

With TENDEX ratings of .394 and .435,

respectively, Maxwell and Johnson are not the kind of players a good team can afford to have in its starting lineup.

Still, the Rockets made progress last season. Their 52-30 record was the best since Olajuwon joined the team, 11 games better than the season before, for the second-biggest improvement in the NBA.

Houston had the ninth-best TENDEX rating in the league and the eighth-best record, meaning that coach Don Chaney got good production out of his players. Chaney directed the Rockets to a league-best 21 victories in games decided by six points or less. He tied for fourth place in the TENDEX coaches ratings with his former Boston Celtic teammate, Don Nelson of Golden State.

The Rockets should contend again for the Midwest Division title this season, but climbing over talent-laden San Antonio and Utah could be too much to expect.

Probable finish: Third in Midwest Division.

HAKEEM OLAJUWON

AGE: 28
HEIGHT: 6-11
WEIGHT: 250
POSITION: Center
EXPERIENCE: 7 Seasons
COLLEGE: Houston
BIRTHPLACE: Lagos, Nigeria
1990–91 TENDEX: .867
POSITIONAL RATING: 2 of 21
CAREER TENDEX: .795

A head injury that caused Olajuwon to miss 26 games kept him from having his best NBA season in 1990–91 . . . ranked third in the league in TENDEX rating with a personal career-high .867 . . . led league in blocked shots (3.95) and rebounds per game (13.8) . . . No. 18 in scoring (21.2) and No. 9 in steals (2.16) . . . he is consistently the only NBA center to rank among the league leaders in steals . . . made all-time TENDEX lists in scoring, rebounding, blocked shots, and steals—one of three players to make all-time lists in four categories . . . should block his 2,000th shot this season . . . out of 21 centers, ranked No. 1 in rebounds, No. 1 in steals, No. 1 in blocked shots, No. 3 in scoring, and No. 2 in TENDEX last season . . . career TENDEX rating of .795 is first among active centers with five years experience . . . TENDEX Hall of Famer.

OTIS THORPE

AGE: 29
HEIGHT: 6-11
WEIGHT: 236
POSITION: Power Forward
EXPERIENCE: 7 Seasons
COLLEGE: Providence
BIRTHPLACE: Boynton Beach, FL
1990–91 TENDEX: .605
POSITIONAL RATING: 8 of 22
CAREER TENDEX: .577

Playing well while Hakeem Olajuwon was out of the lineup, Thorpe had his best NBA season in 1990–91. Had personal highs in rebounds (846) and TENDEX rating (.605) . . . tied for 10th in the league in rebounds with a 10.3 average per game . . . seventh in field-goal percentage (.566) . . . No. 12 on the all-time list with a career field-goal percentage of .548 . . . in the power-forward ratings Thorpe was No. 3 in two-point field-goal percentage, No. 1 in three-point field-goal percentage, and No. 8 in TENDEX rating . . . still needs improvement in free-throw percentage (No. 19), turnovers (No. 17), and blocked shots (No. 21) . . . should score his 10,000th point this season . . . ranks No. 7 among active power forwards in career TENDEX rating.

OLAJUWON

1990–91	2PFG	3PFG	F.T.	REB.	AST.	STL.	T.O.	BLK.	PTS.
Per Game	.510	.000	.769	13.8	2.34	2.16	3.11	3.95	21.2
Per Minute	.510	.000	.769	.373	.064	.059	.084	.107	.576
Rating	12	18	6	1	4	1	17	1	3

THORPE

1990–91	2PFG	3PFG	F.T.	REB.	AST.	STL.	T.O.	BLK.	PTS.
Per Game	.557	.429	.696	10.3	2.40	0.89	2.65	0.24	17.5
Per Minute	.557	.429	.696	.278	.065	.024	.071	.007	.472
Rating	3	1	19	6t	11	15	17	21	12

KENNY SMITH

AGE: 26
HEIGHT: 6-3
WEIGHT: 170
POSITION: Point Guard
EXPERIENCE: 4 Seasons
COLLEGE: North Carolina
BIRTHPLACE: Queens, NY
1990–91 TENDEX: .556
POSITIONAL RATING: 9 of 23
CAREER TENDEX: .456

Smith was one of the most improved players in the NBA last season, and his 141-point increase in TENDEX rating (from .415 to .556) was doubly surprising because it occurred suddenly after three seasons of consistent mediocrity . . . had personal one-season highs in two-point field-goal percentage (.545), three-point field-goal percentage (.363), free-throw percentage (.844), steals (106), and scoring average (17.7) . . . good point-guard ratings were No. 2 in two-point field-goal percentage, No. 6 in three-point field-goal percentage, No. 5 in free-throw percentage, No. 8 in scoring, and No. 9 in TENDEX.

VERNON MAXWELL

AGE: 26
HEIGHT: 6-4
WEIGHT: 180
POSITION: Shooting Guard
EXPERIENCE: 3 Seasons
COLLEGE: Florida
BIRTHPLACE: Gainesville, FL
1990–91 TENDEX: .394
POSITIONAL RATING: 26 of 27
CAREER TENDEX: .393

The Houston Rockets can only hope that Maxwell will do the same thing this season that Kenny Smith did in his fourth NBA season. Maxwell had his third straight poor season in 1990–91 (TENDEX ratings .396 in 1988–89, .389 in 1989–90 and .393 in 1990–91) . . . he did establish a career-high with his 17-point scoring average last season, but had to take a bushel-load of shots to do it . . . out of 27 shooting guards he ranked No. 23 in two-point field-goal percentage, No. 24 in free-throw percentage, No. 24 in rebounds, No. 18 in assists, No. 21 in blocked shots, No. 17 in scoring, and No. 26 in TENDEX rating . . . his only top-10 ranking was No. 8 in steals.

SMITH

1990–91	2PFG	3PFG	F.T.	REB.	AST.	STL.	T.O.	BLK.	PTS.
Per Game	.545	.363	.844	2.09	7.10	1.36	3.04	0.14	17.7
Per Minute	.545	.363	.844	.060	.205	.039	.088	.004	.511
Rating	2	6	5	23	15	17	15	14	8

MAXWELL

1990–91	2PFG	3PFG	F.T.	REB.	AST.	STL.	T.O.	BLK.	PTS.
Per Game	.450	.337	.733	2.90	3.70	1.55	2.09	0.18	17.0
Per Minute	.450	.337	.733	.083	.106	.044	.060	.005	.487
Rating	23	11	25	24	18	8	10	21	17

BUCK JOHNSON

AGE: 27
HEIGHT: 6-7
WEIGHT: 200
POSITION: Small Forward
EXPERIENCE: 5 Seasons
COLLEGE: Alabama
BIRTHPLACE: Birmingham, AL
1990–91 TENDEX: .435
POSITIONAL RATING: 27 of 30
CAREER TENDEX: .442

Johnson focused in on his career TENDEX rating last season and almost matched it with his .435 mark. The problem, as far as the Rockets are concerned, is that .435 more closely resembles the rating of a substitute than a starter, 65 percentage points below the norm for small forwards . . . in comparison with 29 other small forwards, Johnson ranked No. 20 in two-point field-goal percentage, No. 26 in three-point field-goal percentage, No. 22 in free-throw percentage, No. 21 in rebounds, No. 24 in assists, No. 24 in points, and No. 27 in TENDEX rating.

JOHNSON

1990–91	2PFG	3PFG	F.T.	REB.	AST.	STL.	T.O.	BLK.	PTS.
Per Game	.483	.133	.727	4.52	1.95	1.11	1.67	0.64	13.6
Per Minute	.483	.133	.727	.145	.062	.036	.054	.021	.435
Rating	20	26	22	21	24	15	9t	10t	24

ABSTRACTION 16

The Rooked Rebounder

Hakeem Olajuwon played 56 games and 2,062 minutes last season. He accumulated 770 rebounds—more than the totals of 12 of the 20 players among the official league leaders. He led the league with a rebounding average of 13.8 per game.

He was not listed among the rebounding leaders.

Isiah Thomas played 48 games and 1,657 minutes last season. He accumulated 446 assists, less than 22 other players.

Thomas was listed as the No. 6 player in the NBA with his average of 9.3 assists.

Although Olajuwon was not credited with leading the league in rebounds, he was the official league-leader in blocked shots with an average of 3.95.

Olajuwon would have been listed as the league leader in blocks with his 3.95 average even if he had played only 26 games. But he could not qualify in rebounds even though he played more than twice that many games.

Why these weird discrepancies? The reason is that the NBA was using an archaic system involving minimums of games played and/or bulk totals in each statistical category.

In rebounds, the minimums were ridiculously hard to achieve. Only nine players in the league reached the minimum of 800 rebounds, meaning that most of the "top" rebounders were listed by virtue of playing 70 games rather than by pulling down 800 rebounds. Not only was Olajuwon left out as the No. 1 rebounder, but Rony Seikaly, who averaged 11.1 also was omitted. So was Charles Barkley, with his 10.1 average.

Seikaly should have been listed as the seventh best rebounder in the NBA and Barkley as the 13th best.

In assists, the minimum of 400 was exactly half of the rebounding minimum, even though John Stockton, the league leader in assists the past four seasons, consistently has had larger totals of assists than the totals of the leading rebounders.

The blocked-shot minimum of 100 is absurdly easy to achieve.

The problem goes back to the 1967–68 season. At that time the NBA awarded titles to players on the basis of bulk totals alone. A player scoring 2,000 points with an average of 25 points per game was listed ahead of a player who averaged 30 points but scored only 1,999 points because of missing 15 games.

Oscar Robertson had the best scoring and assists averages in the NBA in 1967–68, but was not awarded the titles because his bulk totals fell short. He missed 17 games (about 20 percent of the schedule) because of an injury.

The NBA was criticized for its archaic system. The established league was made to appear even more ridiculous because the ABA, in its very first season, was giving awards on the basis of per-game average, not bulk totals.

In order to save face, the NBA devised a complicated set of minimums (which, by the way, Robertson's statistics were good enough to meet). There were many more rebounds than assists in those days, so the minimum for assists was established half as large as the minimum for rebounds.

All of those minimums are archaic now. So is the NBA's complicated system of minimums.

If a player plays 2,000 minutes—half of a season—he should qualify for all league awards. Olajuwon was rooked of the 1990–91 rebounding title.

14
Indiana Pacers

1990–91 Statistics	Per Game	Rating
2-Point FG Percent	.513	3
3-Point FG Percent	.332	8
Free-Throw Percent	.811	2
Shootist	.967	3
Points	111.7	5
Assists	26.6	6
Rebounds	−1.48	18
PAR	−0.43	14
Blocked Shots	4.35	24
Steals	8.02	18
Turnovers	16.5	17
BEST	−4.15	25
TENDEX	100.8	13
Winning Percentage	.500	14t
Coach: D. Versace-B. Hill	−2	16t
Player: D. Schrempf	.617	21
Rookie: D. Davis	.618	9

If you are looking for teams on the rise, take the expansion teams and the Indiana Pacers. The Pacers showed in the first round of the playoffs last spring that they are no longer a team to be taken for granted. They pushed the Boston Celtics to the final minutes of the final game before losing, three games to two.

Veteran Chuck Person was the scoring star for the Pacers in the playoffs, but a lot of his success was due to the problems the Celtics had defending the Pacers' backcourt. Time and again, Michael Williams or Reggie Miller or Vern Fleming penetrated and passed off to Person for wide-open shots.

Williams, who apprenticed in the Continental Basketball Association in 1989–90 before breaking into the Pacers' lineup last season, is the key to this team's improvement. He took the regular point-guard job from Fleming late last season and finished the year with a TENDEX rating of .593 in about 1,700 minutes of playing time.

If Williams can play this season at the same level of skill for more than 2,000 minutes, he'll rank among the NBA's top 10 point guards. Since the point is a position at which the Pacers did not excel with Fleming as the starter, they'll be an improved team. And if Fleming is not exceptional as a regular, he certainly will make a good reserve (TENDEX .517).

Person is, was and always shall be, a gunner who can get hot and win a game for his team, or get cold and lose one.

But the Pacers have two other excellent players in Detlef Schrempf, a forward with the skills of a backcourtman, and guard Reggie Miller, perhaps the best pure shooter in basketball.

Indiana's big men, Rik Smits (TENDEX .517) and LaSalle Thompson (.480) are just ordinary, but that's all they have to be with so much talent surrounding them.

Coaches Dick Versace and Bob Hill did a so-so job last year, according to TENDEX. The Pacers won 41 games, whereas the composite ratings of their players indicated a 43-win season was in order.

The Pacers had strange team ratings last season, outstanding in every category related to the scoring of points and poor in almost everything else.

On the positive side, they ranked No. 3 in two-point field-goal percentage, No. 8 in three-point percentage, No. 2 in free-throw percentage, No. 3 in Shootist (points per shot), No. 5 in points, and No. 6 in assists.

On the negative side, they were No. 18 rebounds, No. 24 in blocked shots, No. 18 in steals, and No. 17 in turnovers.

The overall result was just about what might have been expected—a TENDEX rating (No. 13) and winning percentage (No. 14) right smack in the middle of the pack.

This is a young team with much potential for improvement, especially with Williams opening for 1991–92 season as the starting point guard.

Probable finish: Second in Central Division.

REGGIE MILLER

AGE: 26
HEIGHT: 6-7
WEIGHT: 190
POSITION: Shooting Guard
EXPERIENCE: 3 Seasons
COLLEGE: UCLA
BIRTHPLACE: Riverside, CA
1990–91 TENDEX: .585
POSITIONAL RATING: 5 of 27
CAREER TENDEX: .523

After four seasons of steady improvement the question is: How much better can Reggie Miller get? He's had TENDEX ratings of .419, .467, .569 and .585 so far and could push over the .600 mark this season . . . Miller led the league in free-throw percentage (.918), placed No. 12 in scoring (22.6), and No. 19 in three-point field-goal percentage (.348) last season . . . led the Pacers in two-point and three-point field-goal percentages, free-throw percentage, scoring and minutes played . . . in the shooting-guard rankings he was No. 1 in two-point field-goal percentage, No. 1 in free-throw percentage, No. 3 in scoring and No. 5 in TENDEX rating.

DETLEF SCHREMPF

AGE: 28
HEIGHT: 6-10
WEIGHT: 214
POSITION: Power Forward
EXPERIENCE: 6 Seasons
COLLEGE: Washington
BIRTHPLACE: Leverkusen, West Germany
1990–91 TENDEX: .617
POSITIONAL RATING: 4 of 22
CAREER TENDEX: .532

It took Detlef Schrempf a while to get started, but he's rolling now. Schrempf has improved his TENDEX rating each of his six seasons in the NBA, from a meager beginning at .398 to .449, .462, .522, .599, and .617 last season . . . won the NBA's Sixth Man of the Year award in 1990–91 . . . had personal highs in minutes played, two-point and three-point field-goal percentages, rebounds, assists, and TENDEX . . . in the power-forward listings, Schrempf ranked among the top 10 in seven categories: No. 7 in two-point field-goal percentage, No. 4 in three-point field-goal percentage, No. 5 in free-throw percentage, No. 8 in rebounds, No. 1 in assists, No. 9 in points, and No. 4 in TENDEX rating.

MILLER

1990–91	2PFG	3PFG	F.T.	REB.	AST.	STL.	T.O.	BLK.	PTS.
Per Game	.575	.348	.918	3.43	4.04	1.33	1.99	0.16	22.6
Per Minute	.575	.348	.918	.095	.111	.037	.055	.004	.624
Rating	1	9t	1	17	17	17	8	23	3

SCHREMPF

1990–91	2PFG	3PFG	F.T.	REB.	AST.	STL.	T.O.	BLK.	PTS.
Per Game	.527	.375	.818	8.05	3.67	0.71	2.13	0.27	16.1
Per Minute	.527	.375	.818	.251	.114	.022	.067	.008	.502
Rating	7	4	5	8	1	18	14	20	9

CHUCK PERSON

AGE: 27
HEIGHT: 6-8
WEIGHT: 225
POSITION: Small Forward
EXPERIENCE: 5 Seasons
COLLEGE: Auburn
BIRTHPLACE: Brantley, AL
1990–91 TENDEX: .503
POSITIONAL RATING: 20 of 30
CAREER TENDEX: .509

Person's big playoff series against Boston, in which he averaged 26 points per game, helped Indiana fans forget an otherwise so-so season by the Pacer small forward . . . in his fifth NBA season, when he should have been peaking, he averaged 18.4 points per game, the second-lowest average of his career, and continued to show little interest in anything other than scoring and deriding opponents . . . in small-forward ratings he did well in shooting and scoring categories—No. 5 in two-point field-goal percentage, No. 7 in three-point field-goal percentage, No. 6 in scoring . . . poor ratings in just about everything else: No. 18 in rebounds, No. 28 in steals, No. 22 in turnovers, No. 27 in blocked shots, and No. 20 in TENDEX.

PERSON

1990–91	2PFG	3PFG	F.T.	REB.	AST.	STL.	T.O.	BLK.	PTS.
Per Game	.536	.340	.721	5.21	2.98	0.70	2.30	0.21	18.4
Per Minute	.536	.340	.721	.163	.093	.022	.072	.007	.574
Rating	5	7	25	18	12	28	22	27	6

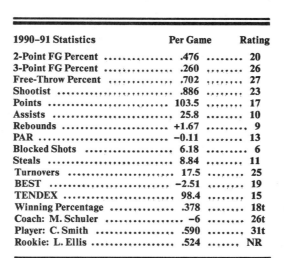

15
Los Angeles Clippers

1990–91 Statistics	Per Game	Rating
2-Point FG Percent	.476	20
3-Point FG Percent	.260	26
Free-Throw Percent	.702	27
Shootist	.886	23
Points	103.5	17
Assists	25.8	10
Rebounds	+1.67	9
PAR	−0.11	13
Blocked Shots	6.18	6
Steals	8.84	11
Turnovers	17.5	25
BEST	−2.51	19
TENDEX	98.4	15
Winning Percentage	.378	18t
Coach: M. Schuler	−6	26t
Player: C. Smith	.590	31t
Rookie: L. Ellis	.524	NR

Shakespeare wrote: "Wise men ne'er sit and wail their loss, but cheerily seek how to redress their harms."

The Clippers have been seeking redress, without much to cheer about, ever since they entered the NBA seven seasons ago. Their record of 163-401 (.289) is the worst in NBA history for any franchise that has existed that long. With the NBA draft set up the way it is, as a great equalizer, their ineptitude is amazing.

If they can't find one way to lose, they try another. The first and best way is the trade: One of the first things they did when they became a franchise was to trade Terry Cummings and Ricky Pierce in the prime of their careers for three aging players. Their most recent wondrous deal was last season when they unloaded Benoit Benjamin (TENDEX .601) to Seattle for Olden Polynice (TENDEX .493).

Between trades, they have taken the injury route to mediocrity. Derek Smith was averaging nearly 30 points a game when he injured a knee early in the 1985–86 season. It was not the injury, but a re-injury when the Clippers returned him to the lineup before the knee was healed, which finished Smith as a good player.

Danny Manning was the No. 1 draft choice in 1988. After an exhausting year in which he led Kansas to an NCAA title and then played for the U.S. Olympic team, the Clippers had him playing 38 minutes per game for two months before he blew out a knee on a no-contact play.

In 1989, they obtained Ron Harper in a good trade with Cleveland. Harper, who at that time was the third-best shooting guard in the NBA, was forced to play 45 minutes per game for a solid month before his knee gave out, also on a no-contact play.

Manning and Harper showed signs of making comebacks last season, and if the Clippers have patience enough not to overwork them, could yet regain most of their former skill. Should this happen, even with Polynice at center, the Clips will have the talent for their first .500 season in history.

Forwards Charles Smith and Ken Norman are excellent players and point guard Gary Grant, when healthy, is good enough. Recovering from a leg injury himself, Grant did not appear to be healthy last season when his TENDEX rating dropped 86 points from the season before his injury.

Since the TENDEX coaches ratings were initiated four years ago, Mike Schuler has consistently been near the bottom. Last year was no exception as he guided the Clippers to a record six games worse than the player talent level of the team. He tied for last place in the 1990–91 ratings with Seattle's K.C. Jones.

In the team statistics, the Clippers did well in rebounding (No. 9) and blocked shots (No. 6), but Benjamin was responsible for a lot of that in his half-season with the team.

On the negative side, they ranked No. 25 in turnovers, No. 20 in two-point field-goal percentage, No. 26 in three-point field-goal percentage, No. 27 in free-throw percentage, and No. 23 in Shootist (points per shot). Harper was to blame for much of this because he shot poorly and did not handle the ball well after returning from his injury. His TENDEX rating plummeted from .613 before the injury to .454 last season.

This is a team at a crossroads: If it has patience with recovering injured players, refuses to make any more foolish trades and finds a coach who can hold his own with the NBA's other top coaches, it could have its first .500 season.

But with this team's front-office record, what do you think are the chances of all this happening?

Probable finish: Sixth in Pacific Division.

DANNY MANNING

AGE: 25
HEIGHT: 6-10
WEIGHT: 230
POSITION: Small Forward
EXPERIENCE: 3 Seasons
COLLEGE: Kansas
BIRTHPLACE: Hattiesburg, MS
1990–91 TENDEX: .580
POSITIONAL RATING: 8 of 30
CAREER TENDEX: .545

Most of the old quickness is back. Quickness was the thing that set Manning apart during this sensational college career, which he capped off with an MVP trophy in the 1988 NCAA Tournament. He seemed to lose it during his rookie NBA season, even before his severe knee injury, and didn't get it back until last season . . . set personal highs in rebounds, assists, steals, and blocked shots . . . led Clippers in steals . . . showed up well in listings of 30 small forwards: No. 8 in two-point field-goal percentage, No. 12 in rebounds, No. 3 in steals, No. 6 in blocked shots, No. 12 in points, No. 8 in TENDEX rating . . . sub-par rankings were No. 26 in free-throw percentage, No. 27 three-point field-goal percentage, and No. 29 in turnovers.

CHARLES SMITH

AGE: 26
HEIGHT: 6-10
WEIGHT: 230
POSITION: Power Forward
EXPERIENCE: 3 Seasons
COLLEGE: Pittsburgh
BIRTHPLACE: Bridgeport, CT
1990–91 TENDEX: .590
POSITIONAL RATING: 9 of 22
CAREER TENDEX: .580

Whatever other problems the Clippers may have, Charles Smith is not one of them. In three seasons, Smith has been nothing but excellent . . . made the All-Rookie Team in 1989 . . . averaged 21.1 and 20.0 points per game the past two seasons . . . set personal highs last season in rebounds, assists, and blocked shots . . . led Clippers in rebounds, free-throw percentage, points, and blocked shots . . . No. 14 in the league in blocked shots, No. 23 in scoring . . . good ratings among power forwards were No. 8 in free-throw percentage, No. 6 in steals, No. 9 in turnovers, No. 3 in blocked shots, No. 5 in scoring, No. 9 in TENDEX . . . needs work on field-goal percentage (No. 18), rebounding (No. 15), and assists (No. 16).

MANNING

1990–91	2PFG	3PFG	F.T.	REB.	AST.	STL.	T.O.	BLK.	PTS.
Per Game	.521	.000	.716	5.84	2.68	1.60	2.58	0.85	15.9
Per Minute	.521	.000	.716	.194	.089	.053	.086	.028	.528
Rating	8	27t	26	12	14	3	29	6	12

SMITH

1990–91	2PFG	3PFG	F.T.	REB.	AST.	STL.	T.O.	BLK.	PTS.
Per Game	.472	.000	.793	8.22	1.81	1.09	2.23	1.96	20.0
Per Minute	.472	.000	.793	.225	.050	.030	.061	.054	.548
Rating	18t	21	8	15	16	6	9	3	5

KEN NORMAN

AGE: 27
HEIGHT: 6-8
WEIGHT: 215
POSITION: Small Forward
EXPERIENCE: 4 Seasons
COLLEGE: Illinois
BIRTHPLACE: Chicago
1990–91 TENDEX: .549
POSITIONAL RATING: 10 of 30
CAREER TENDEX: .499

With the threesome of Charles Smith, Danny Manning, and Ken Norman, the Clippers have one of the best forward combinations in the NBA . . . Norman had the best of his four pro seasons with a .549 TENDEX rating in 1990–91 . . . his No. 10 ranking in TENDEX out of 30 small forwards, coupled with Manning's No. 8, plus Smith's No. 9 in the power-forward ratings, gave the Clippers three of the top 20 forwards in the NBA . . . Norman was the No. 7 small forward in rebounds, No. 7 in blocked shots, No. 10 in two-point field-goal percentage, No. 11 in scoring.

GARY GRANT

AGE: 26
HEIGHT: 6-3
WEIGHT: 195
POSITION: Point Guard
EXPERIENCE: 3 Seasons
COLLEGE: Michigan
BIRTHPLACE: Parson, KN
1990–91 TENDEX: .458
POSITIONAL RATING: 20 of 23
CAREER TENDEX: .489

Grant was becoming one of the better point guards in the NBA in 1989–90 when he suffered a broken leg. He didn't come back completely from the injury in 1990–91. His TENDEX rating of .458 last season was 86 points below his rating (.544) before the injury midway through the previous season . . . despite the overall decline, Grant averaged 8.6 assists per game, eighth best in the NBA . . . in point-guard ratings Grant was No. 10 in rebounds, No. 6 in assists, No. 7 in blocked shots, and below average in everything else . . . worst rankings were No. 20 in free-throw percentage, turnovers, and TENDEX.

NORMAN

1990–91	2PFG	3PFG	F.T.	REB.	AST.	STL.	T.O.	BLK.	PTS.
Per Game	.511	.188	.629	7.10	2.27	0.90	1.99	0.90	17.4
Per Minute	.511	.188	.629	.215	.069	.027	.060	.027	.528
Rating	10	24	30	7	20t	21t	13	7	11

GRANT

1990–91	2PFG	3PFG	F.T.	REB.	AST.	STL.	T.O.	BLK.	PTS.
Per Game	.467	.231	.689	3.07	8.63	1.51	3.09	0.18	8.7
Per Minute	.467	.231	.689	.099	.279	.049	.100	.006	.280
Rating	18	15	20	10	6	13	20	7	19

OLDEN POLYNICE

AGE: 27
HEIGHT: 7-0
WEIGHT: 242
POSITION: Center
EXPERIENCE: 4 Seasons
COLLEGE: Virginia
BIRTHPLACE: Port-Au-Prince, Haiti
1990–91 TENDEX: .493
POSITIONAL RATING: 12 of 21
CAREER TENDEX: .493

In his fourth NBA season, Polynice was well on his way to becoming a career back-up center before the Clippers decided they should trade Benoit Benjamin, one of the NBA's better big men, for him and turn him into a regular . . . he averaged 20 minutes per game for Seattle, with no starts, before the trade. For the Clippers, he started 30 games and averaged 36.5 minutes. The result was predictable—a decline in productivity. As a well-rested reserve for Seattle, Polynice managed a creditable .527 TENDEX rating. Playing heavy-duty minutes for the Clippers, his rating skidded to .465 . . . he shot well (No. 4 among centers in two-point field-goal percentage) but was below average in every other major category.

DOC RIVERS

AGE: 30
HEIGHT: 6-4
WEIGHT: 185
POSITION: Shooting Guard
EXPERIENCE: 8 Seasons
COLLEGE: Marquette
BIRTHPLACE: Maywood, IL
1990–91 TENDEX: .464
POSITIONAL RATING: 15 of 27
CAREER TENDEX: .564

Rivers said he enjoyed playing the shooting guard position in 1990–91 for the first time since his first two NBA seasons; but, from a statistical standpoint, the change was a failure. Rivers did set a personal career mark with his 15.2 scoring average, but dropped off in nearly all other facets of play and his TENDEX rating of .464 was a personal low, 100 points below his career rating . . . Doc ranks among the top 20 players of all-time in assists efficiency, steals efficiency and ratio of steals to turnovers . . . ranked second in the NBA in 1990–91 in ratio of steals to turnovers . . . best ratings among shooting guards were third in turnovers, fourth in steals and fifth in blocked shots . . . worst were 20th in two-point field-goal percentage and 19th in scoring.

POLYNICE

1990–91	2PFG	3PFG	F.T.	REB.	AST.	STL.	T.O.	BLK.	PTS.
Per Game	.561	.000	.579	7.00	0.53	0.54	1.11	0.41	9.8
Per Minute	.561	.000	.579	.264	.020	.021	.042	.015	.372
Rating	4	12t	20	13t	19	14	7	19	13

RIVERS

1990–91	2PFG	3PFG	F.T.	REB.	AST.	STL.	T.O.	BLK.	PTS.
Per Game	.470	.336	.844	3.20	4.30	1.87	1.58	0.60	15.2
Per Minute	.470	.336	.844	.098	.131	.057	.048	.018	.463
Rating	20	12	11	15	10	4t	3t	5t	19

16
Los Angeles Lakers

1990–91 Statistics	Per Game	Rating
2-Point FG Percent	.505	5
3-Point FG Percent	.304	19
Free-Throw Percent	.798	5
Shootist	.950	4
Points	106.3	13
Assists	25.5	11
Rebounds	42.4	7
PAR	+10.3	6
Blocked Shots	4.68	19
Steals	7.83	21
Turnovers	14.7	5
BEST	−2.16	13
TENDEX	105.8	6
Winning Percentage	.707	3
Coach: M. Dunleavy	+2.5	7t
Player: E. Johnson	.818	5
Rookie: A. Jones	NR	NR

Want to know why the Lakers are one of the top franchises in the NBA? Try this for an explanation: They're smarter than everybody else, except maybe old Red Auerbach.

When Kareem Abdul-Jabbar finally retired after the 1988–89 season, it looked as if the Lakers were finished, at least for a few years, as a contending team. Because of their great record the previous season, they had the No. 26 selection in the 1989 draft. Last year they were even worse off with the No. 27 choice.

So what did they do? Got the best center in the draft both years, that's what.

In 1989, for some reason that will forever go unexplained, all of the NBA teams that drafted ahead of the Lakers passed on 6-foot-11 Vlade Divac, star of the Yugoslavian Olympic team the year before at the age of 20. The Lakers selected him and all Divac did was play about the same number of minutes Jabbar had played the season before, with much greater effectiveness (TENDEX .635, compared with Kareem's .444).

Needless to say, the Lakers didn't exactly fall apart. They had the best winning percentage in the league in Divac's rookie season, which entitled them to draft last in 1990.

But with Divac playing only about half of the minutes, they still needed another big man. This time they came up with 6-foot-11 Elden Campbell of Clemson.

Campbell had played poorly his senior season at Clemson. He did not play well in pressure situations and, at 215 pounds, was underweight. But the Lakers must not have limited their scouting to Campbell's senior season because he had shown excellent potential as a scorer during his sophomore and junior campaigns, with TENDEX ratings above .700 both seasons.

The Lakers drafted Campbell, bulked him up on weights, and worked him gradually into the lineup to keep his confidence level up. By playoff time last spring, Campbell was playing more of the crunch-time minutes.

Although Campbell played only bout 400 minutes, that was enough for his TENDEX rating of .544 to have some meaning. It was the best rating of a rookie center, four points better than Felton Spencer of Minnesota, although Spencer did play five times as many minutes.

Campbell has more potential for improvement than Spencer and in three years could rank among the NBA's better centers.

The Lakers, of course, are still Magic's team, but Johnson himself was heard to say last year: "Man, I wish I knew which Vlade Divac would show up tonight."

Johnson was again the NBA's best point guard and Divac, when he did show, was rated by TENDEX as the sixth-best center in the league.

The other Lakers played their roles well: James Worthy and Terry Teagle scoring, Sam Perkins and Sidney Green rebounding, Byron Scott backcourt defense and three-point shooting.

The only thing this team lacks is a substitute for Magic.

Pat Riley, the TENDEX Coach of the Year in 1988, quit, but his replacement, Mike Dunleavy, did almost as well, tying for seventh place in the TENDEX listings last season.

Except for three-point shooting (No. 19), steals (No. 21) and blocked shots (No. 19), the Lakers have no apparent weaknesses. Campbell should take care of the blocked-shots problem as he plays more minutes. He was one of the all-time leading shotblockers in the Atlantic Coast Conference.

In most other statistical categories the Lakers ranked among the top seven teams in the NBA last season.

Don't expect any slipping by this team, at least not during the 1991–92 season. They should contend with Portland and Phoenix for the Pacific Division title from the beginning of the season until the end.

Probable finish: Second in Pacific Division.

MAGIC JOHNSON

AGE: 32
HEIGHT: 6-9
WEIGHT: 226
POSITION: Point Guard
EXPERIENCE: 12 Seasons
COLLEGE: Michigan State
BIRTHPLACE: Lansing, MI
1990–91 TENDEX: .818
POSITIONAL RATING: 1 of 23
CAREER TENDEX: .758

Johnson seems to be improving with age, peaking with TENDEX ratings above .800 four of the past five years . . . broke Oscar Robertson's career assist record last season and should become the first player in history to reach 10,000 assists early this season . . . TENDEX All-NBA First Team honoree 10 times . . . led NBA last season with 13 triple-double games of 10 or more points, assists and rebounds; no other player did it more than four times . . . has won every major award in basketball: NCAA Tournament MVP in 1979, NBA regular-season MVP three times, NBA All-Star Game MVP in 1990, NBA Playoff MVP three times . . . ranked No. 2 in the NBA in assists, No. 5 in free-throw percentage last season . . . excelled with point-guard ratings of No. 4 in two-point field-goal percentage, No. 1 in free-throw percentage, No. 2 in rebounds, No. 2 in assists, No. 4 in blocked shots, No. 6 in scoring, and No. 1 in TENDEX rating . . . No. 1 point guard of all-time in career TENDEX rating.

VLADE DIVAC

AGE: 23
HEIGHT: 6-11
WEIGHT: 243
POSITION: Center
EXPERIENCE: 2 Seasons
COLLEGE: None
BIRTHPLACE: Belgrade, Yugoslavia
1990–91 TENDEX: .632
POSITIONAL RATING: 6 of 21
CAREER TENDEX: .633

Divac proved his excellent rookie season (TENDEX .635) was no accident by practically matching it last season (.632) while playing nearly 50 percent more minutes . . . had problems with erratic play, excelling in first- and third-round playoff series only to be shut down in the second round by Golden State . . . during the regular season he led the Lakers in field-goal percentage, rebounds, steals, and blocked shots . . . No. 5 in the NBA in field-goal percentage . . . out of 21 regular centers, ranked No. 3 in two-point field-goal percentage, No. 2 in three-point field-goal percentage, No. 9 in rebounding, No. 2 in steals, No. 8 in blocked shots, No. 9 in points, and No. 6 in TENDEX rating.

JOHNSON

1990–91	2PFG	3PFG	F.T.	REB.	AST.	STL.	T.O.	BLK.	PTS.
Per Game	.532	.320	.906	6.97	12.5	1.29	3.97	0.26	19.4
Per Minute	.532	.320	.906	.188	.337	.035	.107	.007	.522
Rating	4	12	1	2	2	20	23	4	6

DIVAC

1990–91	2PFG	3PFG	F.T.	REB.	AST.	STL.	T.O.	BLK.	PTS.
Per Game	.570	.357	.703	8.12	1.12	1.29	1.78	1.55	11.2
Per Minute	.570	.357	.703	.288	.040	.046	.063	.055	.399
Rating	3	2	14	9	13	2	14	8	9

JAMES WORTHY

AGE: 30
HEIGHT: 6-9
WEIGHT: 235
POSITION: Small Forward
EXPERIENCE: 9 Seasons
COLLEGE: North Carolina
BIRTHPLACE: Gastonia, NC
1990–91 TENDEX: .525
POSITIONAL RATING: 15 of 30
CAREER TENDEX: .554

Worthy set a personal high in scoring with his 21.4 average last season—No. 1 on the Lakers and No. 18 in the NBA—but he did not have a good season in other phases of play. His TENDEX rating of .525 was the lowest of his nine-year career . . . he had a career field-goal percentage of .555 before last season, but shot only .492 in 1990–91 . . . still ranks No. 10 on the all-time list of field-goal percentage leaders . . . a sure-handed player, Worthy was No. 2 among small forwards in turnovers . . . No. 7 in scoring . . . lows were No. 26 in rebounds and No. 21 in blocked shots . . . No. 15 out of 30 small forwards in TENDEX . . . No. 10 among active small forwards in career TENDEX rating.

SAM PERKINS

AGE: 30
HEIGHT: 6-9
WEIGHT: 235
POSITION: Power Forward
EXPERIENCE: 7 Seasons
COLLEGE: North Carolina
BIRTHPLACE: Brooklyn, NY
1990–91 TENDEX: .515
POSITIONAL RATING: 17 of 22
CAREER TENDEX: .524

Perkins is a steady player who helped solidify the Lakers' defense after being signed as an unrestricted free agent last year . . . out of 22 power forwards, he had good ratings of No. 10 in two-point field-goal percentage, No. 8 in three-point field-goal percentage, No. 3 in free-throw percentage, No. 4 in turnovers, and No. 7 in blocked shots . . . weak ratings were No. 16 in rebounds, No. 17 in assists, No. 15 in scoring, and No. 17 in TENDEX.

WORTHY

1990–91	2PFG	3PFG	F.T.	REB.	AST.	STL.	T.O.	BLK.	PTS.
Per Game	.505	.289	.797	4.56	3.53	1.33	1.63	0.45	21.4
Per Minute	.505	.289	.797	.118	.091	.035	.042	.012	.555
Rating	12t	15	15	26	13	16	2	21	7

PERKINS

1990–91	2PFG	3PFG	F.T.	REB.	AST.	STL.	T.O.	BLK.	PTS.
Per Game	.515	.281	.821	7.37	1.48	0.88	1.41	1.07	13.5
Per Minute	.515	.281	.821	.215	.043	.026	.041	.031	.393
Rating	10	8	3	16	17	13	4	7	15

BYRON SCOTT

AGE: 30
HEIGHT: 6-4
WEIGHT: 195
POSITION: Shooting Guard
EXPERIENCE: 8 Seasons
COLLEGE: Arizona State
BIRTHPLACE: Ogden, UT
1990–91 TENDEX: .420
POSITIONAL RATING: 22 of 27
CAREER TENDEX: .462

Scott sacrifices offense for defense as the complementary guard to Magic Johnson, but has proved when Johnson has been injured that he can step up his scoring and playmaking if necessary . . . it wasn't necessary last season as Johnson missed only three games . . . because Johnson handled the ball so much, Scott led shooting guards in least turnovers but was No. 26 out of 27 shooting guards in assists . . . shot sparingly but well with rankings of No. 5 in two-point field-goal percentage and No. 20 in scoring . . . other below-average ratings were No. 19 in free-throw percentage, No. 18 in rebounds, No. 18 in steals and No. 22 in TENDEX rating . . . ranked fifth in the NBA in ratio of steals to turnovers.

SCOTT

1990-91	2PFG	3PFG	F.T.	REB.	AST.	STL.	T.O.	BLK.	PTS.
Per Game	.517	.324	.797	3.00	2.16	1.16	1.04	0.26	14.5
Per Minute	.517	.324	.797	.094	.067	.036	.032	.008	.453
Rating	5	15	19	18	26	18	1	14	20

ABSTRACTION 17

The Intimidators

The word intimidation is bandied about in the NBA. It's often used to describe an exceptional defensive player, who blocks a lot of shots or forces opponents to alter their shots.

But there's another kind of intimidation. The following players, I suggest, are among the best intimidators in the NBA. It's not that they intimidate other players so much, but they sure do a number on the officials.

The statistic is the ratio between the number of free throws they were awarded and the number of personal fouls charged to them during the 1990–91 season:

Player, Team	Ratio
1. Magic Johnson, LA Lakers	3.82
2. Charles Barkley, Philadelphia	3.80
3. Dominique Wilkins, Atlanta	3.68
4. Reggie Miller, Indiana	3.64
5. Kevin Johnson, Phoenix	3.54
6. Karl Malone, Utah	3.31
7. Chris Mullin, Golden State	3.30
8. Michael Adams, Denver	3.27
9. Joe Dumars, Detroit	3.09
10. Brad Daugherty, Cleveland	3.03

If not superstars, most of these players are at least above average and certainly should have good ratios. But the way Charles Barkley muscles people around, should he really go to the foul line nearly four times as often as he is whistled for personal fouls? Magic Johnson is a great penetrator, but should even his disparity be *that* great?

Why is Brad Daugherty on this list? Is he really more difficult to defend in the low post than David Robinson, Hakeem Olajuwon and Patrick Ewing, or does he just do a better job of flopping to the floor to coax whistles?

I don't know how an NBA official thinks, but I would be more than a little suspicious of seeing 260-pound monsters like Barkley and Daugherty bouncing on the floor as much as they do.

Robinson and Michael Jordan are just outside the top 10 with ratios just under 3.00. No surprise there. But Ewing's ratio of 2.17 is surprisingly low and Olajuwon's ratio of 1.25 is ridiculous. Doesn't Hakeem ever get a call? Maybe he just doesn't whine as much as those other guys. He plays the game like a man.

Just as some players are more intimidating than others, so are some teams. Here are the top teams in intimidation. The statistic here is the difference between a team's free throws and its opponents' free throws for the 1990–91 season. All of the listed teams are on the positive side:

Team	Free-Throw Surplus
1. Philadelphia 76ers	572
2. Los Angeles Lakers	561
3. Atlanta Hawks	475
4. Phoenix Suns	436
5. Utah Jazz	382
6. San Antonio Spurs	272
7. New York Knicks	244
8. Portland Trail Blazers	197
9. Houston Rockets	114
10. Chicago Bulls	94

How is it that the slow-footed 76ers, who have neither a standout penetrating point guard, nor an exceptional low-post center, can lead the NBA in this category?

Golden State coach Don Nelson suggested during the Warriors-Lakers playoff series last spring that maybe the Lakers were getting more than their share of the benefit of the doubt from referees too. Said Nelson:

"Of the 600 more points they (Lakers) scored than their opponents, 500 of them (actually 527) were free throws."

17
Miami Heat

1990–91 Statistics	Per Game	Rating
2-Point FG Percent	.470	22
3-Point FG Percent	.302	20
Free-Throw Percent	.715	26
Shootist	.884	24
Points	101.8	21
Assists	23.2	20
Rebounds	−0.07	14
PAR	−7.31	21
Blocked Shots	4.72	18
Steals	9.23	8
Turnovers	18.9	27
BEST	−4.96	26
TENDEX	94.1	25
Winning Percentage	.293	26
Coach: R. Rothstein	−2	16t
Player: R. Seikaly	.579	36
Rookie: S. Smith	.583	6

With Ron Rothstein's departure last year and the hiring of Kevin Loughery as the new head coach, the Heat is entering a new era. The question is: Will the coaching change and the addition of rookie Steve Smith to the roster be enough to push the Heat past the middle level of the Eastern Conference and into contention with Detroit, Chicago, and Boston? This team isn't likely to get many more shots at the lottery with the young talent it has.

Rothstein was an adequate coach for an expansion team and should be given credit for his perseverance. He was hounded by the South Florida media throughout his final season, and it is likely that he did indeed resign without much pressure from upper management.

In the end, a change was necessary. Rothstein was not a player's coach. He was criticized for giving rookie Alec Kessler too few minutes of playing time. He tied for 16th place in the TENDEX coaches ratings.

One of the reasons the Heat can expect continued improvement this season is depth. Willie Burton and Kessler showed potential as rookies.

Burton, a good athlete, is excellent at driving to the hoop, and if his outside shooting improves, he will be a good NBA small forward.

Burton's attitude however is a big question-mark. He likes to talk a big game, but he didn't produce one often with his .402 TENDEX rating last season.

Kessler bulked up before last season, as Rony Seikaly had done the year before. The only problem is that Kessler's mobility may have been hindered by the extra weight. He does have a good jumpshot from free-throw distance, but inside the paint he is awkward at best. With good coaching he could become a good rebounder and scorer.

Of the Heat's veteran players, room for development is also evident. Their top players, Seikaly and Sherman Douglas, need improvement in free-throw shooting and ball-handling. Douglas was 21st in free-throw percentage and 22nd in turnovers out of 23 point guards,

Seikaly was 19th and 20th respectively out of 21 centers.

The Heat as a team was last in turnovers and next to last in free throws.

Glen Rice made great strides last season. He improved his TENDEX rating by 75 points over his rookie season and that number would have been higher except for a shooting slump at the end of the season. Rice and Douglas should anchor a strong backcourt for years to come.

The Heat is a young team with a lot of players who could develop into NBA talents. Getting all these youngsters was the easy part. Now the hard part is developing that talent and forming a contending team. Look for improvement this season, maybe enough to get out of the lottery, but probably not.

Probable finish: Sixth in Atlantic Division.

—DAN HEEREN

SHERMAN DOUGLAS

AGE: 25
HEIGHT: 6-0
WEIGHT: 180
POSITION: Point Guard
EXPERIENCE: 2 Seasons
COLLEGE: Syracuse
BIRTHPLACE: Washington, DC
1990–91 TENDEX: .567
POSITIONAL RATING: 7 of 23
CAREER TENDEX: .559

Despite being only a second-round draft choice, Douglas was an excellent point guard from the minute he entered the NBA two years ago and got even better last year, improving his TENDEX rating from .550 to .567 . . . his biggest improvement was in scoring, from 14.3 to 18.5 points per game . . . led Miami in scoring, assists, and field-goal percentage . . . No. 9 in the NBA in assists . . . best point-guard ratings were No. 7 in two-point field-goal percentage, No. 8 in assists, No. 4 in scoring, and No. 7 in TENDEX . . . still needs improvement in three-point field-goal percentage (No. 19), free-throw percentage (No. 21), and turnovers (No. 22).

RONY SEIKALY

AGE: 26
HEIGHT: 6-11
WEIGHT: 250
POSITION: Center
EXPERIENCE: 3 Seasons
COLLEGE: Syracuse
BIRTHPLACE: Athens, Greece
1990–91 TENDEX: .579
POSITIONAL RATING: 8 of 21
CAREER TENDEX: .542

The NBA's Most Improved Player in 1989–90, Seikaly took a step backward last season, mostly because of injury problems. After improving his TENDEX rating from .437 to .594 from his first to his second season, he slid back to .579 last season, but remained one of the top five young centers in the NBA . . . led Miami in rebounds and blocked shots . . . ranked No. 7 in the league in rebounding with his average of 11.1 per game . . . good rankings among centers were No. 4 in rebounds, No. 7 in scoring, and No. 8 in TENDEX . . . needs improvement in free-throw percentage (No. 19) and turnovers (No. 20).

DOUBLAS

1990–91	2PFG	3PFG	F.T.	REB.	AST.	STL.	T.O.	BLK.	PTS.
Per Game	.516	.129	.686	2.86	8.55	1.66	3.70	0.07	18.5
Per Minute	.516	.129	.686	.082	.244	.047	.105	.002	.528
Rating	7	19	21	15	8t	15	22	21	4t

SEIKALY

1990–91	2PFG	3PFG	F.T.	REB.	AST.	STL.	T.O.	BLK.	PTS.
Per Game	.482	.333	.619	11.1	1.48	0.80	3.20	1.34	16.4
Per Minute	.482	.333	.619	.327	.044	.024	.094	.040	.484
Rating	17t	3	19	4	10	11	20	11	7

GLEN RICE

AGE: 24
HEIGHT: 6-7
WEIGHT: 215
POSITION: Shooting Guard
EXPERIENCE: 2 Seasons
COLLEGE: Michigan
BIRTHPLACE: Flint, MI
1990–91 TENDEX: .472
POSITIONAL RATING: 12 of 27
CAREER TENDEX: .437

Rice may be a year away from joining team-mates Sherman Douglas and Rony Seikaly as first-rate NBA players. Playing more aggressively in his second season, he improved his TENDEX rating 75 points from .397 to .472 in 1990–91. The 1989 NCAA Tournament MVP has the potential to be one of the best shooting guards in the NBA . . . led the Heat last season in minutes played, free-throw percentage, and three-point field-goal percentage while averaging 17.4 points, second best on the team . . . among shooting guards he excelled in three-point shooting (No. 4) and rebounding (No. 5) . . . needs work on playmaking (No. 24 in assists).

KEVIN EDWARDS

AGE: 26
HEIGHT: 6-3
WEIGHT: 200
POSITION: Shooting Guard
EXPERIENCE: 3 Seasons
COLLEGE: DePaul
BIRTHPLACE: Cleveland Heights, OH
1990–91 TENDEX: .431
POSITIONAL RATING: 20 of 27
CAREER TENDEX: .416

Edwards has had three seasons of playing 2,000 or more minutes for Miami without showing significant improvement. He is unlikely to play another season for the Heat and, if he isn't traded, will have to content himself with much less playing time . . . in 1990–91 shooting-guard listings he ranked high only in steals (No. 3) and blocked shots (No. 3) . . . far down the list in everything else, including two-point field-goal percentage (No. 26), three-point field-goal percentage (No. 20), free-throw percentage (No. 16), turnovers (No. 25), scoring (No. 18), and TENDEX (No. 20).

RICE

1990–91	2PFG	3PFG	F.T.	REB.	AST.	STL.	T.O.	BLK.	PTS.
Per Game	.475	.386	.818	4.95	2.45	1.31	2.16	0.34	17.4
Per Minute	.475	.386	.818	.144	.071	.038	.063	.010	.507
Rating	18	4	15	5	24	14t	13	13	14

EDWARDS

1990–91	2PFG	3PFG	F.T.	REB.	AST.	STL.	T.O.	BLK.	PTS.
Per Game	.422	.286	.803	2.59	3.04	1.65	2.06	0.58	12.1
Per Minute	.422	.286	.803	.103	.120	.065	.082	.023	.478
Rating	26	20t	16	13	13	3	25t	3	18

GRANT LONG

AGE: 25
HEIGHT: 6-8
WEIGHT: 225
POSITION: Power Forward
EXPERIENCE: 3 Seasons
COLLEGE: Eastern Michigan
BIRTHPLACE: Wayne, MI
1990–91 TENDEX: .479
POSITIONAL RATING: 19 of 22
CAREER TENDEX: .487

Like Edwards, Long will be phased out as a regular as soon as the expansion Heat finds a capable replacement, and they are likely to do so this season . . . undersized as a power forward, Long holds his own tenaciously on defense but contributes little to the offense. This is reflected by the fact that he led all power forwards last season in steals, but was no better than ninth in any other statistical category . . . especially weak in scoring (No. 22) and TENDEX rating (No. 19).

LONG

1990–91	2PFG	3PFG	F.T.	REB.	AST.	STL.	T.O.	BLK.	PTS.
Per Game	.495	.167	.787	7.10	2.20	1.49	1.95	0.54	9.2
Per Minute	.495	.167	.787	.226	.070	.047	.062	.017	.292
Rating	15	12t	9	13t	9	1	11	17	22

18
Milwaukee Bucks

1990–91 Statistics	Per Game	Rating
2-Point FG Percent	.497	12
3-Point FG Percent	.341	5
Free-Throw Percent	.801	3
Shootist	.950	5
Points	106.4	12
Assists	25.3	13
Rebounds	−2.22	21
PAR	+0.89	12
Blocked Shots	4.02	25
Steals	10.9	1
Turnovers	16.1	15
BEST	−1.18	8
TENDEX	101.7	11
Winning Percentage	.585	10
Coach: D. Harris	+3	6
Player: A. Robertson	.598	29
Rookie: K. Brooks	NR	28

Milwaukee is an old team that should have died five years ago, but refuses to be buried.

Led by Sidney Moncrief, the Bucks won a remarkable seven divisional titles in a row from 1980 through 1986, but even when Moncrief slumped during the latter years of the 1980s, they remained respectable.

The 1989 trade of Terry Cummings for Alvin Robertson and Greg Anderson helped a lot. For Milwaukee, Robertson has been a Moncrief-like player the past two seasons, playing excellent defense and respectable offense. He even attended the same university as Moncrief (Arkansas).

The Bucks made another trade last season, exchanging shooting guards with Seattle, Ricky Pierce for Dale Ellis. This one may not turn out quite so well.

Ellis, 31, has been susceptible to injuries the past two seasons, averaging about 1,700 minutes per season. His TENDEX ratings for the two seasons (.531 and .488) have not been exceptional.

Although Pierce is a year older than Ellis, his career seems to be peaking. He won the NBA's Sixth Man of the Year award in 1990 and the TENDEX Sixth Man award in 1991. His TENDEX ratings for the past two seasons have been .624 and .590—the highest ratings of his nine-year career.

Ellis must remain healthy in 1991–92 and regain his form of three years ago for the Bucks to have any chance to match their record of last season (48-34).

The point-guard position is in the capable hands of Jay Humphries (TENDEX .536), but up front this team is in big trouble.

The best of the front-liners is Frank Brickowski (TENDEX .579). Brickowski, 32, was obtained in another "steal-deal" with San Antonio, for Paul Pressey. But he played only 1,912 minutes last season and might not play that many this season.

The other frontcourtmen last season were one-time great Jack Sikma, 36, TENDEX .504; Danny Schayes, 32, TENDEX .531; Brad Lohaus, 27, TENDEX .445; and Fred Roberts, 31, TENDEX .439. Moses Malone has been added for this season.

Paced by Robertson, the league-leader in steals, Milwaukee led the NBA in team steals and placed second to the Chicago Bulls in ratio of steals to turnovers.

Good team shooting percentages: No. 12 in two-point field goals, No. 5 in three-point field-goals, No. 3 in free-throws, and No. 5 in Shootist (points per shot).

Below-average team ratings in rebounds (No. 21), blocked shots (No. 25), and turnovers (No. 15).

Coach Del Harris has done a good job of holding this team together. He won TENDEX Coach of the Year honors in 1990 and last year he was the No. 6 rated coach when he directed the Bucks to three more victories than they probably should have won, according to their team TENDEX rating.

Don't expect Harris to be able to repeat the performance this season.

Probable finish: Fifth in Central Division.

ALVIN ROBERTSON

AGE: 29
HEIGHT: 6-4
WEIGHT: 190
POSITION: Shooting Guard
EXPERIENCE: 7 Seasons
COLLEGE: Arkansas
BIRTHPLACE: Barberton, OH
1990–91 TENDEX: .598
POSITIONAL RATING: 3 of 27
CAREER TENDEX: .584

One of the NBA's best defensive guards, Robertson led the league in steals (3.04) last season and was a member of the All-Defensive First Team . . . the TENDEX Hall of Famer ranks No. 1 on the all-time lists in steals-per-game and steals-per-minute . . . had his sixth straight PAR-5 season in 1990–91, averaging at least five points, five assists and five rebounds per game . . . had three triple-double games with at least 10 points, rebounds and assists . . . ranked third in the NBA in ratio of steals to turnovers . . . had a personal-best three-point shooting percentage (.365) and ranked sixth out of 27 shooting guards in that category . . . other good ratings were No. 2 in rebounds, No. 3 in assists, No 1 in steals, No. 3 in TENDEX . . . could stand improvement in free-throw percentage (No. 24), turnovers (No. 25), and points (No. 23) . . . No. 4 among active shooting guards in career TENDEX rating.

JAY HUMPHRIES

AGE: 29
HEIGHT: 6-3
WEIGHT: 185
POSITION: Point Guard
EXPERIENCE: 7 Seasons
COLLEGE: Colorado
BIRTHPLACE: Los Angeles
1990–91 TENDEX: .536
POSITIONAL RATING: 11 of 23
CAREER TENDEX: .472

Humphries is thriving in Milwaukee's guard-oriented system, has had his best two seasons the past two years with the Bucks, with TENDEX ratings of .516 and .536 . . . led Bucks in assists and ranked 18th in the NBA with his 6.7 average in 1990–91 . . . steady with point-guard ratings of No. 5 in two-point field-goal percentage, No. 3 in three-point percentage, No. 6 in turnovers, No. 12 in scoring, and No. 11 in TENDEX.

ROBERTSON

1990–91	2PFG	3PFG	F.T.	REB.	AST.	STL.	T.O.	BLK.	PTS.
Per Game	.493	.365	.757	5.67	5.48	3.04	2.62	0.20	13.6
Per Minute	.493	.365	.757	.177	.171	.095	.082	.006	.423
Rating	12	6	24	2	3	1	25t	3	18

HUMPHRIES

1990–91	2PFG	3PFG	F.T.	REB.	AST.	STL.	T.O.	BLK.	PTS.
Per Game	.528	.373	.799	2.75	6.73	1.61	1.89	0.09	15.2
Per Minute	.528	.373	.799	.081	.197	.047	.055	.003	.446
Rating	6	5	13	17	18	14	6	19	12

DAN SCHAYES

AGE: 32
HEIGHT: 6-11
WEIGHT: 260
POSITION: Center
EXPERIENCE: 10 Seasons
COLLEGE: Syracuse
BIRTHPLACE: Syracuse, NY
1990–91 TENDEX: .531
POSITIONAL RATING: 11 of 21
CAREER TENDEX: .538

Schayes is not as well known as his father, Dolph, a TENDEX Hall of Famer, but is a solid player himself, a 10-year man in the NBA . . . led Bucks in rebounds last season . . . ranked No. 2 in free-throw percentage out of 21 regular centers . . . consistent in other categories: No. 9 in assists, No. 9 in steals, No. 9 in turnovers, No. 10 in scoring, and No. 11 in TENDEX rating.

FRED ROBERTS

AGE: 31
HEIGHT: 6-10
WEIGHT: 220
POSITION: Small Forward
EXPERIENCE: 8 Seasons
COLLEGE: Brigham Young
BIRTHPLACE: Provo, UT
1990–91 TENDEX: .439
POSITIONAL RATING: 26 of 30
CAREER TENDEX: .416

Roberts had one of his best seasons in 1990–91, establishing a personal high with his scoring average of 10.8 . . . led the Bucks in field-goal percentage (.533) . . . out of 30 small forwards had good ratings of No. 4 in two-point field-goal percentage, and No. 9 in free-throw percentage . . . but check out these other ratings: No. 25 in three-point field-goal percentage, No. 23 in rebounds, No. 23 in assists, No. 26 in scoring, and No. 26 in TENDEX rating.

SCHAYES

1990–91	2PFG	3PFG	F.T.	REB.	AST.	STL.	T.O.	BLK.	PTS.
Per Game	.503	.000	.835	6.52	1.20	0.67	1.29	0.74	10.6
Per Minute	.503	.000	.835	.240	.044	.025	.048	.027	.390
Rating	13	19	2	19	9	9	9	13	10

ROBERTS

1990–91	2PFG	3PFG	F.T.	REB.	AST.	STL.	T.O.	BLK.	PTS.
Per Game	.547	.160	.813	3.43	1.65	0.77	1.65	0.35	10.8
Per Minute	.547	.160	.813	.133	.064	.030	.064	.014	.420
Rating	4	25	9	23t	23	17	16t	18	26

19
Minnesota Timberwolves

1990–91 Statistics	Per Game	Rating
2-Point FG Percent	.458	27
3-Point FG Percent	.284	22
Free-Throw Percent	.735	23
Shootist	.873	26
Points	99.6	26
Assists	23.0	21
Rebounds	−1.04	17
PAR	−8.10	23
Blocked Shots	5.37	11
Steals	8.68	13
Turnovers	13.0	1
BEST	+1.10	1
TENDEX	95.4	22
Winning Percentage	.354	21
Coach: B. Musselman	0	11t
Player: F. Spencer	.540	51
Rookie: L. Longley	.656	5

Unlike the other expansion teams, the Timberwolves started out with only one young player (Pooh Richardson) in their starting lineup during their first season. In their second season, they added one more (Felton Spencer). Now it's time to add one or two more.

The vulnerable Timberwolves are shooting guard Tony Campbell, who after one excellent season in Minnesota slumped in 1990–91; and power forward Sam Mitchell, who has yet to prove he doesn't belong back with the Rapid City Thrillers in the Continental Basketball Association, where he played in 1988–89.

Campbell's TENDEX rating slipped from .524 to .466 last season, while his field-goal percentage declined from .457 to .434. For a guy who is mostly a scorer to begin with, field-goal percentage is a vital statistic.

Mitchell played better than expected in the Timberwolves' first season, 1989–90, although his TENDEX rating of .485 was 40 points below the norm for a power forward. Last year his rating was only .411, 21st out of 22 regular power forwards.

Second-year man Gerald Glass is a candidate for Campell's job. He had a creditable .482 TENDEX rating in sparse playing time last season as a rookie and should improve this year.

At the other three positions, the Timberwolves are in fine shape. Third-year point guard Pooh Richardson improved his TENDEX rating by 21 points last season to .535 while at the same time playing a staggering total of 3,154 minutes.

At 28, Tyrone Corbin is peaking at the small forward position. The versatile Corbin has had TENDEX ratings of .553 and .533 the past two seasons while playing more than 3,000 minutes both seasons. He's an excellent all-around basketball player.

Second-year center Felton Spencer exceeded the expectations of even his biggest boosters by becoming a starter in his rookie season and earning TENDEX All-Rookie honors with his .540 rating—best on the Timberwolves team.

Coach Bill Musselman was criticized for playing his starters too many minutes, for not using young players enough, and for not communicating well with players. He was replaced at the end of the season by Jimmy Rodgers. Under Musselman, the Wolves won 29 games in 1990–91, precisely the number that their player talent called for.

This is a team with a few tremendous strengths and many glaring weaknesses. Thanks mostly to the sure hands of Richardson, Minnesota ranked No. 1 in the NBA last season in turnovers and No. 1 in BEST (combination of blocked shots, steals, and turnovers).

But they were abysmal in most everything else: No. 27 (last) in two-point field-goal percentage, No. 22 in three-point field-goal percentage, No. 23 in free-throw percentage, No. 26 in Shootist (points per shot), No. 26 in points, No. 21 in assists, No. 17 in rebounds, No. 23 in PAR (combination of points, assists and rebounds), and No. 22 in TENDEX rating.

Thanks to rookie Luc Longley the Timberwolves can expect some improvement this season but not much. Probable finish: Fourth in Midwest Division.

POOH RICHARDSON

AGE: 25
HEIGHT: 6-1
WEIGHT: 180
POSITION: Point Guard
EXPERIENCE: 2 Seasons
COLLEGE: UCLA
BIRTHPLACE: Philadelphia
1990–91 TENDEX: .535
POSITIONAL RATING: 12 of 23
CAREER TENDEX: .526

In his second NBA season, Richardson improved in nearly every statistical category. Biggest improvement was in scoring, from 11.4 to 17.1 points per game . . . led Timberwolves in assists and ranked No. 7 in the NBA with his 9.0 average . . . No. 5 in minutes played (3,154) . . . Richardson's biggest strength as a point guard is he does not turn the ball over much (No. 5 out of 23 point men) . . . his biggest weakness is incredibly low free-throw percentage of .539. No other point man shot worse than .604.

TYRONE CORBIN

AGE: 29
HEIGHT: 6-6
WEIGHT: 222
POSITION: Small Forward
EXPERIENCE: 6 Seasons
COLLEGE: DePaul
BIRTHPLACE: Columbia, SC
1990–91 TENDEX: .533
POSITIONAL RATING: 12 of 30
CAREER TENDEX: .502

Versatile Corbin had a career season in 1990–91 with personal highs in minutes played (3,196), free-throw percentage (.798), assists (347), blocked shots (53) and points (18.0) . . . No. 4 in the NBA in minutes played . . . seems to be improving with age, had his best two TENDEX ratings the past two seasons (.553 and .533) . . . registered the first triple-double in Timberwolf history with 10 points, 13 rebounds and 10 assists in a game against Dallas . . . ranked No. 5 in assists and No. 5 in rebounds last season out of 30 small forwards . . . weakest statistic was two-point field-goal percentage (No. 28) . . . overall, he's one of the better players at his position (No. 12 in TENDEX).

RICHARDSON

1990–91	2PFG	3PFG	F.T.	REB.	AST.	STL.	T.O.	BLK.	PTS.
Per Game	.485	.328	.539	3.49	8.95	1.60	2.12	0.16	17.1
Per Minute	.485	.328	.539	.091	.233	.042	.055	.004	.444
Rating	13	10	23	14	12	16	5	13	13

CORBIN

1990–91	2PFG	3PFG	F.T.	REB.	AST.	STL.	T.O.	BLK.	PTS.
Per Game	.450	.200	.798	7.18	4.23	1.98	2.55	0.65	18.0
Per Minute	.450	.200	.798	.184	.109	.051	.065	.017	.461
Rating	28	22t	14	14	5	5	19	17	10t

TONY CAMPBELL

AGE: 29
HEIGHT: 6-7
WEIGHT: 215
POSITION: Small Forward
EXPERIENCE: 7 Seasons
COLLEGE: Ohio State
BIRTHPLACE: Teaneck, NJ
1990–91 TENDEX: .466
POSITIONAL RATING: 13 of 27
CAREER TENDEX: .462

After having a career season in 1989–90, Campbell took a big step backward last season. He ranked No. 15 in the NBA with his 21.8 scoring average, but experienced sharp declines in field-goal percentage (from .457 to .434) and TENDEX rating (from .524 to .466) . . . good ratings out of 27 shooting guards were No. 9 in rebounds, No. 7 in blocked shots and No. 6 in scoring . . . bad ones were No. 24 in two-point field-goal percentage, No. 22 in three-point percentage, and No. 23 in assists.

FELTON SPENCER

AGE: 23
HEIGHT: 7-0
WEIGHT: 265
POSITION: Center
EXPERIENCE: 1 Season
COLLEGE: Louisville
BIRTHPLACE: Louisville, KY
1990–91 TENDEX: .540
POSITIONAL RATING: 10 of 21
CAREER TENDEX: .540

Made the TENDEX All-Rookie Team last season with his rating of .540, best of the first-year centers who played at least 1,500 minutes . . . proved pundits wrong who had said he would be a career NBA backup by earning a starting job in his first year . . . led Minnesota in field-goal percentage, rebounds and blocked shots . . . compared with other centers he more than held his own with ratings of No. 9 in two-point field-goal percentage, No. 11 in free-throw percentage, No. 6 in rebounds, No. 2 in turnovers, No. 6 in blocked shots, and No. 10 in TENDEX . . . improvement in assists (No. 21) and points (No. 18) would make him an NBA star.

CAMPBELL

1990–91	2PFG	3PFG	F.T.	REB.	AST.	STL.	T.O.	BLK.	PTS.
Per Game	.441	.262	.803	4.49	2.78	1.57	2.47	0.62	21.8
Per Minute	.441	.262	.803	.120	.074	.042	.066	.017	.580
Rating	24	22	17	9	23	11t	15	7	6

SPENCER

1990–91	2PFG	3PFG	F.T.	REB.	AST.	STL.	T.O.	BLK.	PTS.
Per Game	.513	.000	.722	7.91	0.31	0.59	0.95	1.49	7.1
Per Minute	.513	.000	.722	.305	.012	.023	.037	.058	.273
Rating	9t	12t	11	6	21	12	2t	6	18

SAM MITCHELL

AGE: 28
HEIGHT: 6-7
WEIGHT: 210
POSITION: Power Forward
EXPERIENCE: 2 Seasons
COLLEGE: Mercer
BIRTHPLACE: Columbus, GA
1990–91 TENDEX: .411
POSITIONAL RATING: 21 of 22
CAREER TENDEX: .443

In fairness to Mitchell, he played too many minutes last season and was out of position at power forward. Those are problems Minnesota should remedy this season . . . he ranked No. 6 in the NBA with 3,121 minutes . . . in league-wide power forward ratings he did not fare well at all: No. 22 (last place) in two-point field-goal percentage, No. 22 in three-point percentage, No. 21 in rebounds, No. 18 in assists, No. 19 in steals, No. 14 in blocked shots, No. 16 in points, and No. 21 in TENDEX . . . saving grace was No. 2 rating in turnovers.

MITCHELL

1990–91	2PFG	3PFG	F.T.	REB.	AST.	STL.	T.O.	BLK.	PTS.
Per Game	.445	.000	.775	6.34	1.62	0.81	1.27	0.70	14.6
Per Minute	.445	.000	.775	.167	.043	.021	.033	.018	.384
Rating	22	22	11	21	18	19	2	14t	16

20
New Jersey Nets

1990–91 Statistics	Per Game	Rating
2-Point FG Percent	.458	26
3-Point FG Percent	.275	24
Free-Throw Percent	.740	22
Shootist	.870	27
Points	102.9	19
Assists	21.7	27
Rebounds	−0.80	16
PAR	−4.77	18
Blocked Shots	7.32	1
Steals	9.12	9
Turnovers	17.4	24
BEST	−0.92	5
TENDEX	96.4	20
Winning Percentage	.317	23t
Coach: B. Fitch	−5	23t
Player: D. Coleman	.614	22
Rookie: K. Anderson	.514	4

The Nets filled one of the holes in their lineup last season with Rookie of the Year Derrick Coleman.

Now all they have to do is fill the other four.

It was thanks only to Coleman's excellent play that the Nets didn't join the Denver Nuggets at the bottom of the league standings. Coleman's TENDEX rating was an excellent .614 and he showed potential to become one of the NBA's elite players.

The other four New Jersey starters are below average, with the possible exception of small forward Chris Morris. Morris can be good when he decides to be good, but has not shown consistent motivation during his three NBA seasons. He has the talent of a Scottie Pippen, but seems content to play an up-and-down role like a Chuck Person.

Point guard Mookie Blaylock improved enough in his second season to show that there may be hope for him yet, but since he was rated No. 21 out of 23 point guards last season, he has a long way to go.

Shooting guard Reggie Theus is 34 and shows it at both ends of the court. He can still score (18.6 points per game) but not as well as he once did. And he gives up more points to players he is assigned to defend than he scores himself.

Drazen Petrovic, obtained in a three-way trade with Denver and Portland last season, is a better shooting guard than Theus. Petrovic's TENDEX rating was a very good .519, although he played only 1,015 minutes.

Sam Bowie and Chris Dudley shared the center duties for the Nets and neither proved adequate. The chronically injured Bowie had a TENDEX rating of .516, 34 points below normal for a center. Dudley, the world's worst free-throw shooter, had a rating of .511.

The Nets got a predictably poor coaching job by Bill Fitch. Never one of TENDEX's favorites, Fitch masterminded the Nets to five fewer victories than they should have won in 1990–91. He tied Boston's Chris Ford for the 23rd spot in the coaches' ratings.

Bowie, Dudley, and Coleman all are good shot-blockers, so the Nets led the NBA in that category. Blaylock and Morris stole the ball a lot, so they were ninth in that category. And fifth in BEST, which combines blocked shots, steals and turnovers.

Otherwise, forget it: No. 26 in two-point field-goal percentage, No. 24 in three-point field-goal percentage, No. 22 in free-throw percentage, No. 27 in Shootist (combining the three percentages), No. 19 in points, No. 27 in assists, No. 24 in turnovers, and No. 20 in TENDEX rating.

Expect improvement from Coleman and help from rookie Kenny Anderson this season. The Nets could finish anywhere from second to seventh in the Atlantic Division.

Probable finish: Fifth in Atlantic Division.

DERRICK COLEMAN

AGE: 24
HEIGHT: 6-10
WEIGHT: 230
POSITION: Power Forward
EXPERIENCE: 1 Season
COLLEGE: Syracuse
BIRTHPLACE: Mobile, AL
1990–91 TENDEX: .614
POSITIONAL RATING: 5 of 22
CAREER TENDEX: .614

Coleman proved the Nets did not make a mistake by choosing him No. 1 in the 1990 draft when he earned Rookie of the Year honors last season . . . led all rookies in scoring (18.4 points per game) and rebounds (10.3) . . . tied for 10th in the NBA in rebounds and led the Nets in that category . . . in power forward ratings he was No. 5 in three-point field-goal percentage, No. 4 in rebounds, No. 8 in steals, No. 6 in blocked shots, No. 8 in points and No. 5 in TENDEX . . . trailed only Karl Malone, Larry Nance, Kevin McHale, and Detlef Schrempf in TENDEX . . . needs improvement in two-point field-goal percentage (No. 18) and turnovers (No. 22) to climb even higher on the power-forward list.

CHRIS MORRIS

AGE: 25
HEIGHT: 6-8
WEIGHT: 210
POSITION: Small Forward
EXPERIENCE: 3 Seasons
COLLEGE: Auburn
BIRTHPLACE: Atlanta
1990–91 TENDEX: .502
POSITIONAL RATING: 21 of 30
CAREER TENDEX: .484

Morris had his best NBA season in 1990–91, but still far below what the Nets expected of him when they made him the No. 4 player selected in the 1988 draft . . . set personal highs last season in minutes (2,553), free-throw percentage (.734), rebounds (521), assists (220), steals (138) and blocked shots (96) . . . but his progress was limited because of poor field-goal shooting and decreased scoring (from 14.8 points in 1989–90 to 13.2 last season) . . . in small forward listings he did well in steals (No. 2) and blocked shots (No. 1), not so well in two-point field-goal percentage (No. 26), free-throw percentage (No. 21), turnovers (No. 20), points (No. 28), and TENDEX rating (No. 21).

COLEMAN

1990–91	2PFG	3PFG	F.T.	REB.	AST.	STL.	T.O.	BLK.	PTS.
Per Game	.472	.342	.731	10.3	2.20	0.96	2.93	1.34	18.4
Per Minute	.472	.342	.731	.292	.063	.027	.083	.038	.524
Rating	18t	5	15	4	12	8	22	6	8

MORRIS

1990–91	2PFG	3PFG	F.T.	REB.	AST.	STL.	T.O.	BLK.	PTS.
Per Game	.465	.251	.734	6.59	2.78	1.75	2.11	1.22	13.2
Per Minute	.465	.251	.734	.204	.086	.054	.065	.038	.408
Rating	26	18	21	9t	15t	2	20	1	28

REGGIE THEUS

AGE: 34
HEIGHT: 6-7
WEIGHT: 213
POSITION: Shooting Guard
EXPERIENCE: 13 Seasons
COLLEGE: Nevada-Las Vegas
BIRTHPLACE: Inglewood, CA
1990–91 TENDEX: .448
POSITIONAL RATING: 18 of 27
CAREER TENDEX: .505

Theus has had a long and distinguished NBA career, but it may be coming to an end. His TENDEX rating of .448 last season was his worst since his rookie season of 1978–79. His career rating of .505 is still 55 points above the norm for the position . . . if he decides to play one more season, he could reach the 20,000-point mark in 1991–92—needs 985 more points . . . led the Nets in minutes played, free-throw percentage, three-point field-goal percentage, and scoring last season . . . No. 20 in the NBA in free-throw percentage (.851), No. 18 in three-point field-goal percentage (.361) . . . shooting guard ratings ranged from No. 7 in three-point field-goal percentage to No. 27 (last) in turnovers . . . No. 7 among active shooting guards in career TENDEX rating.

MOOKIE BLAYLOCK

AGE: 24
HEIGHT: 6-0
WEIGHT: 180
POSITION: Point Guard
EXPERIENCE: 2 Seasons
COLLEGE: Oklahoma
BIRTHPLACE: Garland, TX
1990–91 TENDEX: .429
POSITIONAL RATING: 21 of 23
CAREER TENDEX: .416

The Nets probably shouldn't give up on Blaylock as their starting point guard just yet. Although he still ranked far down the list of point men last season, his improvement over his rookie campaign was noteworthy. Playing more than twice as many minutes, he increased his TENDEX rating 40 points from .389 to .429 . . . one of the quickest players in the NBA, he tied for fifth in the league in steals (2.35) . . . led the Nets in steals and assists . . . a good defensive player, he had ratings of No. 4 in steals and No. 1 in blocked shots out of 23 point guards . . . needs work on shooting (No. 22 in two-point field-goal percentage) and playmaking (No. 22 in assists) . . . No. 21 in TENDEX rating.

THEUS

1990–91	2PFG	3PFG	F.T.	REB.	AST.	STL.	T.O.	BLK.	PTS.
Per Game	.481	.361	.851	2.83	4.67	1.05	3.11	0.43	18.6
Per Minute	.481	.361	.851	.077	.128	.029	.085	.012	.511
Rating	16	7	8	25	11	23t	27	9t	13

BLAYLOCK

1990–91	2PFG	3PFG	F.T.	REB.	AST.	STL.	T.O.	BLK.	PTS.
Per Game	.441	.154	.790	3.46	6.13	2.35	2.88	0.56	14.1
Per Minute	.441	.154	.790	.096	.171	.065	.080	.016	.393
Rating	22	18	15	12	22	4	12	1	15

ABSTRACTION 18

The All-Masonry Team

There are basketball awards and all-star teams of all descriptions. Here's one I'd like to see instituted: The All-Masonry Team for guys who shoot nothing but bricks.

One characteristic of these players is that they shoot poorly from the free-throw line. At times they may even shoot a lower percentage on free throws than on field goals.

In the NBA, during the 1990–91 season, nine players had higher field-goal percentages than free-throw percentages. None of them were regulars, which should tell you something about the esteem in which such players are held around the league. Four of the nine played fewer than 100 minutes, so they didn't shoot often enough for their percentages to be meaningful.

The Brick Shooter of the Year Award goes to Larry Smith of Houston, who played more minutes (1,923) than anyone else having a lower free-throw percentage than field-goal percentage. Smith had the worst free-throw percentage in the league (.240) and was the only player whose free-throw percentage was less than half as good as his field-goal percentage. He shot .487 from the field, most of which, obviously, were layups or slam-dunks. His shooting range is about three feet.

Smith now has career percentages of .533 on field goals and .534 on free throws. He has made less than half of his free throws the past four seasons in a row.

Here is the All-Masonry Team:

Player, Team	FG PCT	FT PCT
Larry Smith, Houston	.487	.240
Ralph Sampson, Sacramento ..	.366	.263
Ken Bannister, LA Clippers ..	.531	.385
Jerome Lane, Denver	.438	.411
Randy Breuer, Minnesota	.453	.443

Smith, Lane, and Bannister are repeaters from last year. The shocker is Sampson: How low can he let himself go before he quietly retires?

Another shock is that New Jersey center Chris Dudley didn't make the team. Dudley had an outstanding season (for him) with a .534 free-throw percentage in 1990–91. That pulled his career free-throw mark all the way up to .431, nine points higher than his career field-goal percentage.

Dudley had been one of the most consistent mortar-lobbers from the foul line for two years running. He averaged .364 on free throws in 1988–89 and .319 in 1989–90.

21
New York Knicks

1990–91 Statistics	Per Game	Rating
2-Point FG Percent	.499	10
3-Point FG Percent	.328	9
Free-Throw Percent	.770	10
Shootist	.943	11
Points	103.1	18
Assists	26.5	7
Rebounds	+0.41	13
PAR	+2.29	11
Blocked Shots	5.10	13
Steals	7.78	22
Turnovers	16.8	20
BEST	−3.94	23
TENDEX	101.0	12
Winning Percentage	.476	16
Coach: Jackson-MacLeod	−5.5	25
Player: P. Ewing	.793	7
Rookie: G. Anthony	.483	12

What to do when you have a disappointing season?

Fire the coach, or coaches.

The Knicks began the 1990-91 season with Stu Jackson as the head coach. He was fired after one month. Then came John MacLeod, who lasted until the end of the season before being fired. The two men directed the Knicks to a 39–43 record when TENDEX showed the team should have been 45–37. The Jackson-MacLeod tandem finished ahead of only K.C. Jones and Mike Schuler in the coaches' ratings.

If the Knicks had won 45 games, they would have finished second instead of third in the Atlantic Division, but it is doubtful if they would have survived the first round of the playoffs anyway.

Except for center Patrick Ewing, this is a slow team, an aging team. Ewing had a TENDEX rating of .793 last season, seventh best in the NBA and third best among centers.

At 28, Charles Oakley remains a good power forward, although not as good as he once was (TENDEX .559).

TENDEX Hall of Famer Maurice Cheeks was the point guard last season and, although still intelligent and tough on defense, there is serious doubt whether the Knicks can go with him as the regular point man any longer. Rookie Greg Anthony could replace him.

Mark Jackson, who fell on hard times after winning Rookie of the Year honors in 1988, quietly made a comeback in a reserve role last season. His TENDEX rating for 1,595 minutes was a career-best .589 and he shot the ball well and did not turn it over excessively. But before the Knicks give the job back to Jackson, they have to ask themselves two questions:

⋄ Would Jackson sustain that high level of play if he were required to play more minutes?

⋄ Would he play the same brand of high-intensity defense that Cheeks plays?

The remainder of the Knick roster consists of eight guys who would be replaced if the Knicks could find their replacements.

Kiki Vandeweghe is the latest in a series of failures at the small forward position since the Knicks unceremoniously dumped Bernard King without giving him the opportunity to recover from his severe knee injury. Vandeweghe's TENDEX rating was .409 last season and his defense was as bad as Jackson's.

But Vandeweghe is safe as long as Brian Quinnett (TENDEX .332) is the only guy challenging for his job.

At shooting guard, Gerald Wilkins practically matched his career average with a .430 TENDEX—a rating suitable for a reserve, not a starter. But he's safe too as long as Trent Tucker (TENDEX .373) is his backup.

The Knicks had single-digit rankings in only two statistical categories: No. 9 in three-point field-goal percentage and No. 7 in assists.

They ranked among the worst teams in steals (No. 22), turnovers (No. 20) and BEST (No. 23).

Like everybody else except the Celtics, the Knicks could finish anywhere from second to seventh this season in the Atlantic Division, depending on the genius of new coach Pat Riley.

Probable finish: Fourth in Atlantic Division.

PATRICK EWING

AGE: 29
HEIGHT: 7-0
WEIGHT: 240
POSITION: Center
EXPERIENCE: 6 Seasons
COLLEGE: Georgetown
BIRTHPLACE: Kingston, Jamaica
1990–91 TENDEX: .793
POSITIONAL RATING: 3 of 21
CAREER TENDEX: .742

Ewing earned TENDEX Second Team All-NBA honors last season. His TENDEX rating was the seventh best in the league . . . it was the second-best TENDEX mark of Ewing's career, trailing only the .829 he achieved in 1989–90 when he broke Willis Reed's New York Knicks team record of .788 . . . the TENDEX Hall of Famer ranks second among active centers with five years experience with a career rating of .742 . . . should score his 10,000th point and pull down his 5,000th rebound this season . . . ranked No. 3 in the league in blocked shots, No. 5 in scoring and No. 6 in rebounding last season . . . led the Knicks in minutes played, rebounds, blocked shots, and points . . . No. 8 in the NBA with 3,104 minutes played . . . set personal highs in rebounds (11.2) and assists (3.0) . . . excelled with ratings among the top 10 in all center categories except turnovers and three-point field-goal percentage . . . led all centers in scoring, ranked No. 2 in assists, No. 3 in blocked shots, and No. 3 in TENDEX.

CHARLES OAKLEY

AGE: 28
HEIGHT: 6-9
WEIGHT: 245
POSITION: Power Forward
EXPERIENCE: 6 Seasons
COLLEGE: Virginia Union
BIRTHPLACE: Cleveland
1990–91 TENDEX: .559
POSITIONAL RATING: 12 of 22
CAREER TENDEX: .581

Oakley maintained his status as one of the leading rebounders of all-time with his average of 12.1 per game last season, fourth best in the NBA . . . ranks No. 2 in rebounding efficiency on the all-time list . . . career TENDEX rating of .581 places him No. 6 on the list of active power forwards with at least five years of experience . . . led Knicks last season in rebounding and field-goal percentage . . . in power-forward ratings he was No. 1 in rebounds, No. 6 in assists, No. 9 in two-point field-goal percentage, No. 10 in free-throw percentage, and No. 12 in TENDEX . . . weaknesses were No. 20 in turnovers, No. 22 in blocked shots and No. 21 in points.

EWING

1990–91	2PFG	3PFG	F.T.	REB.	AST.	STL.	T.O.	BLK.	PTS.
Per Game	.516	.000	.745	11.2	3.01	0.99	3.59	3.19	26.6
Per Minute	.516	.000	.745	.292	.079	.026	.094	.083	.694
Rating	8	20	10	7t	2	7	19	3	1

OAKLEY

1990–91	2PFG	3PFG	F.T.	REB.	AST.	STL.	T.O.	BLK.	PTS.
Per Game	.518	.000	.784	12.1	2.68	0.82	2.83	0.22	11.2
Per Minute	.518	.000	.784	.336	.075	.023	.079	.006	.311
Rating	9	17t	10	1	6	16	20	22	21

MAURICE CHEEKS

AGE: 35
HEIGHT: 6-1
WEIGHT: 180
POSITION: Point Guard
EXPERIENCE: 13 Seasons
COLLEGE: West Texas State
BIRTHPLACE: Chicago
1990–91 TENDEX: .462
POSITIONAL RATING: 19 of 23
CAREER TENDEX: .515

The all-time NBA official leader in steals, Cheeks increased his total to 2,194 with 128 in 1990–91 . . . ranked first in the NBA in ratio of steals to turnovers last season . . . led Knicks in steals . . . excellent defensive player . . . out of 23 point guards, ranked No. 8 in two-point field-goal percentage, No. 6 in steals, and No. 2 in turnovers . . . poor ratings were No. 18 in rebounds, No. 16 in assists, No. 20 in points and No. 19 in TENDEX rating . . . No. 7 on the active list of point guards in career TENDEX rating . . . ranks No. 5 on the all-time list of assists with 7,100 . . . is among the top 25 on the all-time list of best Shootists (points per shot) . . . TENDEX Hall of Famer.

GERALD WILKINS

AGE: 28
HEIGHT: 6-6
WEIGHT: 190
POSITION: Shooting Guard
EXPERIENCE: 6 Seasons
COLLEGE: Tennessee-Chattanooga
BIRTHPLACE: Atlanta
1990–91 TENDEX: .430
POSITIONAL RATING: 21 of 27
CAREER TENDEX: .433

Wilkins' biggest claim to fame is that Dominique is his brother . . . just about matched his career average of .433 with his .430 TENDEX rating last season . . . out of 27 shooting guards he did not have a single statistical rating among the top 10 . . . several among the bottom 10: No. 24 in three-point field-goal percentage, No. 21 in turnovers, No. 21 in points, and No. 21 in TENDEX.

CHEEKS

1990–91	2PFG	3PFG	F.T.	REB.	AST.	STL.	T.O.	BLK.	PTS.
Per Game	.510	.250	.814	2.28	5.72	1.68	1.42	0.13	7.8
Per Minute	.510	.250	.814	.081	.203	.060	.080	.005	.276
Rating	8	14	11	18	16	6t	2	11	20

WILKINS

1990–91	2PFG	3PFG	F.T.	REB.	AST.	STL.	T.O.	BLK.	PTS.
Per Game	.488	.209	.820	3.04	4.04	1.21	2.37	0.34	13.8
Per Minute	.488	.209	.820	.096	.127	.038	.074	.011	.433
Rating	15	24	14	16	12	14t	21t	11t	21

KIKI VANDEWEGHE

AGE: 33
HEIGHT: 6-8
WEIGHT: 220
POSITION: Small Forward
EXPERIENCE: 11 Seasons
COLLEGE: UCLA
BIRTHPLACE: Weisbaden, Germany
1990–91 TENDEX: .409
POSITIONAL RATING: 29 of 30
CAREER TENDEX: .518

Still an excellent shooter at age 33, Vandeweghe led the Knicks in two-point field-goal percentage and free-throw percentage last season . . . scored his 15,000th point last year . . . ranks No. 6 on the all-time list in free-throw percentage, No. 5 in Shootist (points per shot) . . . No. 7 in the NBA last season in free-throw percentage (.899) and No. 17 in three-point field-goal percentage (.362) . . . out of 30 small forwards, his best ratings were No. 9 in two-point field-goal percentage, No. 2 in three-point field-goal percentage, No. 1 in free-throw percentage, and No. 4 in turnovers . . . worst ones were No. 30 in rebounds, No. 29 in assists, No. 30 in steals, No. 30 in blocked shots, and No. 29 in TENDEX rating.

VANDEWEGHE

1990–91	2PFG	3PFG	F.T.	REB.	AST.	STL.	T.O.	BLK.	PTS.
Per Game	.518	.362	.899	2.40	1.47	0.56	1.44	0.13	16.3
Per Minute	.518	.362	.899	.074	.045	.017	.045	.004	.507
Rating	9	2	1	30	29	30	4	30	16

22
Orlando Magic

1990-91 Statistics	Per Game	Rating
2-Point FG Percent	.466	23
3-Point FG Percent	.358	4
Free-Throw Percent	.743	20
Shootist	.895	20
Points	105.9	14
Assists	22.1	26
Rebounds	+0.82	12
PAR	−6.93	20
Blocked Shots	3.73	26
Steals	7.34	24
Turnovers	17.0	21
BEST	−5.89	27
TENDEX	92.8	26
Winning Percentage	.378	18t
Coach: M. Guokas	+8	2
Player: S. Skiles	.559	41t
Rookie: B. Williams	.617	15

The second-year Orlando franchise performed a lot of magic to win 31 games last season, best of the expansion teams.

The Magic did it with the worst center tandem in the NBA and only one pure power forward on the roster, who played only 20 percent of the time.

Most of the credit for the team's 13-game improvement—most in the NBA—should go to coach Matt Guokas and point guard Scott Skiles. Guokas had the courage to play Skiles as the regular even though the team's management had made a commitment to Sam Vincent, signing him to a long-term contract with the intention of allowing Skiles to become a free agent at the end of the season.

Skiles had been hindered by injuries and personal problems his first four seasons in the NBA, but turned it around last year, becoming one of the league's most improved players with a TENDEX rating that soared from .444 to .559.

Vincent, a former college teammate of Skiles at Michigan State, went the other direction with a TENDEX rating that slid 51 points from .495 to .444 in his fifth NBA season.

Skiles played 2,714 minutes. Vincent played 975.

But it wasn't until the end of the season that management finally gave in and signed Skiles.

The Magic won eight games more than their player talent signified they should have won, so Guokas was the second-rated coach in the league.

If Guokas had a coaching problem, it was at the power forward position. He had only one player, Michael Ansley, capable of playing the position up to NBA standards, but played him only 877 minutes. Ansley's TENDEX rating was an excellent .580 as he shot and rebounded well for the second straight season with abbreviated playing time.

Terry Catledge (TENDEX .454) and Jeff Turner (.409) played most of the minutes at power forward. Neither man was competitive with the opposition.

At center, Guokas really had no choice. He was stuck with Greg Kite (.369) and Mark Acres (.413).

What Guokas did very well was find a way to give significant playing time to four talented players capable of swinging between the small forward and shooting guard positions.

Rookie Dennis Scott (TENDEX .381) and second-year man Nick Anderson (.483) scored well, while veterans Otis Smith (.539) and Jerry Reynolds (.538) were more efficient in other aspects of play.

Statistically, the only real strength of the Orlando team was three-point field-goal shooting. Thanks to Skiles and Scott, both of whom were among the league leaders, Orlando was the No. 4 team in three-point shooting.

For the Magic the label of areas-needing-improvement includes just about everything else: two-point field-goal percentage (No. 23), free-throw percentage (No. 20), Shootist (No. 20), assists (No. 26), PAR (No. 20), blocked shots (No. 26), steals (No. 24), turnovers (No. 21), BEST (No. 27), and TENDEX rating (No. 26).

Rookie Brian Williams should help this team, but it will contend for a playoff berth only if Scott improves his all-around play and Ansley is allowed to play more minutes.

Probable finish: Seventh in Atlantic Division.

SCOTT SKILES

AGE: 27
HEIGHT: 6-1
WEIGHT: 200
POSITION: Point Guard
EXPERIENCE: 5 Seasons
COLLEGE: Michigan State
BIRTHPLACE: LaPorte, IN
1990–91 TENDEX: .559
POSITIONAL RATING: 8 of 23
CAREER TENDEX: .481

In one season, Skiles went from a fringe player earmarked for an unconditional release to the eighth-best point guard in the NBA. Orlando signed Sam Vincent to be the team's point guard before last season and refused to re-sign Skiles until the end of the season after Skiles had established himself as the Magic's best player . . . led the team in minutes played, three-point field-goal percentage, free-throw percentage, assists and points . . . ranked No. 5 in the NBA in three-point field-goal percentage (.373), No. 6 in free-throw percentage (.902), and No. 10 in assists (8.4) . . . out of 23 point guards he had six top-10 ratings in key statistical categories: No. 2 in three-point field-goal percentage, No. 2 in free-throw percentage, No. 9 in rebounds, No. 10 in assists, No. 9 in points, and No. 8 in TENDEX . . . needs improvement in BEST categories: No. 22 in blocked shots, No. 22 in steals and No. 16 in turnovers.

DENNIS SCOTT

AGE: 23
HEIGHT: 6-8
WEIGHT: 230
POSITION: Small Forward
EXPERIENCE: 1 Season
COLLEGE: Georgia Tech
BIRTHPLACE: Hagerstown, MD
1990–91 TENDEX: .381
POSITIONAL RATING: 30 of 30
CAREER TENDEX: .381

Scott made the official NBA All-Rookie Team last season but did not make the TENDEX All-Rookie Team . . . averaged 15.7 points per game, third best of rookies, but trailed 10 rookies with his .381 TENDEX rating . . . ranked No. 11 in the NBA in three-point field-goal percentage (.374) . . . weaknesses in his game showed up in statistical comparisons with 29 other small forwards: No. 29 in two-point field-goal percentage, No. 19 in free-throw percentage, No. 28 in rebounds, No. 25 in assists, No. 21 in steals, No. 23 in blocked shots, and No. 30 in TENDEX rating . . . talented player, expect dramatic improvement from him this season.

SKILES

1990–91	2PFG	3PFG	F.T.	REB.	AST.	STL.	T.O.	BLK.	PTS.
Per Game	.455	.408	.902	3.42	8.35	1.13	3.19	0.05	17.2
Per Minute	.455	.408	.902	.100	.243	.033	.093	.001	.500
Rating	21	2	2	9	10	22	16	22	9

SCOTT

1990–91	2PFG	3PFG	F.T.	REB.	AST.	STL.	T.O.	BLK.	PTS.
Per Game	.445	.374	.750	2.87	1.63	0.76	1.55	0.31	15.7
Per Minute	.445	.374	.750	.101	.057	.027	.054	.011	.550
Rating	29	1	19	28	25	21t	9t	23	9t

GREG KITE

AGE: 30
HEIGHT: 6-11
WEIGHT: 250
POSITION: Center
EXPERIENCE: 8 Seasons
COLLEGE: Brigham Young
BIRTHPLACE: Houston
1990–91 TENDEX: .369
POSITIONAL RATING: 21 of 21
CAREER TENDEX: .348

There must be something good to be said about every NBA player, so here it is about Kite: He led the Magic in rebounds and blocked shots last season . . . now for some candor: Kite is probably the worst center to play a full season as a regular in the NBA since it became possible to do TENDEX ratings 40 years ago . . . his career TENDEX rating is 202 percentage points below the norm for a center . . . out of 21 regular centers last season, his key ratings were: No. 15 in two-point field-goal percentage, No. 21 in free-throw percentage, No. 13 in rebounds, No. 17 in assists, No. 21 in steals, No. 12 in blocked shots, No. 20 in points, and No. 21 in TENDEX . . . his TENDEX was 35 points worse than the player ranked No. 20 . . . was No. 7 in three-point field-goal percentage because he didn't attempt a shot, No. 8 in turnovers because the Magic didn't want him handling the ball.

KITE

1990–91	2PFG	3PFG	F.T.	REB.	AST.	STL.	T.O.	BLK.	PTS.
Per Game	.491	.000	.512	7.17	0.72	0.31	1.24	0.99	4.8
Per Minute	.491	.000	.512	.264	.027	.011	.046	.036	.178
Rating	15	7t	21	13t	17	21	8	12	20

23
Philadelphia 76ers

1990–91 Statistics	Per Game	Rating
2-Point FG Percent	.491	13
3-Point FG Percent	.316	16
Free-Throw Percent	.790	6
Shootist	.930	12
Points	105.4	15
Assists	22.2	24
Rebounds	−2.38	22
PAR	−7.39	22
Blocked Shots	5.84	7
Steals	8.27	15
Turnovers	15.0	6
BEST	−0.89	4
TENDEX	97.9	17
Winning Percentage	.537	11t
Coach: J. Lynam	+8	1
Player: C. Barkley	.833	4
Rookie: A. Teheran	.501	20

The 76ers are a team of contradictions.

Despite having three members of the All-Mean Team—Charles Barkley, Armon (the Hammer) Gilliam, and Rick Mahorn—they were charged with only 1,629 personal fouls last season, second least in the NBA.

But even with these three bruisers in the starting lineup together, they ranked next-to-last in the league in offensive rebounds and 22nd overall in rebounding.

Go figure.

Were it not for an excellent job by TEN-DEX Coach of the Year Jim Lynam, this is a team that probably would not have made the playoffs. Lynam directed the 76ers to eight more victories than their overall performance merited, including a league-record eight overtime wins and a 19–14 record in games decided by six points or less.

Lynam's efforts were aided (at times) and hindered (at times) by Barkley, whose on-court production continued to place him among the top players in the NBA, but whose diarrhea of the mouth may have adversely affected team morale.

Barkley insulted his teammates by implying more than once that they were inferior to those of other teams. He whined about his own plight, as if not winning an NBA championship ring or a Most Valuable Player trophy were a malady that afflicted him alone out of all professional basketball players.

At least one of Barkley's teammates, shooting guard Hersey Hawkins, was decidedly not inferior. In his third NBA season, Hawkins continued his rapid improvement with a TENDEX rating that rose from .480 to .534. Hawkins' rating had improved by 85 points from his rookie to his second season, so in the past two years he was improved by a total of 139 points.

Gilliam is a competent power forward who should do better than his 1990–91 rating of .504 once he becomes accustomed to the 76ers' system.

At age 33, about the only thing Mahorn (TENDEX .459) is capable of any more is hitting opponents with elbows and forearms.

In order to hold on as the No. 2 team in the Atlantic Division, the 76ers need a complete recovery from point guard Johnny Dawkins, who missed all but four games of the 1990–91 season because of an injury. His replacement, 37-year-old Rickey Green, was inadequate (TENDEX .398).

Reserve small forward Ron Anderson is a capable sixth man. Otherwise, the 76ers bench is thinner than Manute Bol. Green and Mahorn were regulars last season who played as if they should have been reserves.

Statistically, Philadelphia's strengths were blocked shots (No. 7), turnovers (No. 6), BEST (No. 4), and free-throw percentage (No. 6).

The weaknesses: assists (No. 24), rebounds (No. 22), and PAR (No. 22).

Probable 1991–92 finish: With a healthy Dawkins, second in Atlantic Division. Without him, anywhere from second to seventh.

CHARLES BARKLEY

AGE: 28
HEIGHT: 6-5
WEIGHT: 265
POSITION: Small Forward
EXPERIENCE: 7 Seasons
COLLEGE: Auburn
BIRTHPLACE: Leeds, AL
1990–91 TENDEX: .833
POSITIONAL RATING: 1 of 30
CAREER TENDEX: .783

Barkley earned TENDEX All-NBA honors for the fifth straight season in 1990–91 and improved his career rating to .783, second-best power forward of all-time behind Bob Pettit . . . his .833 rating last season was No. 1 of all cornermen in the league and the best rating of Barkley's career . . . Barkley is the No. 1 rated player of all-time in two-point field-goal percentage and led the NBA last season with .614 . . . ranked fourth in the league in scoring (27.6), 11th in rebounding (10.1) and fourth in TENDEX rating . . . although he played small forward last season, he has been a power forward most of his career and is the No. 1 rated active power forward in TENDEX . . . led 76ers last season in field-goal percentage, rebounds, and points . . . out of 30 small forwards, he ranked first in two-point field-goal percentage, second in rebounds, fourth in assists, eighth in steals, second in points, and first in TENDEX.

HERSEY HAWKINS

AGE: 26
HEIGHT: 6-3
WEIGHT: 190
POSITION: Shooting Guard
EXPERIENCE: 3 Seasons
COLLEGE: Bradley
BIRTHPLACE: Chicago
1990–91 TENDEX: .534
POSITIONAL RATING: 7 of 27
CAREER TENDEX: .474

Hawkins improved in nearly every phase of play between his rookie 1988–89 season, when his TENDEX rating was .395, and the 1990–91 season, when it was .534 . . . set personal highs last season in minutes played, field-goal percentage, three-point shots made, free-throw percentage, rebounds, assists, steals, blocked shots, and points . . . ranked No. 14 in the NBA in scoring (22.1), No. 16 in free-throw percentage (.871), No. 7 in three-point field-goal percentage (.400) and No. 7 in minutes played (3,110) . . . led the 76ers in three-point field-goal percentage, free-throw percentage, and steals . . . out of 27 shooting guards, had good ratings of No. 2 in three-point field-goal percentage, No. 6 in free-throw percentage, No. 4 in steals, No. 8 in blocked shots, No. 7 in points, and No. 7 in TENDEX rating.

BARKLEY

1990–91	2PFG	3PFG	F.T.	REB.	AST.	STL.	T.O.	BLK.	PTS.
Per Game	.614	.284	.722	10.1	4.24	1.64	3.13	0.49	27.6
Per Minute	.614	.284	.722	.272	.114	.044	.084	.013	.740
Rating	1	16	24	2	4	8	28	19t	2

HAWKINS

1990–91	2PFG	3PFG	F.T.	REB.	AST.	STL.	T.O.	BLK.	PTS.
Per Game	.491	.400	.871	3.88	3.74	2.23	2.66	0.49	22.1
Per Minute	.491	.400	.871	.100	.096	.057	.068	.013	.568
Rating	13	2	6	14	20	4t	19t	8	7

ARMON GILLIAM

AGE: 27
HEIGHT: 6-9
WEIGHT: 230
POSITION: Power Forward
EXPERIENCE: 4 Seasons
COLLEGE: Nevada-Las Vegas
BIRTHPLACE: Gary, IN
1990–91 TENDEX: .504
POSITIONAL RATING: 18 of 22
CAREER TENDEX: .509

The acquisition of Gilliam last season by means of a trade with Charlotte for Mike Gminski gave Philadelphia the most physical, and probably the slowest, frontline in the NBA with Gilliam, Charles Barkley and Rick Mahorn . . . Gilliam set personal highs in minutes played, free-throw percentage, assists, steals, and blocked shots . . . his only top-10 rating out of 21 power forwards was No. 6 in free-throw percentage . . . weak ratings included No. 17 in two-point field-goal percentage, No. 20 in assists, and No. 18 in TENDEX.

RON ANDERSON

AGE: 33
HEIGHT: 6-7
WEIGHT: 215
POSITION: Small Forward
EXPERIENCE: 7 Seasons
COLLEGE: Fresno State
BIRTHPLACE: Chicago
1990–91 TENDEX: .467
POSITIONAL RATING: 23 of 30
CAREER TENDEX: .451

Anderson contributed 14.6 points per game as the 76ers' sixth man last season, the second-best average of his seven-year career . . . although he's a respectable sixth man, he played enough minutes to be listed as a regular and did not fare well in comparisons with other regular small forwards: No. 18 in two-point field-goal percentage, No. 21 in three-point field-goal percentage, No. 19 in rebounds, No. 28 in assists, No. 19 in steals, No. 28 in blocked shots, and No. 23 in TENDEX rating . . . his best rankings were No. 6 in free-throw percentage and No. 3 in turnovers.

GILLIAM

1990–91	2PFG	3PFG	F.T.	REB.	AST.	STL.	T.O.	BLK.	PTS.
Per Game	.487	.000	.815	7.97	1.40	0.92	2.32	0.71	16.6
Per Minute	.487	.000	.815	.226	.040	.026	.066	.020	.470
Rating	17	17t	6	13t	20	11	13	12	13

ANDERSON

1990–91	2PFG	3PFG	F.T.	REB.	AST.	STL.	T.O.	BLK.	PTS.
Per Game	.497	.209	.833	4.48	1.40	0.79	1.22	0.16	14.6
Per Minute	.497	.209	.833	.157	.049	.028	.043	.006	.512
Rating	18	21	6	19	28	19t	3	28	14

RICKEY GREEN

AGE: 37
HEIGHT: 6-0
WEIGHT: 172
POSITION: Point Guard
EXPERIENCE: 13 Seasons
COLLEGE: Michigan
BIRTHPLACE: Chicago
1990–91 TENDEX: .398
POSITIONAL RATING: 23 of 23
CAREER TENDEX: .474

Green had six excellent seasons as a point guard in the NBA, but ran out of steam four years ago and has been hanging on ever since . . . registered the 5,000th assist of his career last season, but otherwise did little to commend himself . . . his TENDEX rating was last out of 23 regular point guards . . . other poor ratings were No. 16 in two-point field-goal percentage, No. 16 in three-point percentage, No. 22 in rebounds, No. 21 in assists, No. 23 in steals, No. 18 in blocked shots, and No. 17 in points . . . led all point guards in least turnovers per minute . . . ranks among the top 20 players of all-time in assists and ratio of steals to turnovers.

RICK MAHORN

AGE: 33
HEIGHT: 6-10
WEIGHT: 255
POSITION: Center
EXPERIENCE: 11 Seasons
COLLEGE: Hampton Institute
BIRTHPLACE: Hartford, CT
1990–91 TENDEX: .459
POSITIONAL RATING: 16 of 21
CAREER TENDEX: .497

Of the 11 seasons Mahorn has played in the NBA, the 1990–91 campaign was his second-worst. His TENDEX rating of .459 was better only than his rating of .416 with Detroit during the 1985–86 season . . . Mahorn made some centers look good by comparison with his 1990–91 rankings of No. 19 in two-point field-goal percentage, No. 21 in three-point field-goal percentage, No. 18 in rebounds, No. 16 in blocked shots, No. 17 in points, and No. 16 in TENDEX rating . . . he did better in free-throw percentage (No. 4), assists (No. 8), and steals (No. 5).

GREEN

1990–91	2PFG	3PFG	F.T.	REB.	AST.	STL.	T.O.	BLK.	PTS.
Per Game	.475	.222	.830	1.73	5.23	0.72	1.37	0.08	10.0
Per Minute	.475	.222	.830	.061	.184	.025	.048	.003	.353
Rating	16	16	8	22	21	23	1	18	17

MAHORN

1990–91	2PFG	3PFG	F.T.	REB.	AST.	STL.	T.O.	BLK.	PTS.
Per Game	.475	.000	.788	7.76	1.48	0.99	1.59	0.70	8.9
Per Minute	.475	.000	.788	.255	.048	.032	.052	.023	.292
Rating	19	21	4	18	8	5	11t	16	17

ABSTRACTION 19

Sir Charles and the Skeptical Writer

Here's a partly real but mostly imaginary conversation between Charles Barkley and a sportswriter:

WRITER: Is it true that you are the biggest whiner since Julio Gallo?

CHARLES: Hey, I never get a call. The referees are against me.

WRITER: In games I've seen, you've swung a bigger hatchet than Paul Bunyan and they still call four times as many fouls in your favor as against you.

CHARLES: They call more for Magic than me.

WRITER: Is that because he whines more?

CHARLES: It's because me and him are the greatest, but I'm the greatest of the greatest.

WRITER: Greater than Robinson? Or Olajuwon? Or Karl Malone? Or Jordan? Michael tore you up in the playoffs the past two seasons. The only playoff game you won against Michael last season was when they gave your team 40 free throws and his got only 15.

CHARLES: Michael and me are friends, but most of those other players are jerks.

WRITER: I've heard some of them say the same thing about you.

CHARLES: I'll never be MVP because I don't kiss butt like those guys.

WRITER: You'll never be MVP because your team hasn't gotten past the second round of the playoffs since Moses Malone was the star player.

CHARLES: Moses was a wimp.

WRITER: Magic makes his teammates better; Bird makes his teammates better. What about you?

CHARLES: It's a lot easier to make James Worthy better. I've got to make Shelton Jones better.

WRITER: According to the TENDEX rating system, Hersey Hawkins is a better player than James Worthy.

CHARLES: What the hell is TENDEX?

WRITER: It's a system based on 10 stats that says you are the fifth-best player in the NBA. Or maybe the sixth or seventh. Depends on your interpretation of the bottom line.

CHARLES: Bad system. I'm like Dave Stewart of the Oakland As: I don't get no respect.

WRITER: Stewart's a whiner too. He's been a good pitcher for five years after being a lousy one for seven. All he does is complain about not winning the Cy Young Award. Nolan Ryan has been a great pitcher for 20 years and never complained once about not winning a Cy Young.

CHARLES: I don't care about Cy Young. I want MVP.

WRITER: Want to bet you never get it?

CHARLES: I'll bet on anything, sure.

WRITER: Let's bet on who will be the all-time record holder for technical fouls, or do you hold that record already?

CHARLES: I told you, the refs are against me.

WRITER: Fans, too?

CHARLES: Them, too.

WRITER: What about the little girl you spat on?

CHARLES: Hey, I admitted that was a bad thing I did. I didn't mean that.

WRITER: What did you mean?

CHARLES: What do you mean?

WRITER: Who did you mean to spit on?

CHARLES: Her mother.

24
Phoenix Suns

1990–91 Statistics	Per Game	Rating
2-Point FG Percent	.508	4
3-Point FG Percent	.319	14
Free-Throw Percent	.770	11
Shootist	.946	9
Points	114.0	4
Assists	26.9	5
Rebounds	+2.89	6
PAR	+13.1	3
Blocked Shots	6.52	4
Steals	8.38	14
Turnovers	15.9	11
BEST	−0.98	6
TENDEX	107.1	4
Winning Percentage	.671	5t
Coach: C. Fitzsimmons	−4	21t
Player: K. Johnson	.699	9
Rookie: R. Dumas	NR	23

There are injuries and then there are *injuries.*

The Suns were afflicted at the worst possible time by a rash of injuries last season. They had made a late-season rally and closed to within two games of first-place Portland and one game of the second-place Los Angeles Lakers with two weeks left in the season. But then injuries slowed down three of their top players—point guard Kevin Johnson, small forward Dan Majerle and power forward Tom Chambers.

During the final two weeks, the Suns slumped, finishing eight games behind the Trail Blazers and three behind the Lakers.

Chambers managed to get well by playoff time, but Majerle continued to have back problems, and it was sad to watch Kevin Johnson trying to keep up with John Stockton in a first-round series. This is normally an even matchup, but with Johnson hobbling on a gimpy leg, Stockton demolished him. Stockton shot .622 from the field and averaged 12.8 assists and 18 points per game for a TENDEX rating of .751.

Johnson shot .302 from the field, and averaged 9.8 assists and 12.8 points per game. His TENDEX rating was .326—less than half as good as his .699 rating during the regular season—and the Suns were eliminated in four games.

It was a shame, because the Suns had finished second in the Western Conference to Portland in the team TENDEX ratings and had a good chance of emerging as the West's representative in the championship series.

A season later, the outlook doesn't look quite so good for the Suns. At age 32, Chambers is getting a bit long in the tooth. His TENDEX rating dropped 105 points last season, from .625 to .520. Center Mark West, 31, lost 22 points off his TENDEX rating, from .577 to .555. The rating of shooting guard Jeff Hornacek fell 42 points, from .586 to .544.

Sixth man Xavier McDaniel did not seem to fit as well in the Suns' system late last season as the man they traded to get him, Eddie Johnson. Johnson, meanwhile, led Seattle with a 24-point scoring average in five playoff games.

The Suns still have the potential to challenge for divisional and conference titles, but they'll need a better coaching job from Cotton Fitzsimmons. Fitzsimmons has had some excellent seasons as a coach, but 1990–91 wasn't one of them. He tied for 21st place in the TENDEX coaches' ratings as the Suns lost four more games than they should have lost.

Statistically, the Suns were a powerful team in most categories in 1990–91: No. 4 in two-point field-goal percentage, No. 9 in Shootist (points per shot), No. 4 in points, No. 5 in assists, No. 6 in rebounds, No. 3 in PAR (combination of points, assists and rebounds), No. 4 in blocked shots, No. 6 in BEST (combination of blocks, steals and turnovers), and No. 4 in TENDEX rating.

Phoenix was no worse than 14th in any category. Only Chicago, Boston, and Portland had better team TENDEX ratings than the Suns.

Even assuming a return to 100 percent by Johnson, the Suns could have difficulty challenging the Trail Blazers and Lakers again for Pacific Division supremacy. Majerle is not expected to be completely recovered from back surgery at the outset of the season and may never play at 100 percent efficiency again.

Probable finish: Third in Pacific Division.

KEVIN JOHNSON

AGE: 25
HEIGHT: 6-1
WEIGHT: 180
POSITION: Point Guard
EXPERIENCE: 3 Seasons
COLLEGE: California
BIRTHPLACE: Sacramento, CA
1990–91 TENDEX: .699
POSITIONAL RATING: 3 of 23
CAREER TENDEX: .642

Johnson is headed for the Hall of Fame, if his first four seasons in the NBA are a preview of years to come. Ranks No. 3 on the all-time assists efficiency list . . . has improved each season with TENDEX ratings of .512, .644, .673, and .699 . . . missed joining the TEN-DEX 700 Club by one point in 1990–91 because of an injury that bothered him at the end of the season and during the playoffs . . . despite the injury, he set personal highs in field-goal percentage (.516), and steals (2.12 per game) . . . ranked fourth in the NBA in assists (10.1), ninth in steals, 13th in scoring (22.2), and ninth in TENDEX rating . . . led Phoenix in minutes played, assists, steals and scoring . . . in point-guard ratings he excelled in two-point field-goal percentage (No. 5), free-throw percentage (No. 6), assists (No. 5), steals (No. 9), points (No. 2), and TENDEX rating (No. 3) . . . worst category was turnovers (No. 18).

JEFF HORNACEK

AGE: 28
HEIGHT: 6-4
WEIGHT: 190
POSITION: Shooting Guard
EXPERIENCE: 5 Seasons
COLLEGE: Iowa State
BIRTHPLACE: Elmhurst, IL
1990–91 TENDEX: .544
POSITIONAL RATING: 6 of 27
CAREER TENDEX: .518

Hornacek was cruising along with an ordinary NBA career until the last two seasons when he ranked among the better shooting guards in the NBA . . . although his TEN-DEX rating of .544 in 1990–91 fell 42 points short of his career-high the season before, he set personal highs in minutes (2,733), free-throw percentage (.897), three-point field-goal percentage (.418), and rebounds (321) . . . tied for second in the NBA in three-point field-goal percentage and ranked eighth in free-throw percentage . . . an excellent shooter, he had shooting-guard ratings of No. 3 in two-point field-goal percentage (.534), No. 1 in three-point field-goal percentage, and No. 4 in three-throw percentage . . . also did well in assists (No. 4), turnovers (No. 3) and TENDEX rating (No. 6) . . . weakest category was scoring (No. 15) . . . ranks No. 6 among active shooting guards with career TENDEX rating of .518.

JOHNSON

1990–91	2PFG	3PFG	F.T.	REB.	AST.	STL.	T.O.	BLK.	PTS.
Per Game	.529	.205	.843	3.52	10.1	2.12	3.49	0.14	22.2
Per Minute	.529	.205	.843	.098	.282	.059	.097	.004	.617
Rating	5	17	6	11	5	9	18t	15	2

HORNACEK

1990–91	2PFG	3PFG	F.T.	REB.	AST.	STL.	T.O.	BLK.	PTS.
Per Game	.534	.418	.897	4.01	5.11	1.39	1.63	0.20	16.9
Per Minute	.534	.418	.897	.117	.150	.041	.048	.006	.494
Rating	3	1	4	11	4	13	3t	20	15

DAN MAJERLE

AGE: 26
HEIGHT: 6-6
WEIGHT: 220
POSITION: Small Forward
EXPERIENCE: 3 Seasons
COLLEGE: Central Michigan
BIRTHPLACE: Traverse City, MI
1990–91 TENDEX: .515
POSITIONAL RATING: 17 of 30
CAREER TENDEX: .451

Majerle is a defensive specialist who also played his share of offense last season, averaging 13.6 points per game and shooting well from all distances . . . improved his TENDEX rating for the third season in a row (.369, .434, .515) . . . set personal highs in minutes played (2,281), two-point field-goal percentage (.499), three-point field-goal percentage (.349), free-throw percentage (.762), assists (216), steals (106), blocked shots (40), and points (1,051) . . . out of 30 small forwards, he ranked No. 4 in three-point field-goal percentage, No. 7 in steals, and No. 6 in turnovers.

XAVIER McDANIEL

AGE: 28
HEIGHT: 6-8
WEIGHT: 205
POSITION: Small Forward
EXPERIENCE: 6 Seasons
COLLEGE: Wichita State
BIRTHPLACE: Columbia, SC
1990–91 TENDEX: .512
POSITIONAL RATING: 19 of 30
CAREER TENDEX: .555

McDaniel averaged more than 20 points per game for four straight seasons in Seattle and started out last season with a 21.8 average in 15 games for the Supersonics, but was unable to get anything going after being traded to Phoenix. He averaged 15.8 points in 66 games with the Suns and had the worst TENDEX rating of his six-year NBA career . . . had only one top-10 rating in the small-forward listings, No. 8 in rebounds . . . below-average ratings included No. 30 in three-point field-goal percentage, No. 23 in free-throw percentage, No. 19 in assists, No. 18 in steals, No. 21 in turnovers, and No. 19 in TENDEX . . . ranks No. 9 among active small forwards with a career TENDEX rating of .555.

MAJERLE

1990–91	2PFG	3PFG	F.T.	REB.	AST.	STL.	T.O.	BLK.	PTS.
Per Game	.499	.349	.762	5.43	2.81	1.38	1.48	0.52	13.6
Per Minute	.499	.349	.762	.183	.095	.046	.050	.018	.461
Rating	17	4	17	15	10t	7	6t	15t	20t

McDANIEL

1990–91	2PFG	3PFG	F.T.	REB.	AST.	STL.	T.O.	BLK.	PTS.
Per Game	.501	.000	.723	6.88	2.31	0.94	2.27	0.57	17.0
Per Minute	.501	.000	.723	.211	.071	.029	.070	.018	.521
Rating	16	30	23	8	19	18	21	15t	13

TOM CHAMBERS

AGE: 32
HEIGHT: 6-10
WEIGHT: 230
POSITION: Power Forward
EXPERIENCE: 10 Seasons
COLLEGE: Utah
BIRTHPLACE: Ogden, UT
1990–91 TENDEX: .520
POSITIONAL RATING: 16 of 22
CAREER TENDEX: .549

Maybe it was age, or maybe it was injuries, but whatever the reason, Chambers had one of his worst NBA seasons in 1990–91. His TENDEX rating fell 105 points, from .625 in 1989–90 to .520 in 1990–91 . . . The 32-year-old forward is a scorer, so his most alarming dropoff was 7.3 points in scoring average, from 27.2 to 19.9 . . . also shot poorly with a .437 field-goal percentage that was the worst of his 10-year career . . . good ratings out of 22 power forwards were No. 9 in three-point field-goal percentage, No. 2 in free-throw percentage, No. 4 in assists, No. 3 in points . . . poor ratings were No. 21 in two-point field-goal percentage, No. 18 in rebounds, No. 18 in turnovers, and No. 16 in TENDEX.

CHAMBERS

1990–91	2PFG	3PFG	F.T.	REB.	AST.	STL.	T.O.	BLK.	PTS.
Per Game	.447	.274	.826	6.45	2.55	0.86	2.33	0.71	19.9
Per Minute	.447	.274	.826	.198	.078	.026	.072	.021	.611
Rating	21	9	2	18	4	10	18	11	3

25
Portland Trail Blazers

1990–91 Statistics	Per Game	Rating
2-Point FG Percent	.501	9
3-Point FG Percent	.377	1
Free-Throw Percent	.753	18
Shootist	.950	6
Points	114.7	3
Assists	27.5	1
Rebounds	+4.02	4
PAR	+15.2	1
Blocked Shots	5.00	14
Steals	8.83	12
Turnovers	16.0	13
BEST	−2.13	12
TENDEX	107.8	3
Winning Percentage	.768	1
Coach: R. Adelman	+2.5	7t
Player: C. Drexler	.686	10t
Rookie: M. Kennedy	NR	NR

With all of the talent the Trail Blazers have, in the starting lineup and on the bench, it's a wonder that this team doesn't just blow everybody else away. But the truth is, even with all of their talent, they are vulnerable in two areas:

⬧ The half-court offense.

⬧ The low post.

Portland is basically a fast-breaking team. It can run off 10 points in a minute and a half. But the opposing team that can lull the Trail Blazers into a half-court game has a good chance to beat them, as the Lakers did in the playoffs last spring.

Centers and power forwards are key men in half-court offenses. Portland power forward Buck Williams is still an exceptional player at age 31 (TENDEX .576), but he's not the kind of guy you can ask to generate half-court offense. Neither is center Kevin Duckworth (.452).

Stung by criticism that he was the weak link in the Trail Blazers' starting lineup, and that maybe they should have tried harder to sign Lithuanian center Arvidas Sabonis, Duckworth put forth a good effort to prove his

231

detractors wrong last season. He improved his defense and rebounding, but in key situations during the playoffs, as often as not, it was Cliff Robinson (TENDEX .477) who was called on to play the center position, even though Robinson is a natural forward.

Robinson fits in with the other Portland players for one reason: He can run. This team is appropriately nicknamed the Blazers, because when Clyde Drexler and Terry Porter and Jerome Kersey and Danny Ainge and Robinson are on the move, they play at a breathtaking pace.

Drexler played with his usual magnificence in 1990–91, ranking second to Michael Jordan among shooting guards and 10th overall in the NBA with a .686 TENDEX rating.

Porter made his sixth NBA season his best to date with his rating of .659, placing him 16th in the league and fourth best among point guards. He has developed into one of the most dangerous three-point shooters in the NBA.

Kersey's TENDEX rating (.529 last season) never seems to tell the full story of how good he is. In tandem with Williams he keys the defense. And he zealously fills a lane running the break with Porter and Drexler.

Ainge (TENDEX .555), Robinson, and TENDEX Hall of Famer Walter Davis are excellent reserves who contribute instant offense when they set foot on the court.

In just three seasons with Portland, Rick Adelman has earned respect as one of the better coaches in the NBA. Not only has he taken a malcontent bunch of players and given them a winning attitude, but he's also a fine tactical coach. He guided Portland to a 16–6 record in games decided by six points or less last season and tied for seventh place in the coaches rankings for squeezing more victories out of his team than it should have been expected to win. The more talented a team is, the more difficult this is to accomplish, because of the already-high expectations.

Statistically, the Blazers were among the lower echelons in only one category, free-throw percentage (No. 18). They ranked among the top 10 teams in the NBA in two-point field-goal percentage (No. 9), three-point field-goal percentage (No. 1), Shootist (No. 6), points (No. 3), assists (No. 1), rebounds (No. 4), PAR (No. 1), TENDEX rating (No. 3), and winning percentage (No. 1).

This is not an old team, so there is no reason to expect any less from it this season.

Probable finish: First in Pacific Division.

CLYDE DREXLER

AGE: 29
HEIGHT: 6-7
WEIGHT: 215
POSITION: Shooting Guard
EXPERIENCE: 8 Seasons
COLLEGE: Houston
BIRTHPLACE: New Orleans
1990–91 TENDEX: .686
POSITIONAL RATING: 2 of 27
CAREER TENDEX: .652

A TENDEX Hall of Famer, Drexler is the No. 2 shooting guard of all-time with his .652 TENDEX rating . . . also ranks among the all-time leaders in steals and assists . . . twice has made the TENDEX 700 Club with ratings above .700 . . . rating of .686 last season was the 10th best in the NBA and ranked second among shooting guards to Michael Jordan . . . Drexler was 17th in the NBA in scoring (21.5) and 17th in steals (1.76) . . . led Portland in minutes played and points . . . achieved PAR-6 status by averaging over six points, assists and rebounds per game . . . had four triple-double games with at least 10 points, 10 assists and 10 rebounds . . . in shooting-guard ratings, Drexler was among the top 10 in seven of 10 statistical categories last season: No. 7 in two-point field-goal percentage, No. 1 in rebounds, No. 2 in assists, No. 7 in steals, No. 4 in blocked shots, No. 4 in points, and No. 2 in TENDEX . . . worst ratings were No. 24 in turnovers and No. 20 in free-throw percentage.

TERRY PORTER

AGE: 28
HEIGHT: 6-3
WEIGHT: 195
POSITION: Point Guard
EXPERIENCE: 6 Seasons
COLLEGE: Wisconsin-Stevens Point
BIRTHPLACE: Milwaukee
1990–91 TENDEX: .659
POSITIONAL RATING: 4 of 23
CAREER TENDEX: .578

Porter has improved every season since his first with TENDEX ratings of .461, .535, .561, .566, .627, and .659 . . . he isn't a TENDEX Hall of Famer yet, but will be if he can sustain his career rating of .578 until his retirement . . . ranked 12th in the NBA last season in assists (8.0), fourth in three-point field-goal percentage (.415), and 14th in steals (1.95) . . . led Trail Blazers in the same three statistical categories . . . led point guards in two-point field-goal percentage and three-point field-goal percentage . . . ranked No. 9 in free-throw percentage, No. 6 in rebounds, No. 8 in assists, No. 8 in steals, No. 7 in points, and No. 4 in TENDEX . . . worst rating was No. 12 in blocked shots . . . ranks No. 4 among active point guards with career TENDEX rating of .578.

DREXLER

1990–91	2PFG	3PFG	F.T.	REB.	AST.	STL.	T.O.	BLK.	PTS.
Per Game	.509	.319	.794	6.66	6.01	1.76	2.83	0.73	21.5
Per Minute	.509	.319	.794	.191	.173	.050	.081	.021	.620
Rating	7	17	20	1	2	7	24	4	4

PORTER

1990–91	2PFG	3PFG	F.T.	REB.	AST.	STL.	T.O.	BLK.	PTS.
Per Game	.564	.415	.823	3.48	8.01	1.95	2.33	0.15	17.0
Per Minute	.564	.415	.823	.106	.244	.059	.071	.005	.518
Rating	1	1	9	6	8t	8	10	12	7

BUCK WILLIAMS

AGE: 31
HEIGHT: 6-8
WEIGHT: 225
POSITION: Power Forward
EXPERIENCE: 10 Seasons
COLLEGE: Maryland
BIRTHPLACE: Rocky Mount, NC
1990–91 TENDEX: .576
POSITIONAL RATING: 10 of 22
CAREER TENDEX: .600

Williams may specialize in rebounding and defense, but that doesn't mean he can't shoot. He led the NBA in field-goal percentage last season . . . his .602 percentage was the only one in the league over .600 and was a personal high for Williams . . . career field-goal percentage of .554 is the ninth best of all-time . . . he's also among the top 15 rebounders of all-time . . . ranked 15th in the league in rebounds last season and led Portland with 9.4 per game . . . needs 873 rebounds to reach 10,000 . . . in the power-forward ratings Williams' strong points are two-point field-goal percentage (No. 1), rebounds (No. 5), turnovers (No. 7), and TENDEX (No. 10) . . . weak points are assists (No. 21), steals (No. 20), and points (No. 20) . . . ranks No. 5 of active power forwards with career TENDEX rating of .600.

JEROME KERSEY

AGE: 29
HEIGHT: 6-7
WEIGHT: 222
POSITION: Small Forward
EXPERIENCE: 7 Seasons
COLLEGE: Longwood
BIRTHPLACE: Clarksville, VA
1990–91 TENDEX: .529
POSITIONAL RATING: 13 of 30
CAREER TENDEX: .551

Kersey's TENDEX ratings have diminished each season for the past five, but that is misleading. He has become a defensive specialist during recent years as the Trail Blazers have come to rely on backcourtmen for most of their offense . . . out of 30 rated small forwards last season, he was No. 9 in rebounds, No. 9 in assists, No. 9 in steals, No. 3 in blocked shots, and No. 13 in TENDEX . . , poor ratings were No. 21 in two-point field-goal percentage, No. 27 in free-throw percentage, and No. 22 in points.

WILLIAMS

1990–91	2PFG	3PFG	F.T.	REB.	AST.	STL.	T.O.	BLK.	PTS.
Per Game	.602	.000	.705	9.39	1.21	0.59	1.71	0.59	11.7
Per Minute	.602	.000	.705	.291	.038	.018	.053	.018	.361
Rating	1	16	17	5	21	20	7	16	20

KERSEY

1990–91	2PFG	3PFG	F.T.	REB.	AST.	STL.	T.O.	BLK.	PTS.
Per Game	.481	.308	.709	6.59	3.11	1.38	2.04	1.04	14.8
Per Minute	.481	.308	.709	.204	.096	.043	.063	.032	.460
Rating	21	12t	27	9t	9	9	15	3	22

KEVIN DUCKWORTH

AGE: 27
HEIGHT: 7-0
WEIGHT: 280
POSITION: Center
EXPERIENCE: 5 Seasons
COLLEGE: Eastern Illinois
BIRTHPLACE: Harvey, IL
1990–91 TENDEX: .452
POSITIONAL RATING: 17 of 21
CAREER TENDEX: .471

After a fast start last season, a late-season slump knocked Duckworth's TENDEX rating down to .452, second lowest of his five-year career . . . had a personal high .772 free-throw percentage . . . in the center rankings, he was No. 5 in free-throw percentage and No. 5 in points . . . but he was at least two-thirds of the way down the list of 21 centers in everything else: No. 17 in two-point field-goal percentage, No. 21 in rebounds, No. 14 in assists, No. 19 in steals, No. 16 in turnovers, No. 20 in blocked shots, and No. 17 in TENDEX.

DUCKWORTH

1990–91	2PFG	3PFG	F.T.	REB.	AST.	STL.	T.O.	BLK.	PTS.
Per Game	.482	.000	.772	6.56	1.10	0.41	2.30	0.42	15.8
Per Minute	.482	.000	.772	.211	.035	.013	.074	.014	.511
Rating	17t	15	5	21	14	19	16	20	5

ABSTRACTION 20

Draft-Day Dealings

There have been some strange dealings on NBA draft day during recent seasons.

In the 1988 and 1989 expansion drafts we witnessed such bizarre things as strong teams giving up draft choices to prevent expansion teams from selecting unprotected players like Kareem Abdul-Jabbar and Dennis Johnson.

In the 1990 draft, the Miami Heat made an unusual draft-day deal with Houston. Instead of exchanging draft choices outright, the two teams went ahead and selected players the other team wanted and then traded the players.

Houston made Alec Kessler the No. 12 selection. Miami picked Dave Jamerson No. 15 and Carl Herrera No. 30, and then traded both of them to Houston for Kessler.

Here are a few unusual draft-day events that didn't happen but should have:

⬥ In 1984, the Portland Trail Blazers should have traded their No. 2 choice in the draft even-up for Utah's No. 16. Then maybe they would have taken John Stockton instead of Sam Bowie.

⬥ In 1986, someone should have asked Bill Russell to explain to every team in the NBA that defense was an important part of basketball. Then maybe a team would have picked Dennis Rodman in the first round, instead of letting him slide all the way down to the second round.

⬥ Since 1978, the Atlanta Hawks' first-round draft choices have been Butch Lee, Jack Givens, Don Collins, Al Wood, Keith Edmonson, Kevin Willis, Jon Koncak, Billy Thompson, Dallas Comegys, Roy Marble, and Rumeal Robinson. The Hawks could have done better by trading away those draft choices and saving the millions of dollars they wasted on those players.

⬥ In 1980, the Philadelphia 76ers—in their own best interests—should have traded one of their two first-round draft choices to Golden State in exchange for a promise that the Warriors would not trade Robert Parish and draft rights to Kevin McHale to the rival Boston Celtics in exchange for two draft choices that turned out to be Joe Barry Carroll and Rickey Brown.

⬥ The Denver Nuggets should have traded down in the 1990 draft. That way maybe they could have avoided selecting Chris Jackson. Then again, he still might have been there for them if they had selected No. 10 or No. 20. If all 27 NBA teams had been smart, Jackson would have been fair game as a free agent.

26
Sacramento Kings

1990–91 Statistics	Per Game	Rating
2-Point FG Percent	.460	25
3-Point FG Percent	.374	2
Free-Throw Percent	.732	24
Shootist	.889	22
Points	96.7	27
Assists	24.3	17
Rebounds	−5.63	27
PAR	−11.5	25
Blocked Shots	6.26	5
Steals	7.70	23
Turnovers	15.5	8
BEST	−1.56	9t
TENDEX	94.9	23
Winning Percentage	.305	25
Coach: D. Motta	−3	19t
Player: A. Carr	.609	24t
Rookie: B. Owens	.633	3

The Kings have the right idea, building with young players. They set the cornerstone in place with small forward Lionel Simmons, the NBA's second-best rookie last season. At the same time, they mortared three other first-round bricks on top of the cornerstone (center Duane Causwell, guard Travis Mays, forward Anthony Bonner). And from the 1991 draft they have cemented in one more—Billy Owens.

Now that the building blocks are in place, all they have to do is smooth out the cracks. But that could take a couple of years for a team so bad that it managed to score only 59 points in a game against Charlotte last season.

It was the lowest single-game point total in the NBA in 36 years.

The instant success of Simmons in 1990–91 was counterbalanced by the struggles of the other three rookies. Mays (TENDEX .384) scored explosively at times, but more often than not the fireworks were generated by players he was attempting to guard. Mays played aggressive defense, but misunderstood the difference between hand-checking and karate-chopping.

Causwell (.510) improved steadily through the season, becoming an efficient rebounder and shot-blocker. But his offense consisted mostly of slam-dunks when opponents forgot about guarding him. They'll be less inclined to ignore him in his second NBA season.

Bonner (.432) was afflicted with so many injury problems that the Kings must wonder about his ability to stand the grind of an 82-game schedule. He played a 34-game schedule, one game more than he had played the previous season for the St. Louis University Billikens.

The Kings are in good shape at the power forward position, no matter who wins the starting job between Antoine Carr (.609) and Wayman Tisdale (.605). Tisdale was the starter at the beginning of last season, but when he missed 49 games because of an injury, Carr stepped in and played just as well offensively and better defensively than Wayman had done.

Whoever loses out in the Carr-Tisdale tussle could be trade bait for future draft choices to add to Sacramento's edifice of young players.

Rory Sparrow is on his way out as the starting point guard. Sparrow (TENDEX .423) was actually outplayed last season by backup point man Jim Les (.476), the league-leader in three-point field-goal percentage.

Another player who could be on his last legs, in more ways than one, is 7-foot-4 center Ralph Sampson, a former Rookie of the Year and All-Star Game MVP, whose knees were ruined while trying to play the corner position in Houston.

Kings' coach Dick Motta struggled to get the team chemistry together last season, so perhaps he wasn't fully to blame for the 25–57 record. But the statistical fact of life is this: The Kings won three less games than the performance ratings of their players indicated they should have won. Motta tied for 20th place in the coaches' ratings.

In comparison with the NBA's other teams, the Kings had four areas of excellence: No. 2 in three-point field-goal percentage, No. 5 in blocked shots, No. 8 in turnovers, and No. 9 in BEST.

But the negatives outweighed the positives: No. 25 in two-point field-goal percentage, No. 24 in free-throw percentage, No. 22 in Shootist, No. 27 in points, No. 27 in rebounds, No. 25 in PAR, No. 23 in steals, No. 23 in TENDEX rating, and No. 25 in winning percentage.

The Kings should win five to 10 more games this season, but that won't be enough to move them up in the standings.

Probable finish: Seventh in Pacific Division.

ANTOINE CARR

AGE: 30
HEIGHT: 6-9
WEIGHT: 235
POSITION: Power Forward
EXPERIENCE: 7 Seasons
COLLEGE: Wichita State
BIRTHPLACE: Oklahoma City, OK
1990–91 TENDEX: .609
POSITIONAL RATING: 6 of 22
CAREER TENDEX: .549

It is unusual for a player to peak at the age of 30, but that is what Carr has done. He had the best season of his career in 1990–91, exceeding a .600 TENDEX rating (.609) for the first time in his seven-season career . . . had personal highs in minutes, rebounds, assists, steals, blocked shots, and points . . . led the Kings in scoring (20.1) . . . in power-forward ratings, he excelled in assists (No. 5), blocked shots (No. 5), points (No. 2) and TENDEX (No. 6) . . . weaknesses were rebounding (No. 22, last place), and steals (No. 21) . . . in spite of his great 1990–91 season, he faces a battle for a starting job this season with Wayman Tisdale, who missed most of last season because of an injury.

LIONEL SIMMONS

AGE: 23
HEIGHT: 6-7
WEIGHT: 220
POSITION: Small Forward
EXPERIENCE: 1 Season
COLLEGE: LaSalle
BIRTHPLACE: Philadelphia
1990–91 TENDEX: .549
POSITIONAL RATING: 10 of 30
CAREER TENDEX: .549

Simmons was the second-best rookie in the NBA last season, but was a lot closer to being No. 1 than indicated by the 65-point difference between his TENDEX rating and Rookie of the Year Derrick Coleman's. Simmons played small forward, while Coleman played power forward. Power forwards normally have 25-point higher ratings than small forwards. Also, Simmons played 376 more minutes than Coleman, continuing the iron-man characteristic he displayed while earning TENDEX Hall of Fame honors as a collegian . . . for a rookie, Simmons showed remarkable versatility with his averages of 18.0 points, 8.8 rebounds and 4.0 assists per game . . . ranked No. 19 in the NBA in rebounds . . . led the Kings in minutes, rebounds, and steals . . . among small forwards he had good ratings of No. 4 in rebounds, No. 6 in assists, No. 5 in blocked shots and No. 10 in TENDEX . . . problem was two-point field-goal percentage (No. 30).

CARR

1990–91	2PFG	3PFG	F.T.	REB.	AST.	STL.	T.O.	BLK.	PTS.
Per Game	.513	.000	.758	5.45	2.48	0.58	2.22	1.31	20.1
Per Minute	.513	.000	.758	.166	.076	.018	.068	.040	.614
Rating	11t	20	13	22	5	21	15t	5	2

SIMMONS

1990–91	2PFG	3PFG	F.T.	REB.	AST.	STL.	T.O.	BLK.	PTS.
Per Game	.423	.273	.736	8.82	3.99	1.43	2.91	1.08	18.0
Per Minute	.423	.273	.736	.234	.106	.038	.077	.029	.477
Rating	30	17	20	4	6	12	25t	5	18

RORY SPARROW

AGE: 33
HEIGHT: 6-2
WEIGHT: 175
POSITION: Point Guard
EXPERIENCE: 11 Seasons
COLLEGE: Villanova
BIRTHPLACE: Suffolk, VA
1990–91 TENDEX: .423
POSITIONAL RATING: 22 of 23
CAREER TENDEX: .422

In his 11th season, Sparrow practically matched his career TENDEX rating with a .423 mark. Although that wasn't bad for Sparrow, it is doubtful that he will be the starting point guard any longer . . . Sparrow shot a career-high .397 from three-point range last season . . . led the Kings in assists . . . weak player in comparison with 22 other point guards: No. 19 in free-throw percentage, No. 20 in rebounds, No. 23 (last place) in assists, No. 19 in steals, No. 18 in points, No. 22 in TENDEX . . . but he did have good ratings of No. 9 in two-point field-goal percentage, No. 3 in three-point field-goal percentage, No. 4 in turnovers, and No. 5 in blocked shots.

BRIAN SHAW*

AGE: 25
HEIGHT: 6-6
WEIGHT: 190
POSITION: Point Guard
EXPERIENCE: 2 Seasons
COLLEGE: UC-Santa Barbara
BIRTHPLACE: Oakland, CA
1990–91 TENDEX: .496
POSITIONAL RATING: 16 of 23
CAREER TENDEX: .473

Shaw returned from a season of European basketball as a better player than when he left. In his second NBA season, sandwiched around the one in Europe, he improved his TENDEX rating by 50 points to .496 and became Boston's regular point guard after the retirement of Dennis Johnson . . . led Celtics in assists (7.6) and was second in steals (1.3) . . . No. 14 in the NBA in assists . . . best point-guard ratings were No. 3 in rebounds and No. 3 in blocked shots . . . TENDEX rating was only sixteenth—out of 23 regular point men.

*As of the date the book went to press, this trade had been announced but not consummated.

SPARROW

1990–91	2PFG	3PFG	F.T.	REB.	AST.	STL.	T.O.	BLK.	PTS.
Per Game	.501	.397	.699	2.33	4.53	1.04	1.58	0.20	10.4
Per Minute	.501	.397	.699	.078	.152	.035	.053	.007	.350
Rating	9	3	19	20	23	19	4	5	18

SHAW

1990–91	2PFG	3PFG	F.T.	REB.	AST.	STL.	T.O.	BLK.	PTS.
Per Game	.480	.111	.819	4.68	7.62	1.33	2.82	.430	13.8
Per Minute	.480	.111	.819	.133	.217	.038	.097	.012	.394
Rating	14t	20	10	3	14	18	18t	3	14

TRAVIS MAYS

AGE: 23
HEIGHT: 6-2
WEIGHT: 190
POSITION: Shooting Guard
EXPERIENCE: 1 Season
COLLEGE: Texas
BIRTHPLACE: Ocala, FL
1990–91 TENDEX: .384
POSITIONAL RATING: 27 of 27
CAREER TENDEX: .384

The Kings insisted they were pleased with the play of Mays during his rookie season, but TENDEX wasn't impressed, rating him in last place out of 27 regular shooting guards . . . he earned his low TENDEX rating with the help of these shooting-guard ratings in other categories: No. 27 in two-point field-goal percentage, No. 22 in free-throw percentage, No. 23 in rebounds, No. 21 in turnovers, No. 22 in blocked shots, and No. 22 in points . . . his only top-10 rating was No. 5 in three-point field-goal percentage.

MAYS

1990–91	2PFG	3PFG	F.T.	REB.	AST.	STL.	T.O.	BLK.	PTS.
Per Game	.421	.366	.770	2.78	3.95	1.27	2.48	0.02	14.3
Per Minute	.421	.366	.770	.083	.118	.038	.074	.005	.427
Rating	27	5	22	23	15	14t	21t	22	22

27
San Antonio Spurs

1990–91 Statistics	Per Game	Rating
2-Point FG Percent	.497	11
3-Point FG Percent	.273	25
Free-Throw Percent	.766	12
Shootist	.930	13
Points	107.1	9
Assists	26.1	9
Rebounds	+4.83	1
PAR	+11.9	4
Blocked Shots	6.96	2
Steals	8.17	17
Turnovers	17.6	26
BEST	−2.49	18
TENDEX	106.0	5
Winning Percentage	.671	5t
Coach: L. Brown	−1	14
Player: D. Robinson	.904	1
Rookie: G. Sutton	NR	27

Mr. Robinson's Neighborhood isn't quite as peaceful and serene as it ought to be. The Spurs had incredible good fortune with the draft during the late 1980s but now seem intent on giving away the players who should have made them the NBA's dominant team of the 1990s.

What happened was this: San Antonio got lucky in the lottery in 1987 and obtained draft rights to David Robinson. The next good break was that Robinson could not play immediately with the Spurs because of a two-year Navy commitment.

How can that be classified as a good break?

Well, try this: If Robinson had been able to play the 1987–88 and 1988–89 seasons, the Spurs would not have been a lottery team. With him in the Navy they continued to play mediocre basketball, however, and picked up two more high draftees, Willie Anderson and Sean Elliott.

Then Robinson joined the team for the 1989–90 season. If the Spurs had simply kept the players they had when they drafted Robinson, making no trades while they picked up Anderson and Elliott, top players on their roster today would be Robinson, Anderson, Elliott, Alvin Robertson, Johnny Dawkins,

Frank Brickowski, Greg Anderson, and Vernon Maxwell.

Instead, the nucleus of the team is Robinson, Willie Anderson, Elliott, Rod Strickland and Terry Cummings. Strickland and Cummings are all they have to show for trades in which they lost Dawkins, Brickowski, Greg Anderson, Maxwell, and Robertson.

Now the Spurs have no depth to speak of.

What team in the NBA has a better backcourt than the might-have-been foursome of Robertson, Dawkins, Maxwell, and Willie Anderson?

That is such a strong group that the 6-foot-7 Anderson could have swung to forward for backup strength behind Elliott and Brickowski.

It's true that Dawkins and Greg Anderson were injured last season. But when healthy Dawkins is as good a point guard as Strickland, and there's no reason to believe he won't be healthy again this season.

It's also true that Cummings is a TENDEX Hall of Fame candidate, but at age 30 he appears to have seen better days. Brickowski (TENDEX .579) played better than Cummings (.557) last season. In fact, Brickowski and Robertson (TENDEX .598) were Milwaukee's best players.

Without having made those trades, the Spurs would be much stronger at shooting guard with TENDEX Hall of Famer Robertson and no weaker at any of the other starting positions. And they would have a much deeper bench, including Maxwell, who would give them a three-point shooting threat, which they don't have now. Yes, I know I criticized Maxwell as a starter for Houston, but he'd be adequate as a reserve.

Coach Larry Brown must bear the blame for these trades, because he has been allowed to make the deals he wanted to make since he became the Spurs' head coach in 1988.

Strategically, Brown did okay as a coach last season. The Spurs lost only one more game than their player ratings warranted, making him the No. 14 rated coach in the NBA.

Team strengths for the Spurs were points (No. 9), assists (No. 9), rebounds (No. 1), PAR (No. 4), blocked shots (No. 2), TENDEX rating (No. 5), and winning percentage (No. 5). They led the league in holding their opponents to the lowest field-goal percentage (.448).

Weaknesses were No. 25 in three-point field-goal percentage and No. 26 in turnovers, two stats that would have been improved with Robertson and Maxwell on the roster.

The single biggest upset of the 1990–91 season was the Spurs' ouster from the playoffs in the first round by the Golden State Warriors. Even having made a few bad trades, the Spurs should have advanced at least to the conference championship series. They had no injury excuses.

A key question is this: Can Larry Brown ever get this team to play up to its potential?

I doubt it.

Probable finish: First in Midwest Division (but a third straight first or second-round exit from the playoffs).

DAVID ROBINSON

AGE: 26
HEIGHT: 7-1
WEIGHT: 235
POSITION: Center
EXPERIENCE: 2 Seasons
COLLEGE: Navy
BIRTHPLACE: Key West, FL
1990–91 TENDEX: .904
POSITIONAL RATING: 1 of 21
CAREER TENDEX: .879

Robinson earned TENDEX Hall of Fame honors as a collegian, and hasn't done anything to tarnish his reputation in two seasons as a professional . . . led the NBA in TENDEX rating last season, ending Michael Jordan's four-season reign . . . became the third player in NBA history to score 1,000 points and block 300 shots in one season . . . won official NBA rebounding title with 13.0 average . . . had three triple-double games with 10 or more points, rebounds and blocked shots . . . ranked No. 2 in blocked shots (3.90), No. 9 in scoring (25.6), and No. 9 in field-goal percentage (.552) . . . led Spurs in minutes, field-goal percentage, rebounds, steals, blocked shots, and points . . . his .904 TENDEX rating was a San Antonio team record . . . in center rankings he placed among the top eight in nine of 10 categories: No. 5 in two-point field-goal percentage, No. 5 in three-point field-goal percentage, No. 8 in free-throw percentage, No. 3 in rebounds, No. 3 in assists, No. 3 in steals, No. 2 in blocked shots, No. 2 in points, and No. 1 in TENDEX.

ROD STRICKLAND

AGE: 25
HEIGHT: 6-3
WEIGHT: 175
POSITION: Point Guard
EXPERIENCE: 3 Seasons
COLLEGE: DePaul
BIRTHPLACE: Bronx, NY
1990–91 TENDEX: .522
POSITIONAL RATING: 13 of 23
CAREER TENDEX: .519

After ranking among the top three collegiate point guards for the decade of the 1980s, Strickland has yet to reach his potential after three seasons in the NBA . . . had a respectable 1990–91 season, ranking 13th in the league in assists with 8.0 per game . . . led Spurs in assists . . . set personal highs in two-point field-goal percentage, three-point field-goal percentage, free-throw percentage, and scoring . . . in point-guard ratings he held his own but did not excel, with a best rating of No. 7 in rebounds and worsts of No. 16 in free-throw percentage and points.

ROBINSON

1990–91	2PFG	3PFG	F.T.	REB.	AST.	STL.	T.O.	BLK.	PTS.
Per Game	.554	.143	.762	13.0	2.54	1.55	3.29	3.90	25.6
Per Minute	.554	.143	.762	.343	.067	.041	.087	.103	.679
Rating	5	5t	8	3	3	3	18	2	2

STRICKLAND

1990–91	2PFG	3PFG	F.T.	REB.	AST.	STL.	T.O.	BLK.	PTS.
Per Game	.490	.333	.763	3.78	7.98	2.02	2.69	0.19	13.8
Per Minute	.490	.333	.763	.106	.223	.056	.075	.005	.385
Rating	12	9	16	7	13	10	11	8	16

TERRY CUMMINGS

AGE: 30
HEIGHT: 6-9
WEIGHT: 235
POSITION: Power Forward
EXPERIENCE: 9 Seasons
COLLEGE: DePaul
BIRTHPLACE: Chicago
1990–91 TENDEX: .557
POSITIONAL RATING: 13 of 22
CAREER TENDEX: .630

Cummings had a "down" 1990–91 season, matching his career-low with a .557 TENDEX rating. His scoring average also skidded to career-low 17.6 . . . despite the bad season, he still ranks No. 4 among active power forwards with his career TENDEX rating of .630 . . . ranks among the all-time leaders in scoring efficiency, averaging 21.7 points per game . . . scored his 15,000th point last season . . . in power-forward ratings he did well in assists (No. 8), steals (No. 7), turnovers (No. 8), and points (No. 6) . . . not so well in two-point field-goal percentage (No. 16), free-throw percentage (No. 20), and blocked shots (No. 19).

WILLIE ANDERSON

AGE: 24
HEIGHT: 6-7
WEIGHT: 190
POSITION: Shooting Guard
EXPERIENCE: 3 Seasons
COLLEGE: Georgia
BIRTHPLACE: Greenville, SC
1990–91 TENDEX: .458
POSITIONAL RATING: 16 of 27
CAREER TENDEX: .509

If you just look at Anderson's TENDEX ratings, you see a guy who mysteriously has skidded from being one of the top shooting guards in the NBA as a rookie three years ago to a below-average one last year. An immensely talented player, Anderson was the TENDEX Rookie of the Year in 1988–89, but slid all the way down to the team's fourth offensive option when David Robinson and Rod Strickland joined the team during the past two seasons. To Anderson's credit, he willingly sacrificed his own statistics for the sake of the team . . . had good 1990–91 shooting-guard ratings of No. 8 in rebounds, No. 7 in assists and No. 5 in blocked shots . . . bad ones of No. 22 in two-point field-goal percentage, No. 25 in three-point field-goal percentage, No. 18 in free-throw percentage, No. 22 in steals, and No. 24 in points.

CUMMINGS

1990–91	2PFG	3PFG	F.T.	REB.	AST.	STL.	T.O.	BLK.	PTS.
Per Game	.493	.212	.683	7.78	2.34	0.91	1.96	0.45	17.6
Per Minute	.493	.212	.683	.237	.072	.028	.060	.014	.536
Rating	16	11	20	10	8	7	8	19	6

ANDERSON

1990–91	2PFG	3PFG	F.T.	REB.	AST.	STL.	T.O.	BLK.	PTS.
Per Game	.467	.200	.798	4.68	4.77	1.05	2.23	0.61	14.4
Per Minute	.467	.200	.798	.135	.138	.030	.064	.018	.418
Rating	22	25	18	8	7	22	14	5t	24

SEAN ELLIOTT

AGE: 23
HEIGHT: 6-8
WEIGHT: 205
POSITION: Small Forward
EXPERIENCE: 2 Seasons
COLLEGE: Arizona
BIRTHPLACE: Tucson, AZ
1990–91 TENDEX: .458
POSITIONAL RATING: 24 of 30
CAREER TENDEX: .444

Elliott is in exactly the same situation as Willie Anderson with the Spurs, and had an identical TENDEX rating last season. At times, the No. 3 selection in the 1989 draft showed talent during his second season, but on the same team with David Robinson, Terry Cummings, Rod Strickland and Anderson, he didn't have the ball enough to demonstrate all of his skills . . . ranked 13th in the league in minutes played with 3,044 . . . exceeded all of his first-year statistics except free-throw percentage . . . in the small forward rankings his only top-10 category was turnovers (No. 5), because he didn't have the ball enough to lose it very often . . . bad ratings were No. 20 in rebounds, No. 27 in steals, No. 22 in blocked shots, No. 25 in points, and No. 24 in TENDEX.

ELLIOTT

1990–91	2PFG	3PFG	F.T.	REB.	AST.	STL.	T.O.	BLK.	PTS.
Per Game	.502	.313	.808	5.56	2.90	0.84	1.79	0.40	15.9
Per Minute	.502	.313	.808	.150	.078	.023	.048	.011	.427
Rating	15	10	11t	20	17	27	5	22	25

28
Seattle SuperSonics

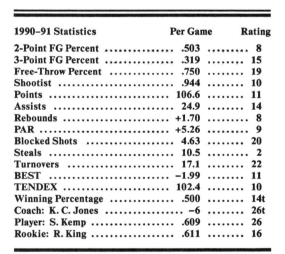

1990–91 Statistics	Per Game	Rating
2-Point FG Percent	.503	8
3-Point FG Percent	.319	15
Free-Throw Percent	.750	19
Shootist	.944	10
Points	106.6	11
Assists	24.9	14
Rebounds	+1.70	8
PAR	+5.26	9
Blocked Shots	4.63	20
Steals	10.5	2
Turnovers	17.1	22
BEST	−1.99	11
TENDEX	102.4	10
Winning Percentage	.500	14t
Coach: K. C. Jones	−6	26t
Player: S. Kemp	.609	26
Rookie: R. King	.611	16

K. C. Jones has come in for his share of criticism in *The Basketball Abstract,* both as a player and as a coach. Now I want to say something good about him: He is an excellent judge of basketball talent.

In a little more than one year as Seattle's head coach, Jones has had a lot to do with personnel decisions resulting in the acquisition of Ricky Pierce, Benoit Benjamin, Eddie Johnson, and Gary Payton.

What the SuperSonics have now, if Jones could coach as well as he can judge talent, is the making of a contending team, even in the talent-laden Pacific Division.

The key moves were even-up trades in which Seattle got rid of Olden Polynice, Xavier McDaniel, and Dale Ellis. Polynice went to the Los Angeles Clippers for Benjamin, McDaniel to Phoenix for Johnson, and Ellis to Milwaukee for Pierce.

The 1990–91 TENDEX ratings of the traded players indicate Seattle came out ahead in all three deals. The ratings of the six players were Benjamin .601 vs. Polynice .493 . . . Pierce .590 vs. Ellis .488 . . . Johnson .526 vs. McDaniel .512. Totaling the difference puts the Sonics 224 percentage points to the good.

But even this fails to tell the whole story: The fact is, all three trades were steals.

In Benjamin, the Sonics got an excellent center for Polynice, a career reserve. It had been said of Benjamin that he didn't put forth effort. For some reason, cumbersome 7-footers often get that reputation. Was it justified? Well, in the playoffs last spring, after TV commentators had boldly predicted that Kevin Duckworth would dominate Benjamin, the opposite happened. Benjamin dominated Duckworth with a TENDEX rating 105 points higher than the Portland center and Seattle surprised the Trail Blazers by pushing the first-round series to five tense games.

In that same series, Johnson averaged 24 points per game to lead Seattle while McDaniel, the man traded for him, was averaging 9.5 points while shooting .415 from the field as Phoenix was being upset by Utah.

Pierce won TENDEX Sixth Man of the Year honors last season and, although he was dominated in the playoffs by Clyde Drexler, at least he played. The chronically-injured Ellis missed the playoffs for the Bucks and they were upset by Philadelphia.

Payton made the TENDEX All-Rookie team last season with his rating of .467, and was the only rookie among the league leaders in two categories (12th in steals and 20th in assists). But he actually was a better player than his statistics, playing excellent defense all season. He saved one of the playoff victories over Portland with a steal in the closing seconds when a basket would have won the game for the Trail Blazers.

Add to these players center-forward Michael Cage (TENDEX .467), guards Nate McMillan (.542) and Sedale Threatt (.465), and forwards Derrick McKey (.513) and Shawn Kemp (.609) and you have the makings of an excellent team. Kemp is perhaps the next emerging superstar in the NBA.

But for Seattle to become a contender, Jones will have to do a better job of strategic coaching. The Sonics had a team TENDEX rating of 102.38 last season—No. 10 in the league—but finished with only a .500 record, winning six fewer games than they would have won with average coaching. They were 13–20 in games decided by six points or less. Jones tied Mike Schuler of the Los Angeles Clippers for last place in the coaches' ratings.

Seattle finished near the middle of the pack in most statistics last season, but did well in two-point field-goal percentage (No. 8), rebounds (No. 8), PAR (No. 9), steals (No. 2), and TENDEX (No. 10).

Weaker categories were No. 20 in blocked shots and No. 22 in turnovers.

With young or mid-career players at most positions, this team should improve if it develops chemistry under Jones' leadership. It might even challenge Portland, the LA Lakers and Phoenix for the Pacific Division title.

Probable finish: Fourth in Pacific Division.

RICKY PIERCE

AGE: 32
HEIGHT: 6-4
WEIGHT: 222
POSITION: Shooting Guard
EXPERIENCE: 9 Seasons
COLLEGE: Rice
BIRTHPLACE: Dallas
1990–91 TENDEX: .590
POSITIONAL RATING: 4 of 27
CAREER TENDEX: .532

Pierce has had TENDEX ratings over .500 for the past seven years, exceptional for a shooting guard . . . had the second-best rating of his career (.590) last season and was chosen the TENDEX Sixth Man of the Year . . . ranks No. 5 among active small forwards with his career TENDEX rating of .532 . . . was No. 3 in the NBA in free-throw percentage (.913) last season and No. 19 in scoring (20.5) . . . led Seattle in three-point field-goal percentage, free-throw percentage, and scoring . . . in shooting-guard ratings, there is no in-between for Pierce. He was near the top last season in two-point field-goal percentage (No. 9), three-point field-goal percentage (No. 3), free-throw percentage (No. 3), points (No. 2), and TENDEX rating (No. 4) . . . near the bottom in rebounds (No. 20), assists (No. 22), steals (No. 25), turnovers (No. 19), and blocked shots (No. 19).

SHAWN KEMP

AGE: 22
HEIGHT: 6-10
WEIGHT: 230
POSITION: Power Forward
EXPERIENCE: 2 Seasons
COLLEGE: None
BIRTHPLACE: Elkhart, IN
1990–91 TENDEX: .609
POSITIONAL RATING: 6 of 22
CAREER TENDEX: .606

Kemp was 21 years old when he completed his second excellent season in the NBA. He more than doubled his minutes played in 1990–91 while improving his TENDEX rating from .600 to .609. Future unlimited . . . Kemp's athletic talent was manifest in the categories in which he excelled in comparison with other power forwards: No. 6 in rebounds, No. 5 in steals, No. 4 in blocked shots, and No. 6 in TENDEX rating . . . needs refinement in skill categories: No. 22 in free-throw percentage, No. 14 in assists, No. 21 in turnovers.

PIERCE

1990–91	2PFG	3PFG	F.T.	REB.	AST.	STL.	T.O.	BLK.	PTS.
Per Game	.495	.397	.913	2.45	2.15	0.77	1.88	0.17	20.5
Per Minute	.495	.397	.913	.088	.078	.028	.068	.006	.737
Rating	9	3	3	20	22	25	19t	19	2

KEMP

1990–91	2PFG	3PFG	F.T.	REB.	AST.	STL.	T.O.	BLK.	PTS.
Per Game	.513	.167	.661	8.38	1.78	0.95	2.49	1.52	15.0
Per Minute	.513	.167	.661	.278	.059	.032	.083	.050	.497
Rating	11t	12t	22	6t	14	5	21	4	10

BENOIT BENJAMIN

AGE: 27
HEIGHT: 7-0
WEIGHT: 245
POSITION: Center
EXPERIENCE: 6 Seasons
COLLEGE: Creighton
BIRTHPLACE: Monroe, LA
1990–91 TENDEX: .601
POSITIONAL RATING: 7 of 21
CAREER TENDEX: .583

Benjamin achieved his third successive TENDEX rating above .600 in 1990–91, even though he switched teams at midseason. Continued to play well after being traded from the Los Angeles Clippers to Seattle and may finally be the answer to the SuperSonics' center problem . . . ranked ninth in the NBA in blocked shots (2.07) and 10th in rebounds (10.3) . . . his total of 723 rebounds was a career high . . . ranks No. 11 on the all-time list in shot-blocking efficiency . . . in center listings last season he was rated No. 5 in rebounds, No. 7 in assists, No. 10 in steals, No. 5 in blocked shots, No. 8 in points, and No. 7 in TENDEX . . . his only bad rating was No. 21 in turnovers . . . ranks No. 7 among active centers with career TENDEX rating of .583.

EDDIE JOHNSON

AGE: 32
HEIGHT: 6-7
WEIGHT: 215
POSITION: Small Forward
EXPERIENCE: 10 Seasons
COLLEGE: Illinois
BIRTHPLACE: Chicago
1990–91 TENDEX: .526
POSITIONAL RATING: 14 of 30
CAREER TENDEX: .500

Johnson made the 10th season of his career in the NBA one of his best. Equaled his second-best TENDEX rating (.526) during the regular season and continued hot in the playoffs, averaging 24 points in a five-game first-round series against Portland . . . ranked ninth in the NBA in free-throw percentage (.891) . . . out of 30 small forwards was No. 9 in three-point field-goal percentage, No. 2 in free-throw percentage, No. 4 in points, and No. 14 in TENDEX . . . poor ratings were No. 25 in rebounds, No. 26 in assists, and No. 29 in blocked shots.

BENJAMIN

1990–91	2PFG	3PFG	F.T.	REB.	AST.	STL.	T.O.	BLK.	PTS.
Per Game	.496	.000	.712	10.3	1.70	0.77	3.36	2.07	14.0
Per Minute	.496	.000	.712	.323	.053	.024	.105	.065	.439
Rating	14	7t	13	5	7	10	21	5	8

JOHNSON

1990–91	2PFG	3PFG	F.T.	REB.	AST.	STL.	T.O.	BLK.	PTS.
Per Game	.503	.325	.891	3.35	1.37	0.72	1.51	.111	16.7
Per Minute	.503	.325	.891	.130	.053	.028	.059	.004	.649
Rating	14	9	2t	25	26	19t	12	29	4

SEDALE THREATT

AGE: 30
HEIGHT: 6-2
WEIGHT: 177
POSITION: Shooting Guard
EXPERIENCE: 8 Seasons
COLLEGE: West Virginia Tech
BIRTHPLACE: Atlanta
1990–91 TENDEX: .465
POSITIONAL RATING: 14 of 27
CAREER TENDEX: .418

In his eighth NBA season, Threatt excelled, setting personal highs in minutes, field-goal percentage, assists, steals, and points . . . led Seattle in field-goal percentage (.519) . . . out of 27 shooting guards he had good ratings of No. 4 in two-point field-goal percentage, No. 9 in assists, and No. 6 in steals . . . low ratings were No. 20 in three-point field-goal percentage, No. 21 in free-throw percentage, No. 27 in rebounds, and No. 24 in blocked shots.

DERRICK McKEY

AGE: 25
HEIGHT: 6-9
WEIGHT: 205
POSITION: Small Forward
EXPERIENCE: 4 Seasons
COLLEGE: Alabama
BIRTHPLACE: Meridian, MS
1990–91 TENDEX: .513
POSITIONAL RATING: 18 of 30
CAREER TENDEX: .501

The good news is that McKey had his best season in 1990–91 (TENDEX .513). The bad news is it wasn't that much better than his first three seasons. Truth is, McKey has not made as much progress as Seattle hoped he would make after drafting him No. 9 in 1987 . . . established new personal highs last season in field-goal percentage (.517) and free-throw percentage (.845) . . . good small-forward ratings were No. 7 in two-point field-goal percentage, No. 5 in free-throw percentage, and No. 9 in blocked shots . . . bad ones were No. 20 in three-point field goal percentage, No. 22 in assists, No. 23 in points, and No. 18 in TENDEX.

THREATT

1990–91	2PFG	3PFG	F.T.	REB.	AST.	STL.	T.O.	BLK.	PTS.
Per Game	.529	.286	.792	1.24	3.41	1.41	1.73	0.10	12.7
Per Minute	.529	.286	.792	.048	.132	.055	.067	.004	.490
Rating	4	20t	21	27	9	6	16t	24	16

McKEY

1990–91	2PFG	3PFG	F.T.	REB.	AST.	STL.	T.O.	BLK.	PTS.
Per Game	.524	.211	.845	5.79	2.32	1.25	2.16	0.77	15.3
Per Minute	.524	.211	.845	.169	.068	.036	.063	.022	.446
Rating	7	20	5	16	22	14	14	9	23

GARY PAYTON

AGE: 23
HEIGHT: 6-4
WEIGHT: 180
POSITION: Point Guard
EXPERIENCE: 1 Season
COLLEGE: Oregon State
BIRTHPLACE: Oakland, CA
1990–91 TENDEX: .467
POSITIONAL RATING: 18 of 23
CAREER TENDEX: .467

Ho-hum, it happened again: Gary Payton didn't have a high scoring average, so he was ignored when it came time for the NBA to pick its official All-Rookie team. However, he did make the TENDEX All-Rookie team, because TENDEX considers statistics other than scoring . . . was the only rookie who ranked among the NBA leaders in two categories: No. 12 in steals (2.01) and No. 20 in assists (6.4) . . . led Seattle in assists and steals . . . best point-guard ratings were No. 2 in steals, No. 5 in rebounds, and No. 6 in blocked shots . . . worst ones were No. 19 in two-point field-goal percentage, No. 21 in three-point field-goal percentage, and No. 21 in points.

MICHAEL CAGE

AGE: 29
HEIGHT: 6-9
WEIGHT: 230
POSITION: Center
EXPERIENCE: 7 Seasons
COLLEGE: San Diego State
BIRTHPLACE: West Memphis, AR
1990–91 TENDEX: .467
POSITIONAL RATING: 14 of 21
CAREER TENDEX: .524

Cage skidded to his lowest TENDEX rating in five years during the 1990–91 season, but he could prove to be an adequate reserve center this season, now that Benoit Benjamin has been obtained to be the regular . . . out of 21 centers last season his good rankings were No. 4 in steals and No. 6 in turnovers . . . the worst sign for him was his No. 15 rating in rebounds: he had led the NBA in rebounding in 1988 . . . other mediocre ratings were No. 18 in free-throw percentage, No. 14 in blocked shots, No. 19 in points, and No. 14 in TENDEX.

PAYTON

1990–91	2PFG	3PFG	F.T.	REB.	AST.	STL.	T.O.	BLK.	PTS.
Per Game	.459	.077	.711	2.96	6.44	2.01	2.20	0.18	7.2
Per Minute	.459	.077	.711	.108	.235	.074	.080	.007	.262
Rating	19t	21	18	5	11	2	13	6	21

CAGE

1990–91	2PFG	3PFG	F.T.	REB.	AST.	STL.	T.O.	BLK.	PTS.
Per Game	.511	.000	.625	6.80	1.09	1.04	1.01	0.71	6.4
Per Minute	.511	.000	.625	.261	.042	.040	.039	.027	.244
Rating	11	16t	18	15	12	4	6	14	19

29
Utah Jazz

1990–91 Statistics	Per Game	Rating
2-Point FG Percent	.504	6
3-Point FG Percent	.323	11
Free-Throw Percent	.789	7
Shootist	.947	7
Points	104.0	16
Assists	27.0	3
Rebounds	−0.46	15
PAR	+7.24	8
Blocked Shots	5.50	9
Steals	7.95	19
Turnovers	15.91	12
BEST	−2.46	17
TENDEX	104.9	7
Winning Percentage	.659	7
Coach: J. Sloan	+1	9t
Player: K. Malone	.808	6
Rookie: E. Murdock	.575	8

Every season I keep wanting to be able to say: This time the Jazz will win it all because they finally got a third outstanding player to complement Karl Malone and John Stockton. I want to say it but I can't, because it hasn't happened yet.

Goodness knows, the Jazz have tried. They picked up Jeff Malone last year from Washington. Malone had averaged 24.3 points per game for the Bullets the season before. But for the Jazz he dropped off six points to 18.6. Jeff Malone is a scorer, and in TENDEX language that means an average player at best. His career TENDEX rating is .460, which is about average for a shooting guard. He practically matched his norm with a .440 rating last season.

The fact is that, other than Karl Malone and John Stockton, the Jazz did not have a single player with a TENDEX rating matching the league-wide average of .500 last season. That should tell you something about how good Karl Malone and John Stockton are because, with minimal help, they almost led the Jazz to a Midwest Division championship over talent-rich San Antonio. The Spurs won by a single game when Utah was upset by Golden State on the final day of the season.

It was more of the same in the playoffs with Stockton and Karl Malone performing super-human feats in a first-round upset over Phoenix but coming up short in the second round against Portland.

With Malone and Stockton, the Jazz were the only team in the NBA with two players among the top 10 in the NBA. Malone was No. 6 with his .808 TENDEX rating. Stockton was No. 8 at .739.

Center Mark Eaton (.438) and sixth man Thurl Bailey (.432) continued the precipitous downward trends they had established during recent seasons.

Backup power forward Mike Brown (.406) and swing man Blue Edwards (.393) had their good moments, but not many of them.

In three seasons, Jerry Sloan has gone from one of the lower-rated to one of the higher-rated coaches in the NBA. Last season he directed the Jazz to a 16–7 record in games decided by six points or less. He tied for ninth place in the coaches' ratings.

Statistically, Utah had eight ratings among the top 10 without having a single one in the 20s.

The good stats were No. 6 in two-point field-goal percentage, No. 7 in free-throw per-centage, No. 7 in Shootist (points per shot), No. 3 in assists, No. 8 in PAR (combination of points, assists and rebounds), No. 9 in blocked shots, No. 7 in TENDEX rating, and No. 7 in winning percentage.

The worst one was No. 19 in steals.

There appears to be little hope of the Jazz winning the Midwest Division this season but, barring an injury to Stockton or Malone, they should have enough to hold off Houston for second place.

KARL MALONE

AGE: 28
HEIGHT: 6-9
WEIGHT: 250
POSITION: Power Forward
EXPERIENCE: 6 Seasons
COLLEGE: Louisiana Tech
BIRTHPLACE: Summerfield, LA
1990–91 TENDEX: .808
POSITIONAL RATING: 1 of 22
CAREER TENDEX: .726

Malone had his second straight season with a TENDEX rating higher than .800 in 1990–91 and pulled his career rating up to .726, making him the fifth-rated power forward of all-time . . . ranks No. 5 on the all-time list in scoring efficiency . . . also is among the all-time leaders in rebounding efficiency . . . has pulled down more than 5,000 rebounds and scored more than 12,000 points in six NBA seasons . . . ranked No. 2 in minutes, No. 2 in scoring, No. 5 in rebounding and No. 17 in field-goal percentage in the NBA last season . . . led Utah in minutes, rebounds and points . . . he is one of eight players in NBA history to average 30 points and 10 rebounds in the same season (1989–90) . . . dominated power-forward ratings last season: No. 6 in two-point field-goal percentage, No. 7 in three-point field-goal percentage, No. 3 in rebounds, No. 2 in assists, No. 9 in steals, No. 9 in blocked shots, No. 1 in points, and No. 1 in TENDEX.

JOHN STOCKTON

AGE: 29
HEIGHT: 6-1
WEIGHT: 175
POSITION: Point Guard
EXPERIENCE: 7 Seasons
COLLEGE: Gonzaga
BIRTHPLACE: Spokane, WA
1990–91 TENDEX: .739
POSITIONAL RATING: 2 of 23
CAREER TENDEX: .693

Stockton has become one of the most consistent players in the NBA. He has led the league in assists with 1,128, 1,118, 1,134 and 1,164 the past four seasons. His TENDEX ratings for those seasons have been .749, .746, .739 and .739 . . . career TENDEX rating of .693 is the third-best of all-time among point guards, trailing only Magic Johnson and Oscar Robertson . . . Stockton is the top-rated player of all-time in assists efficiency . . . his 1990–91 assist total of 1,164 broke his own record for most assists in a season . . . he also holds the record for assists per game (14.5) set in 1989–90 . . . ranked No. 1 in the NBA in assists, No. 2 in steals, No. 20 in three-point field-goal percentage last season . . . led Utah in assists and steals . . . outstanding point-guard ratings were No. 3 in two-point field-goal percentage, No. 8 in two-point field-goal percentage, No. 7 in free-throw percentage, No. 1 in assists, No. 1 in steals, and No. 2 in TENDEX.

MALONE

1990–91	2PFG	3PFG	F.T.	REB.	AST.	STL.	T.O.	BLK.	PTS.
Per Game	.529	.286	.770	11.8	3.29	1.09	2.98	0.96	29.0
Per Minute	.529	.286	.770	.293	.082	.027	.074	.024	.721
Rating	6	7	12	3	2	9	19	9	1

STOCKTON

1990–91	2PFG	3PFG	F.T.	REB.	AST.	STL.	T.O.	BLK.	PTS.
Per Game	.541	.345	.836	2.89	14.2	2.85	3.63	0.20	17.2
Per Minute	.541	.345	.836	.076	.375	.075	.096	.005	.455
Rating	3	8	7	21	1	1	17	9	11

JEFF MALONE

AGE: 30
HEIGHT: 6-4
WEIGHT: 205
POSITION: Shooting Guard
EXPERIENCE: 8 Seasons
COLLEGE: Mississippi State
BIRTHPLACE: Mobile, AL
1990–91 TENDEX: .440
POSITIONAL RATING: 19 of 27
CAREER TENDEX: .460

Utah obtained Malone from Washington to add scoring punch to its lineup, and Malone did that with his 18.6 scoring average last season . . . ranked second in the NBA with a .917 free-throw percentage and shot well from the field (.508) . . . trouble was, the Jazz found out what the Bullets already knew, that scoring is the only thing you get from Malone . . . good shooting-guard ratings in two-point field-goal percentage (No. 6), free-throw percentage (No. 2), and turnovers (No. 2) . . . bad ones in three-point field-goal percentage (No. 26), rebounds (No. 22), assists (No. 27, last place), steals (No. 27), blocked shots (No. 26), and TENDEX (No. 19).

THURL BAILEY

AGE: 30
HEIGHT: 6-11
WEIGHT: 232
POSITION: Small Forward
EXPERIENCE: 8 Seasons
COLLEGE: North Carolina State
BIRTHPLACE: Washington, DC
1990–91 TENDEX: .432
POSITIONAL RATING: 28 of 30
CAREER TENDEX: .492

Bailey was a 19.5 and 19.6-point scorer off the bench at the peak of his career, but his scoring averages have trailed off to 14.2 and 12.4 the past two seasons . . . he was the second-best small forward in blocked shots last season, but was far down the list in most other categories and was getting reduced playing time at the end of the season, perhaps indicating that the Jazz would be seeking someone else to fill his role this season . . . bad ratings out of 30 small forwards were No. 27 in two-point field-goal percentage, No. 27 in three-point field-goal percentage, No. 27 in assists, No. 29 in steals, No. 27 in points, and No. 28 in TENDEX.

MALONE

1990–91	2PFG	3PFG	F.T.	REB.	AST.	STL.	T.O.	BLK.	PTS.
Per Game	.510	.167	.917	2.99	2.07	0.73	1.57	0.09	18.6
Per Minute	.510	.167	.917	.084	.058	.020	.044	.002	.520
Rating	6	26	2	22	27	27	2	26	11

BAILEY

1990–91	2PFG	3PFG	F.T.	REB.	AST.	STL.	T.O.	BLK.	PTS.
Per Game	.459	.000	.808	4.96	1.51	0.65	1.59	1.11	12.4
Per Minute	.459	.000	.808	.164	.050	.021	.052	.037	.409
Rating	27	27t	11t	17	27	29	8	2	27

MARK EATON

AGE: 34
HEIGHT: 7-4
WEIGHT: 290
POSITION: Center
EXPERIENCE: 9 Seasons
COLLEGE: UCLA
BIRTHPLACE: Westminster, CA
1990–91 TENDEX: .438
POSITIONAL RATING: 19 of 21
CAREER TENDEX: .489

Eaton is the second-ranking player of all-time in shot-blocking efficiency, but has slacked off in his specialty during the past two seasons . . . led the Jazz in blocks last season with 188, but had the lowest total of his nine-year career . . . ranked seventh in the NBA in blocks with a 2.35 average per game . . . TENDEX rating of .438 was the second-lowest of his career . . . led the Jazz in field-goal percentage (.579) but did not make enough shots to be listed among the league leaders . . . best ratings among centers were No. 2 in two-point field-goal percentage, No. 4 in turnovers, and No. 4 in blocked shots . . . but had weak ratings of No. 17 in free-throw percentage, No. 17 in rebounds, No. 20 in assists, No. 16 in steals, No. 21 in points, and No. 19 in TENDEX.

EATON

1990–91	2PFG	3PFG	F.T.	REB.	AST.	STL.	T.O.	BLK.	PTS.
Per Game	.579	.000	.634	8.34	0.64	0.49	1.24	2.35	5.1
Per Minute	.579	.000	.634	.259	.020	.015	.038	.073	.159
Rating	2	7t	17	17	20	16	4	4	21

30
Washington Bullets

1990–91 Statistics	Per Game	Rating
2-Point FG Percent	.478	18
3-Point FG Percent	.194	27
Free-Throw Percent	.729	25
Shootist	.894	21
Points	101.4	23
Assists	25.4	12
Rebounds	−1.74	19
PAR	−4.02	17
Blocked Shots	5.71	8
Steals	7.17	25
Turnovers	16.6	19
BEST	−3.71	22
TENDEX	96.9	19
Winning Percentage	.366	20
Coach: W. Unseld	−3	19t
Player: B. King	.583	34
Rookie: L. Smith	.436	NR

Just when the Bullets got their frontcourt together, the backcourt fell apart.

Small forward Bernard King completed his five-year comeback from a serious knee injury by having an all-star 1990–91 season (TENDEX .583) and power forward John Williams began his comeback from a serious knee injury by playing in 33 games.

But the big story for Washington was the improvement of forward Harvey Grant and center Pervis Ellison. Both men were among the NBA's most improved players. Grant improved his TENDEX rating 134 points, from .421 to .555, and Ellison was the league's most improved player with his 176-point increase, from .442 to .618.

The three-way trade in which Washington dealt Jeff Malone to Utah and acquired Ellison from Sacramento may someday be considered one of the greatest trades in the history of the Bullets' franchise. Ellison was the No. 1 draft choice in 1989 and, after an injury-marred rookie season, played like a No. 1 last year.

With Ellison, Williams, and Grant, the Bullets appear set in frontcourt for at least the next five years. But in backcourt, the team's strength in 1989–90, there are problems.

It wasn't the loss of Malone that hurt so much as an injury to point guard Darrell Walker. Walker was the seventh-best point man in the NBA with his .578 TENDEX rating two seasons ago, but spent much of last season trying to recover from an injury while his rating skidded 81 points to .497.

The Bullets were counting on Ledell Eackles to step in as Malone's replacement, but Eackles had other ideas. First, he held out for more money. He missed 15 games, and ultimately made the Bullets pay with his poor performance. He averaged 11 points per game less than Malone and his TENDEX rating of .386 was 133 points lower than Malone's the season before.

So now, instead of having a stable backcourt and a troubled frontcourt, as they did a year ago, the situation is reversed for the Bullets.

In Wes Unseld, Washington has a former TENDEX Coach of the Year (1989). Unseld did not have a good season in 1990–91, when the Bullets won three fewer games than they should have won, according to TENDEX statistics. But that might not have been entirely Unseld's fault. Injuries and the turnover in personnel kept the team from developing good chemistry.

Thanks mostly to Ellison, the 10th-rated shotblocker in the NBA, Washington ranked No. 8 as a team in blocks.

On the negative side, the Bullets were No. 25 in steals, No. 19 in turnovers, No. 22 in BEST (combination of blocked shots, steals and turnovers), No. 18 in two-point field-goal percentage, No. 27 in three-point field-goal percentage, No. 25 in free-throw percentage, No. 21 in Shootist (points per shot), No. 23 in points, No. 19 in rebounds, No. 19 in TENDEX rating, and No. 20 in winning percentage.

The Bullets need a good performance from new point guard Michael Adams, comebacks by Williams and Walker, and a full season of effort from Eackles, in order to make the playoffs this season.

Probable finish: Third in Atlantic Division.

MICHAEL ADAMS

AGE: 28
HEIGHT: 5-11
WEIGHT: 165
POSITION: Point Guard
EXPERIENCE: 6 Seasons
COLLEGE: Boston College
BIRTHPLACE: Hartford, CT
1990-91 TENDEX: .617
POSITIONAL RATING: 5 of 23
CAREER TENDEX: .491

Adams stepped forward and became an outstanding player last season, finishing as the runnerup for TENDEX Most Improved Player honors with an increase of 168 percentage points. Biggest improvements were in scoring, from 15.5 to 26.5 points per game, and in assists, from 6.3 to 10.5 per game . . . finished sixth in the NBA in scoring, third in assists and seventh in steals (2.23 per game) . . . a prolific three-point shooter, in six NBA seasons he has attempted 1,911 shots from long range, an all-time record . . . has made 658 three-pointers for a percentage of .344 . . . led Denver in scoring, steals, assists, and free-throw percentage last season . . . among regular point guards he ranked No. 3 in free-throw percentage, No. 4 in rebounds, No. 3 in assists, No. 5 in steals, No. 1 in points, and No. 5 in TENDEX rating.

BERNARD KING

AGE: 35
HEIGHT: 6-7
WEIGHT: 205
POSITION: Small Forward
EXPERIENCE: 13 Seasons
COLLEGE: Tennessee
BIRTHPLACE: Bronx, NY
1990-91 TENDEX: .583
POSITIONAL RATING: 7 of 30
CAREER TENDEX: .597

If there were still a Comeback Player of the Year award in the NBA, King would have won it last season, 10 years after winning it for the first time . . . at age 34 he had his best season since incurring what was thought to be a career-ending knee injury six years ago . . . averaged 28.4 points per game to rank No. 3 in the league . . . career scoring average is 23.1 . . . a TENDEX Hall of Famer, King ranks among the top 10 players of all-time in scoring efficiency . . . led the league in scoring in 1985 . . . should score his 20,000th point this season . . . a good passer, King ranked No. 3 out of 30 small forwards last season in assists, No. 1 in points, No. 7 in TENDEX rating . . . low ratings in the BEST categories: No. 30 in turnovers, No. 26 in steals, and No. 26 in blocked shots . . . led Washington in scoring and free-throw percentage.

ADAMS

1990-91	2PFG	3PFG	F.T.	REB.	AST.	STL.	T.O.	BLK.	PTS.
Per Game	.459	.296	.879	3.88	10.5	2.23	3.64	0.09	26.5
Per Minute	.459	.296	.879	.109	.295	.063	.102	.003	.747
Rating	19t	13	3	4	3	5	21	20	1

KING

1990-91	2PFG	3PFG	F.T.	REB.	AST.	STL.	T.O.	BLK.	PTS.
Per Game	.478	.216	.790	4.98	4.56	0.88	3.98	0.25	28.4
Per Minute	.478	.216	.790	.133	.122	.023	.106	.007	.757
Rating	18	21	6	19	28	19t	3	28	14

HARVEY GRANT

AGE: 26
HEIGHT: 6-8
WEIGHT: 200
POSITION: Power Forward
EXPERIENCE: 3 Seasons
COLLEGE: Oklahoma
BIRTHPLACE: Augusta, GA
1990–91 TENDEX: .555
POSITIONAL RATING: 14 of 22
CAREER TENDEX: .475

In his third NBA season, Grant improved from a fringe reserve, barely clinging to a job, to an above-average starting power forward . . . TENDEX rating of .555 was 134 percentage points above his 1989–90 rating, making him the fourth most improved player in the league. Teammate Pervis Ellison was No. 1 with an improvement of 176 points . . . led the Bullets in minutes played and steals, ranked second in scoring and rebounding . . . good power forward ratings were No. 7 in assists, No. 4 in steals, and No. 5 in turnovers . . . needs to gain weight so he can improve his rebounding (No. 19).

DARRELL WALKER

AGE: 30
HEIGHT: 6-4
WEIGHT: 180
POSITION: Point Guard
EXPERIENCE: 8 Seasons
COLLEGE: Arkansas
BIRTHPLACE: Chicago
1990–91 TENDEX: .497
POSITIONAL RATING: 15 of 23
CAREER TENDEX: .498

Walker's hopes of matching his career-best TENDEX rating of .578 in 1989–90 were dashed by an injury in the 1990–91 season . . . achieved PAR-6 status, averaging over six points, assists and rebounds per game, but fell short of his PAR-8 the previous season . . . led Bullets in assists, ranked No. 19 in the NBA with his 6.5 average . . . had four triple-double games with 10 or more points, assists and rebounds . . . led point guards in rebounds per minute, placed second in blocked shots, ninth in turnovers . . . but was 23rd (last) in two-point field-goal percentage, No. 22 in three-point field-goal percentage, No. 22 in free-throw percentage, No. 17 in assists, No. 21 in steals, No. 23 in points, and No. 15 in TENDEX.

GRANT

1990–91	2PFG	3PFG	F.T.	REB.	AST.	STL.	T.O.	BLK.	PTS.
Per Game	.502	.133	.743	7.23	2.65	1.18	1.62	0.79	18.2
Per Minute	.502	.133	.743	.196	.072	.032	.044	.022	.494
Rating	14	15	14	19	7	4	5	10	11

WALKER

1990–91	2PFG	3PFG	F.T.	REB.	AST.	STL.	T.O.	BLK.	PTS.
Per Game	.437	.000	.604	7.01	6.46	1.10	2.17	0.47	7.8
Per Minute	.437	.000	.604	.216	.199	.034	.067	.014	.240
Rating	23	22	22	1	17	21	9	2	23

HAYWOODE WORKMAN

AGE: 25
HEIGHT: 6-2
WEIGHT: 180
POSITION: Shooting Guard
EXPERIENCE: 2 Seasons
COLLEGE: Oral Roberts
BIRTHPLACE: Charlotte, NC
1990–91 TENDEX: .420
POSITIONAL RATING: 22 of 27
CAREER TENDEX: .423

The trade of Jeff Malone and the holdout of Ledell Eackles moved Workman up from the No. 3 shooting guard, hanging on to a roster spot, to the starting lineup. Although he was not exceptionally good, neither was he as bad as might have been expected. His .420 TENDEX rating was only 30 points below the league average for shooting guards . . . led the Bullets in three-point field-goal percentage . . . ranked No. 1 among shooting guards in assists per minute, No. 9 in steals, No. 10 in rebounds . . . poor ratings were No. 23 in three-point field-goal percentage, No. 23 in free-throw percentage, No. 25 in blocked shots, No. 27 in points, and No. 22 in TENDEX.

WORKMAN

1990–91	2PFG	3PFG	F.T.	REB.	AST.	STL.	T.O.	BLK.	PTS.
Per Game	.477	.240	.759	3.32	4.84	1.19	1.86	0.10	8.0
Per Minute	.477	.240	.759	.119	.174	.043	.067	.003	.286
Rating	17	23	23	10	1	9t	16t	25	27